Learn, Teach...

Succeed...

With **REA's PRAXIS II® English Subject Assessments**
test prep, you'll be in a class all your own.

WITHDRAWAL

We'd like to hear from you!

Visit **www.rea.com** to send us your comments
or email us at **info@rea.com**

PRAXIS II® ENGLISH SUBJECT ASSESSMENTS

(0041, 0042, 0043, 0049)

TestWare® Edition

Anita Price Davis, Ed.D.
Professor Emerita
Converse College, Spartanburg, S.C.

The Editors of REA

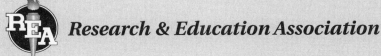

Research & Education Association

Research & Education Association

61 Ethel Road West
Piscataway, New Jersey 08854
E-mail: info@rea.com

**PRAXIS II® English Subject Assessments (0041, 0042, 0043, 0049)
With TestWare® on CD-ROM, 2nd Edition**

Library of Congress Control Number 2011923794

ISBN-13: 978-0-7386-0950-8
ISBN-10: 0-7386-0950-1

Windows® is a registered trademark of Microsoft Corporation.

The competencies presented in this book were created and implemented by Educational Testing Service. For individual state requirements, consult your state education agency. For further information visit the PRAXIS website at *www.ets.org*. PRAXIS II® and The PRAXIS Series™ are trademarks of ETS®.

REA® and TestWare® are registered trademarks of Research & Education Association, Inc.

About Research & Education Association

Founded in 1959, Research & Education Association is dedicated to publishing the finest and most effective educational materials—including software, study guides, and test preps—for students in middle school, high school, college, graduate school, and beyond.

REA's Test Preparation series includes books and software for all academic levels in almost all disciplines. Research & Education Association publishes test preps for students who have not yet entered high school, as well as for high school students preparing to enter college. Students from countries around the world seeking to attend college in the United States will find the assistance they need in REA's publications. For college students seeking advanced degrees, REA publishes test preps for many major graduate school admission examinations in a wide variety of disciplines, including engineering, law, and medicine. Students at every level, in every field, with every ambition can find what they are looking for among REA's publications.

REA's practice tests are always based upon the most recently administered exams and include every type of question that you can expect on the actual exams.

REA's publications and educational materials are highly regarded and continually receive an unprecedented amount of praise from professionals, instructors, librarians, parents, and students. Our authors are as diverse as the fields represented in the books we publish. They are well-known in their respective disciplines and serve on the faculties of prestigious high schools, colleges, and universities throughout the United States and Canada.

Today, REA's wide-ranging catalog is a leading resource for teachers, students, and professionals.

We invite you to visit us at *www.rea.com* to find out how "REA is making the world smarter."

Acknowledgments

We would like to thank Larry Kling, Vice President, Editorial, for his editorial direction; Pam Weston, Senior Vice President and Publisher, for setting the quality standards for production integrity and managing the publication to completion; John Cording, Vice President, Technology, for coordinating the design, development, and testing of REA's TestWare®; Kathleen Casey, Senior Editor, for project management; Alice Leonard, Senior Editor, for preflight editorial review; Diane Goldschmidt and Michael Reynolds, Senior Editors, for post-production quality assurance; Amy Jamison and Heena Patel, Technology Project Managers, for their software testing efforts; Christine Saul, Senior Graphic Artist, for cover design; Maureen Mulligan, Graphic Artist, for post-production file mapping.

We also gratefully acknowledge Dr. Michael D. Amey, University of Maine at Presque Isle, for his valuable critique; Carolyn Duffy for copyediting; CaraGraphics for typesetting; Ellen Gong for proofreading; and Terry Casey for indexing the manuscript.

About the Author

Dr. Anita Price Davis is The Charles Dana Professor Emerita of Education and was the Director of Elementary Education at Converse College, Spartanburg, South Carolina. Dr. Davis earned her B.S. and M.A. from Appalachian State University and her doctorate from Duke University. She also received a postdoctoral fellowship to Ohio State University for two additional years of study.

Dr. Davis had worked more than 36 years at Converse College, where she served as the faculty advisor for Kappa Delta Epsilon, a national education honor organization. She also worked 5 years as a public school teacher.

Dr. Davis has received wide recognition for her work, including a letter of appreciation from the U.S. Department of the Interior, inclusion in Contemporary Authors, and a citation of appreciation from the Michigan Council of the Social Studies. She has authored/coauthored 23 funded grants for Converse College. She has served as a mentor and twice was President of the Spartanburg County Council of the International Reading Association. The state of South Carolina twice named her an outstanding educator, and she was twice a nominee for the CASE U.S. Professor of the Year.

Dr. Davis has authored, co-authored, and edited more than 80 books. She has written two college textbooks, *Reading Instruction Essentials* and *Children's Literature Essentials*. Dr. Davis has published several history books and is also the author of more than 80 papers, book reviews, journal articles, and encyclopedia entries.

CONTENTS

Introduction

ABOUT THIS BOOK AND TestWare®

If you're looking to secure certification as an English teacher at any level, you'll find that many states require one or another of the Praxis II English Language, Literature, and Composition Assessments (Test Codes 0041, 0042, 0043, and 0049). Think of this book and accompanying TestWare® software as your toolkit to pass the test(s). It will help take the mystery and anxiety out of the testing process by equipping you not only with the nuts and bolts, but also, ultimately, with the confidence to succeed alongside your peers across the United States.

In this guide, REA offers our customarily in-depth, up-to-date, objective coverage, with test-specific modules devoted to targeted review, and realistic practice exams complete with the kind of detail that makes a difference when you're coming down the homestretch in your preparation. The first practice tests for the Praxis II 0041, 0042, 0043, and 0049 exams are included in two formats: in printed form in this book and on the enclosed TestWare® on CD-ROM. We strongly recommend that you begin your preparation with the TestWare® tests, which provide timed conditions and instantaneous, accurate scoring. In this book, we include a competency-categorized progress chart to enable you to pinpoint your strengths and weaknesses.

REVIEW AT A GLANCE	0049	0041	0042	0043
Chapter 2 Reading and the Study of Literature				
Know major works and authors of literature appropriate for adolescents.	✔	✔		
Paraphrase, interpret, and compare various types of print/nonprint texts (e.g., fiction, poetry, drama, etc.).	✔	✔		✔
Identify and interpret figurative and other elements of language (e.g., point of view, voice, style, tone patterns and structures, allegory/parable and symbolism, etc.).	✔	✔		✔
Locate and interpret literature within historical/culture context (Middle English, Harlem Renaissance, etc.).	✔	✔	✔	
Recognize various critical approaches to interpreting text (e.g., shared inquiry, reader-response theory).	✔			
Recognize and apply various approaches to teaching reading (e.g., cueing systems, activating knowledge, etc.).	✔	✔		✔
Chapter 3 Language and Linguistics				
Understand and apply conventions of grammar, mechanics, and usage.	✔	✔	✔	✔
Understand the development and structure of the English language (e.g., vocabulary and syntax).	✔		✔	✔
Understand principles of first- and second-language acquisition and development, and the nature of dialects.	✔	✔		
Understand element of the history, development, and structure of the English language, including linguistic change, etymology, and so forth.		✔		
Understand the elements of semantics (e.g., ambiguity, euphemism, connotation, and jargon) and how these elements affect meaning.		✔	✔	
Chapter 4 Composition and Rhetoric				
Understand strategies for teaching writing:	✔		✔	
• Individual/collaborative approaches	✔			
• Common research and documentation techniques (e.g., gathering and evaluating data, etc.)	✔	✔		
• Evaluating and assessing student writing (e.g., peer review, portfolios, holistic scoring, scoring rubrics, self-assessments, etc.)	✔	✔		✔
Recognize, understand, and evaluate rhetorical features of writing:	✔	✔	✔	✔
• Use of thesis statements and appropriate supporting evidence	✔	✔	✔	✔
• Types of audiences and purposes	✔	✔		✔
• Types of discourse	✔	✔	✔	✔
• Coherence and organization (e.g., chronological order, transition, etc.)	✔	✔	✔	✔

REVIEW AT A GLANCE (con't)	0049	0041	0042	0043
• Critical reasoning (e.g., recognition of bias and fallacies, distinctions between fact and opinion, and use of stereotypes, inferences, and assumptions)	✔	✔	✔	✔
• Discourse aims, styles of writing (e.g., creative, expository, persuasive)		✔	✔	✔
• Methods of argument and types of appeals (e.g., analogy, extended metaphor, allusion, and appeals to logic or emotion)		✔		✔
0049 Test-specific strategies and practice exams, **Chapter 5**	✔			
0041 Test-specific strategies and practice exams, **Chapter 6**		✔		
0042 Test-specific strategies and practice exams, **Chapter 7**			✔	
0043 Test-specific strategies and practice exams, **Chapter 8**				✔

ABOUT THE PRAXIS SERIES

Praxis is Educational Testing Service's (ETS) shorthand for Professional Assessments for Beginning Teachers. The Praxis Series is a group of teacher licensing tests that ETS developed in concert with states across the nation. There are three categories of tests in the series: Praxis I, Praxis II, and Praxis III. Praxis I includes the paper-based Pre-Professional Skills Tests (PPST) and the Praxis I Computer-Based Tests (CBT). Both versions cover essentially the same subject matter. These exams measure basic reading, mathematics, and writing skills and are often a requirement for admission to a teacher education program.

Praxis II embraces Subject Assessment/Specialty Area Tests, of which the Praxis II English Assessments (0041, 0042, 0043, and 0049) are a part. The Praxis II examinations cover the subject matter that students typically study in teacher education courses such as language acquisition, school curriculum, methods of teaching, and other professional development courses. In most teacher-training programs, students take these tests after having completed their classroom training, the course work, and practicum.

Praxis III is different from the multiple-choice and essay tests typically used for assessment purposes. With this assessment, ETS-trained observers evaluate an instructor's performance in the classroom, using nationally validated criteria. The observers may videotape the lesson, and other teaching experts may critique the resulting tapes.

PRAXIS Pointer

Work quickly and steadily. Avoid focusing on any one problem too long. Taking the practice tests in this book will help you learn to budget your precious time.

The Praxis II English Assessments (0041, 0042, 0043, and 0049) cover the content areas of reading and language arts, literature, and composition and rhetoric. This study guide will deal with each of these broader content areas and with the subareas such as are found in English.

Who Takes the Test?

Most people who take the Praxis II English Assessments (0041, 0042, 0043, and/ or 0049) are seeking initial licensure. Twenty-eight states require both the English Literature Content Knowledge (0041) and the Middle School English Language Arts (0049) tests to teach middle school English. Seven states require both the Secondary School Language Arts (0041) and the English Language Literature and Composition: Essays (0042) exams; two states—Utah and Arizona—require three of the exams, although Utah notes that in some circumstances all four may be required and to check with the licensing authority. Six states require both the Secondary School Language Arts (0041) and the English Language Literature and Composition: Pedagogy (0043) tests to teach English and additionally require the Middle School English Language Arts (0049) test to teach middle school English. We concluded that there is a significant reason to include the 0041 and 0049 exams in the same book. And our decision to include the 0042 and 0043 exams is supported by the fact that 14 states require the 0041, the 0049, and either the 0042 or the 0043.

You should check with your state's education agency to determine which Praxis examination(s) you should take; the ETS Praxis website (*www.ets.org/praxis/*) and registration bulletin may also help you determine the test(s) you need to take for certification. You should also consult your education program for its own test requirements. Remember that colleges and universities often require Praxis examinations for entry into programs, for graduation, and for the completion of a teacher certification program. These requirements may differ from the baseline requirements the state has for teacher certification. You will need to meet both sets of requirements.

The grid on pages 2 and 3 presents the topics covered in each review chapter and their relative test in each category. Depending on the test(s) for which you are preparing, you will want to focus on the corresponding chapter and section of the review.

When Should I Take the Test?

The Praxis II English Assessments (0041, 0042, 0043, and 0049) are tests for those who have completed or almost completed their teacher education programs. As we mentioned in the previous section, each state establishes its own requirements for certification; some states specify the passing of other tests. Some states may require the test for initial certification; other states may require the test for beginning teachers during their first months on the job. Generally, each college and university establishes its own requirements for program admission and for graduation. Some colleges and universities require certain tests for graduation and/or for completion of a teacher education program. Check with your college and the state teacher certification agency for details.

When and Where Can I Take the Test?

ETS offers the Praxis English Assessments seven times a year at a number of locations across the nation. The usual testing day is Saturday, but examinees may request an administration on an alternate day if a conflict—such as a religious obligation—exists.

How Do I Get More Information on the ETS Praxis Exams?

To receive information on upcoming administrations of any of the Praxis II English Assessments or any other test, consult the ETS registration bulletin or website, or contact ETS at:

Educational Testing Service
Teaching and Learning Division
P.O. Box 6051
Princeton, NJ 08541-6051
Phone: (609) 771-7395
Website: *www.ets.org/praxis*
E-mail: praxis@ets.org

Special accommodations are available for candidates who are visually impaired, hearing impaired, physically disabled, or specific learning disabled. For questions concerning disability services, contact:

ETS Disability Services: (609) 771-7780
TTY only: (609) 771-7714

Provisions are also available for examinees whose primary language is not English. The ETS registration bulletin and website include directions for those requesting such accommodations. You can also consult ETS with regard to available test sites; reporting test scores; requesting changes in tests, centers, and dates of test; purchasing additional score reports; retaking tests; and other basic facts.

Is There a Registration Fee?

To take a Praxis examination, you must pay a registration fee, which is payable by check, money order, or with American Express, Discover, MasterCard, or Visa credit cards. In certain cases, ETS offers fee waivers. The registration bulletin and website give qualifications for receiving this benefit and describe the application process. Cash is not accepted for payment.

Can I Retake the Test?

Some states, institutions, and associations limit the number of times you can retest. Contact your state or other licensing authority to confirm its retest policies.

HOW TO USE THIS BOOK AND TestWare®

What Do I Study First?

Read over REA's subject reviews and suggestions for test taking. On CD-ROM, take Practice Test 1 for the specific Praxis II Assessment which you will be taking. This will help you determine your areas of weakness, so you know how to focus your studies. After further study, make sure to take Practice Test 2 in this book so that you will be familiar with the format and procedures involved with taking the actual test.

When Should I Start Studying?

It is never too early to start studying; the earlier you begin, the more time you will have to sharpen your skills. Do not procrastinate! Cramming is not an effective way to study because it does not allow you the time needed to learn the test material.

FORMAT OF EACH TEST

Test	Multiple-Choice	Essay	Constructed-Response	Exam Length
0049	90	—	2	2 hours (90 minutes for multiple-choice; 30 minutes for constructed response)
0041	120	—	—	2 hours
0042	—	4	—	2 hours
0043	—	—	2	1.5 hours

The multiple-choice questions assess a beginning teacher's knowledge of certain job-related skills and knowledge. Four choices are provided for each multiple-choice question; the options bear the letters A through D. The exams use four types of multiple-choice questions:

1. The Roman numeral multiple-choice question

2. The "Which of the following?" multiple-choice question

3. The complete-the-statement multiple-choice question

4. The multiple-choice question with qualifiers

The essay and constructed-response questions assess the examinee's ability to analyze literary texts and to understand and articulate arguments about issues central to the study of English. The following sections describe each type of question and suggested strategies.

Roman Numeral Multiple-Choice Questions

Perhaps the most difficult of the types of multiple-choice questions is the Roman numeral question because it allows for more than one correct answer. **Strategy**: Assess each answer before looking at the Roman numeral choices. Consider the following Roman numeral multiple-choice question:

The Praxis II English Assessments include

　I.　Middle School English Language Arts 0049
　II.　English Language, Literature, and Composition: Content Knowledge 0041

III. English Language, Literature, and Composition: Essays 0042
IV. Teaching Foundations: English 0048

(A) I and II.
(B) II and III.
(C) I, II, and III
(D) I, II, III, and IV.

In reviewing the questions, you should note that you may choose two or three answers by selecting (A), (B), (C), or (D). The correct answer is (D) because it includes four correct statements. All of the tests named are part of the Praxis II series.

"Which of the Following?" Multiple-Choice Questions

In a "Which of the following?" question, one of the answers is correct among the various choices. **Strategy:** Form a sentence by replacing the first part of the question with each of the answer choices in turn, and then determine which of the resulting sentences is correct. Consider the following example:

Which of the following are all American writers?

(A) Mark Twain, Charles Dickens, William Blake
(B) Mark Twain, Washington Irving, James Fenimore Cooper
(C) William Blake, Charles Dickens, Washington Irving
(D) James Fenimore Cooper, William Blake, Washington Irving

Using the suggested technique, one would read:

(A) Mark Twain, Charles Dickens, and William Blake are all American writers.
(B) Mark Twain, Washington Irving, and James Fenimore Cooper are all American writers.
(C) William Blake, Charles Dickens, and Washington Irving are all American writers.
(D) James Fenimore Cooper, William Blake, and Washington Irving are all American writers.

Read all of the options. If you know that option (A) is incorrect because Mark Twain is the only American author listed, then you know that both (C) and (D) are also incorrect because the two other writers from option (A) also appear in options (C) and (D). The correct answer is (B) since it is the only option that lists *only* American writers.

Not all "Which of the following?" multiple-choice questions are as straightforward and simple as the previous example. Consider the following multiple-choice question that requires reading a passage:

> Language not only expresses an individual's ideology, it also sets perimeters while it persuades and influences the discourse in the community that hears and interprets its meaning. Therefore, the language of failure should not be present in the learning environment (i.e., the classroom) because it will have a prohibitive impact on the students' desire to learn as well as a negative influence on the students' self-esteem. *The Oxford English Dictionary* defines *failure* as "a fault, a shortcoming, a lack of success, a person who turns out unsuccessfully, becoming insolvent, etc." We as educators might well ask ourselves if this is the sort of doctrine that we want to permeate our classrooms. Perhaps our own university axiom, *mens agitat molem* ("the mind can move mountains") will help us discover if, indeed, the concepts of failure are really the types of influences we wish to introduce to impressionable new students. Is the mind capable of moving a mountain when it is already convinced it cannot? One must remain aware that individuals acquire knowledge at independent rates of speed. Certainly, no one would suggest that one infant "failed" the art of learning to walk because she acquired the skill two months after her infant counterpart. Would anyone suggest that infant number one failed walking? Of course not. What would a mentor project to either toddler were he to suggest that a slower acquisition of walking skills implied failure? Yet, we as educators feel the need to suggest that student A failed due to the slower procurement of abstract concepts than student B. It is absolutely essential to shift the learning focus from failure to success.

Which of the following statements best conveys the meaning of the passage?

- (A) Learning is something that happens at different speeds and is, therefore, natural.
- (B) Instructors need to be sensitive to students' individual needs.
- (C) Instructors need to shift the educational focus from failure to success in learning environments.
- (D) Failure is a potential hazard in the classroom and should be avoided at all costs.

The answer is (C). The passage suggests that education today is based primarily on failure and negative reinforcement and that, in order to create a more productive and positive learning environment, the emphasis must shift to success.

> **PRAXIS Pointer**
>
> **Don't make questions more difficult than they are—there are no "trick" questions or hidden meanings.**

Strategy: Underline key information as you read the question. For instance, as you read the previous question, you might underline or highlight the sentence: "Therefore, the language of failure should not be present in the learning environment (i.e., the classroom) because it will have a prohibitive impact on the students' desire to learn as well as a negative influence on the students' self-esteem." This sentence gives you a hint of the thesis, and therefore the meaning of the passage. The highlighting will thus save you time; saving time is helpful when you must answer 90 questions in two hours.

Complete-the-Statement Multiple-Choice Questions

The complete-the-statement multiple-choice question consists of an incomplete statement for which you must select the answer choice that will complete the statement correctly. Here is an example:

The repetition of an initial consonant sound is an example of the literary device known as

    (A) metaphor.
    (B) personification.
    (C) alliteration.
    (D) denouement.

The correct answer is (C). With this type of question your strategy should be to eliminate answer choices you are certain to be wrong, thus reducing your choices.

Multiple-Choice Questions with Qualifiers

Some of the multiple-choice questions may contain qualifiers—words like *not*, *least*, and *except*. These added words make the test questions more difficult because rather than having to choose the best answer, as is usually the case, you must actually select the opposite. **Strategy:** Circle the qualifier. It is easy to forget to select the negative; circling the qualifier in the question stem is a flag. This will serve as a reminder as you are reading the question and especially if you must reread or check the answer at a later time. Now consider this question with a qualifier:

Which of the following is NOT characteristic of Italian Renaissance humanism?

    (A)   Its foundation is in the study of the classics.

    (B)   Intellectual life was its focus.

    (C)   It was noticeable in the artistic accomplishments of the period.

    (D)   It was based on learning and understanding about what it means to be human.

You are looking for the exception in this question, so you want to compare each answer choice to the question to find which answer is not representative of Italian Renaissance humanism. Humanism is *not* learning and understanding, nor is it the study of being human, so (D) is the correct answer. Humanism was an intellectual movement based on the study of the classics. And, artistic accomplishments of the period did reflect the characteristics of the Renaissance.

New question formats will, at times, appear on the Praxis II English Assessments. If such a new format question appears on the test you are taking—don't panic! You have the tools you need to succeed. Simply follow these steps:

1. Read the directions thoroughly.

2. Read the question carefully, as you would any other question.

3. Decide what you should be trying to determine.

4. Look for the details that will help you answer correctly.

You will receive answer sheets, similar to the ones in this volume, on which you will fill in you response: (A), (B), (C), or (D). As the previous example questions have shown, there are four options for each of the multiple-choice questions; questions with more than one correct answer may use Roman numerals. Individual test items require a variety of different thinking levels, ranging from simple recall to evaluation and problem solving.

You should spend approximately one minute on each multiple-choice question on each of the practice tests—and on the real exams, of course.

Constructed-Response and Essay Questions

Test questions on some of the Praxis II English Assessments are constructed-response questions or essay questions. The proctor will supply you with the necessary paper for these questions.

Most of the test directions ask you to write the answer in ink. This means that you must bring your own ballpoint pen(s) and No. 2 pencil(s) for these questions; erasable pens are acceptable.

The allotted time for completing the answer sheets and writing the answers to the constructed-response questions and/or the essay questions varies from test to test. Be sure to study the directions in this guide for the test that you must take and review the test directions on the day of the test.

The reviews in this book will help you sharpen the basic skills needed to approach the exams and offer you strategies for attacking the questions. By using the reviews in conjunction with the practice tests, you will better prepare yourself for the actual tests. You have learned through your coursework and your practical experience in schools most of what you need to know to answer the questions on the test. In your education classes, you gained the expertise to make important decisions about situations you will face as a teacher; in your content courses, you should have acquired the knowledge you will need to teach specific content. The reviews in this book will help you fit the information you have acquired into its specific testable category. Reviewing your class notes and textbooks along with systematic use of this book will give you an excellent springboard for passing any of the Praxis II English Assessments.

SCORING

The numbers of raw points awarded on the Praxis II English Assessments are based on the number of correct answers given or scoring of essays or constructed responses. Most Praxis examinations vary by edition, which means that each test has several variations that contain different questions. The different questions are intended to measure the same general types of knowledge or skills. However, there is no way to guarantee that the questions on all editions of the test will have the same degree of difficulty. To avoid penalizing test takers who answer questions that are more difficult, the initial scores are adjusted for difficulty by using a statistical process known as equating. To avoid confusion between the adjusted and unadjusted scores, ETS reports the adjusted scores on a score scale that makes them clearly different from the unadjusted scores. Unadjusted scores or "raw scores" are simply the number of questions answered correctly. Adjusted scores, which are equated to the scale ETS uses for reporting the scores are called "scaled scores." For each edition of a Praxis test, a "raw-to-scale conversion table" is used to translate raw to scaled scores.

The easier the questions are on a test edition, the more questions must be answered correctly to earn a given scaled score. The college or university in which you are enrolled may set passing scores for the completion of your teacher education program and for graduation. Be sure to check the requirements in the catalogues or bulletins. You will also want to talk with your advisor. The passing scores for the Praxis II tests vary from state to state. To find out which of the Praxis II tests your state requires and what your state's set passing score is, contact your state's education department directly.

Score Reporting

When Will I Receive My Examinee Score Report and in What Form Will It Be?

ETS mails test-score reports six weeks after the test date. There is an exception for computer-based tests and for the Praxis I examinations. Score reports will list your current score and the highest score you have earned on each test you have taken over the last 10 years. Along with your score report, ETS will provide you with a booklet that offers details on your scores. For each test date, you may request that ETS send a copy of your scores to as many as three score recipients, provided that each institution or agency is eligible to receive the scores.

STUDYING FOR THE TESTS

It is critical to your success that you study effectively. Throughout this guide, you will find Praxis Pointers that will give you tips for successful test taking. The following are a few tips to help get you going:

- Choose a time and place for studying that works best for you. Some people set aside a certain number of hours every morning to study; others may choose to study at night before retiring. Only you know what is most effective for you.

- Use your time wisely and be consistent. Work out a study routine and stick to it; don't let your personal schedule interfere. Remember, seven weeks of studying is a modest investment to put you on your chosen path.

- Don't cram the night before the test. You may have heard many amazing tales about effective cramming, but don't kid yourself: most of them are false, and the rest are about exceptional people who, by definition, aren't like most of us.

- When you take the practice tests, try to make your testing conditions as much like the actual test as possible. Turn off your television, radio, and telephone. Sit down at a quiet table free from distraction.

- As you complete the practice test, score your test and thoroughly review the explanations to the questions you answered incorrectly.

- Take notes on material you will want to go over again or research further.

- Keep track of your scores. By doing so, you will be able to gauge your progress and discover your strengths and weaknesses. You should carefully study the material relevant to your areas of difficulty. This will build your test-taking skills and your confidence!

STUDY SCHEDULE

The following study course schedule allows for thorough preparation to pass the Praxis II English Assessments (0041, 0042, 0043, and 0049). This is a suggested seven-week course of study. However, you can condense this schedule if you are in a time crunch or expand it if you have more time. You may decide to use your weekends for study and preparation and go about your other business during the week. You may even want to record information and listen to it on your MP3 player or CD as you travel in your car. However you decide to study, be sure to adhere to the structured schedule you devise.

Week	Activity
1	After reading the first chapter of this book to understand the format and content of the exam you'll be taking, take the first practice test on CD-ROM. Our computerized tests are drawn from the tests presented in this book. They provide a scored report which includes a score analysis chart indicating the percentage right in each category. This will help you to pinpoint your strengths and weaknesses. Make sure you simulate real exam conditions when you take the practice test.
2	Review the explanations for the questions you missed, and review the appropriate chapter sections. Useful study techniques include highlighting key terms and information, taking notes as you review each section, and putting new terms and information on note cards to help retain the information.

Week	Activity
3 and 4	Reread all your note cards, refresh your understanding of the exam's subareas and related skills, review your college textbooks, and read over notes you took in your college classes. This is also the time to consider any other supplementary materials suggested by your counselor or your state education agency.
5	Begin to condense your notes and findings. A structured list of important facts and concepts, based on your note cards, college textbook, course notes, and this book's review chapters will help you thoroughly review for the test. Review the answers and explanations for any questions you missed on the practice test.
6	Have someone quiz you using the note cards you created. Take the second practice test in this book, adhering to the time limits and simulated test-day conditions.
7	Review your areas of weakness using all your study materials. This is a good time to retake the practice tests, if time allows.

THE DAY OF THE TEST

Before the Test

- Dress comfortably in layers. You do not want to be distracted by being too hot or too cold while you are taking the test.

- Check your registration ticket to verify your arrival time.

- Plan to arrive at the test center early. This will allow you to collect your thoughts and relax before the test; your early arrival will also spare you the anguish that comes with being late.

- Make sure to bring your admission ticket with you and two forms of identification, one of which must contain a recent photograph, your name, and your signature (e.g., a driver's license). You will not gain entry to the test center without proper identification.

- Bring several sharpened No. 2 pencils with erasers for the multiple-choice section and pens if you are taking another test that might have essay or constructed-response questions. You will not want to waste time searching for a replacement pencil or pen if you break a pencil point or run out of ink while taking your test. The proctor will not provide pencils or pens at the test center.

- Wear a watch to the test center so you can apportion your testing time wisely. You may not, however, wear one that makes noise or that will otherwise disturb the other test takers.

- Leave all dictionaries, textbooks, notebooks, calculators, briefcases, and packages at home. You may not take these items into the test center.

- Do not eat or drink too much before the test. The proctor will not allow you to make up time you miss if you have to take a bathroom break. You will not be allowed to take materials with you, and you must secure permission before leaving the room.

During the Test

- Pace yourself. The Praxis II English 0041, 0042, and 0049 Assessments are each administered in one two-hour sitting with no breaks; the 0043 exam is an hour and half, also with no breaks. Follow all of the rules and instructions that the test proctor gives you. Proctors will enforce these procedures to maintain test security. If you do not abide by the regulations, the proctor may dismiss you from the test and notify ETS to cancel your score.

- Listen closely as the test instructor provides the directions for completing the test. Follow the directions carefully. Be sure to *mark only one answer* per multiple-choice question, erase all unwanted answers and marks completely, and fill in the answers darkly and neatly. There is no penalty for guessing at an answer, so *do not leave any answer ovals blank.* Remember: a blank oval is just scored as wrong, but a guessed answer has a chance of being right!

- Do your best! Afterward, make notes about the multiple-choice questions you remember. You may not share this information with others, but you may find that the information proves useful on other exams that you take. Relax! Wait for that passing score to arrive.

Reading and the Study of Literature

Reading and the study of literature includes several subtopics. These subtopics include the ability to recognize, know, and discuss the major works and authors of adolescent literature; and paraphrase, compare, and interpret—both inferentially and literally—various types of texts and reading materials: fiction, poetry, drama, graphic representations, and nonfiction. An examinee must be able to identify and interpret figurative language and literary elements, which include tone, figurative language, allusion, diction, voice, point of view, style, character, setting, plot, and theme; and to recognize and apply various instructional approaches to teaching reading such as cueing systems, activating prior knowledge, constructing meaning through context, and using metacognitive strategies.

MAJOR WORKS AND AUTHORS OF LITERATURE FOR ADOLESCENTS

While it is impossible to identify all the major works and authors of literature appropriate for adolescents, these exams attempt to ensure that the candidates are familiar with some of the major works and writers. The list of the "best" works and authors varies from one source to another. A teacher must consider the curriculum guide in selecting the authors and books for use in the class. In addition, the students themselves, various recommended-reading lists, and the parents should be taken into consideration.

Publishers Weekly periodically prepares a list of the all-time best-selling books for children and young people. The most recent list published in 2001 is divided into paperback and hardcover books. The list of hardcover books shows that the first four top sellers are books for children:

1. *The Poky Little Puppy* by Janette Sebring Lowrey

2. *The Tale of Peter Rabbit* by Beatrix Potter

3. *Tootle* by Gertrude Crampton

4. *Green Eggs and Ham* by Dr. Seuss

The next section of the list identifies several books for young adults. Of course, J. K. Rowling ranks in the all-time best-selling category even though her books are relatively recent publications. Here are a few of the books for young people that ranked among the top 20 best sellers:

Harry Potter and the Goblet of Fire by J. K. Rowling

Harry Potter and the Chamber of Secrets by J. K. Rowling

Harry Potter and the Prisoner of Azkaban by J. K. Rowling

Where the Sidewalk Ends by Shel Silverstein

Harry Potter and the Sorcerer's Stone by J. K. Rowling

Some books on top-seller lists may raise objections, either among students or parents. For example, some middle school students may resent reading the Laura Ingalls Wilder books and some of the Judy Blume books. These students may view the books as too "babyish" for them. Other Judy Blume books—like the juvenile novel *Forever*—may offend some parents due to its portrayal of teen sexuality; Blume is one of the most censored writers for young adults. J. D. Salinger's adolescent novel *Catcher in the Rye* has likewise been the subject of controversy.

Other sources offer recommended-reading lists as well. Jim Trelease (2008), the author of numerous books and reading lists for young people, usually cites *Where the Red Fern Grows* by Wilson Rawls and *Stone Fox* by John Gardiner as personal favorites; both animal books include excitement, respect for others, and setting as important features. Trelease's other books and videos on reading are particularly helpful and can be accessed via his Web site, http://*www.trelease-on-reading.com*. Another list of current books to consider is that of the American Library Association's (ALA) annual Newbery Medal winners. Again, the teacher must consider the list in relation to the students in the class. Some classes of mostly boys, for instance, may not enjoy reading about the doll in *Hitty, Her First Hundred Years* by Rachel Field. In 1970, the ALA established the Coretta Scott King Award to recognize outstanding African American authors (and later illustrators). Named for civil rights activist Coretta Scott King and designed to honor the life and works of her husband, Dr. Martin Luther King Jr., the award is given to those whose literary work promotes understanding and appreciation of the culture of all peoples and their contribution to the realization of the American dream. The award has gone to such writers as Christopher Paul Curtis (*Bud, Not Buddy*), Mildred Taylor (*The Land, The Road to Memphis, The Friendship, Let the Circle Be Unbroken*), and Virginia Hamilton (*The People Could Fly*), all of whom have also won the Newbery Medal. Christopher Paul Curtis is the only author to have won both the Coretta Scott King Award and the Newbery Medal in the same year.

Other books frequently included in the middle school curriculum may not appear on the previously mentioned lists. For example, *To Kill a Mockingbird* by Harper Lee has been a popular book for middle school reading classes. Set in the 1930s South, the 1961 Pulitzer Prize winner can also be incorporated into the lesson plans for American history classes studying that time period. The teacher should take care in choosing the book, however, because of some references to rape and racial discrimination (Davis 1994b). Many middle school teachers use Maya Angelou's *I Know Why the Caged Bird Sings*. Also set in the 1930s, the autobiographical account of Angelou's life is not necessarily intended only for young adults (Davis 1994a).

Books used in middle school reading classes may come from adult and from children's literature—with adequate consideration on the part of the teacher, administrators, and parents. In addition to the more current books, middle school students should become familiar with older works. Charles Dickens's novels, for example, are a frequent choice for middle school classes. (Other suggested books and authors from past time periods are discussed later in this chapter.) Nonfiction materials may also be a part of middle school classes.

LITERARY FORMS AND ELEMENTS

Being familiar with the various types of print and nonprint materials is essential to passing the Praxis II 0049, 0041, and 0042 exams. Certain characteristics help the reader to identify the form and structure of writing. Prose is a literary type; it is writing that is not poetry. Prose is what we write and speak most of the time in our everyday discourse; it is unmetered, unrhymed language. This is not to say, however, that prose does not have its own rhythms—language, whether written or spoken, has cadence and balance. Certainly, prose can have instances of rhyme or assonance, alliteration, or onomatopoeia; language is, after all, phonic.

Furthermore, prose—like poetry—may be subdivided into fiction or nonfiction. Even these divisions are not always clear-cut. A novel (or short story) is fiction; an autobiography is nonfiction. A novel (or short story) may have autobiographical elements; conversely, an autobiography may have some fictionalized parts—even though most readers regard an autobiography as entirely factual.

Traditional and Modern Literature

Based on its content and the time period during which it was written, literature may be traditional or modern. **Traditional literature** includes ancient stories, and it has a set form. For generations, people handed these stories down by word of mouth. Later, others, like the Grimm Brothers and Charles Perrault, recorded the stories for other generations. **Modern literature**, on the other hand, is, as its name suggests, much more recent; its categories can overlap some of the categories of traditional literature and can include additional forms of literature.

Types of Traditional Literature

There are seven types of traditional fiction: parables, fables, fairy tales, folktales, myths, noodle-head tales, and legends. Each type has certain characteristics that set it apart from the other types.

Parable.   The parable is a story that is realistic and has a moral. The story is **didactic** because it teaches a lesson. Unlike the fable, the parable can be—but is not necessarily—true. The biblical figure Jesus often taught with parables. One of his best known parables is "The Prodigal Son." His other parables include "The Good Samaritan," "The Lost Coin," and "The Parable of the Seeds on Rich and Fallow Ground."

Fable.   The fable is a nonrealistic story with a moral. The fable often has animals as main characters. **Aesop**, a Greek slave supposedly born around 600 BCE, is often associated with the fable. Whether he actually lived and whether he actually developed the fables are both debatable. Some of the best known fables include "The Fox and the Crane," "The Fox and the Crow," and "The Fox and the Grapes." Some scholars classify fables in which animals behave as humans (as they do in these fables) as **beast tales**.

Over the course of many centuries, Aesop's fables were translated from Greek to Latin and ultimately to English. William Caxton published these fables in England in 1484. It was sometime after the publication of these fables that Charles Perrault and the Grimm Brothers secured the publication of fairy tales.

Fairy tales.   Despite the name, fairy tales do not necessarily include fairies; rather, their key characteristic is the element of magic. Fairy tales usually follow a certain pattern and often present an "ideal" to the listener or the reader. For instance, fairy tales such as "Cinderella," "Snow White," and "Rapunzel" convey a message about the "proper" woman. According to these tales, the ideal woman is beautiful, kind, and long-suffering; she waits for her prince to come and to save her from any disappointment or disaster that may occur.

Charles Perrault recorded the French fairy tales in the 1600s. It was not until the 1800s that the Grimm Brothers recorded German fairy tales, Joseph Jacobs recorded

British fairy tales, Peter Asbjørnsen and Jørgen Moe recorded Scandinavian fairy tales, and Aleksandr Nikolaevich Afanas'ev recorded Russian fairy tales.

Some writers—like Nathaniel Hawthorne, for instance—use the term *wonder tales* to refer to fairy tales with their magical elements. These elements of magic often appear in the characters of witches, wizards, magical animals, and talking beasts. The use of the **magic three** is another frequent feature of the fairy tale; for instance, there are often three wishes, three attempts at achieving a goal, or three siblings.

Another characteristic of a fairy tale is that the listener or reader knows that good will always wins out over evil. A youngster may find frightening witches, wicked ogres, and evil forces, but in the end the protagonist "… will live happily ever after."

Stereotyping is another characteristic of the fairy tale. As soon as the storyteller or the reader says the word *stepmother*, for instance, the listener knows that the woman is wicked. Likewise, mere mention of the setting as being in the *woods* conveys a message of fear, impending doom, and evil. The word *prince* causes one to envision a young, handsome man on a white horse! The *princess* is usually the youngest in the family, beautiful, soft-spoken, kind, inactive, and waiting for her prince to come. The female protagonist in the fairy tale is often a direct contrast to the assertive female of the folktale.

Folktales.   Folktales are told in the language of the people. The stories do not necessarily have a moral. In fact, folktales often have entertainment as their main purpose. In the 1600s and 1700s, early residents of the Appalachian Mountains, for instance, took many of the fairy tales of England, Scotland, and Ireland with them to the "new" country. The fairy tale "Cinderella" became "Ashpet" in the Appalachians. The quiet, passive Cinderella became the hard-working, smart, active Ashpet, a character more like the mountain women who had to work and assist their men. "The Bremen Town Musicians" became "Jack and the Robbers" in another mountain tale.

Noodlehead stories are another type of humorous folktale. The noodlehead stories are those tales that have a character or characters whom the listener can outsmart. The listener often views these stories as particularly humorous because they make the listener feel superior.

The humor in folktales may be coarse, and the diction is often that of the particular group of people who originated the tales. Richard Chase collected many of the Appalachian folktales. He transcribed the tales on paper and told them in personal appearances, on records, and on tapes for the public. He was always careful to use the mountain dialect. His *Jack Tales* and *Grandfather Tales* are among his best known works.

Likewise, other cultures around the world have their own unique folktales and fairy tales. For instance, Charles Perrault's French tale of "Cinderella" is "Tattercoats" in Joseph Jacobs's collection; in this British version the prince falls in love with a dirty, ragged girl, not a beautiful, well-dressed figure at the ball. The Norwegian tale is of Cinderlad, not of Cinderella. The Jewish folktale of *Zlateh the Goat* tells of the survival of a young boy and his goat in a snowstorm.

Myths. Myths are stories designed to explain things that the teller does not understand. Greeks and Romans, for example, used this story type and its associated heroes and heroines to explain thunder, fire, and the "movements" of the sun. Norse myths, too, explain phenomena, especially those associated with the frost, snow, and cold climate of the north. Most cultures have their own myths. Native American myths explain such phenomena as why the rabbit does not have a tail and why the constellations exist. (These Native American myths are sometimes referred to as *legends* instead of myths. Another name for these explanations is **pourquoi tales**.)

Legends. Legends are stories—usually exaggerated—about real people, places, and things. George Washington, for instance, was a real person. However, not all the stories about him are true. For example, because there were no silver dollars minted during the American Revolution, it would have been impossible for him to have tossed a silver dollar across the Potomac. Paul Bunyan may have actually been a logger or lumberjack, but it is doubtful that he owned a blue ox or had a pancake griddle large enough that his cook could tie hams on his feet and skate on it. The careful reader of literature realizes that though legends are generally a part of traditional literature, legends continue to spring up about modern figures, animals, and places.

Movements in Literature

There have been numerous movements in literature; the best known among these are romanticism, realism, symbolism, modernism, surrealism, and existentialism.

Romanticism. Romanticism flourished in the eighteenth and nineteenth centuries, beginning in Germany and England and spreading quickly throughout Europe. It ultimately encompassed the entire Western Hemisphere, making its presence known in musical form around the globe. Romanticism "emphasized imagination, fancy, and freedom, emotion, wildness, beauty of the natural world, the rights of the individual, the nobility of the common man, and the attractiveness of the pastoral life." (Kinsella et.al 2004, 1482). Writers representative of the Romantic Movement include William Wordsworth, Lord Byron, Percy Bysshe Shelley, and Victor Hugo.

Realism.   Realism was a nineteenth-century reaction to romanticism. The form of literature that gained particular popularity during the realist movement was the novel. Realism embraced the true-to-life approach to subject matter. Rejecting the classical themes common in literature such as mythology and ballads, realists preferred to focus on everyday life. Writers who epitomized this movement include Honoré de Balzac, Gustave Flaubert, George Eliot, Fyodor Dostoevsky, and Leo Tolstoy.

Symbolism.   Symbolism was a literary movement that "reached its peak in the last two decades of the nineteenth century":

> It denotes an early modernist literary movement initiated in France during the nineteenth century that reacted against the prevailing standards of realism. Writers in this movement aimed to evoke, indirectly and symbolically, an order of being beyond the material world of the five senses. Poetic expression of personal emotion figured strongly in the movement, typically by means of a private set of symbols uniquely identifiable with the individual poet. The principal aim of the Symbolists was to express in words the highly complex feelings that grew out of everyday contact with the world. In a broader sense, the term 'symbolism refers to the use of one object to represent another. Early members of the Symbolist movement included the French authors Charles Baudelaire and Arthur Rimbaud; William Butler Yeats, James Joyce, and T. S. Eliot were influenced as the movement moved to Ireland, England, and the United States. Examples of the concept of symbolism include a flag that stands for a nation or movement, or an empty cupboard used to suggest hopelessness, poverty, and despair. (*www.answers.com/topic/symbolism*)

Modernism. Modernism is associated with the first decades of the twentieth century. The term *modernist* can describe the content and the form of a work, or either aspect alone. Typical of modernism is experimentation and the realization that knowledge is not absolute. Common themes in modernist literature are the loss of a sense of tradition and the dominance of technology. Several theories put forth at the turn of the twentieth century influenced modernist writers, including Albert Einstein's theory of relativity, Max Planck's quantum theory, and Sigmund Freud's theories on the unconscious.

Surrealism. Surrealism is another literary movement of the twentieth century. Works from this period feature the element of surprise, unexpected juxtapositions, and non sequitur. André Breton is considered the leader of this movement, which began in Paris in the early 1920s, and soon spread around the world. Surrealists aimed to free people from what they saw as false rationality and restrictive customs and structures. Breton proclaimed the true aim of surrealism is "long live the social revolution and it alone!" To this goal, at various times surrealists aligned with communism and anarchism. Surrealists thought to use Freud's free association work, dream analysis, and the unconscious to free imagination.

Existentialism. The existentialism emphasized individual existence, freedom, and choice and influenced writers in the nineteenth and twentieth centuries. The Danish philosopher Søren Kierkegaard, the first writer to refer to himself as an existentialist, stated, "The highest good for the individual is to find his or her own unique vocation" (Microsoft Encarta Online Encyclopedia 2008). Traditionalists argue that moral choice involves an objective judgment of right and wrong, while existentialists contend that there is no objective, rational basis for moral choice. In addition to Kierkegaard, other noted existentialist writers are Blaise Pascal, Friedrich Nietzsche, Martin Heidegger, and Jean-Paul Sartre.

Types of Modern Fiction

An easy way of classifying modern fiction is simply to decide whether a book is **realistic** or **fanciful**. There are times, however, when a more discrete classification method is in order. In this case, modern fiction may be classified into four categories: **novels**, **romance**, **confession**, or **Menippean satire**.

Novels. Novels recount realistic stories that really could happen or could have happened. A novel's setting and characters are thus realistic. The setting can be any city, any country, even another planet, as long as the author can convince the reader that the setting is real. Likewise, anyone can serve as a main character as long as the author can make that character believable to the reader.

Romance.   A romance, on the other hand, presents an idealized view of life in which the characters, setting, and action are better than what one would experience in real life. An ocean cruise in a romance book might, for example, involve characters who are young, handsome or beautiful, and rich. Romances may—or may not—feature a love story, but they always involve fantasy.

Confession.   In a confession, one character reveals thoughts and ideas. This particular character is a **round character**, whom the reader knows in detail. In Laura Ingalls Wilder's books, for example, the reader knows exactly what the character Laura is thinking; the reader, however, does not know what Mary (Laura's sister) is thinking. In this case, the confession allows the reader to view only one character.

Menippean satire.   A Menippean satire allows the reader to see the world through the eyes of another. In Roald Dahl's *Charlie and the Chocolate Factory*, the reader sees the world through Charlie's eyes. The desire for candy becomes almost overpowering for the reader— just as it does for Charlie. The reader has a different outlook on life, candy, and others as a result of experiencing *Charlie and the Chocolate Factory*.

Literary Elements

An important part of reading and literature study is the identification and interpretation of literary elements. These literary elements include:

1. tone: condescension, didacticism, irony, humor, parody, sentimentality

2. figurative language: simile, metaphor, analogy, personification, clichés

3. allusion

4. diction

5. voice

6. point of view

7. style

8. plot

9. setting

10. character

11. theme

In the following subsections, we use excerpts from Homer Hickam's semiautobiographical work *October Sky* (1999) to provide concrete examples of many of these literary elements. Hickam's memoir, which is often found on the reading lists of middle school students, is the story of some West Virginia high school students who manage to launch their own rockets in the late 1950s and pursue their life dreams.

Tone

The **tone** in literature reveals the author's attitude toward the writing, the reader, the subject and/or the people, places, and events in a work. The author's feelings might be serious or ironic, sad or happy, private or public, angry or affectionate, bitter or nostalgic, or any of the other attitudes and feelings that human beings experience. The author's style reveals these attitudes to the reader. There are several frequently used tones in literature.

Condescension occurs when the writer talks down to the reader. The writer addresses the audience as if they are beneath him or her in age, in knowledge, or in class.

Didacticism embodies a teaching tone. The writer addresses the readers as if they must learn something. Sometimes this didactic tone can reach the point of condescension.

Irony is the incongruity between what one expects and what actually happens. A pervasive quality in fiction, irony may appear in three main forms: language, incidents, and point of view; whatever the form, there is a contrast or discrepancy between one thing and another. With **verbal irony**, there is a contrast between what is said and what is meant. With **situational irony**, there is a discrepancy between what happens and what the reader expects to happen. With **dramatic irony**, there is a contrast between what a character believes or says and what the reader understands to be true.

Irony is one of the many stylistic devices used by Homer Hickam in *October Sky*. An instance of irony occurs when Homer attempts to use a telescope to look at his own town of Coalwood but is unable to do so—an unexpected happening to Homer:

> I thought how ironic it was that Jake's telescope could see stars a million light-years away, but not the town it was in. Maybe I was that way myself. I had a clear vision of my future in space, but the life I led in Coalwood sometimes seemed to blur. (162)

Humor in writing conveys fun. It can be precise and exacting, Hickam's *October Sky* provides an example. When Homer wears his Sunday shoes to the creek, his mother punishes him by making him go to church in his stocking feet. Everyone hears of his punishment and turns out to see:

> I didn't disappoint, walking down the church aisle in my socks while everybody nudged their neighbor and snickered. The thing was, though, I had picked out the socks, and my big toe poked through a hole in one of them. Mom was mortified. Even the preacher couldn't keep a straight face. (49)

A **parody** is a humorous or ridiculing imitation of something else. In *October Sky*, the principal announces that the football team will not be able to compete that year; he proclaims that there will be a concentrated curriculum and more homework than ever. After his announcement, the principal calls the cheerleaders to the front and tries to make the occasion into a joyous pep rally—a parody of the actual event.

Sentimentality—the excessive use of feeling or emotion—is another tone an author might employ.

Figurative Language

Using figurative language, such as similes, metaphors, and personification, is a way of adding information and description to the writing and of encouraging the reader to think about the text. All of the details are not "spoon-fed" to the reader.

A **simile** is a description that uses *like*, *than*, or *as* to draw a comparison between two dissimilar things. In describing Jake Mosby, the new junior engineer, Homer remarks, "He's got more money than Carter's got little liver pills" (145). Homer overhears a secretary tell some other women, "He looks just like Henry Fonda" (146). This figurative language brings imagery to the mind of the reader, requires the reader to think, and adds information to the description.

A **metaphor** is a figure of speech containing an implied comparison in which a word or phrase ordinarily and primarily used for one purpose is applied to another which is not literally applicable. In *October Sky*, Jake calls the local newspaper, the *McDowell County Banner*, "a grocery-store rag" (154). Homer calls the rocket fuel "rocket candy" (181) because of its sweet odor and refers to a cord as "a thick electrical umbilical" (199).

An **analogy** is a comparison of one thing to another thing. For instance, comparing the world to a stage or the heart to a pump would be examples of analogies.

Personification is the attribution of human characteristics to inanimate objects. For instance, Homer states that the "big golden moon hovered overhead" (53). Later he says that "a shuttle car darted in, its crablike arms sweeping up the coal thrown out" (99).

Clichés are phrases that have become meaningless because of their frequent use; "Have a good day" and "Look on the bright side" are examples of clichés. The listener wonders whether the speaker is sincere in the sentiment expressed or truly understands the situation. A writer might have a character speak in clichés to indicate that the character is a shallow person, has difficulty expressing thoughts, or does not think before speaking.

Allusion

An allusion is a reference to a historical, literary, or otherwise generally familiar character or event that helps make an idea understandable. Hickam employs this device when he gives the family pets the names Daisy Mae (a character in a comic strip popular in the 1950s) and Lucifer (another name for the devil). The pets' names give the readers a hint to the "characters" of the animals.

Diction

Diction is the author's choice of words. Hickam uses a colloquial diction in the dialogue of his characters to enhance the reader's image of the people of Coalwood, West Virginia:

> "We ought to just shoot that damn Sputnikker down." There was a pause while the men all thoughtfully spat tobacco juice into their paper cups, and then one of them said, "Well, I'll tell you who we oughta shoot. Makes me madder'n fire"—he pronounced the word as if it rhymed with *tar*—"them damn people up in Charleston who's tryin' to cheat Big Creek out of the state champs. I'd like to warp them upside the head." (32)

Other examples include Homer's mother stating that his dad "would have a hissy" (51) and Roy Lee telling Homer to "have at it" (37) when Homer says he plans to build a rocket. Quentin, unlike most of the residents of the West Virginia town, speaks in his own dialect: " 'O'Dell,' Quentin replied, in all sincerity, 'I'm worried that your insatiable cupidity will ultimately prove to be something less than a virtue for our club' " (105).

Voice

The literary term that describes a writer's individual writing style and combines an author's use of dialogue, diction, alliteration, and other devices within the body of the text is referred to as **voice.** Because every author has a different style of writing, voice is the fingerprint of the author.

Voice in nonfiction is similar to the narrator's tone in fiction; the major difference is in who is "speaking." In fiction, the author is not usually the speaker; the narrator is the speaker. Students sometimes have difficulty with this distinction, but it is necessary to make this distinction to preserve the integrity of the fictive "story."

In an essay, however, the author speaks directly to the reader, even if presenting ideas that the writer may not actually espouse personally—as in a satire. This directness creates the writer's tone or the attitude toward his subject.

Point of View

Point of view is a stylistic device that an author needs to determine as soon as the composing begins. There are several views a writer might use.

A narrator who knows all about the characters and the actions and shares this information with the audience presents an **omniscient point of view**. A narrator who does not share all the information about all the characters or all the events with the readers presents a **limited omniscient point of view**.

A writer may assume an **objective point of view** and simply tell the happenings without voicing an opinion; with the objective point of view, the narrator never reveals what the characters are thinking or feeling.

A story told from the **first-person singular point of view** unfolds through the eyes of one central character. The reader should realize that the account may be biased by the person telling the story. The writer will have the narrator speak of him- or herself using first-person pronouns: *I, me,* and *my.* The **second-person point of view** employs the word *you.* Sometimes this point of view poses a problem for the reader. Who is *you*? The reader? Everyone in the world? Without knowing the antecedent for the pronoun *you,* the reader experiences problems in understanding the piece. In stories told from the **third-person point of view**, the narrator does not participate in the action. The narrator can, however, reveal thoughts and actions of the characters. The writer usually employs either the third-person singular pronouns—*he, she,* and *it*—or the third-person plural—*they* and *them.*

Style

In addition to the elements already discussed, there are many devices that the writer can employ to enhance the flow of the words, make the writing more appealing, and clarify the meaning. Style incorporates such devices as denotation and/or connotation, alliteration, consonance, assonance, onomatopoeia, rhythm, imagery, hyperbole, understatement, wordplay, and symbolism.

All of these stylistic devices—and others—appear in *October Sky* (Hickam 1999).

The **denotation** of a word is its precise meaning. Denotation is evident throughout *October Sky*, which seems logical because as a scientist, Hickam would use accurate, clear descriptions and would say precisely what he means. Homer uses denotation when he describes Emily Sue's family and where they live:

> Emily Sue lived in a house built on the side of a nearly vertical mountain across the creek and not more than a hundred yards from Big Creek High School. Her father owned a big scrap yard in War [the actual name of a town], and her mother was the third-grade schoolteacher at War Elementary. (148)

The **connotation** of a word is the impression or feeling a word gives beyond its exact meaning. Sometimes the reader must have some prior knowledge to understand the term. For example, Homer's statement that "Mr. Turner was a banty-rooster type of man" (139–40) gives a unique impression of Mr. Turner. However, a reader with no previous experience with a banty rooster may not get much insight into the character of the man.

Alliteration is the repetition of initial sounds in two or more words in a sentence or phase. In Homer's description of riding the bus to school on a snowy morning, he uses the repetition of the *s* sound, certainly fitting for the slippery, snowy season: ". . . we were faced with a steep, straight stretch followed by a series of curves that dipped and turned" (162).

Consonance, like alliteration, involves sounds of words; consonance is the repetition of, consonant sounds, especially at the end of stressed syllables. The short, staccato sound of the hard *c* builds tension when Homer reports that the mining town is about to experience change that may result in the loss of jobs and company housing for Coalwood residents:

> In May, the company announced that its big new coal-preparation plant in Caretta was complete, and all the coal from both the Coalwood and Caretta mines would henceforth be loaded into coal cars over there. (148)

Assonance is the repetition of vowel sounds. In *October Sky*, the Rocket Boys work to build a blockhouse for protection during their rocket launchings. They chant as they work. The use of similar vowel sounds (and final consonant sounds) is necessary for the chant's rhyming pattern:

> "I'm not the carpenter or the carpenter's son," he chanted as we sawed and drove nails, "but I'll do the carpentryin' until the carpenter comes."

> "Anybody here ever pour concrete?" I asked the group. "I'm not the concrete pourer or the concrete pourer's son . . ." came back the cheerful chorus of replies. (139–40)

The school fight song also uses assonance:

> "On, on, green and white . . .We are right for the fight tonight!
> Hold that ball and hit that line, every Big Creek star will shine.
> We'll fight, fight, fight for the green and white." (133–34)

Onomatopoeia is a stylistic device in which the sound of the word imitates the sound it represents. Comic book authors often use onomatopoeic words like *pow*, *bop*, *splat*, and *pop* to create sound effects for the story's action; sometimes the words even appear on the screen of an animated feature.

October Sky contains many instances of onomatopoeia. For instance, Homer wonders if Sputnik, the Russian satellite, will "zip along or dawdle" and notes that his father "plopped on his hat" (37). Later, Homer remarks that his father's "door banged open and I heard him thumping down the stairs. . . . At the bottom of the stairs he started to cough, a racking, deep, wet hack" (54).

The **rhythm**, or flow or cadence, of the words can help create a mood, or feeling, in the reader. When Homer and the Rocket Boys attempt to launch their first rocket, the sentences and thoughts that follow the "blastoff" are short and choppy—almost staccato—evoking the tension and excitement the boys felt. These brief sentences and concise thoughts are in marked contrast to Hickam's typical style of longer, more descriptive sentences:

Wooden splinters whistled past my ears. Big clunks of the fence arced into the sky. Burning debris fell with a clatter. A thunderous echo rumbled back from the surrounding hollows. Dogs up and down the valley barked and house lights came on, one by one. People came out and huddled on their front porches. (45)

The reader senses the tension subsiding when Hickam returns to his more usual style of longer, less stressful sentences:

Later, I would hear that a lot of them were wondering if the mine had blown up or maybe the Russians had attacked. At that moment, I wasn't thinking about anything except a big orange circle that seemed to be hovering in front of my eyes. When I regained some sensibility and my vision started to come back, the circle diminished and I started to look around. (45)

Imagery is descriptive language designed to create a mental image for the reader of the smells, feelings, sounds, or sights of a person, place, thing, or event. Hickam employs imagery to describe many of the places and events surrounding the activities of the Rocket Boys. Particularly important are his descriptions of the town of Coalwood and how the town appeals to the many senses of its inhabitants:

Every weekday, and even on Saturday when times were good, I could watch the black coal cars rolling beneath the tipple to receive their massive loads and then smoke-spouting locomotives straining to pull them away. All through the day, the heavy thump of the locomotives' steam pistons thundered down our narrow valleys, the town shaking to the crescendo of grinding steel as the great trains accelerated. Clouds of coal dust rose from the open cars, invading everything, seeping through windows and creeping under doors. Throughout my childhood, when I raised my blanket in the morning, I saw a black, sparkling powder float off it. My socks were always black with coal dirt when I took my shoes off at night. (2)

Hickam's description of Buck, a football player, employs the senses of sight, smell, sound, and touch:

> "You really are a little sister, ain't you?" He pulled his face in close to us, his chin prickly with whiskers. There was a brown chewing-tobacco stain in the lower left corner of his mouth. I could smell its sweetness on his breath. (93)

Another stylistic device that a writer may use for effect is **hyperbole**. A hyperbole is an exaggeration; it describes something—or someone—as larger or more important than is the case. Hickam makes use of many hyperboles in *October Sky*. For instance, Hickam notes, "There was . . . a huge flash in the Hickams' yard and a sound like God Himself had clapped His hands" (44).

An **understatement** underplays something and presents it to be less significant than is actually true. Whereas a hyperbole exaggerates to the maximum, an understatement minimizes. For example, a hospitalized patient may say that a medical procedure "smarts a little," when in fact the procedure was actually extremely painful. Although a gift may be extravagant, a suitor may say, "I bought you a little something." Both of these comments are understatements.

Wordplay is a stylistic device that many writers employ. It is essentially as it sounds: the playful and creative use of words for a witty effect. A **pun**, for example, is a humorous wordplay in which the two meanings of a word or two similar-sounding words are deliberately confused. Hickam makes use of a pun when he describes Homer losing a wheel off his wheelbarrow:

> I'd spotted some great flower dirt up in the mountains and would've brought Mom some home with me "if this blame ol' 'wheelbare' hadn't fallen apart!" (47)

Symbolism is the use of one person, place, or thing to represent another. A common symbol in juvenile literature is the loss of an animal to represent the death of childhood; this symbol appears in *Old Yeller* by Fred Gipson, *The Yearling* by Marjorie Kinnan Rawlings, and *Where the Red Fern Grows* by Wilson Rawls.

Plot

The plot of a book is its story line and is usually the element that keeps one interested in reading. The plot has a definite order, involves conflict, has a pattern, and may be of two types.

Order of the Plot. The events of the plot may occur in **chronological**, or sequential, order, or the events may occur in a more random order. In some books or stories, the plot may carry the reader from the present to events in the past **(flashback)** and then back again. This pattern of action may occur only once within the story or several times. There may even be a hint of the future or of what is to come (**foreshadowing**).

Conflict in the Plot. There must be conflict, or unsettled issues, in the plot to keep the reader interested. The conflict can be internal, with self; or external, with others, with society, or with nature. Of course, *Robinson Crusoe* by Daniel Defoe is an excellent example of conflict with nature. In *Gulliver's Travels* by Jonathan Swift, the protagonist encounters conflict with the Lilliputians, small people though they are. Jerry Renault in *The Chocolate War* by Robert Cormier faces conflicts with himself (e.g., "Am I strong enough to refuse to sell the chocolates that the rest of the school is selling?"), with others who try to force him to sell, and with society because the entire school community is at odds with him for not selling.

Patterns of Action. There are several possible patterns of action in juvenile fiction. These patterns include suspense, cliff-hanger, foreshadowing, sensationalism, climax, and denouement.

Suspense is the state of uncertainty or not knowing. A book or story that employs suspense keeps the reader in doubt or uncertainty as to the outcome until the end. *Robinson Crusoe* is such a book.

Chapter books and books that are part of a series often featuring **cliffhangers**, endings in which an exciting event is left unresolved so that the reader is prompted to keep turning the pages or to read the next book in the series. Television programs—especially soap operas—and movies often incorporate cliffhanger plots.

Foreshadowing is a literary effect in which a character or event gives a clue or a hint as to what will occur in future action. For example, in *The Chocolate War* (Cormier

1974/1977), the narrator foreshadows the novel's later plot developments when he says, "They shouldn't have picked Frankie Rollo for an assignment, of course" (130).

Sensationalism is the use of emotionally charged words, expressions, or events in order to provoke a strong reaction in the reader. "Hansel and Gretel" is a piece of traditional literature that features sensationalism. The evil stepmother sends the father out into the woods to lose the children; they find their way back; the father takes them out again; the birds eat the crumbs they have scattered as landmarks; the children become lost; the witch takes them captive; Hansel eventually pushes the witch into the oven. Certainly these are ample examples of the sensationalism in the fairy tale. Many action movies—like the Indiana Jones and the James Bond series—also contain elements of sensationalism in the pattern of action of the plot.

The **climax** is the highest point of interest in a book or story; the climax is the point at which the reader says, "Ah-ha! Now I am sure of the outcome of the conflict!" Some books feature a **false climax**. The reader mistakenly believes that all the story's questions have been answered only to find that the story or book has new twists and turns. In "Hansel and Gretel," for instance, the listener or reader believes that when the children find their way home after the first time their father abandons them in the woods, the conflict is resolved; it is a false climax. It is only later in the story that the reader has all questions answered.

The **denouement** is the ending of the book. There are two types: an **open denouement** leaves some of the reader's questions unanswered, some plot points unresolved; a **closed denouement** answers all the reader's questions. Howard Garis's dime novels about Uncle Wiggly contain an open ending for each story or episode in the volume to keep the reader turning the pages. For instance, Story I ends with

> But then, all of a sudden, a harsh voice cried out: "Ha! Now I have you! I was just wishing some one would come along with my dinner, and you did! Get in there, and see if you can find your fortune, Uncle Wiggly!"
>
> And with that a big, black bear, who had been hiding in the stump, pushed Uncle Wiggly into a dark closet, and locked the door! And there the poor rabbit was, and the bear was getting ready to have him for dinner.

> But don't worry, I'll find a way to get Uncle Wiggly out. And
> in case we have ice cream pancakes for supper, with strawberry
> jam pudding sauce, I'll tell you, in the next story, how Uncle
> Wiggly got out of the bear's den, and went fishing. (Garis 14)

It is the open ending of some of the horror movies that keep viewers attending the numerous sequels. Some of the horror films with open endings include *Friday the 13th*, *Nightmare on Elm Street*, *Halloween*, and *I Know What You Did Last Summer*. Of course, the *Rocky* movies are also good examples of movies with an open denouement. Soap operas are notorious for their open endings. The American public waited a whole summer in 1980 to find out "Who shot J.R.?" after the television series *Dallas* ended its season with a cliffhanger.

Plots may be progressive or episodic. A **progressive plot** requires one to read the entire book or story to find the answers to the question(s) in the plot. An **episodic plot** features individual chapters or episodes that are related to each other but each of which is a story unto itself. Robert Newton Peck's *Soup* series contains chapters that are episodic.

Setting

The setting, or the time and place in which a story or book occurs, is important to juvenile literature. An essential element of the setting is that it is believable. The plot and the setting together make up the **structure** of the story.

A setting may be one of two types: backdrop or integral. A **backdrop setting** is one that is not essential to the plot. The setting in many of the Nancy Drew books is a backdrop setting because the plot could have happened in almost any American city. This backdrop setting is figurative. The **figurative setting** simply serves as an illustration.

An **integral setting** is a setting that is essential to the plot. It actually occurs where the author states that it does. The setting of Wilson Rawls's *Summer of the Monkeys*—the Ozarks—is literal and integral:

> It was in the late 1800s, the best I can remember. Anyhow—at
> the time, we were living in a brand-new country that had just
> been opened up for settlement. The farm we lived on was called

Cherokee land because it was smack dab in the middle of the Cherokee Nation. It lay in a strip from the foothills of the Ozark Mountains to the banks of the Illinois River in northeastern Oklahoma. (Rawls 9–10)

Character

As important as the plot and action are, it is the **characters**—or the personalities— who make many books live on for many years. It is Tom Sawyer, Long John Silver, Meg, Beth, Jo, and Amy who helped to make *The Adventures of Tom Sawyer*, *Treasure Island*, and *Little Women* classics; the characters have withstood the test of time.

Characters may be **round** (fully described or revealed) or **flat** (not fully developed, described, or revealed), **dynamic** (developing or changing) or **static** (unchanging).

Writers use a variety of means to reveal characters to the readers. The writer may tell about the character in detail, as in this passage about the dog Lassie, one of the main characters in *Lassie Come Home* by Eric Mowbray Knight (1938/1966):

> Greenall Bridge was like other Yorkshire villages. Its men knew and understood and loved dogs, and there were many perfect ones that walked at men's heels; but they all agreed that if a finer dog than Sam Carralough's tricolor collie had ever been bred in Greenall Bridge, then it must have been long before they were born.

Another effective way to reveal a character is to describe the character in the character's surroundings, as in this excerpt from *Never Cry Wolf* by Farley Mowat (1963/1984):

> This country belonged to the deer, the wolves, the birds and the smaller beasts. We two were no more than casual and insignificant intruders. Man had never dominated the Barrens. Even the Eskimos, whose territory it had once been, had lived in harmony with it. The little group . . . was the last of the inland people, and they were all but swallowed up in this immensity of wilderness.

The writer might also show the character in action. The following excerpt from *To Kill a Mockingbird* by Harper Lee (1960/1982) describes Atticus, the lawyer and father, in action when a rabid dog enters their neighborhood:

> Atticus pushed his glasses to his forehead; they slipped down, and he dropped them in the street. In the silence, I heard them crack. Atticus rubbed his eyes and chin; we saw him blink hard. . . . With movements so swift they seemed simultaneous, Atticus's hand yanked a ball-tipped lever as he brought the gun to his shoulder.

The **speech**, or dialect or diction, of the character(s) can aid the author in revealing the character(s). The language of the gang members in Frank Bonham's *Durango Street* (1965/1975) helps to disclose Tojo's and Rufus's attitudes:

> Tojo smiled. "Esscuse me, brothers. I meant bloods."
>
> Rufus rocked his head. "That's all right, greaseballs—Esscuse *me:* I mean Spanish-Americans."
>
> "Mexicans," Tojo snapped.
>
> "Sure, man," Rufus said. "Well, if you beans change your minds, you know where to find us. But don't come into Durango unless you're ready to talk business. *Adiòs,* huh?" (Bonham 105)

The author often reveals the thoughts of a character to inform the reader about the character. Billie Jo in the 1998 Newbery Medal winner *Out of the Dust* by Karen Hesse (1997/1999) expresses her thoughts in her diary:

> From the earliest I can remember I've been restless in this little Panhandle shack we call home, always getting in Ma's way with my pointy elbows, my fidgety legs. (4)

A character's appearance can help the reader to understand the character as well. Dori Sanders uses this device in her book *Clover* (1991):

They dressed me in white for my daddy's funeral. White from my head to my toes. I had the black skirt I bought at the six-dollar store all laid out to wear. I'd even pulled the black grossgrain bows off my black patent leather shoes to wear in my hair. But they won't let me wear black. (1)

What others say *about* a character gives the reader additional insight into that character. S. E. Hinton uses this device in *The Outsiders* (1967) to tell the reader about Dallas:

He had quite a reputation. They have a file on him down at the police station. He had been arrested, he got drunk, he rode in rodeos, lied, cheated, stole, rolled drunks, jumped small kids— he did everything. I didn't like him, but he was smart and you had to respect him. (13)

What others say *to* a character is another way of revealing the character to the reader. In *Brighty of the Grand Canyon* by Marguerite Henry (1953/1967), Uncle Jim—a prospector—speaks to the burro Brighty as if it were a human. The reader comes to believe that the burro can understand. When the claws of a mountain lion cut Brighty, Uncle Jim explains to the burro how he plans to help heal the animal's wounds:

"I've an idee!" he crowed, eyes twinkling in triumph. He took out his pocketknife and pierced the denim just above one knee. Then he cut his way around the pants leg and stepped out of it.

"Y'see, boy," he said, "if we hide yer cuts, you can't pick at 'em so easy, and they'll heal nice and clean." (57–58)

Additional details about a character's life and circumstances further inform the reader about the character, as in this passage from Mary Mapes Dodge's *Hans Brinker* (1963):

These queer-looking affairs [homemade skates] had been made by the boy Hans. His mother was a poor peasant woman, too poor even to think of such a thing as buying skates for her little ones. Rough as these were, they had afforded the children many a happy hour upon the ice; and now as with cold, red fingers our young Hollanders tugged at the strings—their solemn faces

bending closely over their knees—no vision of impossible iron
runners came to dull the satisfaction glowing within. (1–2)

The reactions of one character to another and vice versa can help the reader gain insight into both characters. In the following passage from *Anne of Green Gables*, for example, Anne's reactions to Marilla and Marilla's reaction to Anne help the reader to know both characters:

"Will you please call me Cordelia?" she [Anne] asked eagerly.

"*Call* you Cordelia! Is that your name?" [Marilla]

"No-o-o, it's not exactly my name, but I would love to be called Cordelia. It's such a perfectly elegant name."

"I don't know what on earth you mean. If Cordelia isn't your name, what is?"

"Anne Shirley," reluctantly faltered forth the owner of that name, "But oh, please do call me Cordelia. It can't matter much to you what you call me if I'm only going to be here a little while, can it? And Anne is such an unromantic name."

"Unromantic fiddlesticks!" said the unsympathetic Marilla.

"Anne is a real good plain sensible name. You've no need to be ashamed of it." (Montgomery 1908/1935, 34)

Whatever method that the writer chooses to use to reveal a character, a careful writer will avoid **stereotyping**, or typecasting a character based on the character's nationality, religion, size, or age. Gender, too, has been a basis for stereotyping characters in children's books. There have traditionally been fewer female than male characters in books for children. In such traditional works, the female characters often display poorer reasoning skills than do the males and also lead more placid existences. Many of the females depend on males to rescue them and behave more passively than their male counterparts.

An article by Davis and McMillan (1999) shows some gains for girls in the way that Caldecott Medal–winning books depict them, but the researchers were perplexed that the

1950s remained the golden era for females in the text of Caldecott winners. This surprising finding led to the title: "You've Come a Long Way, Baby—or Have You?"

Some teachers who discover stereotyping in a work may wish to exclude it from the required reading list for the class. Other teachers may make a point to include such books with their classes so as to draw attention to stereotyping and indicate to the students the weaknesses of such pigeon-holing.

A **protagonist** is a good, positive force in the book. An **antagonist** is the bad or evil element. Can you identify the protagonist in "Cinderella"? Can you indicate the antagonist(s)?

Theme

The theme is the main idea or central meaning of the book. Three main themes for traditional literature are the survival of the unfittest theme, the picaresque (journey) theme, and the reversal of fortune theme. Whether the theme is **implicit** (suggested) or **explicit** (stated), the reader should immediately recognize these common themes.

The **survival of the unfittest theme** appears in Swift's *Gulliver's Travels* and Defoe's *Robinson Crusoe*, two books that were published in the 1700s for adults but gained broad appeal among children. In the satire *Gulliver's Travels* and the religious writing *Robinson Crusoe*, Gulliver and Crusoe, respectively, face many life-threatening situations; in reality they probably should not have survived. Yet, they manage to endure, thus manifesting the survival of the unfittest theme.

The **picaresque theme** is evident in both *Robinson Crusoe* and *Gulliver's Travels* as well. The journey brings excitement—and danger—into each character's life. This journey provides excitement for the reader too.

The **reversal of fortune theme**, usually played out as a change or even a complete turnabout in the circumstance(s) of a character or characters, is a frequent feature of modern juvenile literature. *Heidi*, for example, is a novel with the reversal of fortune theme. The main character goes to live in the mountains with her grandfather, finds herself in the city with a foster family, and returns to the mountains with her friend to live with Grandfather. Heidi finds not only her own fortune reversed but also that of her crippled friend, whose once useless legs heal thanks to the clean mountain air, fresh food, and proper exercise.

Authenticity

One final, essential element in juvenile books is **authenticity**. Even juvenile fiction books must be authentic, in other words, believable and convincing. This requires that the components (setting, characters, diction, details) must be accurate for the time and place—or at least believable to the reader. A story may, for example, take place on the planet Mars, but as long as the writer can make the facts, setting, and characters seem believable to the reader, at least one ingredient of the story—authenticity—will have been met.

Evaluating Traditional and Modern Fiction

To evaluate a work of literature, the evaluator must take into account all the literary elements just discussed. Figure 2.1 brings together all of the components that form the story.

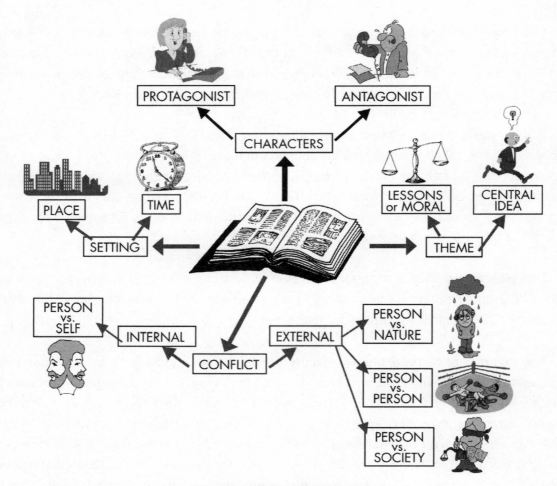

Figure 2.1 Literary Elements

Types of Traditional and Modern Fiction

Fable	Short story or folktale that contains a moral. Aesop's fables include *The Country Mouse.*
Fairy Tale	A narrative made up of fantastic characters and creatures (e.g., *Rupunzel* and *Sleeping Beauty*)
Fantasy	The primary elements of the plot or theme are supernatural or magical (e.g., C. S. Lewis's *The Chronicles of Narnia.*
Historical Fiction	Narrative fiction set in an earlier time; often it uses historical figures, places, or events (e.g., *The Killer Angels: A Novel of the Civil War* by Michael Shaara)
Horror	Frightening and unsettling fiction; can overlap with science fiction (e.g. *The Shining* by Stephen King, *Frankenstein* by Mary Shelley)
Legend	A narrative that recounts human actions perceived to have taken place with human history (e.g., *The Legend of Sleepy Hollow* by Washington Irving, *Paul Bunyon* by Ester Shepherd)
Mystery	A story of suspense dealing with a puzzling crime (e.g., Charles Dickens's *The Mystery of Edwin Drood*).
Myth	Narrative fiction that involves gods and heroes, usually expressing a culture's ideals.
Novel	An extended narrative.
Parody	Text or performance imitating or mocking a person or thing.
Romance	A genre that includes gothic and medieval romance that idealizes events far removed from daily life (e.g., Shakespeare's *Romeo and Juliet*)
Satire	Works that make fun of social conventions (e.g., *The Queen and I* by Sue Townsend)
Science Fiction	Fiction that deals with current or future technology and its advances or threats (e.g., George Orwell's *1984*, Aldous Huxley's *Brave New World*)
Short Story	Brief fictional prose narrative (e.g., *Adventures of Sherlock Holmes* by Sir Arthur Conan Doyle, *The Lottery* by Shirley Jackson)

Nonfiction Prose

Nonfiction prose is sometimes referred to as expository writing. Biographies and autobiographies, reports, and essays are all expository; in other words, they are meant to inform the reader.

Style in nonfiction derives from the same elements as style in fiction: word choice, voice, imagery, and so on. Generally speaking, an argumentative essay may have a more formal style than will a narrative essay; a meditative essay may be less formal than an expository essay.

Structure and thought are two important elements of essays. To change the structure of an essay will often alter the meaning. Thought is perhaps the single element that most distinguishes nonfiction from fiction. The essayist chooses the type of essay not to tell a story but to present an idea. Whether the writer chooses the speculative, narrative, argumentative, or expository format, the author has something on his mind to convey to the reader. It is the idea that the reader is seeking in the final analysis.

Poetry

Poetry is writing that is not prose. Opening a book to study for an examination is perhaps the worst occasion on which to read poetry, or about poetry, because above all, poetry is for enjoyment. It is hard to imagine but poetry was the "current language" for students growing up in the Elizabethan or Romantic eras.

There are many types and forms of poetry. For the exam one may need to determine what sort of poem is under scrutiny. The form may dictate the rhyme or meter and may enhance the meaning. Short, terse lines, for example, give a different feeling to the reader than longer, less compact writing. Stress on a particular word may enhance the meaning, as in "She saw *the* boy at the party."

There are two terms that are essential to understanding the forms of poetry: *stanza* and *rhyme*. A **stanza** is a group of lines to which there is often a metrical order and a repeated rhyme. Students sometimes call the grouping a verse, but the correct term is *stanza*. **Rhyme** can refer to corresponding sounds, to rhyme schemes, and/or to the metrical order. Letters are often used to show the repeated sounds:

> Jack and Jill (a)
> Went up the hill. (a)
> Bill did not go. (b)
> His car was slow. (b)

In the example, the rhyme scheme is aabb. *Jill* and *hill* and *go* and *slow* are examples of **end rhyme**, rhyming that occurs at the end of the line. The end rhyme brings the line to a stop but prepares the reader for a rhyming word in another line. In contrast, **internal rhyme** has one rhyming word within the line. This often speeds up the rhythm.

Forms of Poetry

Form is the pattern or design of a poem. Some poets also add shape to their poem, constructing it such that the poem's appearance (number and length of its lines, placement of individual words) coordinates to or even mimics the appearance of its subject. Such visual poems are not just fun to look at and read, but the form adds to the subject and helps the reader to appreciate the poet's view.

Open-form poems developed from *vers libre*—meaning "free verse," which suggests that little skill or craft went into the poem. Such is not the case, however. Open-form poems do, of course, require skill and craft, but the creativity of this form frees the poet from having to adhere to any specific rules.

Closed-form poems are recognizable because the poet adheres to the form, number of lines, rhyme scheme, meter, and/or shape. There are several types of closed-form poems.

Sonnet.   The sonnet is a closed- or fixed-form poem of 14 lines; it is one of the most easily recognizable types of poem. There are two types of sonnets: the Petrarchan or Italian and the Shakespearean or English.

The word *sonnet* comes from the Italian word *sonnetto*, which means "little song." Petrarch, the fourteenth-century Italian poet, took the form to its peak with his sonnets to Laura, his loved one. Laura died before he could declare his love; such poignant, unrequited love became the theme for many Elizabethan sonnets.

The **Petrarchan sonnet** has two groups: the octave of eight lines and the sestet of six lines. Usually the rhyme scheme is abbaabba-cdecde, but the sestet can vary in its pattern.

The octave may set up a problem or a proposition, the sestet—after a turn or a shift—may provide the answer or resolution.

The **Shakespearean sonnet** organizes the lines into three groups of four lines (quatrains) and two rhyming lines (a couplet). The rhyming scheme is always abab cdcd efef gg. The turn or shift can happen at one of three places, or the resolution or a "twist in the tail" may occur at the end.

Couplet.   The couplet is a closed form of poetry. It is a two-line stanza that usually has an end rhyme. A **heroic couplet** is a couplet that is end-stopped; it is written in iambic pentameter (discussed later in the chapter).

Epic.   An epic is a story poem that is vast in length, that is written with dignified language, and that celebrates the achievements of a hero. Because of the long length, a complete epic will probably not be on your Praxis English exam. You may, however, need to identify a few lines of one.

Translations of epics are often laid out in couplet form, the meter regular with equal line lengths. This is because these story poems have their roots in the oral tradition: they were originally sung aloud or chanted to the beat of drums. Repetition is a key feature of epics, again because of the oral tradition: if the bard, or singer, forgot a line, the audience, who had heard the stories many times before, could help him out.

The subject of the epic is typically a legendary or historical hero and the great deeds, adventures, and trials he experiences. The theme is one of human grief or pride, divided loyalties—but all "writ large." Here are some of the most frequently cited epics:

Paradise Lost, a great English epic by John Milton, tells the story of Adam and Eve and the Fall. Adam thus becomes the great hero; the divided loyalties occur when Adam must choose between obedience to God and love for his wife.

The Iliad by Homer relates events surrounding the final years of the Trojan War. The opening lines begin:

> Sing, O goddess, the anger of Achilles son of Peleus, that brought countless ills upon the Achaeans. Many a brave soul did it send hurrying down to Hades, and many a hero did it yield a prey to dogs and vultures, for so were the counsels of Jove fulfilled from the day on which the son of Atreus, king of men, and great Achilles, first fell out with one another. (Butler 1898)

The Odyssey by Homer tells of the adventures and trials of Odysseus (Ulysses). The opening lines begin:

Tell me, O muse, of that ingenious hero who traveled far and wide after he had sacked the famous town of Troy. Many cities did he visit, and many were the nations with whose manners and customs he was acquainted; moreover he suffered much by sea while trying to save his own life and bring his men safely home; but do what he might he could not save his men, for they perished through their own sheer folly in eating the cattle of the Sun-god Hyperion; so the god prevented them from ever reaching home. Tell me, too, about all these things, O daughter of Jove. (Butler 1900)

Ballads.   Ballads are stories in song. Some date from as early as the fourteenth and fifteenth centuries, having been passed down by word of mouth until the actual recording on paper. Working folk without skills of reading and writing sometimes composed them. Ballads usually are simple in theme and the author anonymous. The stories often center on love and hate, lust and murder, knights, and the supernatural. Like epics, ballads feature repetition, typically incorporating a repeated refrain.

A ballad stanza often has four lines with a rhyme scheme of ab cb. Lines 1 and 3 have 8 syllables; lines 2 and 4 have 6 syllables.

Literary ballads are the composition of later poets, rather than the result of the oral tradition. These later poets used ballads to tell stories; an example is Samuel Taylor Coleridge's "The Rime of the Ancient Mariner." He reconstructs the old folk story but writes it in a very closed form. The reader will notice that the second and fourth lines rhyme and have six syllables. These are perhaps the best known lines from the poem:

> Water, water, every where,
> And all the boards did shrink;
> Water, water, every where,
> Nor any drop to drink.

Lyric.   The lyric moves the listener/reader from the story of the ballad to emotion. The word *lyric* comes from the Greek word *lyre*; often the musical instrument accompanied the reading of this form of the poem. Samuel Taylor Coleridge and William Wordsworth moved away from the ballad form when they used the lyric.

Wordsworth uses six lines in the following poem. Lines 1 and 3 rhyme; 2 and 4 rhyme; and 5 and 6 rhyme:

> I Wandered Lonely as a Cloud
> I wander'd lonely as a cloud
> That floats on high o'er vales and hills,
> When all at once I saw a crowd,
> A host, of golden daffodils;
> Beside the lake, beneath the trees,
> Fluttering and dancing in the breeze.

Although a listener is sometimes inferred, very often the poet seems to be musing aloud in a lyric. Wordsworth, for example, often wrote in praise of nature: birds, flowers, the sea, and rainbows.

The **elegy** is a type of lyric. It is a lament for someone or for something, such as love or an idea. "Elegy Written in a Country Churchyard" by Thomas Gray is one of the most famous elegies; it mourns the passing of individuals:

> For them no more the blazing hearth shall burn,
> Or busy housewife ply her evening care:
> No children run to lisp their sire's return,
> Or climb his knees the envied kiss to share.

The **ode**—another part of the lyric family—is usually longer than an elegy and explores topics other than merely death. The "Ode on a Grecian Urn" by John Keats is perhaps the most famous. His lines give praise to the figures—especially the women—captured forever on the vase:

> She cannot face, though thou hast not thy bliss,
> For ever wilt thou love, and she be fair.

Other forms.   Being able to recognize additional forms of poetry may help in explicating a poem, recognizing the meaning, and doing well on the Praxis 0041. Familiarize yourself with these other forms of poetry: the villanelle, the sestina, the epigram, and the limerick.

The **villanelle** is a courtly love poem from medieval times. It has five, three-line stanzas (tercets) with a rhyme scheme of aba, and then a four-line stanza—a quatrain with the rhyme scheme abaa—ends the poem. There is also a repetition of the poem's first line as the last line of the second and the fourth tercets. The third line appears as the last line of the third and fifth tercet; the two lines appear again as rhyming lines at the end of the poem. The most famous villanelle is "Do Not Go Gentle into that Good Night" by Dylan Thomas. The poem has a controlled structure and a caution to rage against death until the end; there is a reminder, however, that the night, too, is good:

> Do not go gentle into that good night,
> Old age should burn and rave at close of day;
> Rage, rage against the dying of the light.

The **sestina**, a French form of poetry, is the most difficult of all closed forms. In James Joyce's *A Portrait of the Artist as a Young Man*, writing a villanelle on an empty cigarette packet turns a young boy into a poet. The structure consists of six stanzas of six lines. Elizabeth Bishop's "Sestina" and W. H. Auden's "Hearing of Harvests Rotting in the Valleys" are examples.

The **epigram** is a short poem with a clever twist at the end. Samuel Taylor Coleridge wrote some 1,561 epigrams. Here is one example:

> What is an Epigram? A dwarfish whole;
> Its body brevity, and wit its soul.

Likewise, Benjamin Franklin wrote some epigrams:

> Little strokes
> Fell great oaks.
> A stitch in time
> Saves nine.

Limericks have five lines and the rhyme scheme of aabba. Edward Lear specialized in the limerick:

> There was an Old Man with a beard.
> Who said, It is just as I feared.

Two owls and a hen
Four larks and a wren
Have all built nests in my beard.

Types of Rhyme

There are many types of rhyme, and being able to distinguish among them will be important on the Praxis 0041 exam.

PRAXIS Pointer

Be prepared. Don't waste time on "beat-the-test" strategies. Organize a study schedule and keep to it—you will avoid test anxiety.

Slant Rhyme. Slant rhyme—also known as half rhyme, off rhyme, near rhyme, or approximate rhyme—is a device that some poets use to surprise the reader. The audience is expecting a perfect rhyme, but it does not come. Some poets use the slant rhyme to give the reader a let-down or to express disappointment.

Masculine and Feminine Rhyme. Masculine rhyme typically uses one-syllable words to give a feeling of strength or impact. Some poets stress the final syllable of polysyllabic words to add this strength and create a masculine rhyme. Feminine rhyme may use a rhyme of two or more syllables. The stress does not fall upon the final syllable as it does in a masculine rhyme form. The general effect is to give the reader a feeling of softness and lightness. The terms *masculine rhyme* and *feminine rhyme* come from an earlier time. The terms themselves, however, are less important than the effect that the rhyme forms have on the reader.

Unrhymed Verse. Unrhymed verse that varies in its metrical pattern is **free verse**, or according to the French term, "vers libre." Free verse is without rhyme and rhythm. Robert Frost preferred not to use free verse; he likened it to "playing tennis with the net down," meaning he thought that it was easier than rhymed and metrical writing.

Blank verse is also unrhymed, but it has a strict rhythm. William Shakespeare often used blank verse in his plays. John Milton later used blank verse in his English epic, *Paradise Lost*. Contrary to what the term may suggest, blank verse is closed-form poetry because there are rules to writing it: not only must it be unrhymed, but it also must be written in iambic pentameter.

Meter and Feet. **Iambic pentameter** is a poetry meter in which each line contains five measures of one unstressed and one stressed syllable. A **foot** is the basic measuring unit in a line of poetry, and each of these unstressed-stressed syllable pairs is called an **iambic foot**. The following line from Shakespeare's *Henry IV* incorporates 10 syllables with rising and falling stress—an iambic pentameter, or a five-measure line with ten beats:

To BE comMENC'D in STRONDS aFAR reMOTE.

Iambic pentameter is, of course, only one type of meter. Other poetry-line lengths include monometer (one foot), dimeter (two feet), trimeter (three feet), tetrameter (four feet), heptameter (seven feet), and octameter (eight feet).

There are also several foot names worth learning:

An **anapest** is a foot consisting of three syllables in which the first two are short or unstressed and the final one is long or stressed. For example, "in the FIRE." The following is a famous anapestic line from Clement Moore:

Twas the NIGHT before CHRISTMAS, when all THROUGH the HOUSE . . .

A **trochee** is a foot that has two syllables in which the first is long or stressed, and the second is short and unstressed. Shakespeare uses a trochee in this line from *Macbeth*:

DOUble, DOUble, TOIL and TROUble . . .

A **dactyl** is a foot of three syllables in which the first is long or stressed, and the next two are unstressed or short:

TAKE her up TENderly . . .

Rhyme in Open-Form Poems. Open-form poems seem to have spilled on the page in any order; the poet has no rules of rhyme pattern or meter. There may be rhyme, but if there is, the rhyme may seem to have "slipped in" with no formal pattern. The poet may address the reader directly—even in an informal way. The lines break at any point; dashes abound. The poet may seem to have played with words. This type of rhyme dates from after World War I (usually); its classification is modern. Emily Dickinson used the open form in many of her works.

Forms of Poetry

Ballad	A short poem comprised of short verses intended to be sung or recited
Elegy	A poem with a mournful lament for the dead
Epic	A long narrative poem detailing a hero's deeds (e.g., *Beowulf*, and *Don Quixote* by Cervantes)
Haiku	A specific type of Japanese poetry that expresses one thought written in 17 syllables with three lines of five, seven, and five syllables, respectively
Limerick	A humorous verse composed of five anapestic lines with a rhyme scheme of aabbaa
Lyric	Short poem about personal feelings and emotions
Sonnet	Poem with 14 lines written in iambic pentameter, with a varied rhyming scheme

Nonprint Texts

Drama may refer to compositions in prose or poetry that present in pantomime or in dialogue "the conflict or contrast of character." *Drama* originally referred to performances on the stage, but in current usage, the word may refer to programs for television. The word may also refer to the quality of being dramatic and "any situation or series of events having vivid, emotional, conflicting, or striking interest or results: the drama of a murder trial" (Dictionary.com).

Middle school students may read portions of Shakespeare's plays or even part of such plays as *Our Town* by Thornton Wilder. *Our Town* is, in fact, one of the most frequently produced plays by an American playwright; it won the Pulitzer Prize in 1938.

INTERPRETING TEXTS

A key step in interpreting a literary work is situating it within the historical period and cultural context in which it was written. This is often difficult for students as the task requires knowledge beyond the literature itself.

A cursory overview of the historical periods described by Western tradition follows.

Early Periods of Literature

These periods are spans of time in which literature shared intellectual, linguistic, religious, and artistic influences.

Classical Period (1200 BCE–455 CE)

Homeric or Heroic Period (1200–800 BCE). Greek legends are passed along orally, including Homer's *The Iliad* and *The Odyssey*. This is a chaotic period of warrior princes, wandering sea traders, and fierce pirates.

Classical Greek Period (800–200 BCE). Greek writers, playwrights, and philosophers such as Gorgias, Aesop, Plato, Socrates, Aristotle, Euripides, and Sophocles all make their mark during this period. The fifth century (499–400 BCE) in particular is known as the Golden Age of Greece. This is the sophisticated age of the polis, or individual city-state, and early democracy. Some of the world's finest art, poetry, drama, architecture, and philosophy originate in Athens.

Classical Roman Period (200 BCE–455 CE). Greece's culture gives way to Roman power when Rome conquers Greece in 146 CE. The Roman Republic was traditionally founded in 509 BCE, but it is limited in size until later. Playwrights of this time include Plautus and Terence. After nearly 500 years as a republic, Rome slides into dictatorship under Julius Caesar and finally into a monarchial empire under Caesar Augustus in 27 CE. This later period is known as the Roman Imperial period. Roman writers include Ovid, Horace, and Virgil. Roman philosophers include Marcus Aurelius and Lucretius. Roman rhetoricians include Cicero and Quintilian.

Patristic Period (ca. 70 CE–455 CE). Early Christian writings appear such as those by Saint Augustine, Tertullian, Saint Cyprian, Saint Ambrose, and Saint Jerome. This is the period in which Saint Jerome first compiles the Bible, when Christianity spreads across Europe, and the Roman Empire suffers its dying convulsions. In this period, barbarians attack Rome in 410 CE, and the city finally falls to them completely in 455 CE.

Medieval Period (455 CE–1485 CE)

Old English (Anglo-Saxon) Period (428–1066). The so-called **Dark Ages** (455–799) occur when Rome falls and barbarian tribes move into Europe. Franks, Ostrogoths, Lombards, and Goths settle in the ruins of Europe, and the Angles, Saxons, and Jutes migrate to Britain, displacing native Celts into Scotland, Ireland, and Wales. Early Old English epic poems such as *Beowulf*, *The Wanderer*, and *The Seafarer* originate sometime late in the Anglo-Saxon period.

The **Carolingian Renaissance** (800–850) emerges in Europe. In central Europe, texts include early medieval grammars, encyclopedias, and the like. In northern Europe, this time period marks the setting of Viking sagas.

Middle English Period (ca. 1066–1450). In 1066, Norman French armies invade and conquer England under William I. This marks the end of the Anglo-Saxon hierarchy and the emergence of the **Twelfth-Century Renaissance** (ca. 1100–1200). French chivalric romances, such as works by Chrétien de Troyes, and French fables, such as the works of Marie de France and Jean de Meun, spread in popularity. Peter Abelard and other humanists produce great scholastic and theological works.

Late or "High" Medieval Period (ca. 1200–1485). This often tumultuous period is marked by the Middle English writings of Geoffrey Chaucer, the "Gawain" or "Pearl" Poet, the Wakefield Master, and William Langland. Other writers include Italian and French authors like Boccaccio, Petrarch, Dante, and Christine de Pisan.

The Renaissance and the Reformation (ca. 1485–1660)

The Renaissance takes place in the late fifteenth, sixteenth, and early seventeenth centuries in Britain, but somewhat earlier in Italy and southern Europe, and somewhat later in northern Europe.

Early Tudor Period (1485–1558). The War of the Roses ends in England with Henry Tudor (Henry VII) claiming the throne. Martin Luther's split with the Roman Catholic Church marks the emergence of Protestantism, followed by Henry VIII's Anglican schism, which creates the first Protestant church in England. Edmund Spenser is a poet of this period.

Elizabethan Period (1558–1603). Queen Elizabeth I saves England from both Spanish invasion and internal squabbles at home. Her reign is marked by the early works of William Shakespeare, Christopher Marlowe, Thomas Kyd, and Sir Philip Sidney.

Jacobean Period (1603–1625).   Shakespeare writes his later works, and Aemilia Lanyer, Ben Jonson, and John Donne make their mark.

Caroline Age (1625–1649).   John Milton, George Herbert, Robert Herrick, and the "Sons of Ben," among others, write during the reign of Charles I and his Cavaliers.

Commonwealth Period or Puritan Interregnum (1649–1660).   Under Oliver Cromwell's Puritan dictatorship, John Milton continues to write; other writers of the period include Andrew Marvell and Sir Thomas Browne.

Later Periods of Literature

These periods are spans of time in which literature shared intellectual, linguistic, religious, and artistic influences. The following sections describe the later periods of literary history according to the Western tradition.

The Enlightenment (Neoclassical) Period (ca. 1660–1790)

Neoclassical refers to the increased influence of classical literature upon these centuries. The neoclassical period is also called the Enlightenment due to the increased reverence for logic and disdain for superstition. The period is marked by the rise of deism, intellectual backlash against earlier Puritanism, and America's revolution against England.

Restoration Period (ca. 1660–1700).   This period marks the British king's restoration to the throne after a long period of Puritan domination in England. Its symptoms include the dominance of French and classical influences on poetry and drama. Sample writers include John Dryden, John Lock, Sir William Temple, and Samuel Pepys, and Aphra Behn in England. In France, representative authors include Jean Racine and Jean-Baptiste Molière.

Augustan Age (ca. 1700–1750).   This period is marked by the imitation of Virgil and Horace's literature in English letters. The principal English writers include Joseph Addison, Sir Richard Steele, Jonathan Swift, and Alexander Pope. François-Marie Arouet Voltaire is the dominant French writer.

Age of Johnson (ca. 1750–1790).   This period marks the transition toward the upcoming romanticism though the period is still largely neoclassical. Major writers include Dr. Samuel Johnson, James Boswell, and Edward Gibbon, who represent the neoclassical tendencies, while writers like Robert Burns, Thomas Gray, William Cowper, and George Crabbe show movement away from the neoclassical ideal. In America, this period is called the colonial period. It includes colonial and revolutionary writers like Benjamin Franklin, Thomas Jefferson, and Thomas Paine.

Romantic Period (ca. 1790–1830)

Romantic poets write about nature, imagination, and individuality in England. Some romantics include Samuel Taylor Coleridge, William Blake, John Keats, and Percy Bysshe Shelley in Britain and Johann von Goethe in Germany. Jane Austen also writes at this time, though she is not typically categorized with the male romantic poets. In America, this period is mirrored in the transcendental period from about 1830–1850. Transcendentalists include Ralph Waldo Emerson and Henry David Thoreau. **Gothic** writings (ca. 1790–1890) overlap with the romantic and Victorian periods. Writers of Gothic novels (the precursor to horror novels) include Ann Radcliffe, Monk Lewis, and Victorians like Bram Stoker in Britain. American Gothic writers include Edgar Allan Poe and Nathaniel Hawthorne.

Victorian Period and the Nineteenth Century (ca. 1832–1901)

Sentimental novels typify the period of Queen Victoria's reign. British writers include Elizabeth Browning, Alfred Lord Tennyson, Matthew Arnold, Robert Browning, Charles Dickens, and the Brontë sisters, Emily and Charlotte. Pre-Raphaelites like Christina and Dante Rossetti and William Morris idealize and long for the morality of the medieval world. The end of the Victorian period is marked by intellectual movements of aestheticism and "the decadence" in the writings of Walter Pater and Oscar Wilde. In America, **naturalist** writers like Stephen Crane flourish, as do early free verse poets like Walt Whitman and Emily Dickinson.

Modern Period (ca. 1914–1945)

In Britain, modernist writers include W. B. Yeats, Seamus Heaney, Dylan Thomas, W. H. Auden, Virginia Woolf, and Wilfred Owen. In America, the modernist period includes Robert Frost and Flannery O'Connor as well as the famous writers of the Lost Generation (also called the writers of the Jazz Age, 1914–1929) such as Ernest Hemingway, Gertrude Stein, F. Scott Fitzgerald, and William Faulkner. The Harlem Renaissance marks the rise of black writers such as James Baldwin and Ralph Waldo Ellison. Realism is the dominant fashion, but the disillusionment in the aftermath of the World Wars leads to new experimentation.

Postmodern Period (ca. 1945 onward)

T. S. Eliot, George Bernard Shaw, Samuel Beckett, Sir Tom Stoppard, John Fowles, Italo Calvino, Allen Ginsberg, Thomas Pynchon, and other modern writers, poets, and playwrights experiment with metafiction and fragmented poetry. Multiculturalism leads to increasing canonization of non-Caucasian writers such as Langston Hughes, Toni Morrison, Sandra Cisneros, and Zora Neale Hurston. Magic realists such as Gabriel García Márquez, Luis Borges, Alejo Carpentier, Günter Grass, and Salman Rushdie flourish with surrealistic writings embroidered in the conventions of realism.

Literature from Various Cultures

Cultures around the world have their own unique folktales, fairy tales, and other traditional literature and writings. For instance, Charles Perrault's French tale of "Cinderella" is "Tattercoats" in Joseph Jacobs's collection; in Jacob's British version, the prince falls in love with a dirty, ragged girl—not a beautiful, well-dressed figure at the ball. The Norwegian tale is of Cinderlad, not Cinderella, in "East o' the Sun and West o' the Moon."

Promoting respect for and appreciation of cultural diversity and pluralism through literature in the classroom is an important purpose of reading. Dolores B. Malcolm, president of the International Reading Association (IRA) in the late 1990s, stated:

> Only through the acceptance of the presence of "all" will the true concept of pluralism be realized. . . . Every culture has a heritage, and all children need to know and respect their own heritage and that of other people. (Micklos Jr. 1995–96, 1–8)

Teachers should heighten students' appreciation for the importance of cultural pluralism—as opposed to separatism or elitism—by using a variety of readings in the classroom. For example, Carmen Agra Deedy is a well-known writer, storyteller, and speaker who focuses on her Cuban background in her work. Her works add to the literature of a classroom. A teacher might use *Faithful Elephants: A True Story of Animals, People, and War* by Yukio Tsuchiya, which requires the reader to consider war through its impact on animals, particularly the animals in Japan; it is a children's book, but its message is not childlike. *Sadako and the Thousand Paper Cranes* by Eleanor Coerr enables the reader to consider war through the eyes of an innocent child.

In the classroom the students might explore the history of rhymes, riddles, superstitions ("unlucky 13"), customs, symbols (Yule logs, menorahs), chants, songs ("Star-Spangled Banner"), foods, dances, and games. Students might try writing haiku (an ancient Japanese verse form), make origami cranes after reading *Sadako and the Thousand Paper Cranes* (Coerr 1977), and experiment with rope rhymes after reading Eloise Greenfield's poem "Rope Rhyme."

Native American legends describe the beliefs and customs of the people. Many of the myths (legends) explain things that the Native Americans did not understand: the patterns of stars in the sky, why rabbits have short tails, and the reason for seasons.

African American literature features the unique culture of various times in history. Literary works about the pre- and post-Civil War era in the rural South often focus on oppression, slavery, and reconstruction. Poet Phillis Wheatley (1753–84) was America's first known African American poet. Harriet Beecher Stowe, a white abolitionist, wrote the influential, antislavery novel *Uncle Tom's Cabin* during this pre-Civil War period. Joel Chandler Harris, a white Georgian, collected many African American stories in his *Uncle Remus: His Songs and His Sayings*.

The early twentieth-century writings of African Americans often explore the issues of single parenting, inner city strife, drug abuse, lack of opportunities in education and the workplace, a biased society. Later writings also record realistically events of the period. The Newbery Medal winner *Sounder* (1970) by William Armstrong, for example, is a novel of the Depression-era South.

Study guides such as those written by Anita Price Davis and Marla Selvidge (1995) help teachers use the works of women writers—like the Newbery Medal winner Mildred Taylor (*Roll of Thunder, Hear My Cry*)—in the classroom. REA MAXNotes for Maya Angelou's autobiographical *I Know Why the Caged Bird Sings* (Davis 1994a) and the Pulitzer Prize winner *To Kill a Mockingbird* by Harper Lee (Davis 1994b)—both set in the Depression-era South—are available as well.

Literature of the civil rights era of the 1950s and 1960s includes works of a biographical and autobiographical nature. The topics of these writings are often black history, the black movement, and black individuals, like Malcolm X and Martin Luther King, Jr.

Writings of the late twentieth century continue to reveal the African American culture to the reader. Although the poetry of Eloise Greenfield, Nikki Giovanni, Gwendolyn Brooks, and Lee Bennet Hopkins has not yet endured a century, the quality of their work ensures that their poems will become classics. Their poems (and prose) honor and make others aware of their rich African American heritage.

Teachers must make certain to include poetry of all cultures in their classrooms. Charlotte Pomerantz writes about her winters in Puerto Rico. Louise Bennett writes of Jamaica. The teacher and students should research other poems about various cultures and experiences, and students should try crafting their own. As mentioned earlier, writing haiku—the Japanese verse form of three lines with five, seven, and five syllables, respectively—is an excellent poetic exercise for children.

Scandinavian literature such as Hans Christian Anderson's *Fairy Tales*, Henrik Ibsen's plays (*The Wild Duck*, for example), and Selma Langerlof's *The Wonderful Adventures of Nils* should be easy inclusions in the classroom. Comparing and contrasting fairy tales of various cultures could be interesting exercises, too. Excerpts from Dante Alighieri's *The Inferno* (Italy), Victor Hugo's *The Hunchback of Notre Dame* and *Les Misérables*, Alexandre Dumas's *The Three Musketeers* (France), and Miguel de Cervantes *Don Quixote* (Spain) are readily available reading selections as well.

Critical Approaches to Interpreting Text

Reader-Response Critical Approach

The reader-response critical approach focuses on the reader and the reading process—not on the author or the text itself (McManus 1998). The reader in this approach responds to the text personally. The real meaning is that which the reader's psyche—conscious and unconscious—creates in response to the work. There is a rejection of the idea that there is a fixed meaning in a work of literature. Because each individual creates the meaning from personal concerns, experiences, knowledge, and emotions, people do not derive the same interpretation of a text.

Many associate this approach with the 1938 method of Louise Rosenblatt. Rosenblatt opposed the ideas of reading with detachment and of barring personal interpretations into the reading—"close reading." She did not see writing as an entirely objective process; instead, she viewed it as an individual process that was unique for a particular person at a particular time. The method has become firmly established in American classrooms. Language arts teachers at all levels now widely accept the method. The method has led to the use of reading circles, journal writing, and peer writing exercises.

Shared Inquiry Approach

The shared inquiry approach involves a leader and a group. The leader in this approach does not present information or express opinions; instead, the participants are guided in reaching their own interpretation of the writing. This active approach involves using the text, one's own experience, and reasoning to reach an interpretation.

With the shared inquiry approach, each member listens and gives consideration to the opinions of others in the group. Members learn to modify their opinions and to communicate their ideas effectively to others. Debate is a characteristic of the method. A desired outcome of the method is lifelong reading. The approach is associated with the Great Books Program (Great Books Foundation 2008).

Literary Criticism

Literary criticism defines, classifies, analyzes, interprets, and evaluates works of literature. Types of literary criticism include the following:

Historical criticism uses history to understand a literary work more clearly. It looks at the social and intellectual currents in which the author wrote.

Textual criticism uses two main processes: recension and emendation. **Recension** is the selection, after thorough examination of all possible material, of only the most trustworthy evidence on which to base a text. **Emendation** is the effort to eliminate all the errors found in even the best manuscripts.

Feminist criticism seeks to correct or to supplement what is regarded as a predominantly male-dominated critical perspective with a female consciousness. It attempts to understand literature from a woman's point of view.

Biographical criticism uses knowledge of the author's life experiences to gain a better understanding of the writer's work.

Cultural criticism focuses on the historical, social, and economic contexts of a work.

Formal criticism pays particular attention to formal elements of the work, such as the language, structure, and tone. It analyzes form and meaning, paying special attention to diction, irony, paradox, metaphor, and symbols. It also examines plot, characterization, and narrative technique.

TEACHING READING

Instructional approaches to teaching reading should include cueing systems (constructing meaning through context and activating prior knowledge) and metacognitive strategies. Every teacher should be a reading teacher. This topic includes various instructional approaches for the content areas.

Reading Strategies

Looking at strategies used by proficient readers helps teachers make skillful choices of activities to maximize student learning in subject area instruction. Anne Goudvis and Stephanie Harvey (2000) offer the following list:

Activating prior knowledge: Readers pay more attention when they relate to the text. Readers naturally bring their prior knowledge and experience to reading, but they comprehend better when they think about the connections they make between the text, their lives, and the larger world.

Predicting or asking questions: Questioning is the strategy that keeps readers engaged. When readers ask questions, even before they read, they clarify understanding and forge ahead to make meaning. Asking questions is at the heart of thoughtful reading.

Visualizing: Active readers create visual images based on the words they read in the text. These created pictures enhance their understanding.

Drawing inferences: Inferring occurs when the readers take what they know, garner clues from the text, and think ahead to make a judgment, discern a theme, or speculate about what is to come.

Determining important ideas: Thoughtful readers grasp essential ideas and important information when reading. Readers must differentiate between less important ideas and key ideas that are central to the meaning of the text.

Synthesizing information: Synthesizing involves combining new information with existing knowledge to form an original idea or interpretation. Reviewing, sorting, and sifting important information can lead to new insights that change the way readers think.

Repairing understanding: If confusion disrupts meaning, readers need to stop and clarify their understanding. Readers may use a variety of strategies to "fix up" comprehension when meaning goes awry.

Confirming: As students read and after they read, they can confirm the predictions they originally made. There is no wrong answer. One can confirm negatively or positively. Determining whether a prediction is correct is a goal.

Using parts of a book: Students should use book parts—such as charts, diagrams, indexes, and the table of contents—to improve their understanding of the reading content.

Reflecting: An important strategy is for students to think about, or reflect on, what they have just read. Reflection can be simply thinking, or it can be more formal, such as a discussion or writing in a journal.

While providing instruction in a subject area, the teacher needs to determine if the reading material is at the students' level of reading mastery. If not, the teacher needs to make accommodations either in the material itself or in the manner of presentation.

Cueing Systems

Three cueing systems can help increase comprehension: semantics, syntax, and activating prior knowledge.

Semantics is the same as the context. As students read, they can guess at words they do not know by considering the rest of the passage. The context restricts the words that can fit.

Syntax is the second cue. The English language restricts the order of words in a meaningful sentence. If the readers consider both syntax and semantics, they can make better educated guesses about unknown words.

Cueing places less emphasis on "sounding out words" (phoneme-grapheme relationships) and on the individual words (morphemes) themselves than on syntax and semantics.

Students should begin focusing not just on individual parts of words but on whole words, phrases, grammar (the arrangement of words), and sentences. Noting these basic units and patterns of language can increase understanding. Figuring out unknown words by noting if they make sense in the passage increases one's comprehension.

> **PRAXIS Pointer**
>
> By eliminating even one answer choice, you increase your odds of answering correctly. You will have a 1–in–3 chance of choosing the correct answer. Without elimination, you would have only a 1–in–4 chance.

Students should learn to ask, "Does it make sense?" (meaning), "Does it sound right in the passage/sentence?" (grammar), and "Does it look right?" (phoneme-grapheme relationship).

Activating prior knowledge is the third cue. When students make connections to the text they are reading, their comprehension increases. Other names for these connections include *prior knowledge*, *schema*, *relevant background knowledge*, or *experience*. Good readers will try to fit the reading with what they already know *before*, *during*, and *after* they read. Students should eventually use this critical comprehension skill unconsciously. Using these skills helps to create independent readers.

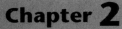

Metacognition

Metacognition is that vital component of reading that calls for critical thinking or "thinking about thinking." Poor readers approach reading material or begin their reading in a different way than good readers. The following table illustrates the differences:

Reading Stage	Good Readers	Poor Readers
Begin reading	• Activate prior knowledge • Read with purpose • Read with a plan on approach to the task • Focus attention on the task at hand • Attempt to predict and anticipate as they read	• Start without activating prior knowledge, without purpose, and without considering *how* to approach the task • Are distracted easily • Read just to "get it done" • Are not independent readers and are unaware of what to do when they encounter comprehension problems
During reading	• Employ reading and comprehension strategies—particularly when they encounter problems • Use context clues and text structure to increase comprehension • Organize and integrate the new information that they gain from the text • Monitor themselves and their comprehension as they read • Continue to reflect on what they have read	• Do not recognize important information and important vocabulary as they read • Do not recognize or use the organization of the text • Do not integrate the information that they read • Stop their reading and their thinking about the passage
After reading	• Believe that success is a result of their efforts—not of luck • Attempt to summarize the major points of what they read	• Believe that their success—or their lack thereof—is a matter of luck

It is important for the students and the teacher to note that the skills that good, mature readers employ are all skills that can be taught and learned (Cook and Mayer 1988).

Miscue analysis is the process of assessing the strategies that students use in their reading. Kenneth Goodman (1965) indicated that the processes occurring during reading were significant. He believed that any departure from the written text could provide a picture of the underlying cognitive processes that the student used. Readers' miscues include substitutions of the written word with another, additions and omissions of words, and alterations to the word sequence.

After determining the words that the child did not read successfully, the teacher can analyze the missed words to determine the reason that the child missed them. This assessment of missed words is miscue analysis. The teacher is looking for a pattern in the student's mistakes in order to provide help to the student.

Levels of Comprehension

Reading is more than calling words; reading must result in comprehension, or understanding. Comprehension skills include the ability to identify supporting details and facts, the main idea or essential message, the author's purpose, fact and opinion, point of view, inference, the conclusion, and other information.

To help students develop these reading and comprehension skills, teachers can consistently emphasize meaning in the classroom and should focus on the four comprehension levels: the literal, the interpretive, the critical, and the creative. These four levels encompass the skills of paraphrasing, comparing, inferentially interpreting, and literally interpreting reading materials—all of which are topics on the Praxis II English Assessments.

Literal Comprehension. The literal level of comprehension, the lowest level of understanding, involves reading the lines; one reads the words and understands exactly what is on the page. When the students give back facts or details directly from the passage or when they paraphrase what they have read, they are demonstrating the literal level of comprehension.

Interpretive or Inferential Comprehension. The interpretive level of comprehension is the second level of understanding; it is the next-to-lowest level of comprehension, just above literal comprehension. The interpretive level of comprehension requires the student to read between the lines; all the answers are not spelled out in print. This level may require readers to define figurative language or to identify terms. They may have to figure out the meaning or answers on their own; the text may not give all the correct information explicitly. Inferential comprehension or interpretive comprehension requires the students to *infer*, or figure out, the answers.

Determining the author's purpose, the main idea of the passage, the point of view of the author, the conclusion, or the essential message is an example of inferential comprehension—unless the passage states the information explicitly. Inferential comprehension may require a reader to make inferences, to draw conclusions, to generalize, to derive meaning from the language, to speculate, to anticipate, to predict, and/or to summarize.

Critical Comprehension.   The critical level of comprehension is one of the highest of the levels of understanding. This level may require one to read and think beyond the printed lines. Examples of critical thinking might include indicating whether text is true or false, distinguishing between fact and opinion, detecting propaganda, judging whether the author is qualified to write the text, recognizing bias and fallacies, identifying stereotypes, and making assumptions.

Creative Comprehension.   The creative level of comprehension requires readers to respond—often emotionally—to something they are reading. The student may reply to a story by stating another way of treating a situation, by indicating another way of solving a problem in the story, or by speculating whether the plot could have occurred in a different place or time.

  Story mapping or webbing helps students think about a passage and its structure. Webs or maps, in which the student charts out a concept or section of text in a graphic outline, are useful organizers. The web begins with the title or concept written in the middle of the page and branches out in web fashion; students will note specific bits of information on the branches or strings of the web. Arrows or lines in other formats can make connections from one bit of information to another. Some typical devices in good narrative fiction that might be useful on a story map or web include setting, stylistic devices, characters, and plot. A class reading Wilson Rawls's *Where the Red Fern Grows* created the story map shown in Figure 2.2.

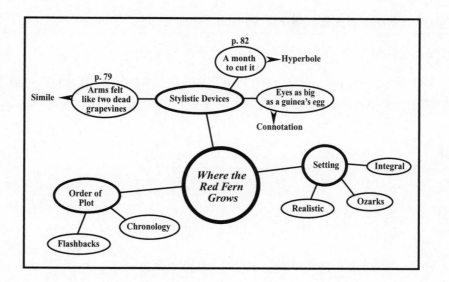

Figure 2.2 Story Map for *Where the Red Fern Grows*

Venn diagrams (overlapping concentric circles) enable a reader to compare two characters, concepts, places or things by placing specific criteria or critical attributes for one in the left circle, for the other in the right circle, and attributes or characteristics that are shared by the two in the overlapping section in the center.

Another useful graphic organizer is the **fishbone organizer** (see Figure 2.3). This type of graphic can help the reader to illustrate cause and effect. A reader viewing the completed fishbone organizer can immediately see the cause and the direct result of the cause.

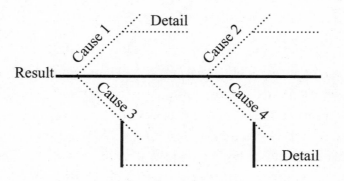

Figure 2.3 Fishbone Organizer

Instructors, writers, and speakers may use these strategies across the curriculum in any subject area.

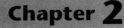

Methods of Assessing Reading Progress

Daily Observation

Skilled teachers can use daily observation to gather data to record on checklists, rubrics, running records, and informal reading inventories.

Checklist

Criteria	3	2	1
Blends	Uses blends consistently	Uses blends inconsistently	Has difficulty blending
Punctuation	Uses voice inflection to reflect written punctuation	Attends to some types of punctuation	Reads through punctuation
Sight words	Recognizes most	Recognizes some	Fails to recognize
Word structure	Uses to derive meaning	Sometimes uses to derive meaning	Fails to use to derive meaning
Main idea	Consistently able to identify	Usually able to identify	Usually unable to identify
Inference	Able to draw from most text	Able to draw from some text	Usually unable to draw from text
Vocabulary	Knows meaning of most words encountered	Knows meaning of many words encountered	Does not know meaning of most words encountered
Total			

A checklist is easily and quickly constructed and can be used to record dichotomous data indicating on a yes/no basis what a student is capable or incapable of doing. Some checklists include a rating scale. When categories on this type of checklist are evaluated, a numerical or letter rating is given to each item. In this way, not only is the presence or absence of a characteristic indicated but also the degree to which it is present. Items such as the following might typically appear on a reading checklist: *uses prior knowledge, makes reasonable predictions, uses context clues to construct meaning, uses word structure to construct meaning, uses metacognition to monitor reading, chooses books at an appropriate reading level*, and *reads a variety of genres* (Bromley 1992).

Rubric

A rubric is defined as a form that "enables the user to rate the quality of student performance according to a predetermined set of criteria and standards" (Roe and Ross 2006, 520). Usually, rubrics have a rating scale in which the biggest number represents the best score.

Running Record

A running record documents a child's reading as he or she reads out loud. This type of assessment allows you to evaluate the reading level as well as to note explicit types of miscues. Specific marks are used to indicate the kinds of errors the reader makes, such as substitutions, omissions, insertions, self-corrections, and so on. You need some training to use this form of assessment, but with practice, it can be done quickly and easily.

Informal Reading Inventory

An informal reading inventory is very similar to a reading record in that for part of the assessment, the student reads aloud, and the teacher uses symbols to note the types of miscues the student makes. However, this tool differs from a running record in that the student reads graded passages and then responds to comprehension questions specifically designed to detect the ability to grasp the main idea of the passage, to use inference to draw conclusions, to remember details, and to understand vocabulary. For the second part of this assessment, the student reads the passages silently and then responds to comprehension questions. The amount of time it takes for the youngster to read the passage is also noted.

PRAXIS Pointer

Cueing systems help comprehension: semantics, syntax, and activating prior knowledge.

Diagnosis of Errors

Searching for patterns of errors can help teachers to diagnose weaknesses as well as strengths. Noting specific types of errors leads to detecting certain weaknesses such as that made by a student who misreads a word because he reads without regard for meaning, and that made by another student who may misread a word by substituting a synonym without regard for the visual appearance of the word. As a teacher your attempts to remediate this difficulty would differ with the student, as even though both misread the same word, the causes of the miscue are completely different. Therefore, diagnosis of specific errors leads to targeted remediation that is far more likely to be successful than general correction.

REFERENCES

Answers.com. Symbolism. The New Oxford Companion to Literature in French, Oxford University Press, 1995, 2005. *http://www.answers.com/topic/ symbolism.*

Bromley, K. D. 1992. *Language Arts: Exploring Connections.* Upper Saddle River, NJ: Prentice Hall.

Butler, Samuel, trans. 1898 *The Illiad* by Homer. Project Gutenberg. *www.gutenberg. org.*

————. 1900. *The Odyssey* by Homer. Project Gutenberg. *www.gutenberg.org.*

Cook, L., and R. Mayer. 1988. Teaching Readers About the Structure of Scientific Text. *Journal of Educational Psychology*, 80: 448–56.

Cormier, Robert. 1974/1977. *The Chocolate War*. New York: Dell.

Davis, Anita P., and Marla Selvidge. 1995. *Focus on Women*. Westminster, CA: Teacher Created Materials, Inc.

Davis, Anita P., and Thomas R. McMillan. 1999. You've Come a Long Way, Baby— or Have You? *Reading Teacher,* 52: 532–35.

Davis, Anita Price. 1994a. *MAXNotes: I Know Why the Caged Bird Sings*. Piscataway, NJ: Research and Education Association.

————. 1994b. *MAXNotes: To Kill a Mockingbird*. Piscataway, NJ: Research and Education Association.

————. 2005. *Reading Instruction Essentials*. Boston: American Press

Dictionary.com. Drama. *Webster's Revised Unabridged Dictionary*. MICRA, Inc. *http://dictionary.reference.com/browse/drama.*

Goodman, Kenneth 1965. "A Linguistic Study of Cues and Miscues in Reading." Elementary English. 42: 639–43.

Goudvis, Anne, and Stephanie Harvey. 2000. *Strategies that Work*. Portland, ME: Stenhouse.

Great Books Foundation, The. 2008. The shared inquiry method of learning. *www.greatbooks.org/programs-for-all-ages/junior/jgbsharedinquiry/shared-inquiry.html.*

Kinsella, Kim, Kevin Feldman, Colleen Shea, Ph.D., Joyce Armstrong Carroll, and Edward E. Wilson. 2004. *Prentice Hall Literature: The British Tradition*. Upper Saddle River, NJ: Prentice Hall.

McManus, Barbara. 1998. Reader-Response Criticism. *www.cnr.edu/home/bmcmanus/ readercrit.html*.

Micklos, B., Jr. 1995–96. Multiculturalism and Children's Literature. *Reading Today* December/January:1, 8.

Microsoft Encarta Online Encyclopedia. 2008. Existentialism. http://encarta.msn. com/text_761555530__-0/Existentialism.html.

Publishers Weekly. 2001. All-time bestselling children's books. December 17. *www.publishersweekly.com/article/CA187127.html?text=bestselling*.

Roe, B. C. and E. P. Ross. 2006. *Integrating Language Arts through Literature & Thematic Units*. Boston: Allyn & Bacon.

Rosenblatt, Louise. 1938. *Literature as Exploration*. New York: Appleton-Century.

Children's Literature

Aesop. 1950. *The Fables of Aesop: Selected, Told Anew, and Their Social History Traced by Joseph Jacobs*. New York: Macmillan.

Afanas'ev, Aleksandr Nikolaevich. 1975. *Russian Fairy Tales*. Trans. Norbert Guterman. New York: Pantheon.

Alcott, Louisa Mae. 1868/1968. *Little Women*. Boston: Little, Brown.

Asbjørnsen, Peter, and Jørgen Moe. 1946. *East o' the Sun and West o' the Moon*. Evanston, IL: Row, Peterson.

Banks, Lynne Reid. 1980. *The Indian in the Cupboard*. Garden City, NY: Doubleday.

Beim, Lorraine, and Jerrold Beim. 1945. *Two Is a Team*. New York: Harcourt, Brace.

Bonham, Frank. 1965/1975. *Durango Street*. New York: Dell.

Bryant, Sara Cone. 1938. *Epaminondas and His Auntie*. Boston: Houghton.

Byars, Betsy. 1970. *The Summer of the Swans*. New York: Viking Press.

Capote, Truman. 2004. *Complete Stories of Truman Capote*. New York: Random House.

Chase, Richard. 1943. *Jack Tales*. New York: Houghton Mifflin.

_____. 1948. *Grandfather Tales*. New York: Houghton Mifflin.

Cleaver, Vera, and Bill Cleaver. 1969. *Where the Lilies Bloom*. New York: Lippincott.

Coerr, Eleanor. 1977. *Sadako and the Thousand Paper Cranes*. New York: Putnam.

Cormier, Robert. 1974/1977. *The Chocolate War*. New York: Dell.

Dahl, Roald. 1972. *Charlie and the Chocolate Factory*. New York: Knopf.

Davis, Anita P., and Ed Y. Hall. 1993. *Harriet Quimby: First Lady of the Air (an activity book for children)*. Spartanburg, SC: Honoribus Press.

_____. 1998. *Harriet Quimby: First Lady of the Air (an intermediate biography)*. Spartanburg, SC: Honoribus Press.

Davis, Anita P., and Katharine Preston. 1996. *Discoveries*. Hillsborough, ID: Butte Publications.

De Angeli, Marguerite. 1946. *Bright April*. Garden City, NY: Doubleday.

Defoe, Daniel. 1719/1972. *Robinson Crusoe*. Boston: Houghton Mifflin.

Dodge, Mary Mapes. 1963. *Hans Brinker*. New York: Grosset and Dunlap.

Garis, Howard. 1912/1915. *Uncle Wiggly's Adventures*. New York: Platt and Munk.

Gipson, Fred. 1956. *Old Yeller*. New York: Harper.

Golding, William. 1954. *Lord of the Flies*. New York: Perigee.

Grimm, Jacob, and Wilhelm Grimm. 1968. *Grimm's Fairy Tales*. Chicago: Follett.

Henry, Marguerite. 1953/1967. *Brighty of the Grand Canyon*. New York: Scholastic.

Hesse, Karen. 1997/1999. *Out of the Dust*. New York: Scholastic.

Hickam, Homer H., Jr. 1999. *October Sky*. New York: Dell. (Originally published in 1998 as *Rocket Boys*.)

Hinton, S. E. 1967/1983. *The Outsiders*. New York: Dell.

Jackson, Jesse. 1945. *Call Me Charley*. New York: Harper.

Jacobs, Joseph. 1959. *Favorite Fairy Tales Told in England*. Boston: Little, Brown.

Keats, Ezra Jack. 1962. *The Snowy Day*. New York: Viking Press.

Kellogg, Steven. 1938/1986. *Paul Bunyan*. New York: Morrow.

Knight, Eric. 1938/1966. *Lassie Come Home*. New York: Scholastic.

Konigsburg, E. L. 1967. *From the Mixed-Up Files of Mrs. Basil E. Frankweiler*. New York: Atheneum.

Lee, Harper. 1960/1982. *To Kill a Mockingbird*. New York: Warner Books.

Lewis, C. S. 1950/1988. *The Lion, the Witch, and the Wardrobe*. New York: Macmillan.

Miles, Miska. 1965. *Mississippi Possum*. Boston: Little, Brown.

Montgomery, L. M. 1908/1935. *Anne of Green Gables*. New York: Farrar, Straus, and Giroux.

Mowat, Farley. 1963/1984. *Never Cry Wolf*. Toronto: Bantam Books.

Norton, Mary. 1953. *The Borrowers*. New York, Harcourt, Brace.

O'Dell, Scott. 1960. *Island of the Blue Dolphins*. New York: Houghton Mifflin.

Peck, Robert Newton. 1974. *Soup*. New York: Knopf.

Perrault, Charles, et al. 1959. *Favorite Fairy Tales Told in France: Retold from Charles Perrault and Other French Storytellers*. Virginia Haviland, ed. Boston: Little, Brown.

Peterson, Jeanne Whitehouse. 1977. *I Have a Sister—My Sister is Deaf*. New York: Harper and Row.

Rawlings, Marjorie Kinnan. 1938. *The Yearling*. New York: Scribner.

Rawls, Wilson. 1961/1976. *Where the Red Fern Grows*. New York: Bantam.

_____. 1977. *Summer of the Monkeys*. New York: Dell.

Sanders, Dori. 1991. *Clover*. New York: Fawcett Columbine.

Shotwell, Louisa Rossiter. 1963. *Roosevelt Grady*. Cleveland: World.

Shreve, Susan. 1984. *The Flunking of Joshua T. Bates*. New York: Knopf.

Singer, Isaac Bashevis. 1966. *Zlateh the Goat and Other Stories*. New York: Harper.

Spinelli, Jerry. 1990. *Maniac Magee*. Boston: Little, Brown.

Spyri, Johanna. 1884/1982. *Heidi*. New York: Messner.

Steinbeck, John. 1939. *The Grapes of Wrath*, New York: Viking.

Steptoe, Javaka, ed. 1997. *In Daddy's Arms I Am Tall: African Americans Celebrating Fathers*. New York: Lee and Low Books.

Steptoe, John. 1969. *Stevie*. New York: Harper and Row.

Stevenson, Robert Louis. 1883/1981. *Treasure Island*. New York: Scribner.

Swift, Jonathan. 1726/1945. *Gulliver's Travels*. Garden City, NY: Doubleday.

Taylor, Mildred D. 1976. *Roll of Thunder, Hear My Cry*. New York: Dial Press.

Tsuchiya, Yukio. 1988. *Faithful Elephants: A True Story of Animals, People, and War*. Boston: Houghton Mifflin.

Twain, Mark. 1876/1989. *The Adventures of Tom Sawyer*. New York: Morrow.

————. 1884/1991. *The Adventures of Huckleberry Finn* (1991). New York: Knopf.

Ward, Lynd. 1952. *The Biggest Bear*. New York: Houghton Mifflin.

White, E. B. 1952. *Charlotte's Web*. New York: Harper and Row.

Wilder, Laura Ingalls. 1953. *Little House in the Big Woods*. New York: Harper.

Wyss, Johann. 1814/1981. *Swiss Family Robinson*.

Yarbrough, Camille. 1979. *Cornrows*. New York: Coward, McCann, and Geoghegan.

Yashima, Taro. 1955. *Crow Boy*. New York: Viking Press.

Webliography

www.ala.org/ala/yalsa/booklistsawards/margaretaedwards/maeprevious/winners.cfm

www.ala.org/ala/alsc/awardsscholarships/literaryawds/newberymedal/ newberywinners/medalwinners.htm

www.answers.com/topic/symbolism

www.learner.org/channel/workshops/hslit/session1/index.html#1

www.assumption.edu/users/ady/HHGateway/Gateway/Approaches.html#New% 20Historicism

www.gutenberg.org/catalog/world/readfile?fk_files=715&pageno=1

www.gutenberg.org/catalog/world/readfile?fk_files=715&pageno=39177

www.literatureclassics.com/ancientpaths/litcrit.html#feminist

www.muskingum.edu/~cal/database/general/reading.html#

www.trelease-on-reading.com/video_bibliography.html.

CHAPTER

3

Language and Linguistics

FIRST AND SECOND LANGUAGE ACQUISITION AND DEVELOPMENT

Until about 1957, the general belief was that children acquired language through imitation. In 1964 Noam Chomsky revolutionized the study of language acquisition with his *Aspects of the Theory of Syntax* in which he advanced his belief that language acquisition was innate—not acquired. This innate faculty, or set of rules about language, he refers to as the *Universal Grammar (UG)*.

Universal grammar is the basis upon which all human languages are built. For Chomsky, if an alien linguist visited Earth, she would deduce from the evidence that there was only one language, with a number of local variants. This is true for a number of reasons, the most important of which is the ease with which children acquire their mother tongue. Chomsky claims that it would be nothing short of a miracle if children were to learn language the same way that they learn mathematics. This, he says, is because, children are exposed to very little correctly formed language. When people speak, they constantly interrupt themselves, change their minds, and make slips of the tongue and so on. Yet, children manage to learn their language all the same. This claim is usually referred to as the Poverty of the Stimulus argument.

The second reason supporting the UG case is that children do not simply copy the language that they hear around them. They deduce rules from it—rules from which they use to produce sentences that they have never heard before. They do not learn a repertoire of phrases and sayings, as the behaviorists believe, but a grammar that helps the child generate an infinite number of new sentences.

Chomsky saw language as a specific skill, its acquisition governed by an inborn program, and requiring no direct intervention from parents or teachers. Chomsky distinguished between language acquisition (which is subconscious, has an emphasis on communication and reception, and results in fluency) and language learning (which is conscious, has an increased emphasis on syntax and grammar, and fluency is not a guarantee).

Arguing that six universal stages govern language acquisition and development, Chomsky defined them as the **prelinguistic stage**, which includes a silent period with only crying and later cooing and babbling; the **holophrastic stage** with one-word communication; the **two-word stage**; the **telegraphic stage** (about 28 months) when the child may omit some syllables in words, substitute sounds, and use only a pivot word with other words—much like a telegram; the **intermediate development stage**; and the **adult stage**.

The theory of language acquisition through imitation lost many followers after Chomsky's work. One of the primary reasons for not accepting imitation alone is that children overgeneralize with words and phrases (*holded*, *tooked*) that they could not have copied from hearing adult speech; young deaf and hard-of-hearing children also extract grammar from language. Chomsky explained that analogy alone couldn't explain language acquisition and language use.

PRAXIS Pointer

Mark up your test book. Crossing out answer choice(s) you know are inappropriate will save you time.

There are, of course, linguists who do not agree with Chomsky and they point to several problems: Chomsky differentiates between competence and performance. Performance is what people actually say, which is often ungrammatical, whereas competence is what they instinctively know about the syntax of their language—and this is more or less equated with the Universal Grammar. Chomsky concentrates upon this aspect of language and ignores the things that people actually say. The problem here is that he relies upon people's intuitions as to what is right or wrong—but it is not at all clear that people will all make the same judgments, or that their judgments actually reflect the way people really do use the language.

Chomsky distinguishes between the "core" or central grammar of a language, which is essentially founded on the Universal Grammar, and peripheral grammar. To Chomsky, the real object of linguistic science is the core grammar. But how do we determine what belongs to the core, and what belongs to the periphery? To some observers, all grammar is conventional, and there is no particular reason to make the Chomskian distinction.

Chomsky also appears to reduce language to its grammar. He seems to regard meaning as secondary—a sentence such as "Colorful blue seas sleep furiously" may be considered as part of the English language, for it is grammatically correct, and therefore worthy of study by *Transformational Grammarians*. A sentence such as "My father, she no like oranges," on the other hand, is of no interest to the Chomskian linguist. Nor would he be particularly interested in most of the utterances heard in normal discourse. Because he disregards meaning, and the social situation in which language is normally produced, he disregards in particular the situation in which the child learns her first language.

Language Acquisition Support System

The psychologist Jerome Bruner (1983), holds that while there very well may be, as Chomsky suggests, a *Language Acquisition Device*, or LAD, there must also be a *Language Acquisition Support System,* or LASS. He is referring to the family and its extensions. If we watch closely the way a child interacts with the adults around her, we will see that they constantly provide opportunities for her to acquire her mother tongue. Mother or father provide ritualized scenarios—the ceremony of having a bath, eating a meal, getting dressed, or playing a game—in which the phases of interaction are rapidly recognized and predicted by the infant.

It is within such clear and emotionally charged contexts that the child first becomes aware of the way in which language is used. The utterances of the mother or father are themselves ritualized, and accompany the activity in predictable and comprehensible ways. Gradually, the child moves from a passive position to an active one, taking over the movements of the caretaker, and, eventually, the language as well.

Bruner cites the example of a well-known childhood game, in which the mother, or other caretaker, disappears and then reappears. Through this ritual, which at first may be accompanied by simple noises, or "Peek-a-boo . . . Good-bye . . . Hello," and later by lengthier commentaries, the child is both learning about separation and return, and being offered a context within which language, charged with emotive content, may be acquired. It is this reciprocal and affective nature of language that Chomsky appears to leave out of his hypotheses.

Bruner's conception of the way children learn language is taken a little further by John Macnamara (1972), who holds that children, rather than having an in-built language device, have an innate capacity to read meaning into social situations. It is this capacity that makes them capable of understanding language, and therefore learning it with ease, rather than an LAD.

Chomsky sees the child as essentially autonomous in the creation of language. She is programmed to learn, and will learn as long as minimal social and economic conditions are realized. In Bruner's version, the program is indeed in place, but the social conditions become more important. The child is still an active participant and is still essentially creative in her approach to language acquisition, but the role of the parents and other caretakers is also seen as primordial. Finally, Macnamara sees language learning as being subordinate to and dependent upon the capacity to understand and participate in social activities.

For most children, acquiring their mother tongue is a seamless process, although at least two conditions must be fulfilled for this to happen: (1) the child must not be deaf, and (2) the child must be exposed to language before a certain age. At the age of one month, most children are able to distinguish between their mother's voice and the voices of other people, as well as some differences in the rhythm of speech and intonation. Children are also able to understand the tone of voice as early as at the age of two to four months, differentiating between joyful, angry, or soothing tones. When the child is between six and nine months old, some simple utterances of parents are associated with situations in which they are used, and thus infants learn the meanings of the first words. By the end of the first year, babies usually understand about 20 words.

Each child needs to learn the "codes of his or her culture" because the language of each culture is different. Yet, if a child is to learn about his or her world, the ability to communicate must exist. Even after a baby learns the rudiments of communication through touch, vision, and hearing, those skills need to continue to be refined until, at about age seven, the brain is ready to deal with the abstract concepts involved in reading, writing, comprehension, math "language" or concepts, and body language.

Language acquisition is divided into several parts:

Receptive language is language that is spoken or written by others and received by an individual, that is listening or reading (decoding or getting meaning from spoken words or written symbols). In order to receive language, the individual must be able to attend to, process, comprehend, retain, and/or integrate spoken or written language. In order to do proper auditory processing, the individual needs to have phonemic awareness, the ability to notice, think about, and manipulate the individual sound in words and phonemes (sound-symbol correspondence); and phonological awareness, sound-symbol recognition or the ability to recognize specific sounds, which is necessary for good reading and spelling. Good visual processing demands the ability to interpret visual symbols, to differentiate visual figure from background, to have a functional visual memory and, for writing, good visual-motor activity.

Cognitive language is that which is received, processed into memory, integrated with knowledge already integrated, and made a part of the knowledge of the individual from which new ideas and concepts can be generated. It is a part of the creative process that shapes the thought of each person.

Expressive language is communication through speaking, writing, and/or gestures, that is, selecting words, formulating them into ideas, and producing them through speaking, writing, or gesturing (encoding or the process of expressive language). Expressive language involves word retrieval, rules of grammar (syntax), word and sentence structure (morphology), and word meaning (semantics).

The National Institute for Literacy asserts the principle that a child must be able to form and hold mental pictures if he or she is to acquire language fundamentals; the child must also have the ability to use tools to express those symbols. By the time a child is five years old, speech skills should be such that the child can be understood 100 percent of the time. The ability to read easy words and comprehend them should be in place for most children by the time a child is seven or eight years old. If children are not ready to read by fourth grade, they will not be able to keep up with the curriculum designated by the state.

Second Language Acquisition

The University of Southern California's Steven Krashen developed the predominant theory of second language acquisition. Krashen is a specialist in language development and acquisition, and his influential theory is widely accepted in the language learning community.

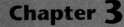

Five Components of Second Language Acquisition Theory

There are five main components of Krashen's theory. Each of the components relates to a different aspect of the language learning process. The five components are as follows:

1. The acquisition-learning hypothesis

2. The monitor hypothesis

3. The natural order hypothesis

4. The input hypothesis

5. The affective filter hypothesis

The Acquisition-Learning Hypothesis. This hypothesis actually fuses two fundamental theories of how individuals learn languages. Krashen has concluded that there are two systems of language acquisition that are independent but related: the acquired system and the learned system.

The **acquired system** relates to the unconscious aspect of language acquisition. When people learn their first language by speaking the language naturally in daily interaction with others who speak their native language, this acquired system is at work. In this system, speakers are less concerned with the structure of their utterances than with the act of communicating meaning. Krashen privileges the acquired system over the learned system.

The **learned system** relates to formal instruction in which students engage in formal study to acquire knowledge about the target language. For example, studying the rules of syntax is part of the learned system.

The Monitor Hypothesis. The monitor hypothesis illustrates how the acquired system is affected by the learned system. When second language learners monitor their speech, they are applying their understanding of learned grammar to edit, plan, and initiate their communication. This action can only occur when speakers have ample time to think about the form and structure of their sentences.

The amount of monitoring occurs on a continuum. Some language learners overmonitor and some use very little of their learned knowledge and are said to undermonitor.

Ideally, speakers strike a balance and monitor at a level in which they use their knowledge but are not overly inhibited by it.

The Natural Order Hypothesis.   This hypothesis argues that there is a natural order to the way second language learners acquire their target language. Research suggests that this natural order seems to transcend age, the learner's native language, the target language, and the conditions under which the second language is being learned. The order that the learners follow has four steps:

1. They produce single words.

2. They string words together based on meaning and not syntax.

3. They begin to identify elements that begin and end sentences.

4. They begin to identify different elements within sentences and can rearrange them to produce questions.

The Input Hypothesis.   This hypothesis seeks to explain how second languages are acquired. In its most basic form, the input hypothesis argues that learners progress along the natural order only when they encounter second language input that is one step beyond where they are in the natural order. Therefore, if a learner is at step 1 from the above list, they will only proceed along the natural order when they encounter input that is at the second step.

The Affective Filter Hypothesis.   This hypothesis describes external factors that can act as a filter that impedes acquisition. These factors include motivation, self-confidence, and anxiety. For example, if a learner has very low motivation, very low self-confidence, and a high level of anxiety, the affective filter comes into place and inhibits the learner from acquiring the new language. Students who are motivated, confident, and relaxed about learning the target language have much more success acquiring a second language than those who are trying to learn with the affective filter in place.

A Final Point on Grammar

According to second language acquisition theory, the role of grammar in language acquisition is useful only when the learner is interested in learning grammar. Otherwise,

Krashen argues, studying grammar equates to language appreciation and does not positively influence language acquisition. (Krashen 1982)

Social and Cultural Influences on Language

We have established that an awareness of the social use of language appears to occur before the first words. Interaction with parents and siblings, care, and environment all enhance language acquisition (American Speech-Language-Hearing Association). Mastering the language includes mastering the rules for social language known as *pragmatics*. Pragmatics involves three primary communication skills:

1. Using language appropriately for different social situations, such as greeting, requesting, demanding, promising, and informing

2. Changing one's language according to the listener's needs, such as speaking at a different volume in a hospital and using different words when speaking to a child rather than an adult

3. Following rules for conversing with others, such as taking turns, staying on topic, not standing too close when speaking to someone, and rephrasing when necessary.

The Role and Nature of Dialects

The first step in the process of forming a dialect is communicative isolation. Historically, the separation of groups from one another—for whatever reason—often resulted in the development of new or different dialects.

A dialect is a subdivision of a language—subdivisions that are related to regional differences and/or to social class. Dialects may differ in sound (phonology), in vocabulary, and in grammar from the original language.

American English derives from seventeenth-century British English. The majority of the Europeans who settled in Virginia and Massachusetts, the "original colonies, were from the south of England, especially London. The mid-Atlantic area—Pennsylvania in particular—was settled by people from the north and west of England and by the Scots-Irish (descendants of Scottish people who settled in Northern Ireland). These sources resulted in three dialect areas—northern, southern, and midland. Over time, other dialects developed.

The Boston area and the Richmond, Virginia, and Charleston, South Carolina, areas maintained strong commercial—and cultural—ties to England and looked to London for guidance as to what was "class" and what was not. So, as the London dialect of the upper classes changed, so did the dialects of the upper-class Americans in these areas. For example, in the late 1700s and early 1800s, *r* dropping spread from London to much of southern England and to places like Boston and Virginia. New Yorkers, who looked to Boston for the latest fashion trends, adopted it early, and in the south, it spread to wherever the plantation system was. On the other hand, in Pennsylvania, the Scots-Irish, and the Germans as well, kept their heavy *r*'s.

Vocabulary in America was much more open to change than back in the old country. The names for many North American indigenous plants, animals, foodstuffs, clothing, housing, and other items derived from native and immigrant languages and have been absorbed into American English.

Richard Effland and his colleagues at the University of Arizona give some hints for recognizing a dialect:

> We commonly know that we are in the presence of a person speaking a different dialect of English than our own when that person "sounds funny" or uses "strange words" to describe something. Even though we can understand what the person is saying we realize that their dialect is different from our own.

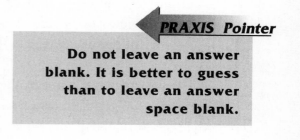

PRAXIS Pointer

Do not leave an answer blank. It is better to guess than to leave an answer space blank.

Linguistic anthropologists who study dialects have found that the distinctions between a language, a dialect, and a substandard variety of that language are often unclear. For instance, Ebonics ("Black English") emerged in the 1960s as a topic of much discussion, particularly in the United States. Some people have argued that Ebonics is an English dialect with an African influence. Others have argued, "Ebonics is simply a sub-standard form and degradation of English" (Trainor).

The Center for Applied Linguistics (CAL) in Washington, D.C., gave special consideration to the study of Ebonics and expressed its opinion this way:

> African American Vernacular English is a dialect of American English used by many African Americans in certain settings and circumstances. It is not slang, as people sometimes say. Like

other dialects of English, African American Vernacular English
is a regular, systematic language variety that contrasts with other
dialects in terms of its grammar, pronunciation, and vocabulary.

Many linguistic scholars believe that the first step in the development of multiple languages from one ancestral language is the formation of dialects.

HISTORY, DEVELOPMENT, AND STRUCTURE OF THE ENGLISH LANGUAGE

A branch of linguistics—historical linguistics—focuses on the development of the more than 6,000 different human languages and the connections among languages. Historical linguists study the change and the evolution of languages, how languages may develop from an original language, and how cultural contacts between those who speak different languages may affect language development and evolution.

Ethno linguistics is a study of how language determines and reflects
worldviews of people. Most contemporary linguists stress the importance of one's language to the group and the individual.

Human language is a signaling system operating with symbolic vocal sounds used for the purposes of communication and social cooperation. The more than 6,000 languages spoken in the world today vary widely but nevertheless fall under the definition of language.

Various attempts have been made to classify languages into different types: analytic and synthetic. An **analytic language** is one that uses very few bound morphemes—prefixes and suffixes (e.g., *re-*, *-ly*) and inflections or grammatical endings of nouns (e.g., *-es*, *-ing*, *-ed*). A **synthetic language** uses large numbers of bound morphemes and often combines strings of them to form a single word. This system of classification has one main weakness: most languages are mixed. Few are either analytic or synthetic; rather, they lie on a continuum and occupy points between the two extreme poles. For instance, the English language in the course of its history has become less synthetic and more analytic.

Language is born out of the need for people to communicate, to preserve their oral stories, to retain the stories of others, and to make a record of important events. Most people had difficulty remembering everything they wanted to remember. These needs led to the development of a written language. This development occurred over a vast period of time and evolved through several levels:

Concrete level: The first way of preserving the memories of an event, the parts of a story, or the history of a person, family, or place was with souvenirs, or concrete reminders. Without artifacts and living persons as remembrances, people began to search for another way to document.

Semiconcrete level: People began using pictography, or drawings, to tell their stories. Pictography, the first stage in writing, began to appear after speech began, sometime around 30,000 BCE. This semiconcrete level enabled the recorder to chronicle events and tell stories about the fish that got away, about the number of possessions a neighbor owned, about natural disasters, about hairy mastodons, about actions of their friends, or about occurrences that were humorous, daring, important, sad, or frightening. Drawings in the sand, on cave walls, on papyrus scrolls, on pottery, on cloth and canvas, and later on paper, communicated messages to their readers. Record keeping seems to have been an important original purpose of "writing."

Semiabstract level: Animal bones with notches dated to somewhere between 20,000 BCE and 6,500 BCE indicate to the historians and archaeologists a more sophisticated system of record keeping than pictography. These same notches or symbols could represent many different things (days, number of people, the number of possessions, etc.) and were at the semiabstract level—the next-to-the-highest level of representation.

Abstract level: The earliest writing in Mesopotamia was picture writing, or pictographs, invented by the Sumerians (ca. 3100 BCE), who wrote on clay tablets using long reeds. The script the Sumerians invented and handed down to the Semitic peoples who conquered Mesopotamia in later centuries is called *cuneiform*, which is derived from two Latin words: *cuneus*, which means "wedge," and *forma*, which means "shape." This picture language, similar to but more abstract than Egyptian hieroglyphics, eventually developed into a syllabic alphabet under the Semites (Assyrians and Babylonians) who eventually came to dominate the area.

About 2000 BCE, Crete "invented" writing also. The writing in Crete at this time was a series of lines—not pictures or pictures and symbols. The Phaistos disk (found in the Phaistos castle) was made of clay and contained linear script. A stamp—not a stylus—was the tool for creating the symbols.

In Asia Minor in 1500 BCE, the Hittite hieroglyphs had a unique direction. The writer arranged the symbols—410 of them—in the same manner as a plowed field: right to left, left to right, right to left, and so on. In the 1800s, archaeologists and other scholars took decades to decipher the hieroglyphs.

About the same time (1500 BCE) the Hittite hieroglyphs were being developed, the Chinese invented a writing system. The materials (bamboo and silk) were unique, as were the pictorial symbols. Modern Chinese writing descends directly from the ancient writing and is the oldest writing with a continuous history still in use.

Ideographic and Phonetic Writing

The written abstract symbols that represent ideas—not just concrete objects and actions—are ideographic writing. Several thousand years passed between the development of ideographic writing and the development of writing that represented sounds (phonetic writing).

The year 449 CE is the accepted date of the birth of the English language. In that year, the British or Celtic king (Vortigern) invited the Angles (led by Hengist and Horsa) to join in helping his forces resist and defeat the Picts. The Angles received land in the southeast for their help. Additional aid came from "three peoples of Germanie." During the next 150 years, newcomers established seven kingdoms. Interestingly, the language that developed did not come primarily from the Celts who preceded some of the newcomers (Mosser). The resulting language—Old English—reflected aspects of those who moved to the new land.

The English language has changed over time and is still changing; English is not static and is a dynamic part of culture. Our language is so different from Old English that English-speaking Americans could not easily understand someone speaking Old English today. Some current words—for example, *Internet, electron*—were unknown a century ago.

Etymology is the study of the history of words, when they entered a language and

> its development since its earliest recorded occurrence in the
> language where it is found, by tracing its transmission from one
> language to another, by analyzing it into its component parts,
> by identifying its cognates in other languages, or by tracing it
> and its cognates to a common ancestral form in an ancestral lan-
> guage. (Merriam-Webster Online Dictionary 2008)

As mentioned earlier, the Celtic language is not the primary root of words in Old English. The Old English language is a synthetic language, as opposed to present-day English, which is analytic. A synthetic language—like Old English—uses inflections to signal grammatical functions and relationships.

Elements of the History and Development of American English

The American English language seems to have come as a result of the desire of the people in America to assert their complete political independence from England. Congress instructed Benjamin Franklin—minister to France—to use "the language of the United States" in his "replies or answers" to Louis XVI. Franklin was presumably amenable to the idea because he had proposed eight years before the writing of the Declaration of Independence a new alphabet to reflect changes in pronunciation and spelling that were already apparent. He did not, however, propose a completely new language.

Further evidence of the revolutionary attitude appeared in *Dissertations on the English Language* by Noah Webster. Webster urged:

> Let us seize the present moment, and establish a national lan-
> guage as well as a national government … [a]s an independent
> nation our honor requires us to have a system of our own, in lan-
> guage as well as government. (Mencken 1921)

Webster was not, however, calling for a completely new language but was instead encouraging the establishment of a distinct and independent dialect, which was already forming. This language—American English—has persisted through the years. (Mencken 1921)

An analytic language—like present-day English—depends on word order and function words for meaning. There are only eight inflectional endings to signal use in present-day English; linguists refer to the ending on a word to signal the use of the word as *inflection*.

Meaning or Function of Endings	Inflection
Indication of third-person singular, present tense for verbs	*-s*
Plural of regular nouns	*-s*
Possession of regular nouns	*-'s*
Indication of past tense of regular verbs	*-ed*
Indication of present participle of regular verbs and/or the progressive aspect of a verb	*-ing*
Indication of past participle of regular verbs and/or the perfect aspect of a verb (In weak verbs this is indicated by *-ed*.)	*-en*
Comparative case of adjectives	*-er*
Superlative case of adjectives	*-est*

The inflections used with pronouns signal the function, role, or case that the word performs in a phrase or sentence. The present-day English pronouns continue to use an array of changes for inflection. Pronouns change for objective and nominative case, for number (singular and plural), and for possession.

Nominative Case	Objective Case
I, we	*me, us*
he, she, who, they	*him, her, whom, them*

Pronominal Genitive	Adjectival Genitive
mine, ours	*my, our*
your, yours	*your, your*
he, she, who	*him, her, whom*
his, hers, its, theirs	*his, her, its, their*

Syntax, then, is the study of the rules for combining morphemes or words into complete, meaningful sentences. Its primary concern is the arrangement of words or phrases into sentences.

The creation of new words in present-day English may be the result of several processes, according to Johanna Rubba (2004) of California Polytechnic State University–San Luis Obispo. These processes of word formation include:

Affixation: Adding a prefix or suffix to a word

Compounding: Joining two or more words, like *whitewash* and *skateboard*

Conversion: Using a word of one category in another category without change; for instance, using the noun *comb* also as the verb *comb*

Stress shift: Changing the stress from one syllable to another changes the meaning and the pronunciation, as in re*cord* (noun) and *record* (verb)

Clipping: Shortening words, as in *math* for *mathematics* and *doc* for *doctor*

Acronym formation: Forming a word from the initials of a group of words; for example, AIDS (Acquired Immune Deficiency Syndrome) and NASA (National Aeronautics and Space Administration)

Blending: Combining two words, such as *breakfast* and *lunch* to form *brunch* and *smoke* and *fog* to form *smog*

Backformation: Rubba explains, "A suffix identifiable from other words is cut off of a base which has previously not been a word; that base then is used as a root, and becomes a word through widespread use." She gives as examples *self-destruct,* which derives from *self-destruction,* and *burger,* which derives from *hamburger*. Rubba explains that this differs from clipping because

> . . . in clipping, some <u>phonological</u> part of the word which is not interpretable as an affix or word is cut off (e.g., the '-essor' of 'professor' is not a suffix or word; nor is the '-ther' of 'brother.' In backformation, the bit chopped off is a recognizable affix or word ('ham' in 'hamburger').

Using brand names as common words: Using the name of a product (without initial capitalization) to act as a noun or verb. Companies often object to the use of their product names in public documents without their consent. Examples might include using the brand name when speaking of a soft drink or when referring to an adhesive bandage.

Onomatopoeia: Words invented to imitate the sound they represent; for example, *pow*, *bop, splat,* and *pop*.

Borrowing: Taking a word from another language. Words borrowed from the African languages, for instance, include *yam* and *tote*; *macho* and *spaghetti* come from European languages.

CONVENTIONS OF STANDARD ENGLISH

All of the PRAXIS II English Assessments assess the ability of candidates to apply traditional grammar elements such as syntax, sentence structure, sentence types, parts of speech, modifiers, sentence combining, phrases, clauses, capitalization, and punctuation.

Grammar, Usage, and Mechanics

Properly applying the conventions of grammar, usage, and mechanics—including sentence types, sentence structure, parts of speech, modifiers, phrases, clauses, capitalization, and punctuation—helps to ensure good communication.

Sentence Types

There are three types of sentences:

1. The **declarative sentence** makes a statement:

   Jane's dress is blue.

2. The **interrogative sentence** asks a question:

   Is Jane's dress blue?

3. The **imperative sentence** gives a command or makes a request:

> Open the closet door. Look inside. Find my sweater.

Sentence Structure

There are four sentence structures:

1. A **simple sentence** has a subject and verb:

> The first president of the United States was George Washington.

2. A **compound sentence** is made up of two **independent clauses**—clauses that have a subject and a verb and express a complete thought—joined by a coordinating conjunction (*and*, *but*, *or*), a correlative conjunction (*either-or*, *neither-nor*), or a semicolon:

> George cooked the eggs for breakfast, and Jane prepared the oatmeal.

> Either Jane will go, or I will go.

> Sam reads well; Bill does not.

3. A **complex sentence** has a **dependent clause**—a clause that contains a subject and a verb and that does not express a complete thought—and an independent clause:

> Because I do not feel well, I will not be attending the concert.

4. A sentence with at least two independent clauses and at least one dependent clause is a **complex-compound sentence** (or compound-complex sentence):

> I am going to town, and Bill is going when he gets his car repaired.

Run-on sentences with several thoughts incorrectly joined are not grammatically correct. Here is an example:

> I like to ice skate my brother does not.

A **sentence fragment** is an incomplete thought and is not grammatically correct. Here is an example of a sentence fragment:

> Making his way in the world today.

Parts of Speech

There are eight parts of speech: nouns, pronouns, verbs, adjectives, adverbs, prepositions, conjunctions, and interjections.

A **noun** is the name of a person, place, or thing. Examples of nouns include Jill, America, and dog.

A **pronoun** is a word that can replace a noun. There are several categories of pronouns, as shown in the following table:

Type of Pronouns	Examples of Pronouns
Personal	*I, you, he, she, it, we, you, they, them, us, my, mine, me, your, yours, her, hers, its, our, ours, us, their, theirs*
Relative	*who, which, that, whose, whom*
Interrogative	*who, what, when, where, how*
Demonstrative	*this, that, these, those*
Indefinite	*one, any, each, anyone, somebody, all*, and so on
Reciprocal	*each other, one another*
Intensive	*myself, yourself, himself*, and so on
Reflexive	*myself, yourself, herself*, and so on

A **verb** is a word or phrase that shows action or a state of being. Examples of state-of-being verbs are *is, are, am, was*, and *were*. Examples of phrases that show action include *was writing* and *has been sewing*.

In addition, verbs may be transitive or intransitive. **Transitive verbs** may take a direct object, as is in *Bob beat the rug*; *beat* is the transitive verb, and *the rug* is the direct object, or the recipient of the action. **Intransitive verbs** do not require an object: *The chorus was singing as they entered the building*; there is no recipient for the action *was singing*. Some transitive verbs can act as both active verbs or linking:

> Jane *felt* the prickly bush. (Transitive active)

> Bill *felt* dizzy when he got up suddenly. (Transitive linking verb
> followed by an adjective)

An **adjective** modifies or limits a noun or pronoun. There are several types of adjectives:

> A **descriptive adjective** names a quality of an object: *blue* notebook.

> A **limiting adjective** restricts the meaning or indicates quantity or number.

> A **possessive adjective:** *her* jacket, *their* house

> A **demonstrative adjective:** *this* automobile

> An **interrogative adjective:** *Which* cat belongs to you?

> **Articles:** *a, an, the*

> **Numerical adjectives:** one ticket, second half of the game

> **Comparative** and **superlative adjectives** indicate degree:

> > *bigger, rounder, hotter* (comparative)

> > *biggest, roundest, hottest* (superlative)

An **adverb** is a word that limits or describes a verb, an adjective, or another adverb:

> Herman walks *quickly*. (*Quickly* describes the verb *walks*.)

Jane colors *very well*. (The adverb *very* modifies the adverb *well*, which modifies the verb *color*.)

Billy put the cat *outside earlier*. (The adverb *outside* modifies the verb *put*; *outside* tells where Billy put the cat. The adverb *earlier* modifies the verb *put* and tells when Billy put the cat outside.)

A **preposition** relates a noun or pronoun to another word in the sentence; the preposition and its object form a **prepositional phrase**:

Bill drew a circle *around the subject*. (*Around* is the preposition; *subject* is the object of the preposition; *around the subject* is the prepositional phrase.)

A **conjunction** is a word that may connect words, phrases, and clauses. Conjunctions may be coordinating or subordinating. A **coordinating conjunction** joins words, phrases, or clauses of equal rank; examples include *and, but, or, nor*. **Subordinating conjunctions**—examples include *although, after, because, if*—join subordinate clauses with main clauses, as in the following:

Because he was better, Billy went home from the hospital. (*Billy went home from the hospital* is the main clause; *Because he was better* is the subordinate clause.)

By changing to a coordinating conjunction, one can make both clauses of equal rank:

Billy was better, and he went home from the hospital. (*And* shows that both clauses are of equal importance.)

An **interjection** is a word inserted or interjected to show emotion:

Wow! That was a surprise.

Ouch! That sting hurt.

Modifiers may describe or limit the meaning of a word or group of words. Both adjectives and adjective phrases or clauses can modify a noun:

> The *red* boat won the race. (The adjective *red* modifies the noun *boat*.)

> The boat *that won the race* was a red one. (*That won the race* is an adjective phrase modifying the noun *boat*.)

Both adverbs and adverbial phrases or clauses can modify a verb:

> *Tomorrow* I will begin driving. (*Tomorrow* is an adverb telling when.)

> *When I am older*, I will begin driving. (*When I am older* is a subordinate clause telling when and modifying the verb phrase *will begin*.)

A **phrase** is a group of words without a subject and predicate. A phrase can function as a noun, an adjective, an adverb, or a verb. Phrases may be prepositional, participial, gerunds, infinitives, and verbs.

> The team ran *across the field*. (A prepositional phrase used as an adverb.)

> The horse *winning the race* belongs to me. (A participial phrase used as an adjective.)

> *Writing the book* was a pleasure. (A gerund phrase used as a noun and the subject of the sentence.)

> *To walk* was his goal. (An infinitive used as a noun and the subject of the sentence.)

> The writer *had been working* on his book for weeks. (The phrase functions as a verb.)

A **clause** contains a subject and a verb. A clause may be independent or subordinate (dependent). An **independent clause** is a complete thought. Consider this example:

When the siren sounded, *the dog began to howl.*

The dog began to howl is an independent clause. It contains the subject *dog* and the verb *began*. *When the siren sounded* is a dependent clause. It contains a subject (*siren*) and a verb (*sounded*), but it does not contain a complete thought and is thus dependent.

Capitalization

Capitalization is an important element of writing. When a word is capitalized, it calls attention to itself. This attention should be for a good reason. There are standard uses for capital letters. In general, capitalize (1) all proper nouns, (2) the first word of a sentence, and (3) the first word of a direct quotation. The following lists outline specific guidelines for capitalization.

What Should Be Capitalized

Capitalize the names of ships, aircraft, spacecraft, and trains:

> *Apollo 13*
>
> Boeing 767
>
> DC-10
>
> HMS *Bounty*
>
> *Mariner 4*
>
> *Sputnik II*

Capitalize the names of divine beings:

> God
>
> Allah
>
> Buddha
>
> Holy Ghost
>
> Jehovah

Jupiter

Shiva

Venus

Capitalize the geological periods:

Cenozoic era

Neolithic age

Ice Age

late Pleistocene times

Capitalize the names of astronomical bodies:

Big Dipper

Halley's comet

Mercury

the Milky Way

North Star

Ursa Major

Capitalize personifications:

Reliable Nature brought her promised Spring.

Bring on Melancholy in his sad might.

She believed that Love was the answer to all her problems.

Capitalize historical periods:

Age of Louis XIV

Christian Era

the Great Depression

the Middle Ages

Reign of Terror

the Renaissance

Roaring Twenties

World War I

Capitalize the names of organizations, associations, and institutions:

Common Market

Franklin Glen High School

Girl Scouts

Harvard University

Kiwanis Club

League of Women Voters

Library of Congress

New York Philharmonic

New York Yankees

North Atlantic Treaty Organization

Smithsonian Institution

Unitarian Church

Capitalize government and judicial groups:

Arkansas Supreme Court

British Parliament

Committee on Foreign Affairs

Department of State

Georgetown City Council

Peace Corps

U.S. Census Bureau

U.S. Court of Appeals

U.S. House of Representatives

U.S. Senate

A general term that accompanies a specific name is capitalized only if it follows the specific name. If it stands alone, comes before the specific name, or is used on second reference, it is lowercased:

Central Park, the park

Golden Gate Bridge, the bridge

the Mississippi River, the river

Monroe Doctrine, the doctrine of expansion

President Obama, the president of the United States

Pope Benedict XVI, the pope

Queen Elizabeth I, the queen of England

Senator Dixon, the senator from Illinois

Treaty of Versailles, the treaty

Tropic of Capricorn, the tropics

Webster's Dictionary, the dictionary

Washington State, the state of Washington

Capitalize the first word of a sentence:

Our car would not start.

When will you leave? I need to know right away.

Never!

Let me in! Please!

When a sentence appears within a sentence, start it with a capital letter:

We had only one concern, When would we eat?

My sister said, "I'll find the Monopoly game."

He answered, "We can only stay a few minutes."

The most important words of titles are capitalized. Those words not capitalized are conjunctions (*and*, *or*, *but*) and short prepositions (*of*, *on*, *by*, *for*). The first and last word of a title must always be capitalized:

A Man for All Seasons

Crime and Punishment

Of Mice and Men

Rise of the West

Strange Life of Ivan Osokin

Sonata in G Minor

"Let Me In"

"Ode to Billy Joe"

Rubaiyat of Omar Khayyam

All in the Family

Capitalize newspaper and magazine names:

the *New York Times*

the *Washington Post*

National Geographic

U.S. News & World Report

Capitalize radio and TV network abbreviations or station call letters:

ABC

CNN

HBO

NBC

WBOP

WNEW

Capitalize regions:

> the Northeast, the South, the West
>
> Eastern Europe
>
> but: the south of France, the east side of town

Capitalize specific military units:

> the U.S. Army, but: the army, the German navy, the British air force
>
> the Seventh Fleet
>
> the First Infantry Division

Capitalize political organizations, and in some cases, their philosophies and members:

> Democratic Party, the Communist Party
>
> Marxist
>
> Whigs
>
> Nazism
>
> Federalist (in U.S. history contexts)

But do <u>not</u> capitalize systems of government or individual adherents to a philosophy:

> democracy, communism
>
> fascist, agnostic

Do <u>not</u> capitalize compass directions or seasons:

> north, south, east, west
>
> spring, summer, winter, autumn

Punctuation

Commas.   Commas should be placed according to standard rules of punctuation for purpose, clarity, and effect. The proper use of commas is explained in the following rules and examples.

In a series.   When more than one adjective describes a noun, use a comma to separate and emphasize each adjective. The comma takes the place of the word *and* in the series:

> the long, dark passageway
>
> another confusing, sleepless night
>
> an elaborate, complex, brilliant plan
>
> the old, grey, crumpled hat

Some adjective-noun combinations are thought of as one word. In these cases, the adjective in front of the adjective-noun combination needs no comma. If you inserted *and* between the adjective-noun combination, it would not make sense:

> a stately oak tree
>
> an exceptional martini glass
>
> my worst report card
>
> a china dinner plate

The comma is also used to separate words, phrases, and whole ideas (clauses); it still takes the place of *and* when used this way:

> an apple, a pear, a fig, and a banana
>
> a lovely lady, an elegant dress, and many admirers
>
> She lowered the shade, closed the curtain, turned off the light, and went to bed.

The only question that exists about the use of commas in a series is whether or not one should be used before the final item. It is standard usage to do so, although many newspapers and magazines have stopped using the final comma. Occasionally, the omission of the comma can be confusing:

INCORRECT: He got on his horse, tracked a rabbit and a deer and rode on to Canton.
CORRECT: He got on his horse, tracked a rabbit and a deer, and rode on to Canton.

INCORRECT: We planned the trip with Mary and Harold, Susan, Dick and Joan, Gregory and Jean and Charles.
CORRECT: We planned the trip with Mary and Harold; Susan, Dick and Joan; Gregory and Jean; and Charles.

In the latter example, semicolons are correctly used to separate series items that have internal commas.

With a long introductory phrase.   Usually if a phrase of more than five or six words or a dependent clause precedes the subject at the beginning of a sentence, a comma is used to set it off:

After last night's fiasco at the disco, she couldn't bear the thought of looking at him again.

Whenever I try to talk about politics, my wife leaves the room.

Provided you have said nothing, they will never guess who you are.

It is not necessary to use a comma with a short introductory phrase:

In January she will go to Switzerland.

After I rest I'll feel better.

During the day no one is home.

If an introductory phrase includes a verb form being used as another part of speech (a verbal), it must be followed by a comma:

INCORRECT: When eating Mary never looked up from her plate.
CORRECT: When eating, Mary never looked up from her plate.

INCORRECT: Because of her desire to follow her faith in James wavered.
CORRECT: Because of her desire to follow, her faith in James wavered.

INCORRECT: Having decided to leave Mary James wrote her a letter.

CORRECT: Having decided to leave Mary, James wrote her a letter.

To separate sentences with two main ideas.   To understand this use of the comma, you need to be able to recognize compound sentences. When a sentence contains two independent clauses—two complete thoughts each with its own subject and verb—and the two clauses are joined by a conjunction (*and, but, or, nor, for, yet*), use a comma before the conjunction to show that another clause is coming:

I thought I knew the poem by heart, but he showed me three lines I had forgotten.

Are we really interested in helping the children, or are we more concerned with protecting our good names?

He is supposed to leave tomorrow, but he is not ready to go.

Jim knows you are disappointed, and he has known it for a long time.

If the two parts of the sentence are short and closely related, it is not necessary to use a comma:

He threw the ball and the dog ran after it.

Jane played the piano and Michael danced.

Be careful not to confuse a sentence that has a compound verb and a single subject with a compound sentence. If the subject is the same for both verbs, there is no need for a comma:

INCORRECT: Charles sent some flowers, and wrote a long letter explaining why he had not been able to attend.

CORRECT: Charles sent some flowers and wrote a long letter explaining why he had not been able to attend.

INCORRECT: Last Thursday we went to the concert with Julia, and afterwards dined at an old Italian restaurant.

CORRECT: Last Thursday we went to the concert with Julia and afterwards dined at an old Italian restaurant.

INCORRECT: For the third time, the teacher explained that the literacy level for high school students was much lower than it had been in previous years, and, this time, wrote the statistics on the board for everyone to see.

CORRECT: For the third time, the teacher explained that the literacy level for high school students was much lower than it had been in previous years and this time wrote the statistics on the board for everyone to see.

To separate an introductory subordinate clause. Usually, when a subordinate clause is at the end of a sentence, no comma is necessary preceding the clause. However, when a subordinate clause introduces a sentence, a comma should be used after the clause:

NO COMMA: I take extra vitamin C *whenever I catch a cold*.

COMMA: *Whenever I catch a cold*, I take extra vitamins.

Some common subordinating conjunctions are:

after	so that
although	though
as	till
as if	unless
because	until
before	when
even though	whenever
if	while
inasmuch as	since

To slow the flow of the sentence.   In general, commas set off words and phrases that stop the flow of the sentence or are unnecessary for the main idea. Here are some examples:

Appositives (expressions identifying the expressions which come immediately before or after them)

> Did you invite my brother, John Paul Jr., and his sister?
>
> Martha Harris, Ph.D., will be the speaker tonight.

Interjections (an exclamation without added grammatical connection)

> Oh, I'm so glad to see you.
>
> I tried so hard, alas, to do it.
>
> Hey, let me out of here.

Direct address

> Roy, won't you open the door for the dog?
>
> I can't understand, Mother, what you are trying to say.
>
> May I ask, Mr. President, why you called us together?
>
> Hey, lady, watch out for that car!

Tag questions

> I'm really hungry, aren't you?
>
> Jerry looks like his father, doesn't he?

Geographical names and addresses

> The concert will be held in Chicago, Illinois, on August 12.
>
> The letter was addressed to Mrs. Marion Heartwell, 1881 Pine Lane, Palo Alto, California 95824.

(Note: No comma is needed before the ZIP code, because it is already clearly set off from the state name.)

Transitional words and phrases

On the other hand, I hope he gets better.

In addition, the phone rang constantly this afternoon.

I'm, nevertheless, going to the beach on Sunday.

You'll find, therefore, that no one is more loyal than I am.

Parenthetical words and phrases

You will become, I believe, a great statesman.

We know, of course, that this is the only thing to do.

In fact, I planted corn last summer.

The Mannes affair was, to put it mildly, a surprise.

Unusual word order

The dress, new and crisp, hung in the closet.

Intently, she stared out the window.

With nonrestrictive elements. Parts of a sentence that modify other parts are sometimes essential to the meaning of the sentence and sometimes not. When a modifying word or group of words is not vital to the meaning of the sentence, commas set it off. Since it does not restrict the meaning of the words it modifies, it is called **nonrestrictive**. Modifiers that are essential to the meaning of the sentence are called **restrictive** and are not set off by commas:

RESTRICTIVE: The girl *who wrote the story* is my sister. (*Who wrote the story* is a restrictive clause; it is essential to the meaning of the sentence.)

NONRESTRICTIVE: My sister, *the girl who wrote the story*, has always loved to write. (*The girl who wrote the story* is a nonrestrictive clause: though it provides additional information, it is not essential to the sense of the sentence.)

RESTRICTIVE: John Milton's famous poem *Paradise Lost* tells a remarkable story.
NONRESTRICTIVE: Dante's greatest work, *The Divine Comedy*, marked the beginning of the Renaissance.

RESTRICTIVE: The cup *that is on the piano* is the one I want.
NONRESTRICTIVE: The cup, *which my brother gave me last year*, is on the piano.

RESTRICTIVE: The people *who arrived late* were not seated.
NONRESTRICTIVE: George, *who arrived late*, was not seated.

To set off direct quotations.   Most direct quotes or quoted materials are set off from the rest of the sentence by commas:

"Please read your part more loudly," the director insisted.

"I won't know what to do," said Michael, "if you leave me."

The teacher said sternly, "I will not dismiss this class until I have silence."

Who was it who said, "Do not ask for whom the bell tolls; it tolls for thee"?

Note: Commas always go inside the closing quotation mark, even if the comma is not part of the material being quoted.

Be careful not to set off indirect quotes or quotes that are used as subjects or complements:

"To be or not to be" is the famous beginning of a soliloquy in Shakespeare's *Hamlet*. (*To be or not to be* is the subject of the sentence.)

She said she would never come back. (*She would never come back* is an indirect quote.)

Back then my favorite poem was "Evangeline." ("Evangeline" is a complement.)

To set off contrasting elements.

Her intelligence, not her beauty, got her the job.

Your plan will take you a little further from, rather than closer to, your destination.

It was a reasonable, though not appealing, idea.

He wanted glory, but found happiness instead.

In dates. When the month, day, and year are given, a comma follows both the day and the year. When only the month and year are given or when the European style of day, month, year is used, no commas are necessary:

She arrived on April 6, 1998, at Grand Central Station.

On October 22, 1992, Frank and Julie were married.

He left on 5 December 1980.

In January 1967 he handed in his resignation.

Semicolons. Questions testing semicolon usage require you to be able to distinguish between the semicolon and the comma, and the semicolon and the colon. This review section covers the basic uses of the semicolon: to separate independent clauses not joined by a coordinating conjunction, to separate independent clauses separated by a conjunctive adverb, and to separate items in a series with internal commas. It is important to be consistent; if you use a semicolon between *any* of the items in the series, you must use semicolons to separate *all* of the items in the series.

Usually, a comma follows the conjunctive adverb. Note also that a period can be used to separate two sentences joined by a conjunctive adverb. Some common conjunctive adverbs are

accordingly	nevertheless
besides	next
consequentially	nonetheless
finally	now
furthermore	on the other hand
however	otherwise
indeed	perhaps
in fact	still
moreover	therefore

Then is also used as a conjunctive adverb, but it is not usually followed by a comma.

When to Use the Semicolon

To separate independent clauses that are not joined by a coordinating conjunction:

> I understand how to use commas; the semicolon I have not yet mastered.

To separate two independent clauses connected by a conjunctive adverb:

> He took great care with his work; therefore, he was very successful.

To combine two independent clauses connected by a coordinating conjunction if either or both of the clauses contain internal punctuation

> Success in college, some maintain, requires intelligence, industry, and perseverance; but others, fewer in number, assert that only personality is important.

To separate items in a series when the items have internal punctuation:

I bought an old, dilapidated chair; an antique table, which was in beautiful condition; and a new, ugly, blue and white rug.

Call our customer service line for assistance: Arizona, 1-800-555-6020; New Mexico, 1-800-555-5050; California, 1-800-555-3140; or Nevada, 1-800-555-3214.

When *Not* to Use the Semicolon

To separate a dependent and an independent clause:

INCORRECT: You should not make such statements; even though they are correct.
CORRECT: You should not make such statements even though they are correct.

To separate an appositive phrase or clause from a sentence:

INCORRECT: His immediate aim in life is centered around two things; becoming an engineer and learning to fly an airplane.
CORRECT: His immediate aim in life is centered around two things: becoming an engineer and learning to fly an airplane.

To precede an explanation or summary of the first clause:

WEAK: The first week of camping was wonderful; we lived in cabins instead of tents.
BETTER: The first week of camping was wonderful: we lived in cabins instead of tents.

(Note: Although the first sentence in this example is punctuated correctly, the use of the semicolon provides a miscue, suggesting that the second clause is merely an extension, not an explanation, of the first clause. The colon provides a better clue.)

> **PRAXIS Pointer**
>
> **Study the directions and format of each practice test. Become familiar with the structure of the test so that you can save time when you begin taking the actual test. This way, you can cut your chances of experiencing any unwanted surprises.**

To substitute for a comma:

> INCORRECT: My roommate also likes sports; particularly football, basketball, and baseball.
> CORRECT: My roommate also likes sports, particularly football, basketball, and baseball.

To set off other types of phrases or clauses from a sentence:

> INCORRECT: Being of a cynical mind; I should ask for a recount of the ballots.
> CORRECT: Being of a cynical mind, I should ask for a recount of the ballots.

> INCORRECT: The next meeting of the club has been postponed two weeks; inasmuch as both the president and vice president are out of town.
> CORRECT: The next meeting of the club has been postponed two weeks, inasmuch as both the president and vice president are out of town.

(Note: The semicolon is not a terminal mark of punctuation; therefore, it should not be followed by a capital letter unless the first word in the second clause ordinarily requires capitalization.)

Colons.   While it is true that a colon is used to precede a list, one must also make sure that a complete sentence precedes the colon. The colon signals the reader that a list, explanation, or restatement of the preceding will follow. It is like an arrow, indicating that something more is to come.

When to Use a Colon

To introduce a list (one item may constitute a list):

> I hate this one course: English.

> Three plays by William Shakespeare will be presented in repertory this summer at the University of Michigan: *Hamlet*, *Macbeth*, and *Othello*.

To introduce a list preceded by *as follows* or *the following*:

> The reasons he cited for his success are as follows: integrity, honesty, industry, and a pleasant disposition.

> There are a number of well-known American women writers, including the following: Nikki Giovanni, Phillis Wheatley, Emily Dickinson, and Maya Angelou.

To separate two independent clauses when the second clause is a restatement or explanation of the first:

> All of my high school teachers said one thing in particular: college is going to be difficult.

To introduce a word or word group that is a restatement, explanation, or summary of the first sentence:

> These two things he loved: an honest man and a beautiful woman.

To introduce a formal appositive:

> I am positive there is one appeal that you can't overlook: money.

To separate the introductory words from a quotation, if the quotation is formal, long, or paragraphed separately:

> The actor then stated: "I would rather be able to adequately play the part of Hamlet than to perform a miraculous operation, deliver a great lecture, or build a magnificent skyscraper."

When *Not* to Use a Colon

After a verb:

> INCORRECT: My favorite holidays are: Christmas, New Year's, and Halloween.
> CORRECT: My favorite holidays are Christmas, New Year's, and Halloween.

After a preposition:

> INCORRECT: I enjoy different ethnic foods such as: Greek, Chinese, and Italian.
> CORRECT: I enjoy different ethnic foods such as Greek, Chinese, and Italian.

In place of a dash:

> INCORRECT: Mathematics, German, English: These gave me the greatest difficulty of all my studies.
> CORRECT: Mathematics, German, English—these gave me the greatest difficulty of all my studies.

Information preceding the colon should be a complete sentence regardless of the explanatory information following the clause.

Before the words *for example*, *namely*, *that is*, or *for instance* even though these words may be introducing a list:

INCORRECT: We agreed to it: namely, to give him a surprise party.

CORRECT: We agreed to it, namely, to give him a surprise party.

Colon usage questions test your knowledge of the colon preceding a list, restatement, or explanation. These questions also require you to be able to distinguish between the colon and the period, the colon and the comma, and the colon and the semicolon.

Apostrophes. Apostrophe questions require you to know when an apostrophe has been used appropriately to make a noun possessive, not plural. Remember the following rules when considering how to show possession:

Add *'s* to singular nouns and indefinite pronouns:

Tiffany's flowers

a dog's bark

everybody's computer

at the owner's expense

today's paper

Add *'s* to singular nouns ending in *s*, unless this distorts the pronunciation:

Delores's paper

the boss's pen

Dr. Yots' class

for righteousness' sake

the species' distinguishing characteristic

Add only an apostrophe to plural nouns ending in *s* or *es*:

two cents' worth

ladies' night

thirteen years' experience

two weeks' pay

Add *'s* to plural nouns not ending in *s*:

men's room

children's toys

Add *'s* to the last word in compound words or groups:

brother-in-law's car

someone else's paper

Add *'s* to the last name when indicating joint ownership:

Joe and Edna's home

Julie and Kathy's party

women and children's clinic

Add *'s* to both names if the intent is to show ownership by each person:

Joe's and Edna's trucks

Julie's and Kathy's pies

Ted's and Jane's marriage vows

Possessive pronouns change their forms *without* the addition of an apostrophe:

our, ours

her, his, hers

your, yours

their, theirs

it, its

Use the possessive form of a noun preceding a gerund:

His driving annoys me.

My bowling a strike irritated him.

Do you mind *our stopping* by?

We appreciate *your coming*.

So long as no confusion will result, add *s* alone to numbers, symbols, and letters to show that they are plural:

TVs

VCRs

the 1800s

the returning POWs

When confusion could result from the addition of *s* alone, add *'s* to words and initials to show that they are plural:

the do's and don'ts of dating

three A's

M.A.'s and Ph.D.'s

Quotation Marks and Italics.   These Praxis II English Assessments test your knowledge of the proper use of quotation marks with other marks of punctuation, with titles, and with dialogue. There are also questions that test your knowledge of the correct use of italics (or underlining) with titles and words used as sample words (e.g., *The word <u>is</u> is a common verb*).

Guidelines for Using Quotation Marks

Use double quotation marks (" ") to set off quoted words, phrases, and sentences:

"If everybody minded their own business," said the Duchess in a hoarse growl, "the world would go round a great deal faster than it does."
"Then you would say what you mean," the March Hare went on.
"I do," Alice hastily replied: "at least—at least I mean what I say—that's the same thing, you know." (Carroll 1865)

Use single quotation marks (' ') to set off quoted material within a quote:

"Shall I bring 'Rime of the Ancient Mariner' along with us?" she asked her brother.

Mrs. Green said, "The doctor told me, 'Go immediately to bed when you get home!' "

"If she said that to me," Katherine insisted, "I would tell her, 'I never intend to speak to you again! Goodbye, Susan!' "

When writing dialogue, begin a new paragraph each time the speaker changes:

"Do you know what time it is?" asked Jane.

"Can't you see I'm busy?" snapped Mary.

"It's easy to see that you're in a bad mood today!" replied Jane.

Use quotation marks to enclose words used as words (italics can also be used for this purpose):

"Judgment" has always been a difficult word for me to spell.

Do you know what "abstruse" means?

"Horse and buggy" and "bread and butter" can be used either as adjectives or as nouns.

Use quotation marks to set off slang words or phrases within more formal writing:

> Harrison's decision to leave the conference and to "stick his neck out" by flying to Jamaica was applauded by the rest of the conference attendees.

When words are meant to have an unusual or specific significance to the reader, for instance, for irony or humor, they are sometimes placed in quotation marks:

> For years, men did not allow women to buy real estate in order to "protect" them from unscrupulous dealers.

> The "conversation" resulted in one black eye and a broken nose.

Use quotation marks to set off titles of poems, stories, book chapters, and songs:

> The article "Moving South in the Southern Rain," by Jergen Smith in the *Southern News*, attracted the attention of our editor.

> The assignment is "Childhood Development," chapter 18 of *Human Behavior*.

> My favorite essay by Montaigne is "On Silence."

> You will find Keats' "Ode on a Grecian Urn" in chapter 3, "The Romantic Era," in Lastly's *Selections from Great English Poets*.

> She sang "The Star-Spangled Banner" at last night's baseball game.

Book, television show, motion picture, newspaper, and magazine titles are underlined when handwritten and italicized when printed.

Errors to Avoid

Be sure to remember that quotation marks always come in pairs. Do not make the mistake of using only one set:

INCORRECT: "You'll never convince me to move to the city, said Thurman. I consider it an insane asylum."

CORRECT: "You'll never convince me to move to the city," said Thurman. "I consider it an insane asylum."

INCORRECT: "Idleness and pride tax with a heavier hand than kings and parliaments," Benjamin Franklin is supposed to have said. If we can get rid of the former, we may easily bear the latter."

CORRECT: "Idleness and pride tax with a heavier hand than kings and parliaments," Benjamin Franklin is supposed to have said. "If we can get rid of the former, we may easily bear the latter."

When a quote consists of several sentences, do not put the quotation marks at the beginning and end of each sentence; put them at the beginning and end of the entire quotation:

INCORRECT: "It was during his student days in Bonn that Beethoven fastened upon Schiller's poem." "The heady sense of liberation in the verses must have appealed to him." "They appealed to every German." —John Burke

CORRECT: "It was during his student days in Bonn that Beethoven fastened upon Schiller's poem. The heady sense of liberation in the verses must have appealed to him. They appealed to every German." —John Burke

A quote of more than five or six lines is considered a block quotation or extract; set it off from the surrounding text by indenting. Do not use quotation marks with extracts:

In his First Inaugural Address, Abraham Lincoln appeals to the war-torn American people:

> We are not enemies, but friends. We must not be enemies. Though passion may have strained, it must not break our bonds of affection. The mystic chords of memory, stretching from every battlefield and patriot grave to every living heart and hearthstone all over this broad land, will yet swell the chorus of the Union when again touched, as surely they will be, by the better angels of our nature.

Do not use quotation marks with indirect quotations:

> INCORRECT: Mary wondered "if she would get over it."
> CORRECT: Mary wondered if she would get over it.
>
> INCORRECT: The nurse asked "how long it had been since we had visited the doctor's office."
> CORRECT: The nurse asked how long it had been since we had visited the doctor's office.

When you quote several paragraphs, it is not sufficient to place quotation marks at the beginning and end of the entire quote. Place quotation marks at the *beginning of each paragraph*, but only at the *end of the last paragraph*. Here is an abbreviated quotation for an example:

> "Here begins an odyssey through the world of classical mythology, starting with the creation of the world . . .
>
> "It is true that themes similar to the classical may be found in any corpus of mythology . . . Even technology is not immune to the influence of Greece and Rome . . .
>
> "We need hardly mention the extent to which painters and sculptors . . . have used and adapted classical mythology to illustrate the past, to reveal the human body, to express romantic or antiromantic ideals, or to symbolize any particular point of view."

Always enclose commas and periods inside the quotation marks, even if they are not actually part of the quote:

> INCORRECT: "Life always gets colder near the summit". Nietzsche is purported to have said, "—the cold increases, responsibility grows".
> CORRECT: "Life always gets colder near the summit," Nietzsche is purported to have said, "—the cold increases, responsibility grows."

> INCORRECT: "Get down here right away", John cried. "You'll miss the sunset if you don't."
> CORRECT: "Get down here right away," John cried. "You'll miss the sunset if you don't."

> INCORRECT: "If my dog could talk", Mary mused, "I'll bet he would say, 'Take me for a walk right this minute' ".
> CORRECT: "If my dog could talk," Mary mused, "I'll bet he would say, 'Take me for a walk right this minute.' "

Do not enclose marks of punctuation such as question marks, exclamation points, colons, and semicolons inside the quotation marks unless they are part of the quoted material. Be careful to distinguish between the placement of the comma and period, which always go inside the quotation marks, and that of other marks of punctuation:

> INCORRECT: "I'll always love you"! he exclaimed happily.
> CORRECT: "I'll always love you!" he exclaimed happily.

> INCORRECT: Did you hear her say, "He'll be there early?"
> CORRECT: Did you hear her say, "He'll be there early"?

> INCORRECT: She called down the stairs, "When are you going"?
> CORRECT: She called down the stairs, "When are you going?"

> INCORRECT: "Let me out"! he cried. "Don't you have any pity"?
> CORRECT: "Let me out!" he cried. "Don't you have any pity?"

Use only one mark of punctuation at the end of a sentence ending with a quotation mark:

> INCORRECT: She thought out loud, "Will I ever finish this paper in time for that class?".
> CORRECT: She thought out loud, "Will I ever finish this paper in time for that class?"

> INCORRECT: "Not the same thing a bit!", said the Hatter. "Why, you might just as well say that 'I see what I eat' is the same thing as 'I eat what I see'!".
> CORRECT: "Not the same thing a bit!" said the Hatter. "Why, you might just as well say that 'I see what I eat' is the same thing as 'I eat what I see'!"

SEMANTICS

In linguistics, semantics is the study of meaning as conveyed through language. Semantics asks how we can use language to express things about the real world and how the meanings of linguistic expressions can reflect people's thoughts. Semantic knowledge is compositional; the meaning of a sentence is based on the meanings of the words it contains and the order in which they appear. For example, the sentences *Teachers love children* and *Children love teachers* both involve people loving other people, but because of the different order of words, they mean different things.

The following are some other terms relate closely to semantics:

Ambiguity is the use of words that allow alternative interpretations. The use of ambiguity may expand the literal meaning of a passage, but it may promote errors in understanding.

Euphemism is the substitution of less-offensive words for words considered explicitly offensive. For example, the term *passed away* seems less offensive than *died* when speaking to a family member of a deceased (dead) person.

Doublespeak is the misuse of language, often in a deliberate and even calculating way in order to mislead. For instance, the phrase *physical persuasion* may be used instead of *torture*. Or one might, for instance, say *preowned* instead of *second-hand* or *used*.

Connotation is the impression or feeling a word gives beyond its exact meaning; it is the opposite of *denotation*, which is saying exactly what is meant. Instead of saying, "We had two inches of rain in a two-hour period," one might say, "We had a real frog-strangler." Sometimes the reader must have some prior knowledge to understand the connotation of a term. (For more on connotation, see chapter 2.)

Jargon is the vocabulary of a particular profession or may refer to any speech or writing that one does not understand. Educators, for examples, use terms such as *learning styles* and *behavioral objectives* that may not be clear to the public. Other examples of jargon include *organoleptic analysis* to refer to the act of smelling something or (particularly during campaign years) the phrase *distributionally conservative notions* to refer to conservative economic policies.

REFERENCES

American Speech-Language-Hearing Association. *Social Language Use. www.asha.org/public/speech/development/Pragmatics.htm.* (Last accessed 11/10/08.)

Aronson, E., N. Blaney, C. Stephin, J. Sikes, and M. Snapp, 1978. *The Jigsaw Classroom.* Beverly Hills, CA: Sage.

Brown, Keith, ed. 2005. *Encyclopedia of Language and Linguistics* – 2nd Edition. Oxford: Elsevier.

Carroll, Lewis. 1865. *Alice's Adventures in Wonderland. www.online-literature.com/carroll/alice/7/.* (Last accessed 11/07/08.)

Chamot, A., and J. O'Malley, 1994. *The CALLA handbook.* Reading, MA: Addison-Wesley.

Crandall, J. A, ed. 1987. *ESL through content-area instruction: Mathematics, science, and social studies.* Englewood Cliffs, NJ, and Washington, DC: Prentice Hall and Center for Applied Linguistics.

Crystal, David. 2005. *The Cambridge Encyclopedia of the English Language*—2nd edition. Cambridge: Cambridge University Press.

Echevarria, J., D. Short, and K. Powers, 2006. School Reform and Standards-Based Education: A Model for English-Language Learners. *The Journal of Educational Research, 99*(4), 195–211.

Effland, Richard, Shereen Lerner, Stephen Perkins, and David Turkon. *Exploration of Language. Dialects: Small Differences. www.mc.maricopa.edu/dept/d10/asb/language/* (Last accessed 11/10/08.)

Gibbons, P. 2002. *Scaffolding Language, Scaffolding Learning: Teaching Second Language Learners in the Mainstream Classroom.* Portsmouth, NH: Heinemann.

Gottlieb, M. 2006. *Assessing English Language Learners: Bridges from Language Proficiency to Academic Achievement.* Thousand Oaks, CA: Corwin Press.

Hymes, D. 1971. Competence and Performance in Linguistic Theory. In R. Huxley and E. Ingram, eds. *Language Acquisition: Models and Methods.* London: Academic Press.

Krashen, S. D. 1982. *Principles and Practice in Second Language Acquisition.* New York: Pergamon Press.

Long, M. H. 1996. The Role of Linguistic Environment in Second Language Acquisition. In W. C. Ritchie and T. J. Bhatia, eds. *Handbook of Second Language Acquisition* (pp. 413–68). New York: Academic Press.

———. 2007. *Problems in SLA.* Mahwah, NJ: Erlbaum.

McCune, Lorraine. 2008. *How Children Learn to Learn Language.* New York: Oxford University Press, 2008. Oxford Scholarship Online. Oxford University Press. 7 November 2008 *http://dx.doi.org/10.1093/acprof:oso/9780195177879.001.0001* (Last accessed 11/7/08.)

Mencken, H. L. 1921. *The Beginnings of American: The First Differentiation.* In *The American Language. www.bartleby.com/185/7.html.*

Merriam-Webster Online Dictionary. 2008. *Etymology. www.m-w.com/cgi-bin/dictionary?etymology.*

Mohan, B. (1986). *Language and content.* Reading, MA: Addison-Wesley.

Mohan, B., Leung, C., and C. Davison, eds. 2001. *English as a Second Language in the Mainstream: Teaching Learning and Identity.* New York: Longman.

Moore, Barbara, M.A., CCC. *Assessment: What is the Role of the Speech Pathologist in the Assessment of Language/Learning Disordered Students?* OCLDA Newsletter, Vol. 38, No. 6, Nov/Dec, 2000.

Mosser, Daniel W. "Of Saxons, and of Angles and Jutes . . ." *The beginnings of English in England. http://ebbs.english.vt.edu/hel/helmod/oe.html.* (Last accessed 11/10/08.)

Nation, I. S. P. 2004. *Learning Vocabulary in Another Language.* Cambridge, UK: Cambridge University Press.

Nieto, S. 2005. Public Education in the Twentieth Century and Beyond: High Hopes, Broken Promises, and an Uncertain Future. *Harvard Educational Review, 75*(1).

Pica, T. 2005. Classroom Learning, Teaching, and Research: A Task-Based Perspective. *Modern Language Journal, 89,* 339–52.

Pica, T., H. Kang, and S. Sauro, 2006. Information Gap Tasks: Their Multiple Roles and Contributions To Interaction Research Methodology. *Studies in Second Language Acquisition, 28,* 301–38.

Robinson, P., and N. C. Ellis, eds. 2008. *Handbook of Cognitive Linguistics and Second Language Acquisition.* New York: Routledge.

Rubba, Johanna. 2004. *An Overview of the English Morphological System. http://cla.calpoly.edu/~jrubba/morph/morph.over.html#WF.* (Last accessed 11/10/08.)

Schleppegrell, M. J., M. Achugar, and T. Oteiza, 2004. The Grammar of History: Enhancing Content-Based Instruction Through a Functional Focus on Language. *TESOL Quarterly, 38,* 67–93.

Shohamy, E., and O. Inbar, 2006. *Assessment of Advanced Language Proficiency: Why Performance-Based Tasks?* (CPDD 0605). University Park, PA: The Pennsylvania State University, Center for Advanced Language Proficiency Education and Research. Available from *http://calper.la.psu.edu/publications.php.*

Snow, M. A. 2005. A Model of Academic Literacy for Integrated Language and Content Instruction. In E. Hinkel, ed. *Handbook of Research in Second Language Learning* (pp. 693–712). Mahwah, NJ: Erlbaum.

Stoller, F. L. 2004. Content-based Instruction: Perspectives on Curriculum Planning. *Annual Review of Applied Linguistics, 24,* 261–83.

Thomas, W. P., and V. P. Collier, 2002. *A National Study of School Effectiveness for Language Minority Students' Long-Term Academic Achievement.* Santa Cruz, CA: Center for Research on Education, Diversity & Excellence.

Trainor, Erin. Nd. *The History and Sociolinguistic Development of the Jamaican Dialect. http://debate.uvm.edu/dreadlibrary/trainor.html.* (Last accessed 11/10/08.)

Valdez-Pierce, L. 2003. *Assessing English language learners*. Washington, DC: National Education Association.

Wajnryb, R. 1990. *Grammar dictation*. Oxford, England: Oxford University Press.

Wiggins, G., and J. McTighe, 2005. *Understanding by Design*. Alexandria, VA: Association for Supervision and Curriculum Development.

Wilson Robert A., ed. 1999. *The MIT Encyclopedia of Cognitive Sciences*. London: The MIT Press.

Wolfram, Walt. 1969. *A Linguistic Description of Detroit Negro Speech*. Washington, DC: Center for Applied Linguistics.

———. 1991. *Dialects and American English*. Englewood Cliffs, NJ: Prentice Hall and Center for Applied Linguistics.

Wolfram, Walter A., and Donna Christian. 1989. *Dialects and Education: Issues and Answers*. Englewood Cliffs, NJ: Prentice Hall.

Wolfram, Walter A., and Nona. Clarke, eds. 1971. *Black-White Speech Relationships*. Washington, DC: Center for Applied Linguistics

Yule, G. 1996. *The Study of Language*. Cambridge: Cambridge University Press.

CHAPTER 4

Composition and Rhetoric

About 36 (30 percent) of the 120 questions on Praxis II English Language, Literature, and Composition: Content Knowledge exam (Test Code 0041) and approximately 29 questions (25 percent) of the total of 90 questions on the Praxis II Middle School English Language Arts test (0049) are designed to assess your knowledge of composition and rhetoric. Three of the exams covered in this volume—Middle School English Language Arts (0049); English Language, Literature, and Composition: Essays (0042); and English Language, Literature, and Composition: Pedagogy (0043)—include either essay or constructed-response questions that assess your mastery of composition and rhetoric. The two main areas being examined are your knowledge of the strategies for teaching writing, and your ability to recognize, understand, and evaluate rhetorical features of writing. This chapter reviews those areas and the subareas contained within.

TEACHING WRITING

In 2004, the National Council for Teachers of English (NTCE) set forth 11 principles to guide the practice of teaching writing:

1. Everyone has the capacity to write, writing can be taught, and teachers can help students become better writers.

2. People learn to write by writing.

3. Writing is a process.

4. Writing is a tool for thinking.

5. Writing grows out of many different purposes.

6. Conventions of finished and edited texts are important to readers and therefore to writers.

7. Writing and reading are related.

8. Writing has a complex relationship to talk.

9. Literate practices are embedded in complicated social relationships.

10. Composing occurs in different modalities and technologies.

11. Assessment of writing involves complex, informed, human judgment.

We recognize that each of these principles is important. For the purposes of you mastering these tests, however, we will focus on those that directly address the strategies for teaching writing, including evaluating and assessing students' writing.

Everyone Has the Capacity to Write

While some would like to argue that writing is a gift, there is a plethora of evidence to the contrary—writing is a skill that can be learned and honed. Teachers can make a difference in how well students learn the skill of writing; young or new writers require support from peers, from their mentors, and especially from their teachers.

People Learn to Write by Writing

The second principle NCTE espouses, *People learn to write by writing*, suggests that writing be built into all levels of education through projects such as Writing Across the Curriculum (WAC). WAC had its beginnings in higher education, and at that level it has met with a great deal of success as one response to the literacy crisis of the 1970s. Elementary, middle, and secondary schools are just now beginning to introduce WAC into the curriculum, increasing the amount that students write. Students already do a lot of self-sponsored writing by producing Web sites, text messaging their friends, writing in journals, and instant messaging online. Writing instruction can tap into this fact and reflect the student's life outside the school walls so they see the connections between the writing they initiate and that which is assigned to them.

Writing Is a Process

Understanding the elements of writing is key to any writer, or to any reader for that matter. When most people think of writing, they think of the finished product—the poem, the book, the article, and so on. Understanding what writers do, however, involves thinking not just about what texts look like when they are finished but also about the strategies writers employ to produce the texts. Two aspects of the actions in which writers engage are helpful to understand the process of writing. First is the development of routines, skills, strategies, and practices for generating, revising, and editing different kinds of texts. Second is the development of reflective abilities and meta-awareness about writing. This procedural understanding helps writers most when they encounter difficulty or when they are in the middle of creating a piece of writing.

While writing is a process, it should not be reduced to a formula of steps to follow. The process of writing is recursive, which is to say that a writer will draft, revise, edit, revise, shifting between the different operations of writing according to need and circumstance (see Figure 4.1). Almost all writers will tell you that they are never done honing their skills or garnering strategies as they move through their lives.

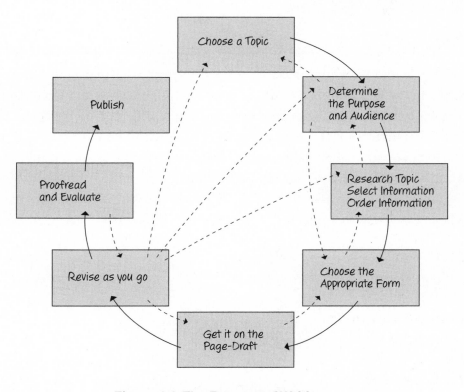

Figure 4.1 The Process of Writing

Students should become comfortable with prewriting techniques, multiple strategies for developing and organizing a message, as well as a variety of strategies for revising and editing, and strategies for preparing products for public audiences and for deadlines. In explaining assignments, teachers should provide guidance and options for ways of approaching the organization of the writing and the writing itself. Evaluating the processes students follow—the decisions they make, the attempts along the way—can be as important as evaluating the final product. Writing instruction must provide opportunities for students to identify what processes work best for them as they move from one writing situation to another.

PRAXIS Pointer

When you feel anxious, close your eyes, and take a couple of long, deep breaths. Then exhale slowly as you imagine a peaceful place.

Writing instruction should take into account that workplace writing and other writing takes place in collaborative situations, at least a good part of the time. Writers must learn to work effectively with one another.

STAGES OF WRITING

Prewriting

Prewriting is the planning phase of the writing process. Everything the writer does before creating the first draft is part of this phase. A great deal of thinking happens during this phase. First, the writer thinks about the topic that will become the focus of the piece and delimits the topic so that it is manageable. Then the writer organizes information on the topic along some dimension and then decides on an organizational format. Next, the writer decides on the audience for the piece. Finally, the writer chooses a point of view for the writing (Roe and Ross 2006). The following prewriting techniques are just a few that can be employed at this stage:

- Brainstorming

- Thinking/reflecting

- Talking/remembering

- Jotting ideas/drawing

- Reading/researching

- Observing/viewing

This first stage includes planning and deciding on the purpose for the writing and the role of the audience. Purposes for writing include engaging in civic discourse; supporting personal and spiritual growth; reflecting on experience; communicating professionally and academically; building relationships with others, including friends, family, and like-minded individuals; and engaging in aesthetic experiences.

There are several structures one may choose to plan a writing task and to organize for writing:

- An outline

- Story maps or diagrams

- Thought or word clusters

- Considering purpose, audience, point of view, and format

Topic Selection

It is typical for teachers to assign writing topics or to provide prompts to which students must respond. However, writers allowed to select their own topics will feel they are in control, enabling them to write about topics they know about and that matter to them. This will allow students to focus on the writing process rather than on gathering information for the content, which ultimately makes the task of writing easier for them. On some occasions, teachers need to assign topics, such as when students are learning how to write a report or to prepare them for standardized tests like the SAT, which requires them to write on a specific topic.

Strategies for identifying a subject include listing interests and experiences, keeping a personal journal, using pieces of literature for inspiration, and a technique called **freewriting** (Senn and Skinner 1995; discussed in the next section). Teachers can use interest inventories (available online or in language arts texts) to assist students in pinpointing their individual interests. These frequently consist of open-ended statements on various subjects for the students to complete. Here are two examples: *When I have some free time, I like to . . .* and *If I could travel to any place in the world, I would visit . . . .* Students can file the results of such an inventory in their respective writing folders for use in future writing exercises.

Some teachers have students keep journals in which to write, on a daily basis, their responses to people and events in their lives or in the world at large. In their journals, students can record ideas they want to explore, questions they have, sketches they have made, and words that intrigue them. All journal entries are possible topics for future writing.

Literature with which students are familiar can also serve as a source of inspiration. Students can write about a particular piece of fiction or a poem that they have read. They might want to focus on the plot of a novel or a particular character, the setting, or the theme. Some students might choose to write their interpretation of a poem, about the message the poet was trying to convey, or about the poet himself.

Freewriting

Freewriting is another technique students can use to reveal topics for future writing assignments. In this approach, students let their minds roam free and write about ideas as they think of them. Another version of this method is called **focused freewriting**. Using this technique, each student focuses on an idea, word, or phrase and then writes everything possible about the focus topic that comes to mind within a given time limit. The student must continue to write for the entire time. If ideas on the topic cease to flow, the student should just write down anything to keep the flow of writing going. The products of a focused freewriting exercise should be saved in the student's writing folder for future development.

Delimiting a Topic

Students need to learn how to delimit a topic, particularly one of their own choosing, so they can address it in the time allowed or within the word or page limits given. Without this ability, a student is apt to select a topic so broad that the student would need to write an entire book rather than a single paper. The teacher needs to model topic selection and the process of delimiting that topic. Students can then do exercises in delimiting topics provided to them and eventually transfer their ability to delimiting topics of their own choice (Roe and Ross 2006).

Teachers can tell students about the following strategies for delimiting a subject and model them as well: "Limit your subject to one person or one example that represents the subject; limit your subject to a specific time or place; limit your subject to a specific event; limit your subject to a specific condition, purpose, or procedure" (Senn and

Skinner 1995, 16). Given a list of topics that are too broad, students would attempt to limit them to those that are more reasonable by using each of the strategies just described. Practice of this kind will furnish students with skills they can apply to their future writing experiences.

Organizing Thoughts

Strategies that can be taught and then later used to help students to organize their thoughts during the prewriting phase include making lists, semantic webbing, drawing or sketching, and discussion (brainstorming) with their teacher and peers. Teachers need to remind students to engage in one of these activities before starting any writing activity, because most students want to rush into the first draft and skip this organizational step entirely. Requiring students to employ organizational strategies does not ensure that the actual writing will be organized, but it does increase the likelihood.

Purpose

The next element that the writer must consider in the prewriting phase is the purpose of and audience for the finished piece. Some possible purposes for writing include these: to explain or inform; to persuade; to express personal thoughts, feelings, or opinions; or to describe. Sometimes a writer combines two or more of these purposes. For example, writers might provide information to their readers and give a personal opinion about the same subject. In another piece, writers might describe somewhere they have visited and attempt to persuade the reader to travel there as well (Senn and Skinner 1995).

Audience

Writers should also consider the audience that they intend to reach before they start writing. Questions writers should ask themselves concerning their target audience include, "Who will be reading my work? How old are they? Are they adults, teenagers, or children? What background do they have in the subject? What interests and opinions are they likely to have? Are there any words or terms I should define for them?" (Senn and Skinner 1995, 17). Students can be given practice in writing two short pieces on the same subject but directed to two very different audiences. This exercise will make students aware of the types of modifications they would want to make to tailor the piece to the intended readers.

Different audiences have different expectations. The writer should consider audience expectations before he or she sits down and begins writing. Michel Muraski, on Colorado State University's writing home page, identifies three different types of audiences:

The untrained or lay audience: This audience expects background information and more description; they may profit from graphics or visuals and may connect with the human interest aspect of the article.

The managerial audience: These individuals may have more information than the lay audience, but they need particulars to make an informed decision.

The experts: This group may be a difficult one for a writer or speaker to address:

> The "experts" may be the most demanding audience in terms of knowledge, presentation, and graphics or visuals. Experts are often "theorists" or "practitioners." For the "expert" audience, document formats are often elaborate and technical, style and vocabulary may be specialized or technical, source citations are reliable and up-to-date, and documentation is accurate. (Muraski)

Point of View

The final aspect of a piece of writing that should be considered during the prewriting phase is the point of view. Authors can choose to tell a story, express an opinion, attempt to persuade, or describe something from their own point of view and write the piece in the first person using *I*, *we*, *us*, and *our*. Alternatively, authors might choose to write in the third person using pronouns such as *she*, *he*, *they*, *their*, *his*, or *her*. To give students repeated opportunities to practice writing from both viewpoints, teachers can provide exercises in changing sentences from first to third person or from third to first person. They should also engage in dialogue on the appropriateness of one over the other depending on the purpose of the piece and the intended effect of the completed writing. Writing in the first person often has more of an emotional impact on the reader than does writing in the third person.

Research and Documentation Techniques

Writing a research paper involves different skills than writing an essay. To the surprise of many students writing a research paper for the first time, the teacher is not interested in just how well a student can find materials and what the sources have to say about a topic but how well the researcher can use the information. Merely reviewing the literature does not make a research paper. "True research papers are more than a loose collection of anecdotal memories or a patchwork of data pulled from several books" (Online Writing Lab).

There are several steps in preparing a research paper. These steps and their order vary from source to source:

1. The researcher establishes a time frame for the work. Often another person or the course requirements set the due dates. These imposed deadlines may determine the time that one can spend.

2. Although most sources encourage one to engage in wide reading as a first step, Empire State College of the State University of New York advises setting a topic for the paper as a first step. Doing too much unfocused, general research can waste time and confuse the researcher. The first step, then, is to choose a topic; as the researcher begins the preliminary reading, the results may indicate a need to narrow and/or modify the original topic slightly. About this time the researcher may begin developing a thesis statement.

3. After these preliminary steps, the researcher will begin to consult identified sources. Consulting the library card catalog (which will probably be in electronic form), both general and trade bibliographies, periodical and newspaper indexes, catalogs at other local libraries through the Internet, and Internet sources is important.

4. Upon the location of pertinent information, the researcher begins the recording of the bibliography information on 3 × 5-inch index cards in correct style.

There are two main styles of documentation: Modern Language Association (MLA) and American Psychological Association (APA). The MLA style is the style most frequently used for work in the liberal arts and the humanities. Here is an example of a citation using MLA style for a book:

> Davis, Anita Price. *Reading Instruction Essentials*. Boston: American Publishing Company, 2005.

This following example shows MLA style for a journal article:

> Davis, Anita. "Sexism in Children's Literature: In Which Direction Are We Moving?" *Reading Matters* 5 Fall (2003): 9–11.

The social sciences commonly use the APA style of citing sources. The following are the APA-style documentation for the same book and journal article as cited above in the MLA style examples:

> Davis, Anita Price. (2005). *Reading instruction essentials*. Boston: American Publishing Company.

> Davis, Anita. (2003) "Sexism in children's literature: In which direction are we moving?" *Reading Matters*, 5 (Fall), 9–11.

Another commonly used method of documenting sources is that of the Chicago or Turabian Manual of Style. Below is the same book and journal article as cited in previous examples, but in Chicago Manual of Style format for reference lists:

> Anita Davis. 2005. *Reading Instruction Essentials*. Boston, MA: American Press.

> Anita Davis. 2003. "Sexism in Children's Literature: In Which Direction Are We Moving?" *Reading Matters* 5 (Fall): 9–11.

Many books and manuals are available to help researchers with proper documentation of resources. Online sources may help also with documentation.

After the preliminary steps (choosing a topic, beginning reading, limiting the topic, developing a thesis) and gathering data (consulting a library and online sources, especially bibliographies, card catalogs, and indexes), preparing bibliography cards, and beginning extensive reading, the researcher should make a preliminary outline and begin taking notes on 3×5-inch index cards. To avoid plagiarizing, the researcher should use quotation marks to indicate comments that are direct quotations.

Last Steps of Prewriting

The last steps involve developing the final outline and organizing the note cards in the same order as the outline. Write the rough draft; check the documentation carefully; revise; rewrite; check all parts: text, citations, bibliography; and finally, proofread (Armstrong Atlanta State University Writing Center).

An important lesson for students is to know that writing is not one thing: it varies in form, structure, and process according to its audience and purpose. A note to a cousin is not written in the same manner as a business report, which is different from writing a poem. The processes and ways of thinking that lead up to various kinds of texts can vary widely, from the quick single-draft email to a friend, to the careful drafting and redrafting of a legal contract. The different purposes and forms create various relationships between the writer and the potential reader. These relationships dictate the degrees of formality in language, assumptions about the knowledge and experience of the audience, and level of explanation needed within the writing. Writing with certain purposes in mind, the writer focuses his or her attention on what the audience is thinking or believing; other times, the writer focuses more on the information he or she is organizing, or on his or her own thoughts and feelings. Therefore, the thinking, the procedures, and the physical format in writing all differ when writers' purposes vary.

Most students will tell you that they write only to prove that they did something they were asked to do—in order to get a grade. Some schools teach a single type of writing, and students are led to believe this type will suffice in all situations. Writers, outside of school, have many different purposes beyond demonstrating accountability, and they practice a myriad of types and genres. In order to make sure students are learning how writing differs when the purpose and the audience differ, teachers must create opportunities for students to be in different kinds of writing situations.

The characteristics of good writing vary among disciplines; what counts as a successful lab report, for example, differs from what constitutes a successful history paper, essay exam, or literary interpretation. Whether writing a grocery list, preparing a paper, writing a letter, or speaking, one's first question should be, "What is my purpose,

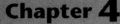

PRAXIS Pointer

Double-check the numbers on the question and on the answer sheet each time you mark your sheet. Put your answers in the right "bubbles."

my aim, my goal?" The immediate purpose may be to remember what one is going to buy, to complete an assignment, to thank someone for a gift, or to pass a course, but the long-range purpose is to communicate something specific with a particular audience.

Drafting

The next phase in the writing process is drafting. In this phase, writers begin to put their ideas on paper. They use everything they have done in the prewriting phase but should not be terribly concerned, at this point, with word choice or other details and technical aspects of the piece. They will address those concerns later. The following are some strategies that teachers can suggest students use to draft their pieces:

- Write an introduction that will capture the reader's interest and express your main idea.

- After you write your introduction, use your organized prewriting notes as a guide but depart from those notes when a good idea occurs to you.

- Write quickly. Do not worry about spelling or phrasing. You will have the opportunity to go back and fix such problems when you revise.

- Stop frequently and read what you have written. This practice will help you move logically from one thought to the next.

- Do not be afraid to return to the prewriting stage if you need more ideas or need to clarify your thinking. You can always stop and freewrite, brainstorm, or cluster to collect ideas.

- Write a conclusion that drives home the point of the composition. (Senn and Skinner 1995, 27)

Young writers need to realize that even a professional writer creates several drafts of a piece and then later revises, edits, and polishes it into a final work. Getting students to revise their writing is often difficult, and they must be taught the steps involved.

Some teachers refer to a first draft as a "sloppy copy" to legitimize the lack of concern and attention to the mechanics of writing that are needed at this phase to focus on content. It is sometimes recommended that when writing their rough drafts, students skip lines to allow room for later changes and revisions. If possible, teachers should allow students to create their rough drafts on computers. Research has shown that when students write on computers, they tend to write six times as much as they would if they wrote by hand. The reason for this is obvious: a computer eliminates the drudgery associated with writing because it can easily check for and correct misspelled words, indicate potential grammatical errors, and allow the writer to insert and delete with ease as well as to completely rearrange a work, using the cut-and-paste feature, without the need to rewrite the entire piece. If students use computers to construct their first drafts, then the later tasks of revising, editing, proofreading, and finally publishing their work will be greatly simplified.

Teachers are encouraged to conduct brief, informal conferences with students as they work on their rough drafts. In this way, they make themselves available to answer questions and provide encouragement. Comments should be as positive as possible. One technique is to use the "sandwich method" when and if it is necessary to offer constructive criticism: any comment that might be construed as negative is sandwiched between two positive remarks, so the overall impression is positive.

To learn to effectively revise their rough drafts, students should first read their work to themselves (some of them will profit from reading their writing aloud to themselves so that they can see and hear their work at the same time) and then read their drafts to one or more peers (after the class has been taught to provide useful, constructive criticism) and seek their comments and suggestions. In addition, students should look for anything in their writing that is unclear or does not communicate ideas effectively.

Revising

The third phase of the writing process is the revision of the first draft. Once again, it is important that students understand the importance of this aspect of the process, because many will consider themselves to be finished with the assigned writing as soon as they complete their rough drafts. Through repeated experiences with the entire writing process—particularly if they have opportunities to compare their rough drafts with revised, edited, and published pieces—they will begin to see how their writing emerges, changes, and improves from the beginning to the end.

At this point in the process, students should be considering adding ideas to their piece, adding details and information, rearranging elements of the piece to make it flow smoothly and logically, deleting unnecessary words, enriching the vocabulary by changing words or ideas that may not express what they want to say as clearly as they want to say it, and possibly using a revision checklist to keep track of revisions they made and to indicate additional revisions they may still want to make. A revision checklist might include the following:

Did you clearly state your main idea?

Does your composition have a strong introduction, body, and conclusion?

Did you support your main idea with enough details?

Did you present your ideas in a logical order?

Do any of your sentences stray from the main idea?

Are your ideas clearly explained?

Are your words specific?

Are any words or ideas repeated unnecessarily?

Are your sentences varied and smoothly connected?

Is the purpose of your composition clear? (Senn and Skinner 1995, 31)

In providing instruction in revision, many teachers find it helpful to put an unrevised rough draft on a transparency and show it to the class on an overhead projector or to show it using a document camera projection system if that is available. The teacher should work with students to review the piece and make appropriate revisions, comparing the original with the revision to enable students to see the improvements as they emerge.

Most of us know that the task of writing is not easy, and taking a draft through several revisions is perhaps the hardest part of writing. Students tend to see revisions as a critique of their first draft rather than a chance to better communicate to their audience about their particular subject. They think that *good* writers produce excellent first drafts without difficulty. When they have to revise, revise, revise they believe themselves to be *bad* at writing. Ideally, we want our students to see the process of writing and revising as a way of learning more about a given topic and clarifying their thinking.

Editing and Evaluation

The next stage in the writing process is editing the piece. "Editing for spelling, grammar, and punctuation is important in writing material that is easily understood by others" (Roe and Ross 2006, 322). Some teachers provide their students with an editing checklist that includes the most common errors that writers make. These would include problems associated with grammar, punctuation, usage, spelling, and capitalization. Common questions frequently included on an editing checklist include the following:

Are your sentences completely free of errors in grammar and usage?

Did you spell each word correctly?

Did you use capital letters where needed?

Did you punctuate each sentence correctly?

Did you indent paragraphs as needed and leave proper margins on each
side of the paper? (Senn and Skinner 1995, 35)

Students can construct personal editing checklists by recording examples of the kinds of errors that frequently occur in their writing along with the page in their English text that addresses that problem and gives examples of the corrected problem. The checklist then becomes a resource to be used for all future writing activities.

The teacher does not have to do all the evaluating. When students collaborate with each other by reading and correcting the work of their classmates, they begin to understand that writing is a process. As they see how their comments guided the writing of another student, they are able to see how their writings are shaped by the input from their peers and their own revisions.

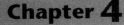

Rewriting: The Final Rewrite

In the next phase of the writing process, students proofread their work and make corrections. Teach students common proofreading symbols such as ^ (insert), ¶ (start a new paragraph), ≡ (capital letter), and so forth. Most dictionaries include lists of proofreading symbols. Once they have learned the symbols, students can use them when editing their own writing, and the teacher can use proofreading symbols to correct student papers quickly and efficiently with confidence that students will understand their meaning. Students should keep a chart containing these symbols and what each represents in their writing folder for easy access and reference.

Publishing

The last phase of the writing process is publishing. This necessitates presenting the writing in final form and sharing it with the target audience. Students need to make a final copy of their writing in which they incorporate all the revisions and corrections indicated in earlier phases. Some ways in which students' work can be published at the school level include displaying the final work on a bulletin board in the classroom or in the school library; having students read their work to their classmates; collecting student work and adding it to a class collection in folders organized according to categories of writing; creating an anthology of students' work and sharing it with other classes; and selecting a student's work to be submitted to a school-wide publication, such as the school newspaper, yearbook, or literary magazine. A teacher interested in having students' work published beyond the school level can encourage them to submit pieces to newspapers or magazines; they can share their writing with an appropriate community group; or students can enter their work in writing contests.

FEATURES OF WRITING

Organization in Writing

Creating and preserving coherence is essential to good writing. Informational writing and literary text commonly use several patterns of organization or structure: descriptive writing, ordered list, sequence, cause and effect, comparison, contrast, chronological order, and problem and solution.

To set the scene for a novel or to describe a place in a geography text, for example, a writer often uses **descriptive writing**. Typically, the writer of fiction describes the time and the characteristics of the setting. The time can be thousands of years in the future, for example, as long as the writer makes the setting believable for the reader. Descriptions should encourage readers to feel some kind of connection to the information. Descriptive writing is usually in paragraph form and differs from the ordered list or sequence.

The **ordered list** is typical in content-area textbooks. Using an ordered list, the author can present facts and information more quickly and concisely than is possible using the paragraph format. Text clues of an ordered list structure are numbers, bullets, or letters or word clues like *first* and *second*.

Sequence organization can be used in both fiction and nonfiction writing. A writer can organize a sequence to suit the purpose of the text—for instance, in alphabetical order, order of occurrence, or geographical placement, among others. A reader who quickly determines the sequence can gain understanding (comprehension) of the material more easily. A perceptive reader watches for word clues like *first*, *next*, *before*, *after*, and *last*.

Cause-and-effect writing does not necessarily have to progress from cause to effect; a writer might decide that presenting the effect and then discussing the cause is the most effective way to present the material. In a social studies text, for instance, the writer might mention the American Revolution first and discuss the causes afterward; an alternative structure, however, would be to give the causes first and then indicate the effect: the American Revolution. Teachers can guide students to watch for key words that indicate the cause-and-effect structure, including *because, resulting in, why, as a result, therefore, if . . . then, cause,* and *effect.*

Comparison writing is writing that explains the similarities between two or more things. The reader can often identify this type of writing by looking for cue words such as *alike, same as,* and *similar to.* Related to this is **contrast writing**, in which the writer contrasts things or indicates how they are different. The cue words that a reader can watch for include *different from, on the other hand,* and *opposite of.*

History books, biographies, and many narratives relate their information in the order in which they happened, or **chronological order**. Watching for words like *first, next, then,* and *last* may cue students that the arrangement is chronological, beginning at the start of the action.

Some writers structure their material according to a **problem-and-solution organization**. The writer can state the problem and then either offer several solutions or present the best answer for the reader (Steele).

Strategies for Organization, Development, and Presentation of Print, Electronic, and Visual Media

As with spoken communication, the organization, development, and presentation of media—whether print, electronic, and/or visual—is essential to understanding. Toward that end, students should first craft an outline that identifies the topics and subtopics of the presentation. The next step is deciding how to present the topics and subtopics to advantage. It may be that some of the subtopics are not important enough to warrant a separate screen in the presentation or a separate heading in print. Students can then rearrange the order of the subtopics—if necessary—until they follow the most logical sequence in the print, visual, or electronic media. The main purpose of the media is always communicating the information—not just decorating the page or the screen. A storyboard or sample layout prepared before the actual media can help the writers determine if they have met their objectives and have presented the information in a way that will be acceptable to the audience for the speaking or writing (Elements of Language). Charts and graphic organizers, some of which were discussed in chapter 2, can help a writer to organize ideas, topics, and subtopics and to communicate this information more effectively. These graphic organizers can facilitate the understanding of the audience—whether it is composed of listeners or readers.

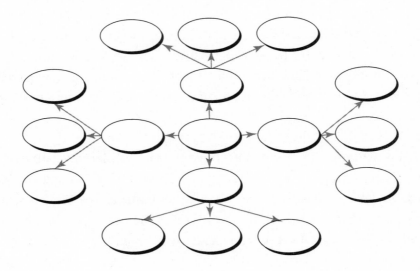

Figure 4.2 Cluster

Clustering is a nonlinear activity that generates ideas, images, and feelings around a stimulus word. As students cluster, their thoughts tumble out, enlarging their word bank for writing and often enabling them to see patterns in their ideas. Clustering may be a class or an individual activity (see Figure 4.2).

Refer to chapter 2 for more graphic organizers that may help with writing.

Discourse Aims

Discourse aims, or the purpose of one's writing or speaking, may be a choice, or the teacher or the employer may determine what needs to be written. The audience, too, helps to determine the purpose or aims of the discourse. The Praxis English Assessments, however, stress three primary aims of discourse: creative, expository, and persuasive.

Creative writing is a type of writing that Heather Abner of Jackson Community College in Jackson, Michigan, distinguishes from academic writing. She excludes academic essays from creative writing, but she does concede that creative writing has structure and form. Creative writing is writing that expresses the writer's thoughts and feelings in an imaginative, often unique, and poetic way. Creative writing is guided more by the writer's need to express feelings and ideas than by the restrictive demands of factual and logical progression of expository writing (SIL International).

Expository writing is typical of that in most textbooks. The primary purpose of the exposition is to explain and clarify ideas. While the expository essay may have narrative elements, that aspect is minor and subservient to that of explanation.

Persuasive writing is a part of nearly all writing. The purpose of most writing is to influence or to persuade the reader in some way. The next section discusses some methods of argument and types of appeals.

Methods of Argument and Types of Appeal

To persuade the audience, the writer may use a variety of methods.

Argumentative strategies. There are two main argumentative strategies to persuade an audience to accept the view of the writer. The first of these strategies dictates that the writer or speaker makes no reference to opposing views. The presenter merely imparts the information that the reading, viewing, or listening audience should know. With the counterargument strategy, the writer or speaker follows the organizational plan of the opposition and rebuts the points of the opposing view. Whichever strategy the presenter uses, it is important to (1) establish facts to support the argument, (2) clarify the writer's perspective for the audience, (3) prioritize the arguments from the least important to the most important, or vice versa, (4) formulate and state the conclusions, and (5) persuade the audience, if possible.

Analogy.   An analogy is a stylistic device that can be used as a method of argument. An analogy compares one thing to another thing. For instance, comparing the world to a stage or life to a box of chocolates would be examples of analogies.

Extended metaphor.   A metaphor is a means of defining one thing in terms of something very different. Every metaphor has two parts: (1) tenor, or the thing being defined, and (2) vehicle, or the thing doing the defining. Here are some examples of metaphors:

> *You* (tenor) *are a hungry wolf* (vehicle) *in sheep's clothing.*

> *Her words* (tenor) *were knife wounds* (vehicle) *to my heart.*

The key to understanding the significance and relevance of metaphors is to uncover the similarities between the tenor and the vehicle.

An extended metaphor is a metaphor that is developed for several lines and sometimes throughout an entire essay or poem. Consider these lines from Robert Burns:

> O, my love is like a red, red rose, that's newly sprung in June.

Allusion.   An allusion is a reference to a historical, literary, or otherwise generally familiar character or event that helps make an idea understandable—or an argument peruasive. To persuade voters, for example, politicians running for office might allude to the term of office of a previous politician. For instance, a Republican candidate who calls for a "return to the principles of the great communicator" is making an allusion to former President Ronald Reagan, as is a Democratic candidate who speaks of "trickle-down economics." In this case, though the candidates are alluding to the same person, they have opposite goals for their arguments.

Style, Tone, Voice, and Point of View

An author's **style** is the result of many factors. The interaction of language, word choice, word order, sentence type, sentence length, use of description, and story elements such as organization, plot, character, theme, and setting all contribute to an author's style.

One can often identify the styles of such diverse writers as Jane Austen, Mark Twain, William Faulkner, and Ernest Hemingway. Austen's style is—to today's reader—very formal and mannered; Twain's is very casual and colloquial. Faulkner's works often spin on without punctuation; his paragraphs sometimes run on far longer than what the reader is used to. Hemingway's dense but spare, pared-down style has earned the epithet, "Less is more."

The **tone** is the writer's attitude toward the writing itself; toward the subject; toward the people, places, time, and events in the passage(s); and/or toward the audience. The tone is often direct and easily discernible in the writing. The author's feelings might be serious or ironic, sad or happy, private or public, angry or affectionate, bitter or nostalgic, or any of the other attitudes and feelings that human beings experience. The author's style may reveal these attitudes to the reader. There are several frequently used tones in literature: condescension, didacticism, irony, humor, parody, and sentimentality. These are discussed in depth in chapter 2.

ANALYZING WRITING

In writing about literature or any specific text, you will strengthen your discussion if you offer specific passages from the text as evidence. Rather than simply dropping in quotations and expecting their significance and relevance to your argument to be self-evident, you need to provide sufficient analysis of the passage. Remember that your overriding goal of analysis writing is to demonstrate some new understanding of the text.

The Keys to Analyzing a Text

1. Read or reread the text with specific questions in mind.

2. Marshal basic ideas, events, and names. Depending on the complexity of the book, this requires additional review of the text.

3. Think through your personal reaction to the book: identification, enjoyment, significance, application.

4. Identify and consider most important ideas (importance will depend on context of class, assignment, study guide).

5. Return to the text to locate specific evidence and passages related to the major ideas.

6. Use your knowledge following the principles of analyzing a passage described in the next section: test, essay, research, presentation, discussion, enjoyment.

Principles of Analyzing a Passage

1. Offer a thesis or topic sentence indicating a basic observation or assertion about the text or passage.

2. Offer a context for the passage without offering too much summary.

3. Cite the passage (using correct format).

4. Follow the passage with some combination of the following elements:

   - Discuss what happens in the passage and why it is significant to the work as a whole.

   - Consider what is said, particularly subtleties of the imagery and the ideas expressed.

   - Assess how it is said, considering how the word choice, the ordering of ideas, sentence structure, and so forth contribute to the meaning of the passage.

   - Explain what it means, tying your analysis of the passage back to the significance of the text as a whole.

5. Repeat the process of context, quotation, and analysis with additional support for your thesis or topic sentence.

Recognizing bias, distinguishing between fact and opinion, and identifying stereotypes, inferences, and assumptions are also important in analyzing writing:

- Judging whether information is fact or opinion involves the highest level of thinking skills: the critical-creative level. A writer might say that the growing up in the South during the 1930s was difficult; that would be an opinion. Others might say that growing up in the rural South during the 1930s limited their opportunities for using public libraries; this would be a fact.

- Identifying stereotypes involves a higher level of thinking than does merely reading the passage. In fairy tales, the older woman—particularly the stepmothers—are wicked and domineering. The youngest daughter is always the most beautiful, the smartest, and the one who will triumph.

- Identifying inferences is a part of the second highest level of comprehension: the literal level. Chapter 2 gives additional information on inferences. Examples of the reader's making inferences include paraphrasing, comparing, and interpreting (inferentially and literally) various types of texts and reading materials.

- Making assumptions suggests taking something for granted. Many readers assume that whatever they read is fact—which is far from the truth. Readers must use a higher level of comprehension than reading literally for facts; checking those facts, the reputation of the author, and the work itself will prevent readers from carelessly taking the work for granted.

Creating an Effective Writing Assignment

- Tie the writing task to specific pedagogical goals.

- Note rhetorical aspects of the task, that is, audience, purpose, writing situation.

- Make all elements of the task clear.

- Include grading criteria on the assignment sheet.

- Break down the task into manageable steps.

ASSESSING STUDENT WRITING

No longer do teachers evaluate all of a student's writing as they did in the past. There are alternative assessment strategies that encourage self-assessment and peer support. Peer review, portfolios, holistic scoring, scoring rubrics, self-assessment, and conferencing are some of the strategies to assess student writing that teachers now use; some of these techniques were not commonly used in the classroom even a few years ago.

Peer Review

An assessment technique now used in many classrooms across the country and an integral part of process writing—discussed earlier in this chapter—is peer review. This technique encourages a student to have a classmate read the writing and make suggestions; the student, meanwhile, reads and reviews the classmate's work. Peer review is a part of the editing/evaluation/postwriting stage in process writing. Students may use a dictionary, thesaurus, and even the spell-check program on the classroom computers to assist in the evaluation. The teacher no longer does all the evaluating.

Portfolios

The portfolio, a collection of a student's work completed over a period of time, is another effective method for assessing student writing. The technique is beneficial to both students and teachers. Students feel a sense of ownership—and can see their own improvement—when they are allowed to select some of the materials to include. For teachers, the portfolio provides an effective way not only to monitor student progress but also to assemble authentic evidence of that progress to share with parents at conferences. Over the last several years, the portfolio has gained widespread support from educators.

Teachers and students must make several decisions before beginning the portfolio:

1. Should only evaluated materials be a part of the portfolio? (Evaluative model)

2. Should only students select items for inclusion? (Showcase model)

3. Should only representative work be a part of the collection—with no attempt at evaluation? (Descriptive model)

The North Central Regional Education Laboratory reports that teachers who use portfolios have found that it helps them evaluate students' learning styles, communicate with the students and parents about the progress, and fulfill the requirement of accountability. If the teacher implements the process well, portfolios can help maintain the focus and content of assessment.

Holistic Scoring

With holistic scoring, the reader or evaluator regards each piece of writing as a unit and assigns a single score based upon the total quality of the essay. When evaluating the work of young writers or those who may be writing a timed essay, the scorers expect some mistakes; an occasional mistake will not affect the evaluation of the paper.

The premise of holistic scoring is that the overall effect of an essay is a combination of several elements, including organization, sentence structure, mechanics, and word choice. Evaluators of the writing samples on the Medical College Admission Test (MCAT), for example, employ a six-point holistic scoring scale that assesses clarity, depth, and unity. If a paper fails to address one of the writing tasks, the evaluator may assign a score no higher than 3. Blank or illegible papers or papers that disregard the writing tasks are marked "Not scorable." Below are the usual criteria for each of the six classifications, beginning with classification 6, the highest possible score:

Score of 6: The features of a six-point essay include (1) a thorough exploration of the topic and (2) a complete answer to the questions or writing tasks. Depth of thought, complexity of thought, superior vocabulary and sentence control, and organization that is both coherent and focused are evident.

Score of 5: A five-point essay addresses all questions. The writer explores the topic substantially (but not thoroughly); there is some control of vocabulary and sentence structure and some depth of thought but not to the extent of the six-point score.

Score of 4: In a four-point essay, the writing addresses all tasks but explores the topic only moderately well. Thoughts in the essay may be clear but not necessarily complex. The organization is largely coherent with only a few digressions. The examinee has used acceptable vocabulary and sentence structure.

Score of 3: A three-point essay neglects or distorts some of the writing tasks. The examinee may show some clarity of thought; the essay is, however, simplistic. There may be some organizational problems. The language may not communicate the ideas effectively, but the writer seems to control the vocabulary and the sentence structure.

Score of 2: In a two-point essay, the writer fails to address the writing tasks seriously. Mechanical errors reoccur. The writing indicates problems with both organization and analysis.

Score of 1: The one-point essay fails to address the topic. There are obvious problems with organization and mechanics. With a score of 1, the essay is difficult for the reader to follow. (Davis 2004, 356)

Ideally, more than one evaluator should evaluate the writing when the holistic scoring method is used.

Scoring Rubrics

Since the second half of the twentieth century, the scoring rubric has been a common method of evaluating student work in kindergarten through grade 12 and even in college classrooms. A scoring rubric is a scoring scheme that the teacher, evaluators, or teacher and class develop.

Scoring rubrics are particularly helpful when one is assessing quality; rubrics can evaluate composition and writing as well as other subjects and other activities.

The rubric for evaluating compositions may vary depending upon the assignment and the goals. Evaluating the linguistic structure of writing might require a different rubric than evaluating the effectiveness of an argumentative essay. Using a predefined scheme helps to eliminate the subjectivity of the scorers and—when shared with the class— enables the students to focus on the goals of the assignment as they work. A high-quality essay probably meets most of the criteria on such a rubric (Moskal 2000).

PRAXIS Pointer

Relax. Bring your shoulders up to your ears, hold still for 10 seconds—release and relax. Do this 2 – 3 times. Then try it with other muscles in your body.

A rubric for evaluating a persuasive writing assignment in a high school class might include these specific criteria:

1. Structuring the essay and the arguments logically

2. Using at least one rhetorical device such as personal anecdote or analogy

3. Defending the position of the paper through at least one type of evidence, such as data, facts, quotations

4. Addressing some of apparent counterarguments (Schools of California Online Resource for Education)

Self-Assessment

Self-assessment helps the students to set realistic goals, monitor their own learning, and evaluate their performance. Perhaps the easiest method of self-assessment is keeping a reflective journal (Srimavin and Darasawang 2004). A reflective journal should develop throughout the semester. With the journal, the students record what they are studying, their progress, their gaps in skills and knowledge, and their reactions to what they are doing. The journal differs from a log: a log records events, but a journal records thoughts and reflections. Teachers may provide guidelines to encourage the learners to consider problems encountered in learning, the causes, and ways to remedy.

The students may prepare a double-entry journal. In a double-entry journal, the student enters direct quotes from reading material (with page number) or quotes from class discussions in the left column and enters "thinking options"—such as "This is important because," "I am confused because," "I think this means"—in the right column The journal involves students in their learning. Journals help students realize that learning is not just something that happens; the students realize that they can enhance their progress themselves.

Although group discussion and classroom observations may help in self-assessment, many students and teachers have found writing to be the best way to collect evidence to help in reflection; students also see the journals as a way to communicate with their teacher. Trainee teachers and practice teachers often employ the reflective journal for enhancing self-assessment. By reading their students' reflective journals, these future teachers may also discover how well they are communicating with their classes (Bartlett 1990).

Although guiding questions may help in the beginning stages of keeping the reflective journal, the students should gradually begin answering more detailed questions and creating their own questions as they assess their learning. Students may also complete inventories to find out more about themselves. Some inventories are helpful in determining one's learning style. These inventories and reflections help to promote independent learning (Srimavin and Darasawang 2004).

Conferencing

An important tool and response strategy for assessing student writing is conferencing. A personal conference may have more impact on the student than handing the student a written evaluation; conferences may also be a way to build rapport between the student and the teacher.

A conference may require less time for the teacher than providing written feedback. A conference may come before the student revises the paper as well as after the student completes the paper. Most students like the individual attention and the help that they receive; the advice can help prevent future misunderstandings about expectations. The teacher and student should sit at adjacent corners or side by side so that both can view the paper together. A good beginning to the conference might be to ask the student if he or she has any questions about the work or the assignment.

The teacher who has looked at the work for the first time may have some notes to read aloud. If the teacher is seeing the paper for the first time, the teacher may want to consider having the student read the paper aloud. The teacher may wish to stop the student at times to discuss a point; the student may add information also and perhaps make a note if something does not sound right. Both the teacher and the student should hold a pen or pencil to make notes during the conference.

It may be too overwhelming to the student and too time consuming if the teacher discusses every weakness in the paper. If mechanics, content, or organization seems to be a major problem, the teacher should try to focus on repeated errors—a pattern—rather than discussing each problem individually.

To keep from putting the writer on the defensive, the teacher should use *I* statements. For instance, the teacher might say, "I had a question about this sentence" and not "Your writing is unclear." Using *I* will remind the student that the purpose of writing is communicating, and the teacher might ask the student to restate an unclear sentence (Kupper-Herr; Case Western Reserve University).

REFERENCES

Armstrong Atlanta State University Writing Center. Writing research papers: A step-by-step checklist. *www.write.armstrong.edu/handouts/ResearchPaperChecklist.pdf.*

Bartlett, L. 1990. Teacher development through reflective teaching. In *Second language teacher education*, ed. J. Richards and D. Nunan. New York: Cambridge University Press, as cited at *http://independentlearning.org/ILA/ila03/ila03_srimavin_and_pornapit.pdf?q=ila03/ila03_srimavin_and_pornapit.pdf.*

Bean, John C. 2001. *Engaging Ideas: The Professor's Guide to Integrating Writing, Critical Thinking, and Active Learning in the Classroom.* San Francisco: Jossey-Bass.

Case Western Reserve University. Conferencing with students about their writing. *www.case.edu/artsci/engl/writing/pedagogy/conference.html.*

Daiker, Donald. "Learning to Praise," *Writing and Response: Theory, Practice, and Research.* Ed. Chris M. Anson. Urbana, IL: NCTE, 1989. 103–13.

Davis, Anita Price. 2004. *Reading Instruction Essentials.* 3rd ed. Boston: American Press.

Elements of Language. Creating a multimedia presentation: Plan your presentation. *http://go.hrw.com/eolang/myomed/plan.htm.*

Emig, J. 1971. The Composing Process of Twelfth Graders. National Council of Teachers of English Research Report No. 13. Urbana, National Council of Teachers of English.

Empire State College, State University of New York. Writing a research paper. *www.esc.edu/ESConline/Across_ESC/WritersComplex.nsf/wholeshortlinks2/Steps?opendocumentKupper-Herr.* Conferencing with students about their writing. *http://emedia.leeward.hawaii.edu/writing/Conferencing.htm.*

Flower, L., and J. R. Hayes, 1981. A Cognitive Process Theory of Writing. College Composition and Communication, 32, 365–87.

Kennedy, Mary L. 2004. *The Online Manual for Writing Across the Curriculum.* SUNY Cortland. *www.cortland.edu/english/wac/index.html.*

Kupper-Herr, Beth. n.d. Conferencing with Students About Their Writing. *http://mps-portal.milwaukee.k12.wi.us/portal/server.pt?open=18&objID=18827&parentname=SearchResult&parentid=1&mode=2&in_hi_userid=2&cached=true.* (Last accessed 12/2/08.)

Lindemann, Erika. 2001. *Rhetoric for Writing Teachers.* 4th ed. NY: Oxford University Press.

Matsuoka, Jan. 1998. "Revising Revision: How My Students Transformed Writers' Workshop." *The Quarterly* (20) 1.

Moskal, Barbara M. 2000. Scoring Rubrics: What, When and How? *Practical Assessment, Research & Evaluation*, 7(3). *http://PAREonline.net/getvn.asp?v=7&n=3.*

Murar, Karen, and Elaine Ware. 1998. "Teacherless Talk: Impressions from Electronic Literacy Conversations." *The Quarterly* (20) 3.

Muraski, Michel. n.d. Writing guides: Adapting to your audience. Three categories of audience. *http://writing.colostate.edu/guides/processes/audmod/pop10c.cfm.*

National Council of Teachers of English. 2004. NCTE beliefs about the teaching of writing. *www.ncte.org/about/over/positions/category/write/118876.htm.*

North Central Regional Education Laboratory. Portfolios. *www.ncrel.org/sdrs/areas/issues/students/earlycld/ea5l143.htm.*

Oglan, G. R. 2003. *Write, Right, Rite!* Boston: Allyn & Bacon.

Online Writing Lab. Writing a research paper. *http://owl.english.purdue.edu/workshops/hypertext/ResearchW/genre.html.*

Roe, B. C., and E. P. Ross. 2006. *Integrating language arts through literature & thematic units.* Boston: Allyn & Bacon.

Rotkow, Debbie. 2003. "Two or Three Things I Know for Sure About Helping Students Write the Stories of Their Lives." *The Quarterly* (25) 4.

Schools of California Online Resource for Education. Writing standard 2.4: Persuasive writing. *www.sdcoe.k12.ca.us/score/actbank/tpers.htm.*

Senn, J. A., and C. A. Skinner. 1995. *Heath English: An integrated approach to writing.* Teacher's ed. Lexington, MA: D. C. Heath & Co.

SIL International. What is creative writing? *www.sil.org/lingualinks/literacy/ReferenceMaterials/GlossaryOfLiteracyTerms/WhatIsCreativeWriting.htm.*

Srimavin, Wilaksana, and Pornapit Darasawang. 2004. Developing Self-Assessment through Journal Writing. *Proceedings of the Independent Learning Conference 2003. http://independentlearning.org/ILA/ila03/ila03_srimavin_and_pornapit.pdf?q=ila03/ila03_srimavin_and_pornapit.pdf.*

Steele, Kim. Kim's korner for teacher talk: Patterns for organization. *www.kimskorner4teachertalk.com/writing/sixtrait/organization/patterns.html.*

Walvoord, Barbara Fassler. 1986. *Helping Students Write Well.* 2nd ed. NY: The Modern Language Association.

CHAPTER

Praxis II English Language, Literature, and Composition: Content Knowledge (0041)

5

The Praxis II English Language, Literature, and Composition: Content Knowledge (0041) assesses whether an examinee has a broad base of knowledge to be licensed as a beginning teacher of English in a secondary school. This subject examination includes three main topics:

- Reading and understanding text

- Language and linguistics

- Composition and rhetoric

The test is a two-hour exam. There are 120 multiple-choice questions based on material typically covered in a bachelor's program in English and English Education. Some questions included in the exam many not count toward your score.

READING AND UNDERSTANDING TEXT

Reading and understanding text, the first topic on the Praxis II 0041 exam, constitutes 66 (55 percent) of the 120 multiple-choice questions on the exam and includes several subtopics. These subtopics include the following skills:

- Paraphrasing, comparing, and interpreting—both inferentially and literally—various types of texts and reading materials: fiction, poetry, essays, and nonfiction

- Identifying and interpreting figurative language and literary elements, which include the stylistic devices of

  1. denotation

  2. connotation

  3. tone: condescension, didacticism, irony, humor, parody, sentimentality

  4. figurative language: simile, metaphor, analogy, personification

  5. alliteration: consonance, assonance, onomatopoeia, rhythm

  6. imagery

  7. exaggeration: hyperbole, understatement

  8. allusion

  9. word play

  10. diction

  11. symbolism

  12. voice

  13. point of view

- Identifying the elements of fiction and other prose and analyzing how these elements—especially setting, plot, and conflict—may affect a work

- Identifying the patterns of action; structures; characters and characterizations; themes; and characteristics of literary genres and forms

- Identifying major works of literature and the major authors of American, British, and World literature for adults and young people; this literature should encompass a variety of time periods, genres, and cultures

- Situating and interpreting various texts within their cultural contexts and historical periods

- Recognizing and applying instructional approaches and elements of teaching reading and interpretation; these approaches should include using cueing systems, activating prior knowledge, constructing meaning through context, and applying metacognitive strategies.

LANGUAGE AND LINGUISTICS

Language and linguistics, the second topic on the Praxis II 0041 exam, constitutes 18 (15 percent) of the 120 multiple-choice questions. The four subtopics require understanding:

- the principles of first- and second-language acquisition and development,

- the elements of history, development, and the structure of the English language,

- and applying the conventions of grammar, mechanics and usage,

- and the elements of semantics.

COMPOSITION AND RHETORIC

About 36 (30 percent) of the 120 questions on the Praxis II 0041 exam focuses on composition and rhetoric. Teachers of English language, literature, and composition must be able to understand and use or apply certain elements of teaching, including the following:

- understanding the elements of teaching writing, including individual and collaborative approaches to teaching writing; tools and response strategies for assessing student writing; and common research and documentation techniques.

- Understanding and evaluating rhetorical features in writing, including the purposes for writing and the nature of audience; organization in writing; strategies for organization, development, and presentation of print, electronic, and visual media; discourse aims; methods of argument and types of appeals; rhetorical strategy; and the ability to recognize bias and fallacies, distinguish between fact and opinion, and identify stereotypes, inferences, and assumptions.

Praxis English Assessment:
Content Knowledge (0041)

Practice Test 1

This test is also on CD-ROM in our special interactive TestWare® for the PRAXIS II English Assessment: Content Knowledge (0041). It is highly recommended that you first take this exam on computer. You will then have the additional study features and benefits of enforced timed conditions and instantaneous, accurate scoring. See page 6 for instructions on how to get the most out of REA's TestWare®.

ANSWER SHEET FOR PRACTICE TEST 1 (0041)

1. (A) (B) (C) (D)
2. (A) (B) (C) (D)
3. (A) (B) (C) (D)
4. (A) (B) (C) (D)
5. (A) (B) (C) (D)
6. (A) (B) (C) (D)
7. (A) (B) (C) (D)
8. (A) (B) (C) (D)
9. (A) (B) (C) (D)
10. (A) (B) (C) (D)
11. (A) (B) (C) (D)
12. (A) (B) (C) (D)
13. (A) (B) (C) (D)
14. (A) (B) (C) (D)
15. (A) (B) (C) (D)
16. (A) (B) (C) (D)
17. (A) (B) (C) (D)
18. (A) (B) (C) (D)
19. (A) (B) (C) (D)
20. (A) (B) (C) (D)
21. (A) (B) (C) (D)
22. (A) (B) (C) (D)
23. (A) (B) (C) (D)
24. (A) (B) (C) (D)
25. (A) (B) (C) (D)
26. (A) (B) (C) (D)
27. (A) (B) (C) (D)
28. (A) (B) (C) (D)
29. (A) (B) (C) (D)
30. (A) (B) (C) (D)

31. (A) (B) (C) (D)
32. (A) (B) (C) (D)
33. (A) (B) (C) (D)
34. (A) (B) (C) (D)
35. (A) (B) (C) (D)
36. (A) (B) (C) (D)
37. (A) (B) (C) (D)
38. (A) (B) (C) (D)
39. (A) (B) (C) (D)
40. (A) (B) (C) (D)
41. (A) (B) (C) (D)
42. (A) (B) (C) (D)
43. (A) (B) (C) (D)
44. (A) (B) (C) (D)
45. (A) (B) (C) (D)
46. (A) (B) (C) (D)
47. (A) (B) (C) (D)
48. (A) (B) (C) (D)
49. (A) (B) (C) (D)
50. (A) (B) (C) (D)
51. (A) (B) (C) (D)
52. (A) (B) (C) (D)
53. (A) (B) (C) (D)
54. (A) (B) (C) (D)
55. (A) (B) (C) (D)
56. (A) (B) (C) (D)
57. (A) (B) (C) (D)
58. (A) (B) (C) (D)
59. (A) (B) (C) (D)
60. (A) (B) (C) (D)

61. (A) (B) (C) (D)
62. (A) (B) (C) (D)
63. (A) (B) (C) (D)
64. (A) (B) (C) (D)
65. (A) (B) (C) (D)
66. (A) (B) (C) (D)
67. (A) (B) (C) (D)
68. (A) (B) (C) (D)
69. (A) (B) (C) (D)
70. (A) (B) (C) (D)
71. (A) (B) (C) (D)
72. (A) (B) (C) (D)
73. (A) (B) (C) (D)
74. (A) (B) (C) (D)
75. (A) (B) (C) (D)
76. (A) (B) (C) (D)
77. (A) (B) (C) (D)
78. (A) (B) (C) (D)
79. (A) (B) (C) (D)
80. (A) (B) (C) (D)
81. (A) (B) (C) (D)
82. (A) (B) (C) (D)
83. (A) (B) (C) (D)
84. (A) (B) (C) (D)
85. (A) (B) (C) (D)
86. (A) (B) (C) (D)
87. (A) (B) (C) (D)
88. (A) (B) (C) (D)
89. (A) (B) (C) (D)
90. (A) (B) (C) (D)

91. (A) (B) (C) (D)
92. (A) (B) (C) (D)
93. (A) (B) (C) (D)
94. (A) (B) (C) (D)
95. (A) (B) (C) (D)
96. (A) (B) (C) (D)
97. (A) (B) (C) (D)
98. (A) (B) (C) (D)
99. (A) (B) (C) (D)
100. (A) (B) (C) (D)
101. (A) (B) (C) (D)
102. (A) (B) (C) (D)
103. (A) (B) (C) (D)
104. (A) (B) (C) (D)
105. (A) (B) (C) (D)
106. (A) (B) (C) (D)
107. (A) (B) (C) (D)
108. (A) (B) (C) (D)
109. (A) (B) (C) (D)
110. (A) (B) (C) (D)
111. (A) (B) (C) (D)
112. (A) (B) (C) (D)
113. (A) (B) (C) (D)
114. (A) (B) (C) (D)
115. (A) (B) (C) (D)
116. (A) (B) (C) (D)
117. (A) (B) (C) (D)
118. (A) (B) (C) (D)
119. (A) (B) (C) (D)
120. (A) (B) (C) (D)

English Language, Literature, and Composition: Content Knowledge
PRACTICE TEST 1 (0041)

**TIME: 120 minutes
120 questions**

In this section, you will find examples of test questions similar to those you are likely to encounter on the Praxis II English Language, Literature, and Composition: Content Knowledge Exam.

1. Goals for an individual student's writing should be
    (A) developed by the teacher based on data from standardized test scores.
    (B) developed by the teacher based on a student's academic record.
    (C) the same for all students.
    (D) developed by the student and teacher together, taking into account the student's ability, academic history, and motivation.

2. Reading through literature is a prevalent instructional strategy today. It is most important that instructors who seek to teach reading through literature choose texts that

    (A) are at the appropriate Lexile range for their students.
    (B) are in the classic cannon.
    (C) reflect the students' backgrounds.
    (D) can be read independently by all the students without teacher support.

3. Teachers use assessment to evaluate student learning and inform both their whole-class and individualized instruction. Which of the following methods of assessment would be the most effective way for a teacher to document students' progress in writing over time in an authentic setting and to keep records of their efforts, progress, and achievements in one or more areas?

    (A) Standardized tests
    (B) Teacher-made tests
    (C) Observation
    (D) Portfolios

4. Which of the following would be the most effective way to evaluate specific learning objectives for student writing?

    (A) Self-evaluation
    (B) Peer evaluation
    (C) Rubrics
    (D) Standardized tests

5. Identify the independent main clause in this famous first line from Thomas Jefferson's *The Declaration of Independence*?

    When in the course of human events, it becomes necessary for one people to dissolve the political bands which have connected them with another, and to assume among the powers of the earth the separate and equal station to which the Laws of Nature and of Nature's God entitle them, a decent respect to the opinions of mankind requires that they should declare the causes which impel them to the separation.

(A) "When in the course of human events"

(B) "it becomes necessary for one people to dissolve the political bands which have connected them with another"

(C) "and to assume among the powers of the earth the separate and equal station to which the Laws of Nature and of Nature's God entitle them"

(D) "a decent respect to the opinions of mankind requires that they should declare the causes which impel them to the separation."

Read the following essay, and then answer question 6.

Creating an English garden on a mountainside in the Ouachita Mountains in central Arkansas may sound like an impossible endeavor, but after two years, this dream is becoming reality. By digging up the rocks and replacing them with bags of topsoil, humus, and peat, the persistent gardener has created an environment that will grow more than just weeds. Gravel paths meander through the beds of Shasta daisies, marigolds, lavender, valerian, iris, day lilies, Mexican heather, and other flowers. Ornamental grasses, dogwood trees, and shrubs create a backdrop for the flowers. Along the periodic waterway created by an underground spring, swamp hibiscus, selenium, hosta, and umbrella plants display their colorful and seasonal blooms. The flower beds are outlined by large rocks dug up by a pickax, but blistered hands are worth the effort when people stop by to view the mountainside beauty.

6. The purpose of this essay is

(A) narrative.
(B) analytical.
(C) argumentative.
(D) descriptive.

7. According to research by Jean Piaget, Noam Chomsky, and others, language acquisition is an innate, developmental process that is also nurtured by the child's environment. For the teacher, this research implies that

(A) there is little she can do in the classroom to address language deficits in at-risk populations.

(B) children with language deficits most often come from deprived backgrounds.

(C) observing children and their language in authentic settings is not as helpful as standardized testing.

(D) early intervention would be the most effective way to address language deficits in children.

8. Current research tells teachers that strong critical readers share the following knowledge and skills.

I. A strong vocabulary as well as vocabulary in context skills

II. Knowledge of the specific names of grammatical terms and constructions

III. An understanding of syntax and the structure of language

IV. An understanding of the structure of a text

(A) I, II, and III
(B) II, III, and IV
(C) I, III, and IV
(D) I, II, III, and IV

9. Knowing that *Cinderella* is one of the world's most famous fairy tales, Ms. Smith decided to stage three different versions of the story with her students. She located Chinese, Native American, and Russian versions of the story and found age-appropriate plays of each that could be staged in her classroom. In addition to acting in these plays, her students created scenery, costumes, and props to use in their performances. Which of the following were

probably Ms. Smith's learning objectives for this activity?

I.   Understanding cultural similarities and differences through dramatic literature
II. Gaining speaking skills and experiencing theatrical practices
III. Understanding the prevalence of universal themes in literature
IV. Gaining experience with adapting stories into plays

(A) I only
(B) I and II
(C) I, II, and III
(D) I, II, III, and IV

10. What is the subject of this famous sentence from the first chapter of Nathaniel Hawthorne's *The Scarlet Letter*?

> The founders of a new colony, whatever Utopia of human virtue and happiness they might originally project, have invariably recognized it among their earliest practical necessities to allot a portion of the virgin soil as a cemetery, and another portion as the site of a prison.

(A) founders
(B) colony
(C) Utopia
(D) they

11. Identify the error in the following sentence.

> Since there will be no place to purchase food, everyone in the class should bring their own lunch on the field trip tomorrow.

(A) pronoun/antecedent agreement
(B) subject/verb agreement
(C) misplaced modifier
(D) comma error

12. Mr. O'Brien's ninth grade class will be reading the novel *Great Expectations* over the next few weeks—a challenging book for most students. He tells his students that they will be keeping a reflective journal on their reading. Every time they are given a reading assignment, they are to record the details of their reading in their journal as well as any questions they may have about the situations and characters. In addition, they are asked to include their reactions to the book as well as any connections they may make to their own lives or the world around them. The primary purpose of this assignment is to provide

(A) a way to help students improve their composition and rhetorical skills.
(B) a way to monitor reading comprehension and help students apply active reading strategies by making connections to the text.
(C) a way to hold students accountable for their reading.
(D) a way to learn more about individual students personal lives and concerns.

Questions 13 to 15 refer to the following scenario.

> It is the first day of class. Ms. Johnson, the composition teacher, tells the students a little about herself. She tells them that she wants to know about each individual student in the class. She asks them to write about themselves and hand in their papers as they leave to go to lunch.

13. Ms. Johnson's primary objective with this activity is to

(A) establish clear guidelines for her writing expectations.
(B) prepare her class to write argumentative essays.

(C) get an early picture of her students' writing skills and at the same time help her to become familiar with her individual students.

(D) follow one of the rules for good classroom management by using all the time in a particular class period.

Read the line below, which is from Edgar Allan Poe, and answer questions 14 and 15.

During the whole of a dull, dark, and soundless day in the autumn of the year, when the clouds hung oppressively low in the heavens, I had been passing alone, on horseback through a singularly dreary tract of country; and at length found myself, as the shades of the evening drew on, within view of the melancholy House of Usher.

14. This famous first line from Edgar Allan Poe's *The Fall of the House of Usher* is an example of

(A) first-person point of view.
(B) third-person omniscient point of view.
(C) third-person limited point of view.
(D) objective point of view.

15. What is the simple subject and verb of the line by Poe?

(A) clouds hung
(B) I had been passing, found
(C) shades drew
(D) length found

16. Classic writers from an earlier time period such as Dickens and Shakespeare are often challenging for students to understand and appreciate. Teachers can support students' understanding of these difficult texts through all of the following instructional strategies EXCEPT

(A) providing context by teaching students about the author's life and times as well as the setting of the text.

(B) showing the film version of the text before the students begin reading.

(C) defining archaic words and idioms for students before they begin their reading.

(D) providing students with graphic organizers for keeping characters and plot lines straight.

17. I went to the woods because I wished to live deliberately, to front only the essential facts of life, and see if I could not learn what it had to teach, and not, when I came to die, discover that I had not lived.

This famous line from Henry David Thoreau's *Walden* is an example of which kind of sentence?

(A) compound
(B) complex
(C) simple
(D) interrogative

18. Consider the following statement:

Another bored teacher found me to pick on as I hid out in the bathroom during language class.

This writing most clearly illustrates

(A) tone.
(B) style.
(C) plot.
(D) analogy.

19. The semantic cueing system refers to the

(A) meaning system of language.
(B) structural system of language.
(C) letter-sound relationships in written language.
(D) social and cultural aspects of language.

20. When reading, the syntactical cueing system refers to

(A) meaning system of language.
(B) structural system of language.

(C) letter–sound relationships in written language.

(D) social and cultural aspects of language.

21. When reading, the phonological cueing system refers to

(A) meaning system of language.

(B) structural system of language.

(C) letter–sound relationships in written language.

(D) social and cultural aspects of language.

22. When reading, the pragmatic cueing system refers to

(A) meaning system of language.

(B) structural system of language.

(C) letter–sound relationships in written language.

(D) social and cultural aspects of language.

23. Identify the error in this sentence.

In the course of his long and productive life, Benjamin Franklin was an inventor, a diplomat, a writer, a philanthropist, founded the University of Pennsylvania, and the first American millionaire.

(A) subject/verb agreement

(B) pronoun/antecedent agreement

(C) parallel construction

(D) punctuating items in a series

24. Identify the error in this sentence.

Arriving at the scene of the accident, the victims of the crash were treated by the paramedics.

(A) dangling participle

(B) subject/verb agreement

(C) verb tense

(D) sentence fragment

25. Consider the following sentence:

Taking computer programming was my Waterloo.

The use of the word "Waterloo" is an example of

(A) connotation.

(B) dialect.

(C) denotation.

(D) foreshadowing.

26. Consider the opening line of Edgar Allan Poe's poem "The Raven."

Once upon a midnight dreary, while I pondered weak and weary.

This is an example of

(A) internal rhyme.

(B) iambic pentameter.

(C) onomatopoeia.

(D) figurative language.

27. Consider the following:

Pretty is
As pretty does.

This is an example of

(A) doubletalk.

(B) hyperbole.

(C) an epigram.

(D) personification.

28. The class has been reading some passages from *The Manchurian Candidate* (1959) by Richard Condon. As a concluding activity, the students are asked to write a research papers discussing the factors that influenced U.S. involvement in the Korean War? The students must include at least two primary sources in their papers. Which of the following would be considered appropriate choices?

I. The personal correspondence of a military man stationed with the Fifth Regimental Combat Team (RCT) in Korea.

II. A biography of Harry S. Truman by David McCullough, published in 1993

III. A journal article about the beginning of the Korean War by a noted scholar

IV. A transcript of an interview with Secretary of Defense George Marshall

(A) I and II
(B) II and IV
(C) II and III
(D) I and IV

29. Consider this statement made by a student:

"The author attended Harvard. I know, therefore, that he was born with a silver spoon in his mouth."

This statement is an example of

(A) an inference.
(B) an understatement.
(C) jargon.
(D) metaphor.

30. Consider the first line of Mark Twain's novel, *The Adventures of Huckleberry Finn*.

You don't know about me, without you have read a book by the name of *The Adventures of Tom Sawyer*, but that ain't no matter.

This line is an example of

(A) hyperbole.
(B) dialect.
(C) jargon.
(D) ambiguity.

31. Which of the following writing assignments or tasks requires synthesizing?

(A) Write a brief scene for a one act play about a student's first day of high school.

(B) Give three reasons why Columbus, in his search for the New World, ended his journey in the Caribbean Islands.

(C) Define what it means to be a true friend using at least three of the characters we have studied in the literature we read this semester.

(D) Describe your favorite place using at least five examples of imagery.

Use the Act II Chorus from Shakespeare's *Romeo and Juliet* to answer questions 32 through 36.

Now old desire doth in his deathbed lie,
And young affection gapes to be his heir;
That fair for which love groaned for and would die,
With tender Juliet matched, is now not fair.
Now Romeo is beloved and loves again,   5
Alike bewitched by the charm of looks;
But to his foe supposed he must complain,
And she steal love's sweet bait from fearful hooks.
Being held a foe, he may not have access
To breathe such vows as lovers use to swear,   10
And she as much in love, her means much less
To meet her new beloved anywhere;
But passion lends them power, time means, to meet,
Temp'ring extremities with extreme sweet.

32. Line 1 is an example of:

I. a pun.
II. personification.
III. alliteration.
IV. dramatic irony.

(A) I only
(B) I and II
(C) II and III
(D) IV only

33. Line 8 is an example of:

(A) simile.
(B) metaphor.
(C) a pun.
(D) allusion.

34. An example of a couplet would be lines:

    (A) 1 and 3.
    (B) 1 and 2.
    (C) 10 and 11.
    (D) 13 and 14.

35. The entire Chorus is an example of:

    I.   iambic pentameter.
    II. a sonnet.
    III. a soliloquy.
    IV. free verse.

    (A) I only
    (B) I and II
    (C) I, II, and III
    (D) I, II, III, and IV

36. Which of the following student activities would be appropriate instructional strategies to support the students' comprehension of this text?

    I.   Student oral reading and performance
    II. Viewing live or film performance
    III. Writing out lines in modern English
    IV. Finding and discussing figures of speech

    (A) I and II
    (B) I and III
    (C) II, III, and IV
    (D) I, II, III, and IV

37. What rhetorical strategies characterize the following lines from Thomas Paine's pamphlet, *The Crisis, No. 1*?

    I call not upon a few, but upon all; not on this state or that state, but on every state: Up and help us; lay your shoulders to the wheel; better have too much force than too little, when so great an object is at stake. Let it be told to the future world that in the depth of winter, when nothing but hope and virtue could survive, that the city and the country, alarmed at one common danger, came forth to meet and to repulse it.

    I.   parallel syntax
    II. sentences utilizing the imperative
    III. a call to action
    IV. citations from well-known political scholars

    (A) I only
    (B) I and II
    (C) I, II, and III
    (D) I, II, III, and IV

38. These are the times that try men's souls. The summer soldier and the sunshine patriot will, in this crisis, shrink from the service of their country; but he that stands it now deserves the love and thanks of man and woman.

    These are the famous opening lines of Thomas Paine's influential pamphlet "The Crisis No. 1." This text is important because it

    (A) emotionally aroused thousands of colonists to the abuses of British rule, to the oppressiveness of the monarchy, and to the advantages of colonial independence.
    (B) asserted the need for the colonists to proceed slowly and explore non-military options before resort to war.
    (C) called for a strong central government to rule the newly independent American states and foresaw the difficulties inherent within the Articles of Confederation.
    (D) asserted to its British readers that they could not beat the American colonists militarily unless they could isolate New England from the rest of the American colonies.

39. Which of the following is characteristic of romantic literature?

    (A) "Every change of season, every change of weather, indeed, every hour of the day, produces some change in the magical hues and shapes of these mountains, and they are regarded by all the good wives, far and near, as perfect barometers."

(B) "Thus his curses light on his own head, and it was an astonishment to all his fellows, for they noted it to be the just hand of God upon him."

(C) "We hold these truths to be self-evident: That all men are created equal; that they are endowed by their Creator with inherent and inalienable rights; that among these are life, liberty, and the pursuit of happiness; that to secure these rights, governments are instituted among men, deriving their just powers from the consent of the governed; that whenever any form of government becomes destructive of these ends, it is the right of the people to alter or to abolish it, and to institute new government, laying its foundation on such principles, and organizing its powers in its foundation on such principles, and organizing its powers in such form, as to them shall seem most likely to effect their safety and happiness."

(D) "Mr. Oakhurst's calm handsome face betrayed small concern in these indications. Whether he was conscious of any predisposing cause was another question. 'I reckon they're after somebody,' he reflected; 'likely it's me.'"

40. Mark Twain is associated with which of the following literary movements?

(A) American Romanticism
(B) American Realism
(C) Naturalism
(D) Rationalism

41. *The Scarlet Letter* by Nathaniel Hawthorne is an example of which of the following literary movements?

(A) American Romanticism
(B) American Realism
(C) Transcendentalism
(D) Puritanism

42. Which of the following authors did not write in the American realistic period?

(A) Mary Wilkins Freeman
(B) F. Scott Fitzgerald
(C) Stephen Crane
(D) Ambrose Bierce

43. Which of the following poets are not associated with the Harlem Renaissance?

(A) Langston Hughes
(B) Claude McKay
(C) Robert Frost
(D) Countee Cullen

44. Harlem Renaissance poetry is known for its

(A) rhythms based on spirituals and jazz.
(B) traditional rhyme schemes.
(C) focus on nature.
(D) exploration of the sonnet form.

45. Mark Twain's *The Adventures of Huckleberry Finn* is controversial today because of

(A) Twain's depiction of African Americans and use of racial slurs.
(B) its negative depiction of religion.
(C) its graphic violence.
(D) its humorous depiction of alcoholism.

Read the following stanza from Samuel Taylor Coleridge's poem "The Rime of the Ancient Mariner" and then answer questions 46 through 48.

Water, water, everywhere
And all the boards did shrink;
Water, water, everywhere
Nor any drop to drink.

46. When Coleridge uses repeated references to "Water," he is really

(A) talking about the fact that he is very thirsty.

(B) referring to the fact that while water covers two-thirds of the earth, not all that water is suitable for human consumption.

(C) using water as a symbolic representation.

(D) looking for words that rhyme.

47. What might an icon such as "oceans of water" represent?

(A) A massive, damp, cold, and dreary element

(B) A gigantic, rough, inhospitable, alien environment

(C) A beautiful recreational, global, environment

(D) An abundant, life-giving element

48. What does Coleridge suggest by juxtaposing images of abundant water supplies with the Mariner's inability to consume that water?

(A) That nourishing and/or life-giving elements surround us, but we are not always able or willing to access them

(B) That the ocean is a big, violent, yet indifferent adversary

(C) That the ocean can either be used by people for fun, nourishment, and recreation or destroyed by pollution, over-fishing, and global warming

(D) Coleridge is metaphorically connecting the human body with the ocean.

49. Romantic poets indicate that isolation and alienation are important components of their poetry. How does alienation impact romantic ideology?

(A) Romantic poets feel isolated and alone.

(B) Romantic poets feel that to commune with nature, one needs to be alone with nature.

(C) Romantic poets feel like aliens in their own country.

(D) Romantic poets feel frustration with foreigners trying to take over their homeland.

50. The repetition of similarly constructed phrases, clauses, or sentences, one after another is called

(A) free verse.

(B) imagery.

(C) parallel structure.

(D) onomatopoeia.

51. Which statement would most accurately identify with Naturalism movement authors such as Stephen Crane?

(A) Colors play the most important role in a story's construction.

(B) Human pain and suffering provide an effective base for a story's composition.

(C) Life is a series of unpredictable and usually depressing events.

(D) Environment is significant in determining human fate.

52. Hamlin Garlin and Bret Harte used realism to create texts. One can define realism best as

(A) the literary technique of realistically representing the nature of life and the social world, as they would appear to the common reader.

(B) an attempt to subject passive representation to the impressions of natural, monolithic, and flagrant social designs and structures.

(C) the representation of the human condition based on loose and freeflowing designs, patterns, and shapes.

(D) the belief that human beings exist entirely in the order of nature and do not have a soul nor any participation in a religious or spiritual world beyond nature.

53. Another, more popular name for regional writing is

(A) national consciousness.
(B) patriotism.
(C) social conservatism.
(D) local color.

54. What are the characteristics of an epic?

(A) A story in prose form that includes both events and characters; it depicts what its characters say and do
(B) Poems that use an ordinary speaking voice and that employ a relaxed, almost satirical treatment of their subject matter
(C) A long narrative poem on a serious subject told in a formal and/or elevated style and centering on a heroic figure
(D) A long, usually depressing poem about heroes and mythical figures, and their relationship to the everyday world

Read the following excerpt from Franz Kafka's *A Hunger Artist* and then answer questions 55 and 56.

During these last decades the interest in professional fasting has markedly diminished. It used to pay very well to stage such great performances under one's own management, but today that is quite impossible. We live in a different world now. At one time the whole town took a lively interest in the hunger artist; from day to day of his fast the excitement mounted; everybody wanted to see him at least once a day; there were people who bought season tickets for the last few days and sat from morning till night in front of his small barred cage; even in the nighttime there were visiting hours, when the whole effect was heightened with torch flames; on fine days the cage was set out in the open air, and then it was the children's special treat to see the hunger artist; for their elders he was often just a joke that happened to be in fashion, but the children stood open-mouthed, holding each other's hands for greater security, marveling at him as he sat there pallid in black tights, with his ribs sticking out so prominently, not even on a seat but down among the straw on the ground, sometimes giving a courteous nod, answering questions with a constrained smile, or perhaps stretching an arm through the bars so that one might feel how thin it was, and then again withdrawing deep into himself, paying no attention to anyone or anything, not even to the all-important striking of the clock that was the only piece of furniture in his cage, but merely staring into vacancy with half-shut eyes, now and then taking a sip from a tiny glass of water to moisten his lips.

55. In this paragraph, Kafka is using hunger as a metaphor for

(A) oil, watercolor, and acrylic paints.
(B) organized religion and spirituality.
(C) nothing; he's talking about food.
(D) social courtesy and social propriety.

56. What do "grown-ups" often think of the hunger artist?

(A) That he is merely a joke.
(B) That he is quality entertainment.
(C) That he is a sensitive artist.
(D) That he is lonely and confused.

57. Who is credited with the introduction of the poetic style known as heroic couplet?

(A) Homer
(B) William Shakespeare

(C) Sophocles

(D) Geoffrey Chaucer

58. A sonnet, whether Italian or English, is

(A) a lyric poem consisting of a single stanza of 14 lines of iambic pentameter linked by an intricate rhyme scheme.

(B) a lyric poem consisting of two stanzas of 12 lines of trochaic meter linked by an intricate rhyme scheme.

(C) an epic poem consisting of 14 lines of iambic pentameter linked by a free-flowing rhyme scheme.

(D) a romantic poem consisting of a single stanza of 15 lines of iambic pentameter linked by an intricate rhyme scheme that ends in an heroic couplet.

59. A soliloquy is

(A) an extended medieval poem that follows a standardized ABAB rhyme scheme whereby an actor reflects on the existence of God.

(B) a monologue in which an actor speaks his or her thoughts and feelings aloud.

(C) a monologue in which an actor confesses his or her innermost feelings to the person whom he or she loves.

(D) an extended dialogue between two principal actors, usually consisting of witty conversation and word play.

60. Who is the writer of *The Iliad* and *The Odyssey*?

(A) Sophocles

(B) Euclid

(C) Homer

(D) Ulysses

61. The art of transmitting culture, beliefs, heritage, and mythologies in the form of either prose or verse and by word of mouth is

(A) a lyrical ballad.

(B) the romantic tradition.

(C) cultural renaissance.

(D) the oral tradition.

62. John Donne is considered by many to be the archetype of the

(A) Cavalier poets.

(B) graveyard school of poets.

(C) Pre-Raphaelite poets.

(D) metaphysical poets.

63. The rhetorical technique of appealing to a reader's sense of emotions is also known as

(A) logos.

(B) pathos.

(C) ethos.

(D) topos.

64. In the construction of an effective persuasive argument, you must include

(A) a detailed explanation of your personal feelings and emotions as they pertain to the subject matter.

(B) a detailed analysis of the social, literary, and historical contexts upon which the argument is based.

(C) a full recognition and clear analysis of the counterargument showing its strengths and weaknesses.

(D) an oversimplification of the opposing argument, which thereby demonstrates the absurdity of the opposition's point of view.

65. Which of the following examples is not considered a logical fallacy?

(A) Paraphrasing

(B) Non sequitur

(C) Post hoc

(D) Stereotypes

66. A short narrative of an interesting, amusing, or biographical incident that serves to elucidate a point or idea is also known as

(A) a protagonist.
(B) onomatopoeia.
(C) an anecdote.
(D) fiction.

Read the following paragraph from Frederick Douglass's essay "An Appeal to Congress for Impartial Suffrage" and then answer questions 67 and 68.

A very limited statement of the argument for impartial suffrage, and for including the negro in the body politic, would require more space than can be reasonably asked here. It is supported by reasons as broad as the nature of man, and as numerous as the wants of society. Man is the only government-making animal in the world. His right to a participation in the production and operation of government is an inference from his nature, as direct and self-evident as is his right to acquire property or education. It is no less a crime against the manhood of a man, to declare that he shall not share in the making and directing of the government under which he lives, than to say that he shall not acquire property and education. The fundamental and unanswerable argument in favor of the enfranchisement of the negro is found in the undisputed fact of his manhood. He is a man, and by every fact and argument by which any man can sustain his right to vote, the negro can sustain his right equally. It is plain that, if the right belongs to any, it belongs to all. The doctrine that some men have no rights that others are bound to respect, is a doctrine which we must banish as we have banished slavery, from which it emanated. If black men have no rights in the eyes of white men, of course the whites can have none in the eyes of the blacks. The result is a war of races, and the annihilation of all proper human relations.

67. What is the most accurate paraphrase of Douglass's thesis?

(A) The most effective way to communicate with branches of government is through "limited statements of argument."
(B) Since "man is the only government-making animal in the world," then it "is no less a crime that he shall acquire property or education."
(C) "If black men have no rights," then only a "war of [the] races" will solve the problems of inequality.
(D) "If the right [of equality] belongs to any, it belongs to all."

68. With Douglass's work in mind, what does enfranchisement mean?

(A) To allow the political privileges of operation and ownership or the license granted to an individual or group to market a company's goods or services in a particular territory
(B) To grant the political privileges of citizenship, especially the right to vote
(C) To grant the right of membership into a professional organization, that is, having such rights of membership
(D) To allow the political freedom and privileges of sincere and honest personal expression

69. What American author is famous for such works as *Life on the Mississippi* and *The Innocents Abroad: Or, the New Pilgrims' Progress*?

    (A) Nathaniel Hawthorne
    (B) Stephen Crane
    (C) Edgar Allan Poe
    (D) Mark Twain

70. A syllogism consists of a

    (A) minor premise, a deduction, and a conclusion.
    (B) major premise, a minor premise, and an induction.
    (C) major induction, a minor premise, and a conclusion.
    (D) major premise, a minor premise, and a conclusion.

71. A rhetorical argument using deductive reasoning builds from

    (A) accepted truths to specific conclusions.
    (B) specific conclusions to a larger premise.
    (C) one minor premise to another.
    (D) one specific conclusion to another.

72. At the end of Shakespeare's *Romeo and Juliet*, Romeo kills himself in Capulet's tomb because he thinks his love, Juliet, is dead. The audience knows, however, that Juliet is alive and waiting for him to come for her. This plot twist is an example of

    (A) verbal irony.
    (B) situational irony.
    (C) dramatic irony.
    (D) epic irony.

73. All of these writers are well known for their essays except

    (A) E.B. White.
    (B) Henry David Thoreau.
    (C) Joan Didion.
    (D) Ernest Hemingway.

74. A metaphor is an example of

    (A) literal interpretation.
    (B) figurative language.
    (C) logical fallacies.
    (D) somnambulism.

75. T. S. Eliot's "The Waste Land" is a poetic example of

    (A) modernism.
    (B) lyricism.
    (C) a ballad.
    (D) an epic.

76. John Bunyan's *The Pilgrim's Progress* and George Orwell's *Animal Farm* are both examples of

    (A) realistic fiction.
    (B) allegorical fiction.
    (C) science fiction.
    (D) young adult literature.

77. Character who are presented in contrast to each other such as Jay Gatsby and Tom Buchanan in F. Scott Fitzgerald's novel *The Great Gatsby* are called

    (A) foils.
    (B) stereotypes.
    (C) dynamic characters.
    (D) static characers.

Read the following poem by Phillis Wheatley, "On Being Brought from Africa to America." Then answer questions 78 and 79.

TWAS mercy brought me from my Pagan land,
Taught my benighted soul to understand
That there's a God, that there's a Saviour too:
Once I redemption neither sought nor knew,
Some view our sable race with scornful eye,
"Their colour is a diabolic die."
Remember, Christians, Negroes, black as Cain,
May be refin'd, and join th' angelic train.

78. What is the overall tone of the poem?

(A) Angry and resentful
(B) Frustrated and contemptuous
(C) Faithful and ironic
(D) Grateful and devoted

79. The poem is written in

(A) couplets.
(B) enjambments.
(C) meters.
(D) stanzas.

80. All of the following writers are British Romantics except for

(A) Lord Byron.
(B) William Wordsworth.
(C) Mary Shelley.
(D) Virginia Woolf.

81. Some scholars contend that Miguel de Cervantes originally intended *Don Quixote* to be "little more than a parody of the popular romantic/chivalric novels of his time." What is a parody?

(A) A literary work holding up human vices and follies scorn, in order to expose or discredit those same social vices and follies

(B) A short fictitious story that illustrates a moral attitude or religious precept

(C) A series or exchange of clever or amusing verbal retorts

(D) A literary or artistic work in which the writer's style imitates that of a serious author or a serious piece of writing to produce comedic effect or ridicule

82. Consider this introductory paragraph in Henry David Thoreau's essay "Civil Disobedience."

I heartily accept the motto,— "That the government is best which governs least"; and I should like to see it acted up to more rapidly and systematically. Carried out, it finally amounts to this, which also I believe,—"That government is best which governs not at all"; and when men are prepared for it, that will be the kind of government which they will have. Government is at best but an expedient; but most governments are usually, and all governments are sometimes, inexpedient. The objections which have been brought against a standing army, and they are many and weighty, and deserve to prevail, may also at last be brought against a standing government. The standing army is only an arm of the standing government. The government itself, which is only the mode which the people have chosen to execute their will, is equally liable to be used and perverted before the people can act through it. Witness the present Mexican war, the work of comparatively a few individuals using the standing government as their tool; for, in the outset, the people would not have consented to this measure.

What is Thoreau's mode of exposition here?

(A) narration

(B) description

(C) argumentation

(D) division and classification

83. An epistolary novel is an extended

(A) narrative poem. Extended narratives came into being during the late Middle Ages.

(B) fictional narrative, written in the form of letters, diaries, and journal entries.

(C) fictional narrative in which an heroic figure embarks on a quest or other perilous journey.

(D) fictional narrative, usually dealing with fantasy and the supernatural.

84. A prominent convention in metaphysical poetry is the paradox. A paradox is a

(A) statement or idea that on the surface seems to be self-contradicting or absurd, yet turns out to make sense or reflect a truth.

(B) romantic representation of rural life and labors, usually involving images of peace and simplicity in country life.

(C) speechless performance in which actors use only posture, gesture, bodily movements, and exaggerated facial expressions.

(D) work of fiction containing supernatural events and situations that are not scientifically explainable.

85. Many modern poets, such as Emily Dickinson, W. B. Yeats, William Blake, and Dylan Thomas, deliberately supplement a perfect rhyme scheme with an imperfect or slant rhyme scheme. What is an imperfect, or slant, rhyme?

(A) A rhyme scheme that is deliberately unfinished, or made to appear incomplete, usually for a dramatic or suspenseful effect

(B) A rhyme scheme in which corresponding vowel sounds are only approximate, and sometimes the rhymed consonants are similar rather than identical

(C) A rhyme scheme that represents a spontaneous overflowing of human emotions and thus seems hastily written or biased in its content

(D) A rhyme scheme that intentionally sacrifices the lyrical rhyme scheme in order to emphasize the importance of its social or political content

Read the following excerpt from Robert Frost's "The Figure a Poem Makes" and then answer questions 86 and 87.

No tears in the writer, no tears in the reader. No surprise for the writer, no surprise for the reader. For me the initial delight is in the surprise of remembering something I didn't know I knew. I am in a place, in a situation, as if I had materialized from cloud or risen out of the ground. There is a glad recognition of the long lost and the rest follows. Step by step the wonder of unexpected supply keeps growing. The impressions most useful to my purpose seem always those I was unaware of and so made no note of at the time when taken, and the conclusion is come to that like giants we are always hurling experience ahead of us to pave the future with against the day when we may want to strike a line of purpose across it for somewhere. The line will have the more charm for not being mechanically straight. We enjoy the straight crookedness of a good walking stick. Modern instruments of precision are being used to make things crooked as if by eye and hand in the old days.

86. When Frost writes, "No tears in the writer, no tears in the reader," he is actually suggesting that

   (A) a poem that is sad or depressing in content will have a lasting or meaningful impression on readers.
   (B) a poem about human suffering or social corruption can affect or influence modern-day readers to read more poetry.
   (C) regardless of subject matter, a poem must be sincere and meaningful to the author before it will be sincere or meaningful to the reader.
   (D) he is frustrated because modern precision instruments are being used to make things appear crooked, thus seemingly replicating handmade items.

87. When Frost writes, "For me the initial delight is in the surprise of remembering something I didn't know I knew," he is actually saying

   (A) that even a poem about the most simple or humble subject matter will move or surprise the reader, if it is written with enthusiasm.
   (B) the poet consciously or unconsciously writes poems based on the influential poetry he or she has read in his or her earlier years.
   (C) the act of writing poetry is an enlightening and cathartic experience for the poet and thus will be enlightening to the reader.
   (D) that he is getting older and it is getting more difficult for him to remember his past. Thus, poetry helps him remember things.

88. A literary symbol is

   (A) a word or phrase that signifies an object or event which in turn signifies something else, or offers a range of interpretations beyond itself.

   (B) a round, concave, brass plate that produces a loud sound when struck with a stick or other stiff object.
   (C) a word or phrase that refers or represents other genres of literary styles of writing.
   (D) anything that motivates a character or moves a story or poem forward, rather than simply allowing the writing to remain stagnant.

89. Alliteration is

   (A) another name for a literary style or structure that uses bright colors to represent ideas or feelings.
   (B) a word (or series of words) like "buzz" that resembles the sound it denotes.
   (C) a word, verse, or sentence that reads the same backward or forward.
   (D) the repetition of usually initial consonant sounds in two or more neighboring words or syllables.

90. Cavalier poets such as Richard Lovelace, Thomas Carew, and Robert Herrick called themselves "Sons of Ben." Who is the "Ben" they refer to?

   (A) Ben Franklin
   (B) Uncle Ben
   (C) Ben Jonson
   (D) Ben Cartwright

91. The Latin phrase "carpe diem" is a familiar paradigm generally associated with the Cavalier poets. What is the translation for carpe diem?

   (A) Seize the love.
   (B) Seize the woman.
   (C) Seize the youth.
   (D) Seize the day.

92. Narrative points of view are influential in the interpretation of both poetry and prose. Which of the following examples is an example of a third-person omniscient narrator?

(A) When I walked into the room, I was overcome with a strange feeling of familiarity. Although I'd never been there before, I felt as if I had.

(B) You know the feeling you get when you walk into a room for the first time, and yet you feel as if you'd been there before.

(C) He walked into the room for the first time, and yet he was overcome with a feeling of peculiar familiarity.

(D) I walked into the room and was overcome with a strange feeling of familiarity. I wondered if I'd been there before.

93. Which of the following best characterizes ambiguous writing?

(A) Using a vague or ambivalent word or expression when a precise word or phrase is necessary

(B) Using a literary text or reference without explicit identification of the text or reference

(C) Using a word or phrase that states specifically what the author is trying to say

(D) Using a literary text or reference that stipulates the continuity of the jargon in a juxtaposing intertextuality

94. Not I, believe me. You have dancing shoes
With nimble soles; I have a soul of lead
So stakes me to the ground I cannot move.

These lines from Shakespeare's *Romeo and Juliet* contain an example of a(n)

(A) pun.
(B) quatrain.
(C) simile.
(D) epithet.

95. What is the definition of grammar?

(A) The branch of language study or linguistic study that deals with the means of showing the relationship between words in use

(B) The branch of language study or linguistic study that deals with the specific origins of word roots and their evolution to current and proper usage

(C) The study that deals with the science of the plant and animal world

(D) The branch of language study or linguistic study that deals with dictionary entries

96. According to the branch of linguistics known as morphology, what is a suffix?

(A) A mark that designates the end of a sentence

(B) A form of affix that follows the morpheme to which it attaches

(C) A form of language that denotes word origins

(D) A style of writing used to report information

97. Syntax is

(A) a division of linguistics that studies synonyms.

(B) a monetary charge applied to recreational goods, services, and activities.

(C) a physiological inability to form coherent sentences.

(D) the order and arrangement of words or symbols forming a logical sentence.

98. Which of the following sentences contains a double-plural noun?

(A) We ain't got nowhere to go.
(B) I have two rabbits.
(C) I don't know whether to choose the green or blue one.
(D) Should we go to Detroit or St. Louis?

99. Irregular verbs

(A) show a vowel alteration when changing to past tense, as in "take/took."

(B) show the difference between a noun and a verb, as in swim/swimming.

(C) show the difficulty in linguistic studies.

(D) work well in any sentence.

100. According to the study of phonetics, what is a fricative?

(A) Two vowels produced consecutively in the same syllable

(B) A word that can be used as either a noun or a verb

(C) A consonant sound made by passing a continuous stream of air through a narrow passage in the vocal tract, creating sounds like "f" and "v"

(D) A stop in the air flow when one is saying a sound

101. Semantically speaking, homonymy refers to

(A) words having identical expression (sound) or pronunciation but different meanings, as in "book a flight" and "read a book."

(B) words in a sentence that begin with a repeating consonant sound, as in "Peter Piper picked a peck of pickled peppers."

(C) words that sound different but have the same meanings, as in "sea" and "ocean."

(D) using a more pleasant or pleasing word to represent something that may be offensive.

102. Paraphrasing is an essential component in the construction of an essay. What is paraphrasing?

(A) Reiterating the argumentative phrasing at least twice in strategic locations within the essay

(B) Restating a text or thesis in your own words thereby making the idea or topic clearer to understand

(C) Using two parallel structures within a sentence

(D) Replacing the author's name with your own and taking credit for the work that he or she has produced

103. Bede's "Caedmon's Hymn" is one of the first known works of Anglo-Saxon poetry written in the vernacular. What does the phrase "written in the vernacular" mean?

(A) Written in the everyday language of the people

(B) Written in Latin

(C) Written in Old English

(D) Written in ink rather than with graphite or carbon

104. "Nothing more and nothing less than the truthful treatment of material" best describes

(A) literary impressionism.

(B) literary regionalism.

(C) literary colonialism.

(D) literary realism.

105. Literary naturalism is

(A) a literary attempt to record accurately and objectively visual reality in terms of transient effects of light and color, thereby representing the various shapes and colors found in nature.

(B) giving the effect that the writing represents the nature of life and the social world as it seems to the common reader.

(C) the belief that human beings exist entirely in the order of nature and do not have a soul or any participation in a religious or spiritual world beyond nature.

(D) the representation of the human condition based on loose and free-flowing designs, patterns, and shapes, like those found in nature.

106. Which of the following was NOT a result of the growth of regional literature?

    (A) The increased popularity of magazines.
    (B) A greater number of female readers.
    (C) A desire to preserve distinct modes of life before industrialization homogenized them.
    (D) A higher literacy rate.

107. Which of the following is the title of the autobiography of Booker T. Washington?

    (A) "The Souls of Black Folk"
    (B) "Uncle Tom's Cabin"
    (C) "Yes, I Can"
    (D) "Up from Slavery"

108. Which of the following sentences uses the colon correctly?

    (A) A dedicated artist requires: brushes, paint, canvas, and an eye for beauty.
    (B) A dedicated artist requires four things: brushes, paint, canvas, and an eye for beauty.
    (C) A dedicated artist requires materials such as: paint brushes, canvas, and an eye for beauty.
    (D) A dedicated artist requires materials: consisting of paint, brushes, canvas, and an eye for beauty.

109. When a verbal phrase does not refer to a specific noun or noun phrase it follows or precedes, it is a

    (A) misplaced modifier.
    (B) past participle.
    (C) predicate.
    (D) independent clause.

110. When two independent clauses are not joined correctly, the sentence is a

    (A) fragmented sentence.
    (B) topic sentence.
    (C) run-on sentence.
    (D) complex sentence.

111. Writing programs may vary from situation to situation, but the most effective writing programs for teaching multicultural students share a main characteristic. The characteristic is that the writing program

    (A) connects students' lives to their classroom writing experience.
    (B) is conducted by a teacher who engages the students in story starters, language games, and worksheets developed for the purpose of creative writing.
    (C) presents the teacher as an authority figure that diverse students can learn from and model.
    (D) has a teacher who is confident, experienced, and willing to present the writing techniques to them systematically.

112. Medieval morality plays, *Everyman* being the most famous, are

    (A) dramatized allegories of proper or acceptable domestic behaviors, presented in the plot form of a day in the life of a feudal family.
    (B) dramatized allegories of proper etiquette for commoners who end up in the presence of social superiors and/or royalty.
    (C) dramatized allegories of Christian life, presented in the plot form of a quest for salvation.
    (D) dramatized allegories satirizing improper social behaviors presented in the form of an early commedia dell'arte.

113. The great error in Rip's composition was an insuperable aversion to all kinds of profitable labor.

    This line from Washington Irving's *Rip Van Winkle* characterizing the title character is an example of

(A) figurative language

(B) cliché

(C) circumlocution

(D) dialect

114. What is the narrative report approach?

(A) Students describe how they feel they are doing.

(B) A formal report card written by the teacher

(C) Teachers provide parents with a written assessment of a student's progress.

(D) Parents and teachers discuss a student's attitude about learning.

115. A very successful high school and college essay typically needs a clear, coherent thesis. What is a working thesis?

(A) A single, solidified idea, stated as an assertion, which responds to a question-at-issue

(B) A general idea that guides your paper, but an idea that may be refined during the course of your writing

(C) A "road map" that guides the reader to the topic and content of the essay

(D) An idea that fits the topic or works well in addressing the assigned question-at-issue

Read the following passage, and then answer questions 116 through 120.

SATIRE is a sort of glass wherein beholders do generally discover everybody's face but their own; which is the chief reason for that kind reception it meets with in the world, and that so very few are offended with it. But, if it should happen otherwise, the danger is not great; and I have learned from long experience never to apprehend mischief from those understandings I have been able to provoke: for anger and fury, though they add strength to the sinews of the body, yet are found to relax those of the mind, and to render all its efforts feeble and impotent.

There are but three ways for a man to revenge himself of the censure of the world: to despise it, to return the like, or to endeavor to live so as to avoid it. The first of these is usually pretended, the last is almost impossible; the universal practice is for the second.

A nice man is a man of nasty ideas.

—Jonathan Swift

116. Which of the following answers best defines satire?

(A) Satire is a form of ridicule towards social inequities, human vice, and folly as a vehicle to promote social awareness and ultimately positive social change.

(B) Satire subtly alters the identity of living individuals, but despite these alterations the reader is still expected to recognize the actual person.

(C) Satire is a form of imitation that pays homage to an actual individual (living or dead) or an actual historical event.

(D) Satire is a form of scathing intellectual humor that was developed in the Middle Ages and is still in use today.

117. What does Swift mean when he says, "SATIRE is a sort of glass wherein beholders do generally discover everybody's face but their own"?

(A) That satire is a vessel that is capable of "holding" or containing social anger and fury.

(B) That satire is fragile like glass; the satirist must "handle" the satire delicately and used it sensitively.

(C) That satire exposes human nature, and human nature is such that people "generally" see the flaws in others but not in themselves.

(D) That satire is a form of literary "mischief," which ultimately renders or reduces the mind to nothing but feeble and impotent thoughts.

118. What does Swift mean when he declares, "A nice man is a man of nasty ideas"?

(A) Swift suggests that people are basically perverse in their nature and in their thinking; as a result, they spend an inordinate amount of time dwelling on perverted and obscene ideas.

(B) Swift suggests that a nice man is an honest man with honest thoughts; society, which does not like to hear honest thoughts or ideas, will thus label him nasty.

(C) Swift suggests that society will externally condemn vulgar ideas but internally support and condone such ideas and behaviors.

(D) Swift suggests that there is actually no such thing as a nice or decent person, because on the inside, all people are inherently vulgar and debased.

119. In the phrase "the censure of the world," censure means

(A) to edit for appropriate moral content.

(B) a device that responds to external stimulus.

(C) a moral thought pattern or process.

(D) to blame or judge in a sternly condemning manner.

120. According to Swift, why is satire "received so kindly" by the world?

(A) Because everyone needs a good laugh, satire is essentially a form of humor that everyone enjoys.

(B) Because satire pokes fun at prominent social figures past and present, and these same social big shots need to be brought down a peg or two.

(C) Because most people are too ignorant or self-absorbed to understand that the satire is making fun of them.

(D) Because satire is fresh and contemporary, the humor doesn't get old or boring like other forms of humor can.

Praxis English Assessment: Content Knowledge (0041)

Answer Explanations for Practice Test 1

ANSWER KEY FOR PRACTICE TEST 1 (0041)

1. (D)	25. (A)	49. (B)	73. (D)	97. (D)
2. (A)	26. (A)	50. (C)	74. (B)	98. (B)
3. (D)	27. (C)	51. (D)	75. (A)	99. (A)
4. (C)	28. (D)	52. (A)	76. (B)	100. (C)
5. (D)	29. (A)	53. (D)	77. (A)	101. (A)
6. (D)	30. (B)	54. (C)	78. (D)	102. (B)
7. (D)	31. (C)	55. (B)	79. (A)	103. (A)
8. (C)	32. (C)	56. (A)	80. (D)	104. (D)
9. (C)	33. (B)	57. (D)	81. (D)	105. (C)
10. (A)	34. (D)	58. (A)	82. (C)	106. (D)
11. (A)	35. (C)	59. (B)	83. (B)	107. (D)
12. (B)	36. (D)	60. (C)	84. (A)	108. (B)
13. (C)	37. (C)	61. (D)	85. (B)	109. (A)
14. (A)	38. (A)	62. (D)	86. (C)	110. (C)
15. (B)	39. (A)	63. (B)	87. (C)	111. (A)
16. (B)	40. (B)	64. (C)	88. (A)	112. (C)
17. (B)	41. (A)	65. (A)	89. (D)	113. (C)
18. (A)	42. (B)	66. (C)	90. (C)	114. (C)
19. (A)	43. (C)	67. (D)	91. (D)	115. (B)
20. (B)	44. (A)	68. (B)	92. (C)	116. (A)
21. (C)	45. (A)	69. (D)	93. (A)	117. (C)
22. (D)	46. (C)	70. (D)	94. (A)	118. (B)
23. (C)	47. (D)	71. (A)	95. (A)	119. (D)
24. (A)	48. (A)	72. (C)	96. (B)	120. (C)

PRACTICE TEST 1 (0041): PROGRESS CHART

Reading and Understanding ____/71

2	9	10	16	17	19	20	21	22	26	27	32	34

35	36	38	39	41	42	43	44	45	46	47	48	49

51	52	53	54	55	56	57	58	59	60	61	65	67

68	72	76	74	76	77	78	79	80	82	83	84	86

87	88	89	90	91	100	101	103	104	105	106	111	115

116	117	118	119	120	106

Language and Linguistics ____/25

5	7	8	11	14	15	23	24	25	30	33	50	66

81	92	93	94	95	96	97	98	99	107	108	109

Composition and Rhetoric ____/24

1	3	4	6	12	13	18	28	29	31	37	40	62

63	64	69	70	71	75	102	110	112	113	114

PRACTICE TEST 1 (0041): ANSWER EXPLANATIONS

1. (D)

Individual goals for a student should be a cooperative effort of teacher and student. This will help ensure that the student can meet the goals. Goals should not be based solely on standardized test scores (A) or based solely on a student's academic record (B). Goals should not be the same for all students (C) because students learn at different levels and aim for different goals.

2. (A)

Lexile range indicates the student's current reading level. For reading instruction to be effective, it is important that reading materials not be too far above or below a student's reading level. Not all literature needs to be in the classic cannon (B). Students can enjoy and learn from literature on a variety of topics beyond their specific experience (C). Teachers must expect to provide support and instruction for students when they teach reading through literature (D).

3. (D)

While all these methods of assessment are useful, the key phrase is "authentic setting." A portfolio is a purposeful collection of work that exhibits efforts, progress, and achievement of students and enables teachers to document teaching in an authentic setting. Standardized tests (A) are commercially developed and are used for specific events; one test would not track changes throughout the semester. A teacher-made test (B) is used to evaluate specific objectives of the course; it might be one element in the portfolio, but it is not the best choice. Observation is used only to explain what students do in classrooms and to indicate some of their capabilities; therefore, (C) is incorrect.

4. (C)

This question relates to evaluating specific learning objectives. A rubric enables the teacher and the student to observe certain things as they write and assess the composition. Choice (C) is the best answer. Although peer evaluation (B) might be helpful on occasion, the teacher would not want to turn the entire evaluation process over to the students in the classroom. Because it may be expensive and difficult to obtain a standardized test to meet the specific content of a composition class at one point in time, (D) would not be the method of choice. Although useful, self-evaluation (A) alone would not be the best way of documenting achievement of specific objectives.

5. (D)

Choices A, B, and C are part of the long introductory subordinate clause. The main independent clause is not found until the end of the sentence, the simple subject being "respect" and the simple predicate being "should declare."

6. (D)

The purpose of this essay is descriptive (D). It describes an English garden created in the Ouachita Mountains in Arkansas. A narrative (A) tells a story and has a discernible plot and characters. An analytical essay (B) shows how something works or is what it is (e.g., a story, a disease, an engine) by breaking it down into its component parts. The purpose of the argumentative essay (C) is always clear: to present a point and provide evidence, which may be factual or anecdotal, and to support the argument. The structure is usually very formal, as in a debate, with counterpositions and counterarguments.

7. (D)

Language acquisition according to Noam Chomsky and Jean Piaget is an innate, developmental process; however, nurture may affect the process. Therefore, early intervention is an effective approach to mitigating language deficits caused by innate or environmental factors.

8. (C)

I, III, and IV are all characteristics of strong readers. While an understanding of syntax and the structure of language are essential critical reading skills, knowledge of specific grammatical terms (II) are not shown to be important.

9. (C)

In using three different versions of this well known story, Ms. Smith is creating an opportunity to bring a multicultural perspective to the drama activity (choice I). In versions of *Cinderella* from around the world, the story of the mistreated but kindhearted protagonist is basically the same, but the characters, settings, and ways in which the plot unfolds are culturally centered. Furthermore, because Ms. Smith is using scripted versions of the story and staging these plays with costumes, scenery, and props, she is making theatrical elements integral to the performances (choice II). Choice III is correct because students will see through this activity the universality of certain themes in literature across time and cultures. Choice IV is incorrect because the students are not the ones who have adapted the stories; and therefore, they are not having firsthand experience with that process. The correct answer is (C), which includes I, II, and III.

10. (A)

This sentence is tricky because the subject, "founders" is separated from the verb "have recognized" by the subordinate clause, "whatever Utopia of human virtue and happiness they might originally project."

11. (A)

The pronoun "everyone" is singular; therefore the plural possessive pronoun "their" does not agree with its antecedent, "everyone." Correct the error by replacing "their" with "his or her."

12. (B)

Students improve their reading skills when they actively engage with the text. The teacher can also check for comprehension of content and the success or failure of class objectives. Journals are usually one-draft writing, and teachers do not usually grade them on their quality of writing; therefore, (A) is incorrect. Choice (C) is irrelevant: no mention is made of giving daily grades on the journal writing. Choice (D) is not an appropriate choice because the objective is student engagement in the text in order to learn, not to disclose their lives to the teacher.

13. (C)

The teacher is encouraging her students to write about a topic with which they are most familiar and at the same time helping her to become familiar with her class. She is also getting an initial impression of their writing strengths and weaknesses. Choices (A), (B), and (D) are irrelevant. The assignment does not establish any "clear guidelines" (A), and choice (B) refers to argumentative essays, a type of essay that the preceding assignment does not address. Choice (D) is not a valid reason for the assignment; a teacher should not give the class an assignment for "busy work," or just to fill the time.

14. (A)

The pronoun "I" tells us right away that Poe is writing in the first-person point of view. The other three would utilize third-person pronouns ("he," "she," or "they").

15. (B)

The long introductory participial phrase and subordinate clause may distract you from the correct answer, (B). The subject, "I," has two verbs, "had been passing" and "found."

16. (B)

Although the students may be fans of this approach, showing the film version before they read the work will not help them develop the skills necessary to read these challenging texts. Teachers should provide context (A) for the students as well as help with archaic language (C). Graphic organizers help students keep track of characters and complicated plot lines (D).

17. (B)

Because this sentence has both an independent and a subordinate clause, it is complex. Compound sentences have two separate independent clauses. Simple sentences have just one independent clause with no subordinate clauses. Interrogative sentences ask a question.

18. (A)

This writing clearly identifies tone. The style of the writer is not clearly apparent through this one sentence, so (B) is not the correct answer. For the same reason, the reader should not select (C). There is no comparison readily apparent; (D) is not the best choice.

19. (A)

Semantic cueing involves using the meaning of the text and the context to figure out an unknown word. The genre of the selection, the illustrations, the reader's knowledge of the topic of the selection, and the context of the written words can provide semantic cues as the reader tries to unlock an unknown word.

The word "semantics" does not directly relate to the sentence structure (B); the phoneme–grapheme, or sound–letter, association (C); or the social and cultural aspects of the writing (D).

20. (B)

Syntactic cueing involves using the reader's grammatical knowledge of spoken and written language to figure out the significance of an unknown word in a text. Semantic cueing involves using the meaning of the text and the context (A)—not the structure of the language—to figure out an unknown word. The phoneme–grapheme, or sound–letter, association (C) is not the same as syntactical cueing. Syntactic cueing does not refer to the social and cultural aspects of the writing (D).

21. (C)

Phonological cueing involves using the knowledge of matching written symbols with their sounds, or grapheme–phoneme relation. This cueing strategy has limitations; for instance, it can be used effectively only for words in which the letter patterns are known by the reader. The reader must also know how to analyze an unknown word. Phonological cueing does not refer to the meaning system (A), or semantics; the structural system (B), or syntax; or the social and cultural aspects of the language (D), or pragmatic cueing.

22. (D)

The pragmatic (practical) cueing system involves the understanding that people use language differently in different contexts. Pragmatic cueing does not refer directly to the meaning system of language (A), or semantics; the structural system of language (B), or syntax; or the letter–sound relationships in written language (C), or phonology.

23. (C)

The items in a series cataloguing Benjamin Franklin's accomplishments are all nouns except for "founded the University of Pennsylvania." To maintain the parallel structure, the item should be "the founder of the University of Pennsylvania."

24. (A)

The victims are not "arriving at the scene of the accident"; the paramedics are. The participial phrase should be kept close to the noun it is modifying.

25. (A)

The word "Waterloo" is a reference to the Battle of Waterloo, which was Napoleon Bonaparte's last battle (June 18, 1815). The writer is referring to the course as being a defeat, just as the battle was Napoleon's defeat. The use of the word requires one to draw on history to gather the meaning; the word is a reference to something else. Choice (A) is, therefore, the best answer. The use of "Waterloo" is not an example of dialect—or a variety of a language; (B) is, therefore, not the best answer. Denotation (C) is the act of saying exactly what one means. "Waterloo" is not an example of speaking precisely; one would have to know the connotation of the word to understand what the writer is saying. The literary device of foreshadowing (D) is a hint of what is to come; that stylistic device is not evident in the sentence.

26. (A)

"Dreary" and "weary" are examples of internal rhyme, in other words, rhyme within a given line of poetry. Iambic pentameter, onomatopoeia, and figurative language are not characteristics of this line.

27. (C)

An epigram is a short, concise poem that deals with a single thought or event and ends with a "twist" or an ingenious turn of thought. *Pretty is/As pretty does* is just such a poem. Doubletalk (A) is meant to deceive, in that it uses big words and nonsensical polysyllables that sound as though they ought to be words, and fuddling syntax to baffle the brains of listeners or readers. A NASA comment illustrates:

"The normal process during the countdown is that the countdown proceeds, assuming we are in a go posture, and at various points during the countdown we tag up on the operational loops and face to face in the firing room to ascertain the facts that project elements that are monitoring the data and that are understanding the situation as we proceed are still in the go condition." (Quoted in Lutz 1989, 223) A hyperbole (B) is an exaggeration, as in this example, "I spent a million hours on my report." Personification (D) is the attribution of human characteristics to inanimate objects, plants, or animals. (D) is not the best answer.

28. (D)

Both the personal correspondence of a military man stationed with the Fifth Regimental Combat Team in Korea (choice I) and an interview with Secretary of Defense George Marshall (choice IV) are primary sources. They involve correspondence or testimony from individuals who were actually involved in the Korean War. The best answer is, therefore, (D). A biography (choice II) published in 1993 would most likely include secondary sources and is itself a secondary source. Answers (A), (B), and (C), all of which include choice II, are, therefore, incorrect. A journal article (choice III) would most likely be a secondary source; any answer that includes choice III, in other words (C), would not be the best choice.

29. (A)

The student—rightly or wrongly—has made an inference: the student has drawn a conclusion about the author based on the fact that the author attended Harvard. Choice (B), an understatement, is not correct because the student has not attempted to represent the author's accomplishments as less impressive than they are. Jargon (C) is confused, unintelligible language; often it involves the terminology of a profession. Choice (C) does not apply here. A metaphor (D) is a figure of speech in which one thing is likened to some wholly different thing; "That lecherous man is a wolf" is an example of a metaphor.

30. (B)

Dialect is language characteristic of a particular region or group of people. Twain's *The Adventures of Huckleberry Finn* is an example of southern dialect.

31. (C)

Putting together or arranging elements to make a whole pattern or product is synthesis. Choices (A) and (D) are creative pieces. Choice (B) is an example of a task requiring analysis (breaking into parts), not synthesis.

32. (C)

Personification entails giving human characteristics to nonhuman things. Alliteration is the repetition of initial consonant sounds. Both of these poetic elements are characteristics of line one.

33. (B)

A metaphor is an abstract comparison between two things: "And she steal love's sweet bait from fearful hooks" is an example of a metaphor. A simile would use the words "like" or "as" to make the comparison.

34. (D)

A couplet is two consecutive rhyming lines. Lines 13 and 14 are an example of a couplet.

35. (C)

The choruses in *Romeo and Juliet* are all examples of Shakespearean sonnets, fourteen lined poems with three stanzas of ABAB rhyme ending in a final rhyming couplet. This poem is in iambic pentameter, five iambs (unstressed, stressed syllables) per line, and it's spoken by one person; thus, it is a soliloquy. Free verse is poetry without set rhyme and meter, which is not a characteristic of this poem.

36. (D)

All of these choices are appropriate instructional strategies to support students' comprehension of this text. As a play, choices I and II are particularly strong approaches to this text, helping students to hear and experience the language in active and engaging ways. Choices three and four will help students grasp both the literal and figurative aspects of the selection.

37. (C)

Choices I, II, and III apply. The first sentence is an example of parallel syntax. Sentences in the imperative make a command utilizing "you" as the understood subject, i.e., "Up and help us." These sentences are a call to action. There are no citations to well-known scholars.

38. (A)

Thomas Paine wrote several pamphlets before and during the American Revolution. "Common Sense" was the most significant because it carefully documented abuses of the British parliamentary system of government, particularly in its treatment of the American colonies. Paine portrayed a brutish monarchy interested only in itself and pointedly argued how independence would improve the colonies' long-term situation. His argument was directed at the common man, and it struck a chord unlike anything previously written in the colonies. Its publication in 1776 was perfect in reaching the public at just the moment that their questions and concerns regarding British rule were peaking. The answers provided in Paine's essays were pivotal in the subsequent behavior of many colonists who, until that time, had been unsure of what they believed regarding independence and British rule.

39. (A)

Choice (A) is a Washington Irving quotation from his story *Rip Van Winkle*. Clearly romantic, it celebrates the natural world and incorporates elements of the supernatural as well. Choice (B) is from Thomas Jefferson's *The Declaration of Independence*, a document from the Revolutionary period which asserts individual freedoms and human rights. Choice (C) was written by William Bradford in his *History of Plymouth Plantation*. A Puritan writer, Bradford believed in predestination. Choice (D) from Bret Harte's *The Outcasts of Poker Flat* incorporates the dialect characteristic of the Realistic period in American Literature.

40. (B)

Twain wrote in the Realistic period, after the American Civil War. This period succeeded American Romanticism, which occurred from about 1820-1860. Naturalism is a school of Realism that emphasized Darwinism, psychology, and environmental factors in human behavior. Writers such as Stephen Crane and Ambrose Bierce were naturalists, but Twain doesn't really fit into that group.

41. (A)

Though *The Scarlet Letter* is a novel set in Puritan times, Nathaniel Hawthorne was a Romantic writer. He published his masterpiece in 1850, right in the middle of the American Romantic period. The novel incorporates many romantic themes including interest in the natural world, emphasis on the emotional and intuitive over the cerebral, and elements of the supernatural.

42. (B)

F. Scott Fitzgerald, author of *The Great Gatsby*, is a modern writer, active in the 1920's and 1930's. The Realistic period characterizes the end of the nineteenth century when Freeman, Crane, and Bierce were writing.

43. (C)

The Harlem Renaissance is associated with African American writers in the 1920's and 30's. Though Frost was active at this time, he was not part of the Harlem Renaissance.

44. (A)

Harlem Renaissance poetry is characterized by its roots in African American spirituals and jazz.

It is associated with the American urban experience rather, not with a focus on nature (C). Choices (B) and (D) are highly structured forms, and not characteristics of the Harlem Renaissance.

45. (A)

This book is one of the most controversial in the canon. While choices (B), (C), and (D) are all true, the novel is controversial because of its depiction of the African American character, Jim, as well as its use of racial slurs. Others see these characteristics as both realistic and satiric, thus an indictment of racism.

46. (C)

Usually, when authors and poets use a word repeatedly, as Coleridge does with "water," they are emphasizing the abstract or symbolic aspect of the language. Coleridge uses water as a symbolic representation. Coleridge was certainly not referring to his body's thirst for water (A). In Coleridge's time, the amount of water on the earth and the amount suitable for consumption was not common knowledge; it is doubtful that he had (B) as a meaning. Coleridge was doing more than looking for rhyming words (D) when he composed "The Rime of the Ancient Mariner."

47. (D)

Water is traditionally thought of as an abundant life-giving element (D). Symbolically, water has come to represent a source of food and safety (e.g., the Bible tells how the baby Moses, placed in a basket by his mother and hidden among the river reeds, was carried to safety by the water). Water is also an infrastructure in the transportation of goods and people, a means of sanitation and personal hygiene, and a source of recreational activities. All of these elements combine to suggest an abundant life-giving element. Coleridge does not depict water primarily as a cold, dreary element (A); an inhospitable, alien environment (B); or a recreational element (C).

48. (A)

Coleridge places the Mariner in a vast surrounding of water not fit for human consumption; Coleridge is emphasizing the aspect that while physical, spiritual, and emotional nourishment surround us, people for various reasons are not always capable or willing to assess it. Thus, the correct answer is (A).

Coleridge is not depicting the ocean as always being a big, violent, yet indifferent adversary (B), nor is he advocating careful management of environment (C), an issue not contemporary to his nineteenth-century life. There is no evidence that Coleridge is metaphorically connecting the human body with the ocean (D).

49. (B)

Romantic poets seem to consider experiencing nature as a cathartic experience; ideally, there should be a one-on-one relationship with no other distractions. Because romantic poets do not necessarily feel isolated and alone, (A) is not the best choice. There is no indication that all the romantic poets feel like aliens in their own country (C). All romantic poets do not necessarily feel frustration with foreigners trying to take over their homeland (D).

50. (C)

Parallel structure is the repetition of similarly constructed phrases, clauses, or sentences. Free verse is a type of poetry that transcends traditional rhythm and rhyme schemes. Imagery is language that appeals to the senses. "Onomatopoeia" refers to words that sound like what they mean.

51. (D)

Crane, like many American authors, grapples with the idea of nature versus nurture. Because he saw the importance of both, (D) is the best answer. Although imagery and colors are a part of Crane's writing, colors (A) is not the best choice. Human pain and suffering are necessarily a part of some of Crane's work, but the two do not provide the only base for his work, so (B) is not the best choice. Crane does not routinely present life as a series of unpredictable and usually depressing events; (C) is not an acceptable choice.

52. (A)

One might correctly consider realism as a literary attempt at photography; realism is a realistic representation as opposed to a romantic one. Realism is not an attempt to subject passive representation to the impressions of natural, monolithic, and flagrant social designs and structures (B), nor is it an attempt to represent the human condition based on loose and free-flowing designs, pattern, and shapes (C). Realism is not the belief that human beings exist entirely in the order of nature, do not have a soul, nor any participation in a religious or spiritual world beyond nature (D).

53. (D)

Regional writing—local color—is the literary use of distinctive characteristics and/or idiosyncrasies of a particular locality and/or its inhabitants. Regional writing may not reflect a national consciousness (A), and it does not necessarily reflect patriotism (B) or social conservatism (C).

54. (C)

An epic poem is a long narrative poem on a serious subject told in a formal and/or elevated style centering on a heroic figure. Choice (A) is incorrect because the story is not in prose form. An epic is in a formal style—not an ordinary speaking voice; (B) is incorrect. An epic is not depressing, but it is about heroes and mythical figures (D). Because all of (D) is not true, (D) is not a good option.

55. (B)

Kafka uses hunger as a metaphor for organized religion and spirituality. The word "hunger" is not a substitute for the media (e.g., oil, watercolor, and acrylic paints) of the artist's trade; (A) is not the best answer. The author is not speaking merely of food (C) or social courtesy and propriety (D); neither answer, therefore, is correct.

Author's note: Because Kafka was born in Prague, he wrote in a language other than English—in this case, German. The following is another version of the opening paragraph. Variations in translations are an important element in literary interpretation. A comparison of the variations might influence one's literary interpretation(s):

In the last decades interest in hunger artists has declined considerably. Whereas in earlier days there was good money to be earned putting on major productions of this sort under one's own management, nowadays that is totally impossible. Those were different times. Back then the hunger artist captured the attention of the entire city. From day to day while the fasting lasted, participation increased. Everyone wanted to see the hunger artist at least daily. During the final days there were people with subscription tickets who sat all day in front of the small barred cage. And there were even viewing hours at night, their impact heightened by torchlight. On fine days the cage was dragged out into the open air, and then the hunger artist was put on display particularly for the children. While for grown-ups the hunger artist was often merely a joke, something they participated in because it was fashionable, the children looked on amazed, their mouths open, holding each other's hands for safety, as he sat there on scattered straw—spurning a chair—in a black tights, looking pale, with his ribs sticking out prominently, sometimes nodding politely, answering questions with a forced smile, even sticking his arm out through the bars to let people feel how emaciated he was, but then completely sinking back into himself, so that he paid no attention to anything, not even to what was so important to him, the striking of the clock, which was the single furnishing in the cage, merely looking out in front of him with his eyes almost shut and now and then sipping from a tiny glass of water to moisten his lips. (Johnston, 2003)

This translation, by Ian Johnston of Malaspina University-College, Nanaimo, British Columbia, Canada, is in the public domain and may be used by anyone, in whole or in part, without permission and without charge, provided the source is acknowledged. (http://www.kafka.org/index.php?id=162, 166,0,0,1,0)

56. (A)

This question is an example of a literal question: the answer is present in the text. Because the answer is clearly stated in the passage, none of the other answers is a suitable response.

57. (D)

Geoffrey Chaucer (1343–1400) used the poetic style of heroic couplet in *The Canterbury Tales* and *The Legend of Good Women*. The other answer choices are all writers of other classic literary genres: Homer (eighth century BCE;

choice A) specialized in the epic; Shakespeare (1564–1616; choice B) has in his surviving works primarily 38 plays, 154 sonnets, 2 long narrative poems, and several other poems; and Sophocles (ca. 496 BCE–406 BCE; choice C) was primarily a Greek tragedian.

58. (A)

A sonnet is a lyric poem consisting of a single stanza of 14 lines of iambic pentameter linked by an intricate rhyme scheme. Choices (B) and (D) can be eliminated on the basis of the number of lines cited in each: 12 lines and 15 lines, respectively. With an intricate rhyme scheme, a sonnet is not an epic poem with a free-flowing rhyme scheme; (C) is also incorrect.

59. (B)

A soliloquy is a monologue in which actors speak their thoughts and feelings aloud. The exact definition does not restrict a soliloquy to a specific period; the soliloquy may be in prose and does not necessarily relate to the existence of God, thus (A) is not appropriate. Because the actor may not be expressing feelings directly to a loved one, (C) is incorrect. A soliloquy is not a dialogue; (D), therefore, is not appropriate.

60. (C)

Homer, a Greek poet (eighth century BCE), appears to be the writer of *The Iliad* and *The Odyssey*. Sophocles (ca. 496 BCE–406 BCE; choice A) was primarily a Greek tragedian. Euclid (300 BCE; choice B) was not an epic writer but a mathematician who is credited as "the father of geometry." Ulysses (D) is the subject, not the writer, of *The Iliad* and *The Odyssey*.

61. (D)

The art of transmitting culture, beliefs, heritage, mythologies, and so on, in the form of either prose or verse, by word of mouth is oral tradition. The lyrical ballads from the late 1700s marked the beginning of the romantic period; the transmission of culture began long before that. Choice (A) is not an appropriate answer. The romantic tradition as an artistic, literary, and intellectual movement originated around the middle of the eighteenth century; it was, in part, a revolt against aristocratic, social, and political norms of the Enlightenment and a reaction to scientific rationalization. Transmitting culture began much earlier; (B) is not a good choice. The Renaissance was a cultural movement of the fourteenth, fifteenth, and sixteenth centuries; the movement began in Italy but gradually expanded to Germany, France, England, and other parts of Europe. Choice (C) is not an appropriate answer.

62. (D)

John Donne is the archetypical metaphysical poet. The metaphysical poets were British lyric poets of the seventeenth century; they were interested in metaphysical concerns, a philosophy that investigates principles of reality transcending those of any particular science. The Cavalier poets (A), also of the seventeenth century, supported King Charles I and consisted primarily of Ben Jonson, Robert Herrick, Richard Lovelace, Thomas Carew, and Sir John Suckling. Their writing featured polished, lyrical, erotically charged poems of gallantry and courtship. The graveyard school of poets (B) focused on death as bereavement and sprang up during the eighteenth century; Donne lived before this time period and is not a part of the movement. The pre-Raphaelites (C) were a group of artists who banded together in 1848 to protest the unimaginative and artificial historical art of the eighteenth and nineteenth centuries; Dante Gabriel Rossetti was one of these.

The period before Raphael was their focus. Donne lived before the mid-1800s, so he could not have been a member of the group.

63. (B)

The word "pathos" comes from the Greek term meaning "to experience suffering or emotion." Logos (A) is a Greek word meaning "to count, to say, to speak, to tell." The word's primary meaning is "something said"; its secondary meaning involves logic, reasoning. Logos is a rhetorical argument based on logic. (A) is not the best answer. Ethos (C) is one of the three modes of persuasion that Aristotle discussed in "Rhetoric." With ethos one appeals to authority to strengthen an argument; ethos is a starting place. The word "ethics," which refers to character, derives from "ethos." (C) is not a good choice. Topos (D) suggests settings, characters, and themes that appear and reappear in literature; the flood, for instance, is a common theme in literature. (D) is not an appropriate answer.

64. (C)

An effective persuasive argument includes a full recognition and clear analysis of the counterargument showing its strengths and weaknesses. An effective persuasive argument does not necessarily have to include a detailed explanation of your personal feelings and emotions as they pertain to the subject matter (A); a detailed analysis of the social, literary, and historical contexts upon which the argument is based (B); or an oversimplification of the opposing argument, which thereby demonstrates the absurdity of the opposition's point of view (D).

65. (A)

Paraphrasing is a legitimate and effective tool in establishing a comprehensive argument. On the other hand, a non sequitur (an argument that does not logically follow the statement before), post hoc (A occurs before B; therefore A causes B), and stereotypes (generalizations about groups based on one example) do not employ valid logic and are not acceptable elements of a persuasive argument. Thus, (B), (C), and (D) are logical fallacies and do not correctly answer the question.

66. (C)

An anecdote is a short narrative of an interesting, amusing, or biographical incident that serves to elucidate a point or idea. A protagonist (A) is the character who takes the lead, as opposed to the antagonist who opposes. Onomatopoeia (B) is the use of a word that imitates the sound ("bop, pow, bang") it represents. Fiction (D) is not factual and the question refers to an interesting, amusing, or biographical incident which implies a factual basis.

67. (D)

Douglass's thesis can be paraphrased as "If the right [of equality] belongs to any, it belongs to all." Douglass begins his writing with a statement of argument for impartial suffrage; he does not suggest, as choice (A) wrongly does, that a limited statement of argument is the best way to communicate with government. Douglass states both that "man is the only government-making animal in the world" and that man should be able to acquire property and education; both statements are, according to Douglass, true. Answer choice (B) does not equate both as being of equal value and is thus incorrect. Douglass does not advocate a war of the races as a solution; he only mentions it as a hypothetical argument. Choice (C) is not acceptable as the thesis of Douglass's writing.

68. (B)

Only (B) refers to voting rights, or enfranchisement, which Douglass advocates for all. Answers (A) and (C) relate to owning a franchise, such as a McDonald's restaurant. Answer (D) is akin to the definition for frankness.

69. (D)

The association between Mark Twain and the Mississippi River is undeniable, so the title *Life on the Mississippi* should have made the answer clear. Nathaniel Hawthorne (A) lived in and wrote primarily about Massachusetts. Stephen Crane (B) lived in New York, New Jersey, and England; he wrote of the Civil War, not the Mississippi River. Edgar Allan Poe (C) lived in Massachusetts, Virginia, and South Carolina; he did not write of the Mississippi.

70. (D)

A syllogism consists of a major premise, a minor premise, and a conclusion. All the other answer choices include at least one incorrect element.

71. (A)

A rhetorical argument using deductive reasoning builds from accepted truths to specific conclusions, from the top to the bottom. The conclusion logically follows from the premises. One does not build from conclusions to a larger premise; that process describes an inductive argument. Choice (B) is, therefore, not acceptable. Building from one minor premise to another minor premise does not suggest deductive reasoning; (C) is incorrect. Likewise, building from one specific conclusion to another specific conclusion is not deductive reasoning; (D) is not a correct choice.

72. (C)

Dramatic irony occurs when the audience or reader knows something that the characters do not. We know that Juliet is alive, but the devastated and impulsive Romeo does not. Situational irony (B) occurs when the opposite of what we expect to happen actually happens. The audience knows through the entire play that both of the protagonists will die. In verbal irony (A), the speaker says one thing but means another, which is not the case with Romeo and Juliet in this scene—they are entirely sincere. There is no such thing as epic irony (D).

73. (D)

White, Thoreau, and Didion are all well-known for their essays. Hemingway was a fiction writers, known primarily for his short stories and novels.

74. (B)

A metaphor is an example of figurative language. One does not use literal interpretation (A) to determine the meaning of a metaphor; one has to read between the lines to determine the meaning of a metaphor. Logical fallacies (C) are not directly related to determining the meaning of a metaphor. "Somnambulism" (D) is another term for sleepwalking.

75. (A)

T. S. Eliot's "The Waste Land" is a poetic example of modernism. It is not an example of a lyric, or poetry that expresses subjective thoughts and feelings, often in a songlike style or form; (B) is, therefore, inappropriate. A ballad (C) is a narrative poem; it is often of folk origin, intended for singing, contains simple stanzas, and usually has a refrain. "The Waste Land" is not a ballad, so (C) is not a good choice. An epic (D) celebrates the feats of a legendary or traditional hero, often one of mythology; it is a long narrative. This description does not fit "The Waste Land."

76. (B)

The Pilgrim's Progress and *Animal Farm* are both allegorical novels, a story in which characters, settings, and events stand for other people or events or for abstract ideas or qualities. *The Pilgrim's Progress* (1678) chronicles the character Pilgrim's journey to the Celestial City, an allegory for man's journey to salvation. *Animal Farm* is an allegorical expression of the Russian Revolution.

77. (A)

Foils are characters that represent opposite traits or ideas. Tom, the cruel realist, and Gatsby, the romantic dreamer, are perfect examples of this rhetorical device.

78. (D)

Phillis Wheatley's poetry rarely is bluntly critical of slavery, although in this poem she directly addresses the issue of slavery. The overall tone is certainly not (A) angry and resentful, nor is it (B) frustrated and contemptuous. Having eliminated those two choices we are left with the pairs, faithful and ironic or grateful and devoted as our choices. Certainly, the phrases "Twas mercy brought me from my Pagan land," and "Taught my benighted soul to understand that there is a God and a Saviour too:" indicate that she found religious faith as a result of her journey, but the poem is not ironic in tone, so (C) is not a good choice. That leaves (D), grateful and devoted, which is evident in her declaration that there is a God and a Saviour, and her challenge, although somewhat ambiguous, to

Christians that "Negros, black as Cain, may be refin'd, and join th' angelic train."

79. (A)

The poem is written in couplets. A couplet is a unit of verse with two successive lines; these lines usually rhyme, often have the same meter, and frequently form a complete thought or syntactic unit. An enjambment (B) is the "running over of a sentence" from one verse or one couplet into another; closely related words may fall in different lines. No such examples exist in this poem. Meter (C) in poetry is the measured arrangement of words by the rhythm of the accents, the quantity of the syllables, or the number of syllables in a line. (C) is an inappropriate choice. A stanza (D) is a group of verse lines that forms a section of a poem and shares the same structure as some of the other sections in the poem because of the length of the line, the meter, and its rhyme scheme. Sometimes students call stanzas "verses." This is not accurate; a verse is a single line.

80. (D)

Virginia Woolf (1882–1941) is the only one of the authors not part of the British Romantic period (1790–1830). In fact, Virginia Woolf, a member of the Bloomsbury Group, is considered one of the foremost modernist literary figures of the twentieth century.

81. (D)

Parody is defined by *Merriam-Webster Dictionary* as "a literary or musical work in which the style of an author or work is closely imitated for comic effect or in ridicule" which fits choice (D). Answer choice (A) describes satire, which in some forms can also be a parody. Answer option (B)

defines a fable and option (C) since it is an extended narrative would have to be a novel.

82. (C)

Thoreau is writing argument here, using reason and logic to persuade his audience to think and feel as he does. Narration tells a story and has a discernible chronology (A). Description uses words to create a picture for the reader (B). Division and classification divides a subject into its parts and places them in appropriate categories (D). While all modes of exposition can be used for a persuasive purpose, this piece is most clearly classified as argument.

83. (B)

An epistolary novel is an extended fictional narrative, written in the form of letters, diaries, and journal entries. It is not the oldest form of prose fiction (A), nor is it an extended fictional narrative, dealing with fantasy and the supernatural (D). It is the epic that is an extended fictional narrative in which an heroic figure embarks on a quest or other perilous journey; (C) is, therefore, also incorrect.

84. (A)

Choice (A) correctly defines paradox. Choice (B) defines pastoral; (C), pantomime; and (D), paranormal.

85. (B)

An imperfect, or slant, rhyme is a rhyme scheme in which corresponding vowel sounds are only approximate, and sometimes the rhymed consonants are similar rather than identical. None of the other schemes described in choices (A), (C), and (D) fit the definition of slant rhyme.

86. (C)

Frost is suggesting that regardless of subject matter, a poem must be sincere and meaningful to the author before it will be sincere or meaningful to the reader. Frost is not making a reference just to the emotion of sadness; (A) is inappropriate as an answer. Frost does not predict that poems about social corruption or human suffering can bring about an increase in poetry reading; (B) is not the best choice. Frost does not express frustration with modern precision instruments making things appear crooked; (D) is not a good choice.

87. (C)

In the quoted line, Frost suggests that his surprise and enjoyment in writing can be conveyed to the reader: Frost is saying that the act of writing poetry is an enlightening and cathartic experience for the poet, and thus will be enlightening for the reader. Because Frost makes no mention of enthusiasm in writing, (A) is not the best choice. He does not suggest that poems he read earlier influenced his own writing; (B) is incorrect. Frost makes no mention of his age or of forgetting things; therefore, (D) is not a good answer.

88. (A)

A literary symbol is a word or phrase that signifies an object or event which in turn signifies something else, or offers a range of interpretations beyond itself. A "round, concave, brass plate" (B) is a cymbal, not a symbol. A symbol does not necessarily refer to other types of writing, as suggested by choice (C). Something that develops or accelerates the action (D) is not a symbol.

89. (D)

Choice (D) accurately defines alliteration. Choice (A) describes a component of impressionism, (B) defines onomatopoeia, and (C) defines palindrome.

90. (C)

The expression "Sons of Ben" refers to Ben Jonson. "Jonson (1572–1637), a poet, playwright, and scholar, was the dean and the leading wit of the group of writers who gathered at the Mermaid Tavern in the Cheapside district of London. Influenced by Jonson, the young poets were the self-styled 'sons' or 'tribe' of Ben, later called the Cavalier poets, a group which included, among others, Robert Herrick, Thomas Carew, Sir John Suckling, and Richard Lovelace." (Jokinen 2003)

None of the other answers are appropriate. Ben Franklin (A) is from a later period than Ben Jonson, Uncle Ben (B) refers to the name of a brand of rice, and Ben Cartwright (D) is the name of a fictional character from the television series "Bonanza."

91. (D)

The translation of carpe diem is "seize the day." Used by Horace, "carpe diem" is a descriptive term for literature that urges readers to live for the moment. The theme, which was widely used in sixteenth- and seventeenth-century love poetry, is best exemplified by a familiar stanza from Robert Herrick's "To the Virgins, to Make Much of Time." Related to this is the phrase "per diem," Latin for "per day" or "for each day"; this usually refers to the daily rate of any kind of payment. It may also refer to a specific amount of money that an organization allows an individual to spend per day, to cover living and traveling expenses in connection with work.

92. (C)

Only answer (C) is written in the third person, in this case, he. Answer (A) is a first-person point of view, (B) illustrates a second-person narration, and (D) is a first-person limited narration.

93. (A)

Answer (A) correctly describes ambiguous writing. Answer (B) describes allusion, answer (C) describes a concrete word or phrase, and answer (D) is an erroneous example of ambiguous writing.

94. (A)

These lines incorporate a pun, a play on words. In this case, the use of "soles" and "soul" is an example of a pun.

95. (A)

According to the *Oxford English Dictionary*, grammar is defined as "the branch of language study or linguistic study which deals with the means of showing the relationship between words in use." Choice (B) refers to etymology, which has as its concern the branch of language study or linguistic study that deals with the specific origins of word roots and their evolution to current and proper usage. Choice (C) is the definition of biology. Lexicography is the branch of language that deals with dictionary writing (D).

96. (B)

Morphology refers to alterations made to a root word that give it the appropriate grammatical tense, quantity, and so forth. As suffixes such as "-ing" and "-ed" go at the end of the word, the correct answer is (B). The mark that notes the end of sentence (A) is a part of punctuation, the period. It is etymology—not morphology—that notes the origins of words (C). Technical writing is the type of writing style used to report information (D).

97. (D)

Syntax is neither a division of linguistics that studies synonyms (A) nor is it related to a monetary charge (tax) applied to recreational goods, services, and activities (B). The physiological inability to form coherent sentences (C) is aphasia, not syntax.

98. (B)

The sentence, "I have two rabbits," shows agreement between the quantity "two" and the noun "rabbits," which in itself is plural. Choice (A) is an example of a double negative; both "ain't" and "nowhere" indicate negation. The sentences in (C) and (D) do not contain double-plural nouns.

99. (A)

Irregular verbs are those whose past tense and past participle are not formed by adding "-ed," "-d," or "-t" to the present tense and those that do not follow the general rules of inflection. The term irregular verb does not relate to the difference between a noun and a verb (B) or to the difficulty in linguistic studies (C). The statement "work well in any sentence" (D) is inapplicable.

100. (C)

In linguistic studies, a fricative is a consonant sound made by passing a continuous stream of air thought a narrow passage in the vocal tract. Two vowels produced consecutively in the same syllable (A) form a diphthong, not a fricative. Some words can function as a noun or a verb (B); very often the change in part of speech results in a different pronunciation even though the spelling remains the same. They are heteronyms if they are spelled the same but pronounced differently as "row" (argument) and "row" (propel with oars). Fricatives do not necessarily require a stop in the air flow when one is pronouncing a word (D).

101. (A)

"Homonymy" is the semantic term for a word having identical expression but different meanings, such as the word "book" in "book a flight" and "read a book." Homophones are words that sound alike but have different meanings, such as "see" and "sea." Choice (B) describes alliteration, which refers to words in a sentence that begin with a repeating consonant sound, as in "Peter Piper picked a peck of pickled peppers." Words that sound different but have the same meanings, as in "sea" and "ocean," are synonyms (C). A euphemism uses a more pleasing word for something that may be offensive (D); for instance, "senior citizen" could be used as a euphemism for "old man."

102. (B)

Paraphrasing is restating a text or thesis in your own words thereby making the idea or topic clearer to understand for both the writer and the reader. Restating the same information more than once (A) is not paraphrasing. Using parallel structures within a sentence (C) is necessary, but it is not the same as paraphrasing. Replacing the author's name with your own name (D) is plagiarism, not paraphrasing.

103. (A)

"Caedmon's Hymn" was written in the everyday language of the people, or the vernacular. Up until the time of Bede, most literature was written in Latin (B) or other non-vernacular languages. "In the vernacular" does not relate directly to the Old English language (C) or the medium used (D).

104. (D)

Realism was a nineteenth-century literary movement attempting to replicate everyday life situations as realistically as possible. The works of authors William Dean Howells and Hamlin Garland are representative of American realism. Literary impressionism (A) is a literary style that employs details and mental associations to develop subjective and sensory impressions rather than merely recreating objective reality. Literary regionalism (B) was particularly popular in the United States after the Civil War; while these writers included realistic elements such as customs, manners, and dialect in their works, (B) is not the best choice. Literary colonialism (C) typically reflects the people and the place; it may describe the discovery of new lands. Literary colonialism is not the same as realism.

105. (C)

Literary naturalism is the belief that human beings exist entirely in the order of nature and do not have a soul or any participation in a religious or spiritual world beyond nature. Staged in an indifferent, deterministic universe, naturalistic texts often describe the futile attempts of human beings to exercise free will in a universe that reveals free will as an illusion. Literary naturalism is not merely a literary attempt to record accurately and objectively visual reality in terms of light and color in nature (A); neither is it writing that represents the nature of life and the social world as the common reader would see it (B). Literary naturalism does not seek to represent the human condition based on designs, patterns, and shapes, suggestive of those found in nature (D).

106. (D)

The growth of regional literature cannot be proven to have a causal relationship to higher literature. Regional literature is fiction and poetry that focuses on the characters, the dialects, the customs, the topography, and specific features of a region. Regional literature came about with the increased popularity of magazines (A), more female readers (B), and (C) the desire to preserve the unique features of a region.

107. (D)

There are strong ideological differences between Booker T. Washington's *Up from Slavery* (1901) and the book cited in choice (A), W. E. B. Du Bois's *The Souls of Black Folk* (1902). These two texts established lasting battle lines on a variety of major issues dealing with racial identity and civil rights in the United States. *Uncle Tom's Cabin* (B) was written by Harriet Beecher Stowe (1852), and *Yes I Can* (C) was written by Sammy Davis, Jr. (1965).

108. (B)

The colon is one of the most misunderstood and misused punctuation marks. The colon tells the reader that what follows is closely related to the preceding clause, as in the choice (B), "A dedicated artist requires four things: brushes, paint, canvas, and eye for beauty." Do not use a colon between the verb and the direct object except when a phrase "like the following" or "as follows" precedes the direct object. Choice (A), "A dedicated artist requires:

brushes, paint, canvas, and an eye for beauty," incorrectly uses a colon to separate the verb "requires" from the direct objects "brushes, paint, canvas, and an eye for beauty." The lists following the words such as in choice (C) and "materials" in choice (D) should not be preceded by a colon.

109. (A)

When a verbal phrase does not refer to a specific noun or noun phrase it follows or precedes, it is a misplaced modifier. Consider the following example:

Rushing to the checkout line, the eggs fell from my buggy.

"Rushing to the checkout line" is a misplaced modifier because it seems to modify the eggs; the eggs, however, were not rushing to the checkout line. Rather the pusher of my buggy (in other words, I) was rushing to the checkout line. The sentence could be corrected by rephrasing:

As I rushed to the checkout line, the eggs fell from my buggy.

In English, a past participle (B) can function independently as an adjective, as does the past participle "baked" in "We had some baked beans." Past participles can also be used with an auxiliary verb to indicate tense, aspect, or voice, as in the passive sentence "The beans were baked too long." The predicate (C) is the part of the sentence that contains the verb and tells what is being said of the subject. A predicate can but does not necessarily include a verbal phrase; (C) is not the best choice. An independent clause (D) has a subject and a verb and can thus stand alone as a sentence; this choice does not answer the question.

110. (C)

A run-on sentence is a sentence in which two or more independent clauses have been run together without a proper conjunction or proper punctuation. A fragmented sentence (A) is not a complete sentence or complete thought; it does not contain two independent clauses. A topic sentence (B), usually located at the beginning of a paper or paragraph, states the main premise of the writing. A complex sentence (D) is a sentence that includes at least one independent clause and at least one dependent clause. Because a complex sentence is a legitimate type of sentence, it does not fit the definition of "two independent clauses . . . not joined correctly."

111. (A)

Teaching multicultural students effectively should enable them to connect the curriculum to their own lives. Such teaching may not result in a standardized approach to the curriculum (B) but rather varying instructional approaches. Ideally, teachers may continue to examine their own beliefs and those of their students; (C) and (D) do not represent successful styles for teaching writing.

112. (C)

Morality plays dramatize early Christian principles and precepts; they graphically show the final punishment for not following Christian doctrine. Because the plays focus on Christian doctrine, not domestic behaviors (A), etiquette (B), or improper social behaviors (D), only answer (C) is appropriate.

113. (C)

Circumlocution is the indirect, usually wordy way of avoiding saying something directly. When Irving comments on Rip's "insuperable aversion to all profitable labor," he is using circumlocution to avoid directly calling Rip lazy. In this case, the circumlocution is meant for a humorous effect.

114. (C)

Teachers compose narrative reports that describe a student's strengths, weaknesses, behaviors, progress, and any other information to supplement the information that is conveyed in a report card. The narrative report can be helpful if a parent cannot attend a parent-teacher conference, for example. Choice (A) is incorrect because it is the teacher, not the student, who describes how the student is performing. The narrative report is not a formal report card (B) but is a supplement to the information on the report card. Choice (D) is incorrect because narrative reports can be an alternative to parent-teacher conferences.

115. (B)

A working thesis, as opposed to a finished or final thesis, is a general idea of the direction an essay will take, but one that the writer will ultimately refine and clarify as the essay develops. Answers (A), (C), and (D) are not applicable: the working thesis is not solidified (A) and may not fit the assigned topic indefinitely (D); a reader may never see the working thesis statement (C).

116. (A)

Satire is a form of imitative ridicule with subject matter that focuses on social inequities and human corruption. Satire does not necessarily alter the lives of individuals; (B) is inapplicable. Satire ridicules, not imitates; (C) is untrue. Satire is ridicule, not just humor; (D) is inappropriate.

117. (C)

People see the hypocrisy in others but seldom see it in themselves. The glass that Swift describes

is a mirror, not a vessel; (A) is not appropriate. The passage does not suggest fragility; (B) is incorrect. The interpretation that choice (D) suggests is not necessarily true.

118. (B)

In this case, Swift is using the adjective "nice" as a euphemism for honest; by using this adjective, he suggests that society will demonize honesty by labeling it as something "nasty." The statement that Swift makes does not necessarily refer to time dwelling on perverse issues (A). Swift does not suggest that society will condemn vulgar ideas (C) or that there is no such thing as an honest person (D).

119. (D)

In the quote, "censure" means "to blame or judge in a sternly condemning manner." The meaning of censure is not to edit (A). Swift does not see censure as "a moral thought pattern" (C); neither does he define it as a device that responds to stimuli (B).

120. (C)

Scathing commentary—Swift's trademark—is received "kindly" because people are too ignorant or self-absorbed to understand that the humor is representative of and directed at them. Swift's scathing commentary is not accepted just because everyone needs some humor (A) or just because it addresses only important people (B). Swift's satire is not necessarily fresh and contemporary in that it addresses only current figures; (D) is inappropriate.

Praxis English Assessment: Content Knowledge (0041)

Practice Test 2

ANSWER SHEET FOR PRACTICE TEST 2 (0041)

1. Ⓐ Ⓑ Ⓒ Ⓓ
2. Ⓐ Ⓑ Ⓒ Ⓓ
3. Ⓐ Ⓑ Ⓒ Ⓓ
4. Ⓐ Ⓑ Ⓒ Ⓓ
5. Ⓐ Ⓑ Ⓒ Ⓓ
6. Ⓐ Ⓑ Ⓒ Ⓓ
7. Ⓐ Ⓑ Ⓒ Ⓓ
8. Ⓐ Ⓑ Ⓒ Ⓓ
9. Ⓐ Ⓑ Ⓒ Ⓓ
10. Ⓐ Ⓑ Ⓒ Ⓓ
11. Ⓐ Ⓑ Ⓒ Ⓓ
12. Ⓐ Ⓑ Ⓒ Ⓓ
13. Ⓐ Ⓑ Ⓒ Ⓓ
14. Ⓐ Ⓑ Ⓒ Ⓓ
15. Ⓐ Ⓑ Ⓒ Ⓓ
16. Ⓐ Ⓑ Ⓒ Ⓓ
17. Ⓐ Ⓑ Ⓒ Ⓓ
18. Ⓐ Ⓑ Ⓒ Ⓓ
19. Ⓐ Ⓑ Ⓒ Ⓓ
20. Ⓐ Ⓑ Ⓒ Ⓓ
21. Ⓐ Ⓑ Ⓒ Ⓓ
22. Ⓐ Ⓑ Ⓒ Ⓓ
23. Ⓐ Ⓑ Ⓒ Ⓓ
24. Ⓐ Ⓑ Ⓒ Ⓓ
25. Ⓐ Ⓑ Ⓒ Ⓓ
26. Ⓐ Ⓑ Ⓒ Ⓓ
27. Ⓐ Ⓑ Ⓒ Ⓓ
28. Ⓐ Ⓑ Ⓒ Ⓓ
29. Ⓐ Ⓑ Ⓒ Ⓓ
30. Ⓐ Ⓑ Ⓒ Ⓓ

31. Ⓐ Ⓑ Ⓒ Ⓓ
32. Ⓐ Ⓑ Ⓒ Ⓓ
33. Ⓐ Ⓑ Ⓒ Ⓓ
34. Ⓐ Ⓑ Ⓒ Ⓓ
35. Ⓐ Ⓑ Ⓒ Ⓓ
36. Ⓐ Ⓑ Ⓒ Ⓓ
37. Ⓐ Ⓑ Ⓒ Ⓓ
38. Ⓐ Ⓑ Ⓒ Ⓓ
39. Ⓐ Ⓑ Ⓒ Ⓓ
40. Ⓐ Ⓑ Ⓒ Ⓓ
41. Ⓐ Ⓑ Ⓒ Ⓓ
42. Ⓐ Ⓑ Ⓒ Ⓓ
43. Ⓐ Ⓑ Ⓒ Ⓓ
44. Ⓐ Ⓑ Ⓒ Ⓓ
45. Ⓐ Ⓑ Ⓒ Ⓓ
46. Ⓐ Ⓑ Ⓒ Ⓓ
47. Ⓐ Ⓑ Ⓒ Ⓓ
48. Ⓐ Ⓑ Ⓒ Ⓓ
49. Ⓐ Ⓑ Ⓒ Ⓓ
50. Ⓐ Ⓑ Ⓒ Ⓓ
51. Ⓐ Ⓑ Ⓒ Ⓓ
52. Ⓐ Ⓑ Ⓒ Ⓓ
53. Ⓐ Ⓑ Ⓒ Ⓓ
54. Ⓐ Ⓑ Ⓒ Ⓓ
55. Ⓐ Ⓑ Ⓒ Ⓓ
56. Ⓐ Ⓑ Ⓒ Ⓓ
57. Ⓐ Ⓑ Ⓒ Ⓓ
58. Ⓐ Ⓑ Ⓒ Ⓓ
59. Ⓐ Ⓑ Ⓒ Ⓓ
60. Ⓐ Ⓑ Ⓒ Ⓓ

61. Ⓐ Ⓑ Ⓒ Ⓓ
62. Ⓐ Ⓑ Ⓒ Ⓓ
63. Ⓐ Ⓑ Ⓒ Ⓓ
64. Ⓐ Ⓑ Ⓒ Ⓓ
65. Ⓐ Ⓑ Ⓒ Ⓓ
66. Ⓐ Ⓑ Ⓒ Ⓓ
67. Ⓐ Ⓑ Ⓒ Ⓓ
68. Ⓐ Ⓑ Ⓒ Ⓓ
69. Ⓐ Ⓑ Ⓒ Ⓓ
70. Ⓐ Ⓑ Ⓒ Ⓓ
71. Ⓐ Ⓑ Ⓒ Ⓓ
72. Ⓐ Ⓑ Ⓒ Ⓓ
73. Ⓐ Ⓑ Ⓒ Ⓓ
74. Ⓐ Ⓑ Ⓒ Ⓓ
75. Ⓐ Ⓑ Ⓒ Ⓓ
76. Ⓐ Ⓑ Ⓒ Ⓓ
77. Ⓐ Ⓑ Ⓒ Ⓓ
78. Ⓐ Ⓑ Ⓒ Ⓓ
79. Ⓐ Ⓑ Ⓒ Ⓓ
80. Ⓐ Ⓑ Ⓒ Ⓓ
81. Ⓐ Ⓑ Ⓒ Ⓓ
82. Ⓐ Ⓑ Ⓒ Ⓓ
83. Ⓐ Ⓑ Ⓒ Ⓓ
84. Ⓐ Ⓑ Ⓒ Ⓓ
85. Ⓐ Ⓑ Ⓒ Ⓓ
86. Ⓐ Ⓑ Ⓒ Ⓓ
87. Ⓐ Ⓑ Ⓒ Ⓓ
88. Ⓐ Ⓑ Ⓒ Ⓓ
89. Ⓐ Ⓑ Ⓒ Ⓓ
90. Ⓐ Ⓑ Ⓒ Ⓓ

91. Ⓐ Ⓑ Ⓒ Ⓓ
92. Ⓐ Ⓑ Ⓒ Ⓓ
93. Ⓐ Ⓑ Ⓒ Ⓓ
94. Ⓐ Ⓑ Ⓒ Ⓓ
95. Ⓐ Ⓑ Ⓒ Ⓓ
96. Ⓐ Ⓑ Ⓒ Ⓓ
97. Ⓐ Ⓑ Ⓒ Ⓓ
98. Ⓐ Ⓑ Ⓒ Ⓓ
99. Ⓐ Ⓑ Ⓒ Ⓓ
100. Ⓐ Ⓑ Ⓒ Ⓓ
101. Ⓐ Ⓑ Ⓒ Ⓓ
102. Ⓐ Ⓑ Ⓒ Ⓓ
103. Ⓐ Ⓑ Ⓒ Ⓓ
104. Ⓐ Ⓑ Ⓒ Ⓓ
105. Ⓐ Ⓑ Ⓒ Ⓓ
106. Ⓐ Ⓑ Ⓒ Ⓓ
107. Ⓐ Ⓑ Ⓒ Ⓓ
108. Ⓐ Ⓑ Ⓒ Ⓓ
109. Ⓐ Ⓑ Ⓒ Ⓓ
110. Ⓐ Ⓑ Ⓒ Ⓓ
111. Ⓐ Ⓑ Ⓒ Ⓓ
112. Ⓐ Ⓑ Ⓒ Ⓓ
113. Ⓐ Ⓑ Ⓒ Ⓓ
114. Ⓐ Ⓑ Ⓒ Ⓓ
115. Ⓐ Ⓑ Ⓒ Ⓓ
116. Ⓐ Ⓑ Ⓒ Ⓓ
117. Ⓐ Ⓑ Ⓒ Ⓓ
118. Ⓐ Ⓑ Ⓒ Ⓓ
119. Ⓐ Ⓑ Ⓒ Ⓓ
120. Ⓐ Ⓑ Ⓒ Ⓓ

English Language, Literature, and Composition: Content Knowledge
PRACTICE TEST 2 (0041)

TIME: 120 minutes
        120 questions

In this section, you will find examples of test questions similar to those you are likely to encounter on the Praxis II English Language, Literature, and Composition: Content Knowledge Exam.

1. A student portfolio

    (A) contains artwork by a student.
    (B) is for comparing student work.
    (C) has a scale for grading.
    (D) contains documents and/or products to show the student's progress.

2. What is the narrative report approach?

    (A) Students write a narrative report each day to describe how they feel they are doing.
    (B) The teacher writes a formal, narrative report card for each student.
    (C) Teachers provide parents with a written assessment of a student's progress.
    (D) Parents and teacher discuss a student's attitudes about learning.

3. A teacher should discuss a student's permanent school record with the

    (A) student's parents or legal guardians, current teachers, and school administrators.
    (B) parents only.
    (C) school administrators only.
    (D) school administrators and parents only.

4. Which name from the following list is most closely associated with metaphysical poetry?

    (A) Edmund Spenser
    (B) Robert Herrick
    (C) John Donne
    (D) Alfred, Lord Tennyson

5. Reading and then dramatizing a story, using that story as the basis of a puppet play, scripting the story and performing it in the classroom, and attending a performance of that story done as a play by a theater company illustrate which of the following concepts?

    (A) Teachers should work with the material until they find the correct way to use it with students.
    (B) There are multiple ways to express and interpret the same material.
    (C) Plays are more interesting than classroom dramatizations.
    (D) Students learn less as audience members than as participants in drama activities.

6. What is a morpheme?

    (A) A word that combines two or more words and establishes its own meaning, as in "businessperson" ("business" + "person")
    (B) A word that changes from a verb to a noun when "-ing" is added, as in "swim/swimming"

(C) A quantitative noun that changes spelling when going from singular to plural, as in "mouse/mice"

(D) The smallest unit of language that has meaning or serves a grammatical function, as in "cat"

7. An affix, also known as a bound morpheme,

(A) attaches to a word, thus giving it the opposite connotation from its original meaning; for example, "non-" added to "negotiable" creates the word "nonnegotiable."

(B) attaches to a root or stem morpheme and can be either a prefix or suffix.

(C) attaches to a verb, thereby making it an adverb; for example, "-ly" added to "swift" creates the adverb "swiftly."

(D) attaches words via a hyphen, as in "twenty-first-century."

8. A diphthong is

(A) a fluctuation in the pronunciation of consonant sounds, produced by regulating airflow over the vocal cords.

(B) a vowel sound whose production requires the tongue to start in one place and move (or glide) to another.

(C) a consonant sound produced by the fluttering of the tongue behind the upper teeth.

(D) an extended vowel sound whose production is created by slowly releasing air over the vocal cords.

9. Prior to the development of written languages, stories, culture, and traditions were passed down from one generation to the next via

(A) pictures painted on walls, rocks, and other surfaces; this process is also known as pictography.

(B) carvings, drawings, and sand designs; this process is also known as cartography.

(C) word of mouth; this process is also known as oral tradition.

(D) Sanskrit.

10. What is a metaphor?

(A) A figure of speech containing an implied comparison in which a word or phrase ordinarily and primarily used for one thing is applied to another, as in "All the world's a stage."

(B) A figure of speech containing contemporary representation of linguistic ideology, primarily used by fiction writers, as in the slang expression "That car is phat."

(C) A figure of speech containing a reproduction of the sounds that the word is supposed to represent, as in "buzz."

(D) A figure of speech containing the implied thematic representation of a story, fable, or morality tale, as in "Slow and steady wins the race."

11. When two different words share the same or similar meaning, they are

(A) obsequies.
(B) onomatopoeias.
(C) homophones.
(D) synonyms.

12. The word that refers to a verb and its related words in a clause or sentence is a

(A) verb clause.
(B) noun clause.
(C) predicate.
(D) postulate.

13. A first stage in the invention of the oral tradition and writing was

(A) painting visual symbols on rock formations to tell stories and record events.

(B) carving small tokens or "fetishes" to represent important people and places, and to record events.

(C) the use of hieroglyphs to tell stories and record events.

(D) communicated via elaborate pantomime gestures and movements.

14. The phonetic alphabet

   (A) represents sound in a visual fashion, assigning a simple iconic picture to each sound, allowing it to be represented visually.

   (B) represents sound in a way that each sound, regardless of language, has a distinct representation, independent of standard or traditional alphabet.

   (C) represents a lack of effort on the part of orthographies to dissect each linguistic sound phonetically, rather than visually.

   (D) represents an antiquated culture whose linguistic properties have long since been lost to time.

15. All languages contain two basic sound types. What are they?

   (A) Affricates and fricatives
   (B) Flotsam and jetsam
   (C) Phrases and clauses
   (D) Consonants and vowels

16. A language, now extinct, used during the Middle Ages by traders who did not share a common language to communicate among themselves while in Mediterranean ports is

   (A) an indigenous language.
   (B) a pidgin language.
   (C) Pig Latin.
   (D) Lingua Franca.

17. According to the principle of language acquisition, the first aspects of maturation required for a child's language acquisition are the ability to

   (A) form and hold mental pictures, that is, the ability to form, recognize, and use symbols.

   (B) form and generate basic vowel and consonant sounds, such as "dada" and "mama."

   (C) grasp abstract concepts and special relations, for example, pointing at a glass of water when thirsty.

   (D) generalize abstract concepts such as water in a cup, in the bathtub, and from a faucet.

18. According to the National Institute for Literacy, parents and educators can encourage the learning of indirect vocabulary by

   (A) reading aloud to the student, regardless of age or grade level.

   (B) showing pictures to your children and mimicking the sounds associated with those pictures.

   (C) using television and videos designed for young people's learning.

   (D) using classical music.

19. According to the National Institute for Literacy, a program of systematic phonics instruction

   (A) "clearly identifies a carefully selected and useful set of letter–sound relationships and then organizes the introduction of those relationships into logical instructional sequences."

   (B) "clearly articulates a random series of ideas, needs, and principles based primarily on the basic needs of learners."

   (C) "clearly acknowledges that learners independently learn language at various levels and stages of development, thus relieving educators and parents from the responsibility of engaging the learner in conversations."

   (D) "clearly recognizes the need for learners to express their immediate wants and needs in a verbal fashion and to establish a basic cause-and-effect relationship in the child's mind."

20. Which of the following sentences contains an example of a gerund?

    (A) Mother wouldn't say whether we could go to the game on Saturday night.
    (B) Mother walks us to school every day.
    (C) Mother objected to our swimming only 30 minutes after eating.
    (D) Mother thinks I am the star of the team, even though I was picked last.

21. Which of the following sentences includes a prepositional phrase serving as an adverb?

    (A) The police followed the robber until they had enough evidence to convict him.
    (B) The police followed the robber because they knew he was guilty.
    (C) The police followed the robber through the deserted city streets.
    (D) The police followed the robber while his trail was still hot.

22. Literary modernism, seen in works such as T. S. Eliot's "The Waste Land," is an early twentieth-century style of literature involving which of the following essentials?

    (A) A deliberate and radical attempt to reconnect with romanticized Greco-Roman iconic representations and ideologies, including the use of Latin, ancient Greek, and ancient Hebrew
    (B) A deliberate and conscious attempt to represent the early twentieth-century as a period of artistic beauty, social harmony, and historical value
    (C) A deliberate and conscious attempt to avoid early twentieth-century iconic representations and to focus more on the Italian Renaissance period as one of inspiration and social salvation
    (D) A deliberate and radical break with traditional literary conventions by presenting fragmented, opaque, and convoluted images juxtaposed with romanticized classical images and ideologies

23. Sonnets and some other forms of English poetry, such as Thomas Gray's "Elegy Written in a Country Churchyard," are in iambic pentameter. What is iambic pentameter?

    (A) Five lines of poetry with each line consisting of five stressed syllables followed by five light syllables
    (B) Five feet per line of one light syllable followed by a stressed syllable
    (C) A poem limited to five stanzas, with each stanza limited to five lines
    (D) One stressed syllable follow by a light syllable appearing in every fifth word per line

24. Anglo-Saxon literary works, such as *Beowulf*, use kennings to enhance literary style and effect. What is a kenning?

    (A) An archaic form of medieval allegory used to compensate for the limited vocabulary and education of minstrels, poets, and other oral storytellers
    (B) A poetic phrase comprised of figurative language used as descriptive phrases in place of the ordinary name of something
    (C) An ambiguous medieval cryptogram that contemporary scholars are still trying to decipher
    (D) An extended poem in which a heroic figure embarks upon an extended quest in search of some mythical object or creature

25. Courtly love is

    (A) a convention of lyric poetry and chivalric romances whereby a lover, usually a bachelor knight, idealizes and suffers agonies on behalf of his unrequited love interest.
    (B) a convention of romance novels and cavalier and metaphysical poetry, whereby a lover, usually an enamored poet, must separate from his love interest, causing him great anguish.

(C) a convention of premedieval and medieval poetry whereby courtesans and others of high-ranking social status are instructed on the proper behaviors of the king's court.

(D) a convention of children's literature that strives to teach proper behaviors and social etiquette for both domestic and social situations.

Read the following paragraph and then answer questions 26 through 29.

Call me Ishmael. Some years ago—never mind how long precisely—having little or no money in my purse, and nothing particular to interest me on shore, I thought I would sail about a little and see the watery part of the world. It is a way I have of driving off the spleen, and regulating the circulation. Whenever I find myself growing grim about the mouth; whenever it is a damp, drizzly November in my soul; whenever I find myself involuntarily pausing before coffin warehouses, and bringing up the rear of every funeral I meet; and especially whenever my hypos get such an upper hand of me, that it requires a strong moral principle to prevent me from deliberately stepping into the street, and methodically knocking people's hats off—then, I account it high time to get to sea as soon as I can. This is my substitute for pistol and ball. With a philosophical flourish Cato throws himself upon his sword; I quietly take to the ship. There is nothing surprising in this. If they but knew it, almost all men in their degree, some time or other, cherish very nearly the same feelings towards the ocean with me.

26. The overall tone of the paragraph is

(A) slow and/or plodding.
(B) angry and/or resentful.
(C) somber and/or melancholy.
(D) jocular and/or optimistic.

27. What does the narrator mean when he says, "This is my substitute for pistol and ball"?

(A) He means that if he doesn't get to the sea right away, he will kill someone.
(B) He means that if he must go to sea one more time, he will kill someone.
(C) He means that if he must go to sea one more time, he will kill himself.
(D) He means that if he doesn't get to the sea right away, he will kill himself.

28. In what style is the paragraph written?

(A) Prosaic
(B) Poetic
(C) Polymorphic
(D) Parallel

29. When the narrator refers to "a damp, drizzly November in my soul," he is using what type of figure of speech?

(A) Simile
(B) Paradigm
(C) Trope
(D) Metaphor

30. Alliteration is

(A) the repetition of a vowel sound occurring at the beginning of a word or the repetition of a vowel sound within a word.
(B) the repetition of a consonant sound occurring at the beginning of a word or the repetition of a consonant sound within a word.
(C) a repetitive vowel sound occurring at the end of a word or within a word.

(D) is the repetition of a consonant (consonance) or the repetition of a vowel (assonance).

31. A concrete poem

(A) avoids the use of figurative phrases and ambiguous language and uses symbolic representations that are more literal or concrete.

(B) is structured around recurring refrains or poetic choruses and results in a poem that sounds more musical or melodic.

(C) may have the visual shape of their textual content.

(D) was written at the beginning of the Industrial Revolution and lauds the sociopolitical benefits of steel and concrete.

32. Poetry consisting of unrhymed iambic pentameter is called

(A) blank verse.
(B) free verse.
(C) ballad meter.
(D) scansion.

33. When William Shakespeare's Richard III first speaks his thoughts aloud or Christopher Marlowe's Dr. Faustus mutters an extended expository "meditation," these characters are actually performing a

(A) cacophony.
(B) syllogism.
(C) epiphany.
(D) soliloquy.

Read the following passage and then answer questions 34 and 35.

Shall I compare thee to a summer's day?

Thou art more lovely and more temperate: Rough winds do shake the darling buds of May, And summer's lease hath all too short a date: Sometime too hot the eye of heaven shines, And often is his gold complexion dimm'd; And every fair from fair sometime declines, By chance or nature's changing course untrimm'd; But thy eternal summer shall not fade, Nor lose possession of that fair thou owest; Nor shall Death brag thou wander'st in his shade, When in eternal lines to time thou growest:

So long as men can breathe or eyes can see, So long lives this and this gives life to thee.

—William Shakespeare, *Sonnet XVIII*, 1593–1599

34. Sonnets, whether Shakespearean or Petrarchan, contain a heroic couplet. Which two lines in the sonnet comprise the heroic couplet?

(A) "So long as men can breathe or eyes can see, So long lives this and this gives life to thee"

(B) "Nor lose possession of that fair thou owest; Nor shall Death brag thou wander'st in his shade"

(C) "And often is his gold complexion dimm'd; And every fair from fair sometime declines"

(D) "By chance or nature's changing course untrimm'd; But thy eternal summer shall not fade"

35. Which answer best summarizes the theme of Shakespeare's sonnet?

    (A) The metaphors relating to nature suggest that love is a part of nature (a naturally occurring phenomenon of the natural world) and, therefore like Nature itself, transcends death, existing eternally.

    (B) The references to "rough winds," "untrimm'd," and "Death" suggest a tempestuous theme: one of a love relationship that is both difficult and challenging, but perhaps ultimately worth the effort.

    (C) The narrator's hurried tone and references to the passing of time suggests, like Andrew Marvell's enamored plea "To His Coy Mistress," the theme of carpe diem, or the need to hurry up and "seize the day" when it comes to love and intimacy.

    (D) The poet's use of extended apostrophe suggests a self-conscious artistic endeavor whereby the theme is one of aesthetic ability rather than the conceptual theme of love and relationships.

Read the following sonnet and then answer questions 36 to 38.

> Loving in truth, and fain in verse my love to show, That she (dear She) might take some pleasure of my pain: Pleasure might cause her read, reading might make her know, Knowledge might pity win, and pity grace obtain; I sought fit words to paint the blackest face of woe, Studying inventions fine, her wits to entertain: Oft turning others' leaves, to see if thence would flow Some fresh and fruitful showers upon my sun-burn'd brain. But words came halting forth, wanting Invention's stay, Invention, Nature's child, fled step-dame Study's blows, And others' feet still seem'd but strangers in my way.

Thus, great with child to speak, and helpless in my throes, Biting my truant pen, beating myself for spite—"Fool," said my Muse to me, "look in thy heart and write." —Sir Philip Sidney, *Astrophel and Stella*, canto 1, 1877

36. What type of writing is the poem?

    (A) It is a Shakespearean sonnet because the structure, style, and tone of the language are definitely seventeenth-century British.

    (B) It is a Shakespearean sonnet because the thematic idea is expanded in three quatrains.

    (C) It is a Petrarchan sonnet because the metaphors and rhyme scheme are of a more classical nature.

    (D) It is a Petrarchan sonnet because the thematic idea is presented in an octave followed by a sestet.

37. When the narrator says, "helpless in my throes," what does he mean by "throes"?

    (A) Spasms of pain; the effects of an upheaval or struggle

    (B) Fits of uncontrollable laughter; a form of hysteria

    (C) Intense feelings of frustration, isolation, and/or loneliness

    (D) Another word "for dwellings," "rooms," "lodgings," and the like

38. The narrator declares, "great with child to speak." What does he mean?

    (A) The woman that he loves is pregnant and thus, unobtainable.

    (B) For the poet, reciting his poem is a form of "childbirth."

    (C) Children speak the truth while adults tend to corrupt the truth.

    (D) Pregnancy makes the poet's love interest even more beautiful and desirable.

39. The literary periods known as modern and postmodern first emerged as far back as

   (A) 1822.
   (B) 1558.
   (C) 1922.
   (D) 1776.

40. What is the literary term for a fictional work blending elements of fantasy with ordinary situations, people, and events?

   (A) Metafiction or magical realism
   (B) Nouveau Roman or antinovel
   (C) Social or historical novel
   (D) Gothic romance or prose romance

41. Novels that accentuate elements of medieval castles, dungeons, hidden passages with hidden chambers, and the exploits of a sexually perverse, sadistic villain trying to impose himself upon an innocent young maiden are more commonly referred to as

   (A) grotesque.
   (B) episodic.
   (C) Gothic.
   (D) epistolary.

42. These works are examples of satire:

   (A) *Gulliver's Travels* and *Catch 22*.
   (B) *The Old Man and the Sea* and *Equus*.
   (C) *A Raisin in the Sun* and *An American Tragedy*.
   (D) *War and Peace* and *Anna Karenina*.

Read this famous first line from Charles Dickens' *A Tale of Two Cities* and answer questions 43 through 47.

> It was the best of times, it was the worst of times; it was the age of wisdom, it was the age of foolishness; it was the epoch of belief, it was the epoch of incredulity; it was the season of Light, it was the season of Darkness; it was the spring of hope, it was the winter of despair; we had everything before us, we had nothing before us; we were all going directly to Heaven, we were all going the other way.

43. Dickens characterizes the age by presenting a serious of

   (A) symbols.
   (B) paradoxes.
   (C) clichés.
   (D) allusions.

44. This sentence would be classified as

   (A) simple.
   (B) complex.
   (C) compound.
   (D) compound-complex.

45. Twelve of the fourteen independent clauses in this sentence use

   (A) a linking verb followed by a predicate noun or a predicate adjective.
   (B) an action verb followed by a direct object.
   (C) the imperative.
   (D) inversion.

46. The "times" Dickens is speaking of in this novel are

    (A) the Elizabethan era during Shakespeare's life.
    (B) the late eighteenth century at the time of the French Revolution.
    (C) the Victorian era during the industrial revolution.
    (D) the early twentieth century just prior to World War I.

47. The vast comparisons in the passage indicate that the speaker is describing

    (A) a placid historical time period.
    (B) a time of extreme political upheaval.
    (C) a public event.
    (D) a time when anything was possible.

48. While not in direct competition, some seventeenth-century poets, such as John Donne and Andrew Marvell, coexisted with another "school" of poets, which included such alumni as Robert Herrick and Ben Jonson. What is the name of the school of poets of which Herrick and Jonson were members?

    (A) The graveyard school
    (B) The metaphysical school
    (C) The Shakespearean school
    (D) The Cavalier school

49. Thomas Gray's "Elegy Written in a Country Churchyard" (1751) is considered a masterpiece of which school?

    (A) The graveyard poets
    (B) The Pre-Raphaelite poets
    (C) The Homeric poets
    (D) The romantic poets

50. In the mid-1800s, English artisans, including Dante Gabriel Rossetti and his sister Christina, developed a group with the purpose of returning to the truthfulness and spirit of the period before the Italian Renaissance. This group was the

    (A) Gregorian poets.
    (B) modern poets.
    (C) Pre-Raphaelite poets.
    (D) romantic poets.

51. In his poem "Holy Thursday (II)," William Blake denounces the fate of poor children in eighteenth-century England.

    > Is this a holy thing to see
    > In a rich and fruitful land,
    > Babes reduced to misery,
    > Fed with cold and usurous hand?
    > Is that trembling cry a song?
    > Can it be a song of joy?
    > And so many children poor?

    This excerpt is characterized by Blake's use of

    (A) anaphora.
    (B) rhetorical questions.
    (C) apostrophe.
    (D) allusion.

52. Rather than interpreting a text separated from its historical context, what form of literary criticism considers the time period during which the author created it?

    (A) New historicism
    (B) Deconstruction
    (C) Marxism
    (D) Poststructuralism

53. Miracle plays, morality plays, and interludes are types of

    (A) early Edwardian drama, written in a variety of verse and forms.
    (B) late romantic drama, written in a variety of verse and forms.
    (C) early contemporary drama, written in a variety of verse and forms.
    (D) late medieval drama, written in a variety of verse and forms.

54. Mary Ann Evans used the pen name of

    (A) Samuel Langhorne Clemens.
    (B) George Eliot.
    (C) Ellis Bell.
    (D) Currer Bell.

55. The Great Vowel Shift is a feature of the

    (A) Middle English period.
    (B) Old English period.
    (C) Renaissance English period.
    (D) Commonwealth period.

56. Entries in a book's contents pages generally have

    (A) an alphabetical arrangement.
    (B) both concrete and abstract arrangements.
    (C) linear and recursive order.
    (D) order of occurrence in the book.

Read the following paragraphs, which follow from the Charles Dickens' quote on page 228, and then answer question 57.

—in short, the period was so far like the present period, that some of its noisiest authorities insisted on its being received, for good or for evil, in the superlative degree of comparison only.

There were a king with a large jaw, and a queen with a plain face, on the throne of England; there were a king with a large jaw, and a queen with a fair face, on the throne of France. In both countries it was clearer than crystal to the lords of the State preserves of loaves and fishes, that things in general were settled for ever.

57. The last sentence of the passage

    (A) mocks the self-assuredness of the governments of England and France.
    (B) comments on the horrible poverty of the two nations.
    (C) most likely foreshadows an upcoming famine or drought.
    (D) attacks the two governments for neglecting the poor, hungry masses.

Read the following passage and then answer question 58 and 59.

The sun showed its face just as the clock struck 7:00 a.m. The drip, drip, dripping of the rain against the sidewalk below was a thing of the past. The ducks waddled away to find the grubs that were waiting behind the shrubs. Billy was eager to begin his day at the lake.

58. The best example of onomatopoeia is

    (A) the word "drip."
    (B) the word "waddled."
    (C) the word "grub."
    (D) the word "showed."

59. An example of personification is

    (A) "waddled away."
    (B) "were waiting."
    (C) "showed its face."
    (D) "begin his day at the lake."

60. *Paradise Lost*, *Beowulf*, *The Iliad*, and *The Odyssey* are all examples of

    (A) dramatic poetry.
    (B) lyric poetry.
    (C) elegies.
    (D) epic poetry.

61. Identify the structure of the following sentence from Flannery O'Connor's short story, A *Good Man Is Hard to Find*:

    The grandmother had the peculiar feeling that the bespectacled man was someone she knew.

    (A) Simple
    (B) Compound
    (C) Complex
    (D) Compound-complex

Read the following passage and then answer questions 62 and 63.

America's national bird, the mighty bald eagle, is being threatened by a new menace. Once decimated by hunters and loss of habitat, the bald eagle is facing a new danger, suspected to be intentional poisoning by livestock ranchers. Authorities have found animal carcasses injected with restricted pesticides. These carcasses allegedly are placed to attract and kill predators such as the bald eagle in an effort to preserve young grazing animals. It appears that the eagle is being threatened again by the consummate predator, humans.

62. Which sentence would be considered the topic sentence of this paragraph?

    (A) America's national bird, the mighty bald eagle, is being threatened by a new menace.
    (B) Once decimated by hunters and loss of habitat, the bald eagle is facing a new danger, suspected to be intentional poisoning by livestock ranchers.
    (C) Authorities have found animal carcasses injected with restricted pesticides.
    (D) These carcasses allegedly are placed to attract and kill predators such as the bald eagle in an effort to preserve young grazing animals.

63. The author's attitude is one of

    (A) uncaring observation.
    (B) concerned interest.
    (C) uniform acceptance.
    (D) suspicion.

64. An advertisement for Chew-ee Gum—"the gum that most superheroes chew in times of stress"—would be an example of

    (A) expository writing.
    (B) narrative writing.
    (C) explanatory writing.
    (D) persuasive writing.

Answer questions 65 and 67 based upon this excerpt from a poem by Emily Dickinson.

Because I could not stop for Death—
He kindly stopped for me—
The carriage held but just Ourselves—
And Immortality.

65. In this stanza, Emily Dickinson expresses her attitude toward death through

    (A) allusion.
    (B) metaphor.
    (C) personification.
    (D) analogy.

66. This stanza is an example of a

    (A) trochaic tetrameter.
    (B) free verse.
    (C) ballad meter.
    (D) blank verse.

67. This stanza is an example of a

    (A) couplet.
    (B) quatrain.
    (C) refrain.
    (D) sonnet.

Answer questions 68 and 69 based on this stanza from *Tithonus* by Alfred, Lord Tennyson.

The woods decay, the woods decay and fall,
The vapors weep their burthen to the ground,
Man comes and tills the field and lies beneath,
And after many a summer dies the swan.

68. The meter of this stanza is primarily

    (A) trochaic tetrameter.
    (B) dactylic trimeter.
    (C) iambic pentameter.
    (D) anapestic pentameter.

69. This stanza is an example of

    (A) end-stopped line.
    (B) enjambment.
    (C) caesura.
    (D) run-on lines.

Consider the following passage from *Jane Eyre* by Charlotte Brontë, in which Jane is asked if she would like to go to school. Answer questions 70 through 73.

Again I reflected: I scarcely knew what school was; Bessie sometimes spoke of it as a place where young ladies sat in the stocks, wore backboards, and were expected to be exceedingly genteel and precise: John Reed hated his school, and abused his master; but John Reed's tastes were no rule for mine, and if Bessie's accounts of school discipline (gathered from the young ladies of a family where she had lived before coming to Gateshead) were somewhat appalling, her details of certain accomplishments attained by these same young ladies were, I thought, equally attractive. She boasted of beautiful paintings of landscapes and flowers by them executed; of songs they could sing and pieces they could play, or purses they could net, of French books they could translate; till my spirit was moved to emulation as I listened. Besides, school would be a complete change: it implied a long journey, an entire separation from Gateshead, an entrance into a new life.

70. The method of development of this passage is

    (A) narration.
    (B) description.
    (C) cause and effect.
    (D) compare/contrast.

71. The tone of this passage can best be described as

    (A) cynical.
    (B) sentimental.
    (C) didactic.
    (D) conflicted.

72. Jane, the title character who triumphs over her difficult past, is considered to be the novel's

    (A) protagonist.
    (B) antagonist.
    (C) foil.
    (D) static character.

73. The novel, *Jane Eyre*, was first published in Great Britain in the

    (A) Elizabethan era.
    (B) Romantic era.
    (C) Victorian era.
    (D) Modern era.

74. Consider the following:

    "Everyone should bring their paper to the front of the room and begin working on the new assignment."

    Which of the following statements about the sentence is true?

    (A) The sentence is an example of diction.
    (B) The sentence foreshadows what is to come.
    (C) The setting of the writing is clearly a classroom for future police officers.
    (D) The sentence is an analogy.

Read the following passages and then answer questions 75 through 77.

Paragraph I. Once upon a time and a very good time it was there was a moocow coming down along the road and this moocow that was coming down along the road met a nicens little boy named baby tuckoo …

Paragraph II. And thus have these naked Nantucketers, these sea hermits, issuing from their ant-hill in the sea, overrun and conquered the watery world like so many Alexanders …

Paragraph III. A large rose tree stood near the entrance of the garden: the roses growing on it were white, but there were three gardeners at it, busily painting them red. Alice thought this a very curious thing, and she went nearer to watch them, and, just as she came up to them, she heard one of them say "Look out now, Five!"

Paragraph IV. Emma was not required, by any subsequent discovery, to retract her ill opinion of Mrs. Elton. Her observation had been pretty correct. Such as Mrs. Elton appeared to her on this second interview, such she appeared whenever they met again: self-important, presuming, familiar, ignorant, and ill-bred. She had a little beauty and a little accomplishment, but so little judgment that she thought herself coming with superior knowledge of the world, to enliven and improve a country neighborhood …

75. Which passage makes use of allusion?

    (A) Paragraph I
    (B) Paragraph II
    (C) Paragraph III
    (D) Paragraph IV

76. Which passage employs a distinct voice to imitate the speech of a character?

    (A) Paragraph I
    (B) Paragraph II
    (C) Paragraph III
    (D) Paragraph IV

77. Which passage is most likely taken from a novel of manners from the nineteenth century?

    (A) Paragraph I
    (B) Paragraph II
    (C) Paragraph III
    (D) Paragraph IV

78. The narrative perspective paragraph IV is

    (A) first-person point of view.
    (B) third-person limited point of view.
    (C) third-person omniscient point of view.
    (D) third-person objective point of view.

79. Consider Romeo's description of love, in Shakespeare's *Romeo and Juliet*.

    > Feather of lead, bright smoke, cold
    >   fire, sick health,
    > Still-waking sleep, that is not what it is.

    These lines are characterized by Shakespeare's use of

    (A) understatement.
    (B) hyperbole.
    (C) oxymorons.
    (D) puns.

Consider this excerpt from Stephen Crane's short story *The Open Boat* as you answer questions 80 through 82.

> But the thing did not then leave the vicinity of the boat. Ahead or astern, on one side or the other, at intervals long or short, fled the long sparkling streak, and there was to be heard the whirroo of the dark fin.

80. In the second sentence, Crane's syntax combines both

    (A) parallelism and inversion.
    (B) a periodic sentence and the imperative.
    (C) a cumulative sentence and a compound sentence.
    (D) parallelism and an interrogative sentence.

81. In the phrase "sparkling streak," Crane combines both

    (A) a metaphor and onomatopoeia.
    (B) an allusion and alliteration.
    (C) personification and diction.
    (D) imagery and alliteration.

82. The word "whirroo" is an example of

    (A) onomatopoeia.
    (B) an abstract noun.
    (C) assonance.
    (D) consonance.

83. Stephen Crane is considered part of which literary movement?

    (A) American Romanticism
    (B) Naturalism
    (C) Transcendentalism
    (D) Rationalism

Consider the following lines from Robert Browning's *Soliloquy of the Spanish Cloister* as you answer questions 84 and 85.

> Gr-r-r—there go, my heart's abhorrence!
>   Water you damned flower-pots, do!
> If hate killed men, Brother Lawrence,
>   God's blood, would not mine kill you!
> What? your myrtle-bush wants trimming?
>   Oh, that rose has prior claims—
> Needs its leaden vase filled brimming?
> Hell dry you up with its flames!

84. In this poem, the speaker's tone can best be described as

    (A) irate.
    (B) didactic.
    (C) condescending.
    (D) facetious.

85. The poem, called a soliloquy, implies that the speaker

    (A) is alone, and Brother Lawrence is not present to hear him.
    (B) is addressing someone other than Brother Lawrence.
    (C) is directly addressing Brother Lawrence.
    (D) is composing his thoughts in a letter to Brother Lawrence.

86. In the last line, "Hell dry you up with its flames," Browning is using

    (A) understatement.
    (B) hyperbole.
    (C) inflated language.
    (D) circumlocution.

87. Which of the following best defines the sequential steps in gathering data and documenting the results in a formal paper?

    (A) Develop a formal thesis statement; construct an outline; begin collecting data, taking notes, and constructing bibliography cards; write the draft; revise the work; prepare the final paper.
    (B) Develop a working topic for research; begin data collection; take notes and prepare a first draft; prepare a bibliography and an outline; edit and revise the paper.
    (C) Develop a working topic for research; begin collecting data, taking notes, and indicating used sources; prepare an outline and first draft—with a bibliography; edit and revise.
    (D) Formalize the title of the paper; begin a working outline; locate sources for data that might be relevant to the topic; begin a draft; note sources used; prepare the bibliography; write the paper; edit and revise.

88. Which of the following is NOT a frequent means of referencing materials used in a paper?

    (A) MLA citations.
    (B) APA citations.
    (C) CMS citations.
    (D) AHA citations.

89. The method of citation often associated with the sciences is

    (A) MLA.
    (B) APA.
    (C) CMS.
    (D) AHA citations.

90. "Ask not what your country can do for you; ask what you can do for your country." This famous line from John F. Kennedy's presidential inaugural address is an example of a

    (A) periodic sentence.
    (B) cumulative sentence.
    (C) balanced sentence.
    (D) simple sentence.

91. An important technique for proper literary assessment is to

    (A) have students read and reread various texts until they comprehend the symbolic representations.
    (B) have students write what they have read.
    (C) watch and document students, noting the ones who are eager to read.
    (D) watch students' performances in authentic learning situations.

Consider the following passage from Mary Shelley's novel *Frankenstein* as you answer questions 92 through 97.

It was a dreary night of November that I beheld the accomplishment of my toils. With an anxiety that almost amounted to agony, I collected the instruments of life around me, that I might infuse a spark of being into the lifeless thing that lay at my feet. It was already one in the morning; the rain pattered dismally against the panes, and my candle was nearly burnt out, when, by the glimmer of the half-extinguished light, I saw the dull yellow eye of the creature open; it breathed hard, and a convulsive motion agitated its limbs.

92. The dominant mode of exposition in this excerpt is

(A) narration.
(B) description.
(C) process analysis.
(D) cause and effect.

93. The point of view is

(A) first-person.
(B) third-person omniscient.
(C) third-person limited.
(D) third-person objective.

94. The tone of the passage is best described as

(A) objective and detached.
(B) fearful and ominous.
(C) confident and celebratory.
(D) arrogant and condescending.

95. The diction of the passage can be characterized as

(A) erudite and scholarly.
(B) scientific.
(C) educated but conversational.
(D) coarse and colloquial.

96. Shelley's sentence, "With an anxiety that almost amounted to agony, I collected the instruments of life around me, that I might infuse a spark of being into the lifeless thing that lay at my feet," can be characterized as

(A) simple.
(B) compound.
(C) complex.
(D) compound-complex.

97. The main verb in the above sentence is

(A) amounted to.
(B) collected.
(C) infuse.
(D) lay.

98. In the following lines, what does the stage direction "Aside" mean?

King: Take thy fair hour, Laertes; time be thine, And thy best graces spend it at thy will! But now, my cousin Hamlet, and my son,—

Hamlet: (Aside) A little more than kin, and less than kind.

(A) The actor steps aside to make room for other action on stage.
(B) The actor directly addresses only one particular actor on stage.
(C) The actor directly addresses the audience, while out of hearing of the other actors.
(D) The previous speaker steps aside to make room for this actor.

99. A poem necessarily includes

(A) verse.
(B) rhythm.
(C) rhyme.
(D) onomatopoeia.

Read Carl Sandburg's poem "Fog" and then answer questions 100 and 101.

Fog

The fog comes
on little cat feet
It sits looking
over harbor and city
on silent haunches
and then moves on.

—Carl Sandburg (1919)

100. "Fog" is an example of

(A) an elegy.
(B) blank verse.
(C) anode.
(D) free verse.

101. Sandburg characterizes the fog using

(A) personification
(B) a paradox.
(C) symbolism.
(D) a metaphor.

Read the following poem and then answer questions 102 and 103.

Now thou art dead, no eyes shall ever see,
For shape and service, spaniel like to thee.
This shall my love do, give thy sad death one
Tear, that deserves of me a million.

102. The above poem is an example of a(n)

(A) allegory.
(B) elegy.

(C) ballad.
(D) kenning.

103. Lines 3 to 4 of the poem contain an example of

(A) enjambment.
(B) personification.
(C) metaphor.
(D) simile.

Read the following passage and then answer questions 104 and 105.

Study is like the heaven's glorious sun,
That will not be deep-searched with
     saucy looks.
Small have continual plodders won
Save base authority from others' books.
These earthly godfathers of heaven's
     lights,
That give a name to every fixed star
Have no more profit of their shining
     nights
Than those who walk and wot not what
     they are.

104. The speaker of these lines is most likely a

(A) student.
(B) professor.
(C) clergyman.
(D) thief.

105. The lines "Small have continual plodders won/Save base authority from others' books" mean

(A) only one's opinions are important, not facts found in books.
(B) study is long and tedious, but ultimately rewarding.
(C) knowledge and authority are eventually given to those who pursue them.
(D) all that is gained by study are the simple and worthless opinions of others.

Read the following passage and then answer question 106.

There was a time when I went every day into a church, a girl I was in love with knelt there in prayer for half an hour in the evening and I was able to look at her in peace.

Once when she had not come and I was reluctantly eyeing the other supplicants, I noticed a young fellow who had thrown his whole lean length along the floor. Every now and then he clutched his head as hard as he could and sighing loudly beat it in his upturned palms on the stone flags.

106. By using the term "supplicants," the author implies that

(A) everyone in the church is there to celebrate mass.
(B) everyone in the church is devout.
(C) everyone in the church is guilty of something.
(D) everyone in the church is a hypocrite.

Read the following lines from Lord Byron's "Stanzas" and then answer questions 107 through 110.

When a man hath no freedom to fight for at home, Let him combat for that of his neighbors;
Let him think of the glories of Greece and of Rome,
And get knocked on the head for his labors.

107. The writer uses

(A) an elaborate rhyme scheme.
(B) a simple rhyme scheme.
(C) free verse.
(D) denotation without connotation.

108. The poem is

(A) sarcastic.
(B) humorous.
(C) a cliché.
(D) a product of the medieval period.

109. Byron later joined a freedom-fighting group in Greece and died in 1824 of a fever. This event is

(A) ironic.
(B) humorous.
(C) a hyperbole.
(D) comedic.

110. Line 2 of the poem uses

(A) internal rhyme.
(B) alliteration.
(C) a metaphor.
(D) a cliché.

111. A popular theme in literature is

(A) survival of the unfittest.
(B) rite of passage.
(C) reversal of fortune.
(D) All of the above

112. Which of the following are considered picaresque novels?

(A) *The Adventures of Huckleberry Finn* and *Don Quixote*
(B) *Wuthering Heights* and *A Tale of Two Cities*
(C) *The Great Gatsby* and *To Kill a Mockingbird*
(D) *The Lord of the Flies* and *Frankenstein*

113. Abraham Lincoln credited this abolitionist novel published in 1852 for starting the Civil War.

(A) *The Adventures of Huckleberry Finn*
(B) *Native Son*

(C) *Uncle Tom's Cabin*
(D) *The Red Badge of Courage*

114. Which of these pairs of works were products of the 1700s?

(A) *Little Women* and *Little Men*
(B) *A Wonder-Book* and *The House of the Seven Gables*
(C) *The Last of the Mohicans*, *The Deerslayer*, and *A Wonder-Book*
(D) None of the above

115. Which American writers are considered Transcendentalists?

(A) Edgar Allan Poe and Nathaniel Hawthorne
(B) Washington Irving and James Fenimore Cooper
(C) Robert Frost and ee cummings
(D) Ralph Waldo Emerson and Henry David Thoreau

116. Which American poet first established free verse as a poetic form?

(A) Walt Whitman
(B) Henry Wadsworth Longfellow
(C) William Cullen Bryant
(D) Oliver Wendell Holmes

117. *Poor Richard's Almanack* was the work of

(A) Ben Jonson.
(B) William Caxton.
(C) Benjamin Franklin.
(D) many British writers.

118. Characters about which the reader knows most of the unique details are

(A) stereotypical.
(B) flat.
(C) round.
(D) stock.

119. Two works that the writers meant for adults of the 1700s but that young people promptly adopted were

(A) *Robinson Crusoe* and *Gulliver's Travels*.
(B) *Little Women* and *Treasure Island*.
(C) *Rip Van Winkle* and *The Pathfinder*.
(D) *Kidnapped* and *A Christmas Carol*.

120. Which of the following works are examples of dystopic literature?

(A) *The Things They Carried* and *Heart is a Lonely Hunter*
(B) *1984* and *A Handmaid's Tale*
(C) *The Sun Also Rises* and *The Grapes of Wrath*
(D) *The Invisible Man* and *The Sound and the Fury*

Praxis English Assessment: Content Knowledge (0041)

Answer Explanations
for Practice Test 2

ANSWER KEY FOR PRACTICE TEST 2 (0041)

1. (D)	25. (A)	49. (A)	73. (C)	97. (B)
2. (C)	26. (C)	50. (C)	74. (A)	98. (C)
3. (A)	27. (D)	51. (B)	75. (B)	99. (A)
4. (C)	28. (A)	52. (A)	76. (A)	100. (D)
5. (B)	29. (D)	53. (D)	77. (D)	101. (D)
6. (D)	30. (D)	54. (B)	78. (B)	102. (B)
7. (B)	31. (C)	55. (A)	79. (C)	103. (A)
8. (B)	32. (A)	56. (D)	80. (A)	104. (A)
9. (C)	33. (D)	57. (A)	81. (D)	105. (D)
10. (A)	34. (A)	58. (A)	82. (A)	106. (C)
11. (D)	35. (A)	59. (C)	83. (B)	107. (B)
12. (C)	36. (D)	60. (D)	84. (A)	108. (A)
13. (A)	37. (A)	61. (C)	85. (A)	109. (A)
14. (B)	38. (B)	62. (A)	86. (B)	110. (A)
15. (D)	39. (C)	63. (B)	87. (C)	111. (D)
16. (D)	40. (A)	64. (D)	88. (D)	112. (A)
17. (A)	41. (C)	65. (C)	89. (B)	113. (C)
18. (A)	42. (A)	66. (C)	90. (C)	114. (D)
19. (A)	43. (B)	67. (B)	91. (D)	115. (D)
20. (C)	44. (C)	68. (C)	92. (A)	116. (A)
21. (C)	45. (A)	69. (C)	93. (A)	117. (C)
22. (D)	46. (B)	70. (D)	94. (B)	118. (C)
23. (B)	47. (D)	71. (D)	95. (C)	119. (A)
24. (B)	48. (D)	72. (A)	96. (C)	120. (B)

PRACTICE TEST 2 (0041): PROGRESS CHART

Reading and Understanding ____/77

5	22	23	24	25	27	29	30	31	32	33	34	35

36	37	38	39	40	41	42	43	46	47	48	49	50

51	52	53	58	59	60	65	66	67	68	69	71	72

73	75	76	77	78	79	81	82	83	85	86	91	92

93	94	95	98	99	101	102	103	104	105	106	107	108

109	110	111	112	113	114	115	116	117	118	119	120

Language and Linguistics ____/18

6	7	8	9	10	11	12	13	14	15	16	17	18

19	20	21	44	45	54	61	74	80	90	96	97

Composition and Rhetoric ____/18

1	2	3	4	26	28	55	56	57	62	63	64	70

84	87	88	89	100

PRACTICE TEST 2 (0041): ANSWER EXPLANATIONS

1. (D)

A portfolio holds a collection of dated samples of a student's work over a period of time. The student can have a single portfolio for all subjects or separate portfolios for specific subjects. The work contained in a portfolio becomes an accurate representation of a student's progress. The portfolio may contain artwork by a student, but it is not limited to artwork; (A) is, therefore, not a suitable answer. The purpose of the portfolio is not to draw comparisons between students (B), nor is there necessarily a scale for grading the portfolio (C).

2. (C)

In the narrative report approach, teachers compose narrative reports that describe a student's strengths, weaknesses, behaviors, progress, and any other information to supplement the information that is conveyed in a report card. These reports are useful particularly if a parent cannot attend a parent-teacher conference, for example. Choice (A) is incorrect because it is the teacher, not the student, who describes a student's performance. It is not a formal report card (B); it can supplement the information on the report card. Choice (D) is also incorrect because narrative reports may substitute for parent teacher conferences.

3. (A)

A student's permanent record, which is a file containing all aspects of a student's background, should be discussed only with the student's parents, legal guardians, teachers, and school administrators. It is a highly personal and comprehensive student record. It may be discussed with the student's parents (B) and with the school administrators (C); discussions are not limited only to school administrators and parents (D). Teachers also have the right to discuss the student's record with previous teachers who may have information. Therefore, (B), (C), and (D) are incorrect.

4. (C)

John Dryden said in his "Discourse of Satire" (1693) that John Donne's poetry "affects the meta physics," meaning in a sense, that Donne epitomized and/or set the standards for this abstract, intellectualized, and idealized style of poetry. Metaphysics is a branch of philosophy that investigates reality principles that may transcend those of any particular science. The metaphysical poets were the British lyric poets of the seventeenth century; they shared an interest in metaphysics and ways of investigating, but they had no formal affiliation. Edmund Spenser (1552–1599), choice (A), wrote before the period of the metaphysical poets. An English poet, he wrote the epic poem "The Faerie Queen" to celebrate Elizabeth I. Robert Herrick (B) was a Cavalier poet of the seventeenth century; he supported King Charles I and did not use the metaphysical theme. Alfred, Lord Tennyson (1809–1892), choice (D), came after the metaphysical poets. He often used mythology—not metaphysics—as a basis for his poetry.

5. (B)

One of the virtues of using drama or theater with young people is that it challenges them to articulate clearly and to think independently and creatively. Many questions posed in drama or theater have no one right answer or interpretation. Using the same material in a variety of ways offers the following advantages: 1. Information is presented through multiple channels, thereby increasing opportunities for knowing. 2. Using different types of dramatic activities broadens both the appeal of and the learning opportunities inherent in the material. 3. Multiple formats increase opportunities to engage students and to address their learning styles. 4. Students can see that there are various ways of creating meaning and expressing ideas. Choice (A) is incorrect because there may not be only one correct way to use material. As the rationale for the correct answer implies, exploring content is one way to move students beyond the obvious and encourage them to use higher-level thinking skills. Choice (C) is incorrect because it requires a value judgment based upon personal preference; it is not grounded in fact. Likewise, (D) is incorrect because it reflects a value judgment that is without substance. Some students may learn more by directly participating in activities (kinesthetic learners); some may learn more by watching a performance (visual learners). Both creative drama activities and theater performances are educationally sound undertakings.

6. (D)

A morpheme is the smallest meaningful unit that a word can be broken into. "Cat," for example, cannot be broken into a smaller form and still have meaning. Two words combined together are compound words, not morphemes; (A) is inappropriate. A gerund, not a morpheme, is a word that changes from a verb to a noun when "-ing" is added, as in "swim/swimming;" (B) is not correct. Some nouns are irregular in the plural form, that is, the plural is formed by a new spelling—as in "mouse" to "mice"—rather than by adding "-s" or "-es." In such cases, the term irregular, not morpheme, is used; (C) is incorrect.

7. (B)

"Affixes" is a synonym for "bound morphemes." They attach to a root or stem morpheme. A prefix, such as "un-," attaches to the beginning of a word, while a suffix, such as "-ing," attaches to the end of a word. An affix does not necessarily give a word an opposite meaning; (A) is not appropriate. The definition prescribed in (C) is too restrictive to use for an affix; an affix may attach to a verb, but it may also attach to other parts of speech. Choice (D) is also too restrictive; an affix does not have to be a complete word—and it usually is not.

8. (B)

A diphthong is a vowel sound whose production requires the tongue to start in one place and move, or glide, to another; a diphthong contains two vowels. Choices (A) and (C) are incorrect because they refer to consonant, not vowel, sounds. Choice (D) is not the correct answer because it refers to one vowel sound; a diphthong contains two vowel sounds coming together, as in "oil."

9. (C)

Before the advent of writing, people passed along stories, culture, heritage, legends, and traditions by word of mouth, also known as oral tradition. Pictography, cartography or mapmaking, and Sanskrit were only parts in the development of the written language; (A), (B), and (D) are incorrect because they do not reflect stages before written language, but only stages in written language.

10. (A)

A metaphor is a figure of speech containing an implied comparison in which a word or phrase ordinarily and primarily used for one thing is applied to another; it involves calling something by a different name. Metaphors are used for thematic or dramatic effect. An example might be the line from Shakespeare, "All the world's a stage, and all the men and women merely players." Using the slang word "phat" as an adjective is not an example of a metaphor; (B) is inappropriate. Choice (C) defines onomatopoeia, and (D) describes a moral, not a metaphor.

11. (D)

Synonyms are various words that share the same or similar meaning, for example, city and metropolis. Obsequies (A) are funeral rites, onomatopoeias (B) are words whose sound represents their meaning ("drip," "splat"), and homophones (C) are words with the same pronunciation ("sea," "see") but different meanings.

12. (C)

The predicate expresses what the subject does, experiences, or is; it includes all the words related to the verb. For example, in the sentence "The fish swims," the predicate is simply "swims." However, in the sentence, "The partygoers celebrated wildly for a long time," the predicate is "celebrated wildly for a long time." Of course, the noun clause (B) and the verb clause (A) do not necessarily relate to the verb and its related words in a sentence. A postulate (D), or axiom, is a statement or a theory that one can use to prove other statements or other theorems.

13. (A)

Before the invention of a writing alphabet as we know it, people communicated by painting visu-al symbols on rock formations to tell stories and record events. The carving of small tokens, the use of hieroglyphs, and pantomiming were later stages in the writing process; (B), (C), and (D) followed (A) and, therefore, are not the correct answers.

14. (B)

The phonetic alphabet represents sounds as opposed to words. Thus, it is adaptable to writing in all languages; the mark indicates the represented sound. The phonetic alphabet does not use pictures; a rebus story, however, might use such pictures. (A) is not a good choice. The phonetic alphabet is a concerted effort to represent each sound through a visual symbol; (C) is, therefore, incorrect. The phonetic alphabet is not a representation of an antiquated culture, but instead a recent development; (D) is incorrect.

15. (D)

All languages contain vowel and consonant sound types. Consonants are formed by obstructing the flow of air as it passes from the lungs; vowel sounds are formed by allowing the flow of air to pass freely from the lungs. An affricative is a complex speech sound consisting of a stop consonant followed by a fricative—for example, the initial sounds of "child" and "joy." A fricative is a consonant, such as "f" or "s" in English, produced by the forcing of breath through a constricted passage. (A), then, is not the correct answer. Flotsam and jetsam are words that describe goods of potential value that have become floating debris; (B) is a poor choice. Phrases and clauses are parts of sentence structures, not sounds of the language; (C) is incorrect.

16. (D)

"Lingua Franca" was the mother of all pidgin languages and was used in the course of trade along the Mediterranean during the Middle Ages. It was never written and had no poetry or folktales. It was simply utilitarian, used to get the best price on a sale or purchase. It was the original "lingua franca," a term now used to indicate the language used to communicate among groups of countries or nations. Latin, French, and English have held that title at various times in history. An indigenous language is one that is native to a particular locale; (A) is not a fitting answer here. A pidgin language (B) is also a simplified form of speech; it may be a mixture of languages, reflect a rudimentary grammar and vocabulary, and serve as a means of communication between groups with different first or native languages. Pidgin is the term for many such utilitarian "languages" and by its very nature is not extinct. Pig Latin (C) is the result of transposing the initial consonant to the end of the work and adding an additional syllable; an example is "ancay" for "can" and "atcay" for "cat." Thus, choice (C) is clearly not the right answer.

17. (A)

According to the National Institute for Literacy's principles of language acquisition, children must be able to form and hold mental pictures if they are to acquire language fundamentals. Before children can develop language skills, they must first possess the ability to form and recognize symbols and be able to use tools to express those symbols. Imitating language by forming and generating certain sounds (B), grasping abstract concepts (C)—which psychologist Jean Piaget says come much later in a child's development than the beginning of language—and associating water with a faucet (D) are not requisite to language.

18. (A)

Reading aloud increases vocabulary in the listener, regardless of the listener's age. Reading aloud can also augment comprehension when the educa-tor/adult discusses the selection before, during, and after the reading. Pictures and sounds alone (B), television and videos alone (C), and classical music alone (D) do not necessarily enhance vocabulary.

19. (A)

The National Institute for Literacy states that, "A program of systematic phonics instruction clearly identifies a carefully selected and useful set of letter–sound relationships and then organizes the introduction of those relationships into a logical instructional sequence." The National Institute does not note that such a program meets the basic needs of learners (B), releases the educators/parents from the responsibility to engage the learner in conversation (C), or meets a need of the learner to express needs and wants verbally and establish a cause and effect relationship in the learner's mind (D).

20. (C)

Gerunds have the ending "-ing" and function as a noun. Choice (C) contains two gerunds: "swimming" and "eating." There is no "-ing" word in (A), (B), or (D).

21. (C)

Answer (C) contains the prepositional phrase "through the deserted city streets," which serves as an adverb detailing where the police followed the robber. The other choices do not contain adverbial prepositional phrases.

22. (D)

Modernism is a deliberate and radical attempt by early twentieth-century artists to break from traditional artistic conventions by presenting fragmented, opaque, eclectic, and convoluted images juxtaposed with romanticized classical images and ideologies. Choice (A) describes the Renaissance period, which spanned the fourteenth century through the seventeenth century. Eliot does not attempt to represent the early twentieth century as a period of artistic beauty, social harmony, and historical value (B). Neither does he try to avoid early twentieth-century iconic representations or to focus more on the Italian Renaissance period as one of inspiration and social salvation (C).

23. (B)

Used in a variety of English poetry forms including blank verse, sonnets, heroic couplets, and so on, iambic pentameter is five feet per line of one light syllable followed by a stressed syllable.

24. (B)

Kennings, such as "whaleroad" (meaning "ocean") and "ringgiver" (meaning "king"), are poetic phrases comprised of figurative language used as descriptive phrases in place of the ordinary name of something. None of the other answer choices resembles the correct definition.

25. (A)

Courtly love is a staple of lyric poems and chivalric romances whereby a lover, usually a bachelor knight, suffers great agonies and moral victories on behalf of his (usually) unrequited or unobtainable love interest. Choice (B) is incorrect because it attributes the action to an enamored poet instead of a bachelor knight. Courtly love may be included in some romance novels and some cavalier and metaphysical poetry, but courtly love is not necessarily a feature of them as choice (B) suggests. Instruction in proper behavior is not a purpose of courtly love; (C) is unacceptable. Courtly love is not a convention of children's literature; (D) is incorrect.

26. (C)

Phrases such as "growing grim about the mouth" and "a damp, drizzly November in my soul" establish the passage's somber and melancholy tone. There are no words to suggest either a jocular (D) or angry (B) tone. The paragraph is not a plodding one, so (A) is not appropriate.

27. (D)

The narrator means that if he doesn't get to the sea right away, he will kill himself. In other words, the passage suggests that sailing is the only cure for his depression.

28. (A)

The paragraph is in prosaic style. It has the characteristics of a prose narrative, as opposed to a poetic style and structure. It is not poetic (B). The word polymorphic (C) seems to relate more to computer viruses and biology than to literature; (C) is inappropriate. Parallel structure in sentence construction means employing the same word pattern and giving the same level of importance to the words. Consider the following sentence: "Bill likes to read, to hike, and to travel." The way that the sentence reads suggests that Bill gives equal importance to all three activities. Parallel structure (D) is not an applicable answer here.

29. (D)

"A damp, drizzly November in my soul" is a metaphor, whereby symbols replace literal representations. A simile (A) employs "like" or "as"; if the narrator had said, "My soul is like a November day," he would have been using a simile instead of a metaphor. A paradigm (B) is a pattern or a model, not a good answer here. A trope (C) is a common pattern in literature; it can relate to characters (the poor, little rich girl), plot (seeking one's fortune), or setting (outer space). Answer (C) is, therefore, not the best choice.

30. (D)

The correct definition of alliteration is choice (D) the repetition of a consonant or the repetition of a vowel. Choice (A) states that the repetition of a vowel sound occurring at the beginning of a word or the repetition of a vowel sound within a word is alliteration; this is incorrect because alliteration may involve initial consonant sounds and vowel sounds. Choice (B) is, likewise, incorrect; it notes only the consonant sounds. Choice (C) indicates that alliteration involves consonant sounds at the end of the words or in the middle of the word; this is incorrect.

31. (C)

Concrete or pattern poems use a visual shape to present their content; a poem about a goblet might result in the shape of a drinking glass. Concrete poems do not necessarily avoid figurative language and ambiguous language; (A) is inaccurate. All concrete poems do not have recurring refrains or poetic choruses; (B) is not correct. These poems were not necessarily a product only of the period of the Industrial Revolution and do not always praise concrete and steel; (D) is inappropriate.

32. (A)

Blank verse, first solidified by Henry Howard around 1540, consists of unrhymed poetic lines of iambic pentameter (five stress iambic verse). This structure allows for the flexibility to replicate natural speech patterns and the adaptability to accommodate diverse subject matters. Free verse poetry (B) also has no set rhyming pattern; however it

also does not follow a structured rhythmic pattern. In ballad meter (C), iambic tetrameter alternates with iambic trimeter. Scansion is the term used to describe the process of analyzing the number and feet in a line of poetry.

33. (D)

A soliloquy is an action in a performance; the character on stage speaks—as an aside—his or her thoughts. Often the soliloquy provides necessary plot information, personal motives, general exposition, and so forth. A cacophony (A) is a jarring, discordant sound, which is to say, dissonance. A syllogism (B) is a type of argument in which one can infer the conclusion from two premises of a certain form. An epiphany (C) is an appearance, a manifestation, a moment of realization.

34. (A)

Both English and Italian sonnet structures require that the heroic couplet (lines of iambic pentameter that rhyme in pairs: "aa," "bb," "cc," etc.) appear at the end of the stanza; this occurs in answer (A). Choices (B), (C), and (D) do not supply this.

35. (A)

Metaphors of nature saturate the sonnet; they include terms like "summer days" to flower "buds" in "May," intertwined with images of "life" and "death." As the presumably male narrator extends his contemplations, he realizes that as long as people "live," "see," and "breathe," his affection will continue. There is no indication that the relationship is tempestuous (B) or that speed is imperative (C). The theme of love and relationships is more important than the aesthetic ability, contrary to what (D) suggests.

36. (D)

A Petrarchan sonnet, such as the opening canto from Sidney's "Astrophel [Astrophil] and Stella," presents the thematic idea in two main parts. The first is the octave (eight lines), which contemplates an idea, conflict, or issue; the second is a sestet (six lines), which attempts to resolve the idea, conflict, or issue. Choices (A) and (B) do not apply because the poem is not a product of the seventeenth century. Because a Petrarchan sonnet is more than just representing a classical style, (C) alone is insufficient for categorization.

37. (A)

A throe is a spasm, usually implying a negative connotation: pain or the effect of an upheaval or struggle. Here the love smitten narrator suffers over his desire for a lady who is not his social equal and, therefore, is unobtainable. The poem does not suggest mirth (B). Frustration is not the predominant mood so (C) is inappropriate. Throe is not a synonym for dwelling; (D) is inappropriate.

38. (B)

Poets often equate the act of creating a poem with that of giving birth to a child. The reader should not take the expression literally as in (A) or (D). The narrator is not referring to the honesty of children, so (C) is inappropriate.

39. (C)

While some scholars consider the onset of the modern period to extend as far back as the 1860s, it is generally accepted that it began in earnest right after World War I ended, circa 1922. The period that includes 1822 (A) would be the nineteenth century period or, in America, the romantic period. The Renaissance and Elizabethan periods encompass 1558 (B); this is much earlier—and, therefore, inappropriate—for a poem characterized as modern. The year 1776 (D) would be a part of the American Revolutionary War period, not the modern era.

40. (A)

The prose fiction of authors like Gabriel García Márquez combines the extraordinary elements of fantasy and mundane elements of reality and is known as magical realism, or meta-fiction. Nouveau Roman refers to a movement in French literature that flourished in the 1950s and early 1960s and that questioned the traditional literary realism that was prominent at the time; (B) is incorrect. The answer (C) is inappropriate. A Gothic romance combines elements of horror and romance, not fantasy and ordinary situations. Choice (D) is not a correct response to the question.

41. (C)

Gothic novels, such as Horace Walpole's *The Castle of Otranto* (1764), emerged in the later part of the eighteenth century and are still a popular form of literary entertainment today. The word "grotesque" (A) is not a common literary term used to categorize writings and is not appropriate here. An episodic novel (B) has a complete story within each chapter; it is not the answer to the question. An epistolary work (D) is a letter or a series of letters; (D) is not the best choice here.

42. (A)

Satire is a subgenre of comedy that ridicules the failings of human beings and society in order to make a point or effect change. Jonathan Swift's *Gulliver's Travels* and Joseph Heller's *Catch 22* are two famous examples of satire.

43. (B)

Dickens presents a series of paradoxes, contradictory ideas that characterize the contradictory elements, the good and the bad, of the time. Symbols (A) are an object, action, or event that represents something beyond itself. While this line is so famous that it might seem clichéd (C), Dickens thought of it first, so it was original when he wrote it. An allusion (D) would be a reference to an earlier work or source.

44. (C)

This is a very long compound sentence, with fourteen discrete independent clauses held together by commas and semicolons. There are no subordinate clauses, so it is not complex (B) nor is it compound complex (D). A simple sentence (A) would have just one independent clause.

45. (A)

"Was" is the past tense of the verb "to be," a linking verb. Twelve of the fourteen clauses in this sentence are followed by either a predicate noun or adjective that links directly back to the subject. Active verbs (B), show action and take direct objects. The imperative (C) is a form of command where the subject is the understood second person "you." An inversion (D) is an atypical sentence order. Though this sentence is unusually long, each clause presents in the expected subject verb order.

46. (B)

Though Dickens is a Victorian writer, *A Tale of Two Cities* is set in London and Paris, during the French Revolution.

47. (D)

The passage, which opens Charles Dickens's *A Tale of Two Cities*, contains numerous comparisons. By making these comparisons and descriptions of the time period ("we had everything before us, we had nothing before us, we were all going direct to Heaven, we were all going direct the other way," etc.), Dickens is illustrating how during this period (just before the French Revolution) anything was possible: "wisdom," "foolishness," "Light," or "Darkness." This "anything is possible" tone also foreshadows the French Revolution, which the aristocracy never expected. Dickens does not describe extreme political upheaval in this passage; (B) is a wrong choice. Choice (A) is wrong because "placid" implies settled and calm; if "anything is possible," then the times are the exact opposite. There is no mention of a public event, so (C) is also incorrect.

48. (D)

The Cavalier poets, who included Robert Herrick, Thomas Carew, and Richard Lovelace, wrote in polished, lyrical, erotically charged poems of gallantry and courtship. They were followers of King Charles I. The graveyard school was a group of eighteenth-century British poets who focused their works on death and bereavement; (A) is not a good answer. The metaphysical school included as a focus its speculation on questions that science could not answer; because this was not a focus of Herrick or Jonson, answer (B) is not acceptable. Neither the style nor the subject of Herrick's and Jonson's work is suggestive of the Shakespeare school; (C) is an inappropriate answer.

49. (A)

The graveyard poets were a group of eighteenth-century poets (including Thomas Gray, Edward Young, and Thomas Parnell) who wrote—

often in a cemetery—meditative poems that usually had a cemetery and that contemplated the happenstances of life and death. The Pre-Raphaelites (B) were poets who attempted to return to the ideals of truthfulness, simplicity, and art prior to the Italian Renaissance. The graveyard poets did not write in the style of Homer or in the epic style; (C) is incorrect. The language of the people and creative expression were not characteristics of Gray's poem; (D) is not a suitable answer.

50. (C)

The Pre-Raphaelites were poets who attempted to return to the ideals of truthfulness, simplicity, and art prior to the Italian Renaissance. The poets mentioned were not modeling after the Gregorian chants of 540 to 604, or perhaps even earlier; (A) is not appropriate. Modern poets (B) date from after World War I, and the romantic poets (D), including John Keats, Percy Bysshe Shelley, Mary Shelley, Samuel Taylor Coleridge, and William Wordsworth, date from the 1700s until about the early 1800s.

51. (B)

A rhetorical question is a figure of speech in which a question is posed where the answer is already assumed and obvious to the audience. Anaphora (A) is the repetition of words or phrases at the beginning of successive lines, stanzas, sentences, or paragraphs. An apostrophe is an address to a dead or absent person or to an inanimate object or abstract idea. An allusion (D) is an indirect reference to an earlier work, history, folklore, mythology, etc.

52. (A)

New historicism deals with texts with respect to their historical and cultural context. Deconstruction (B) has as its basis the premise that human history in trying to understand and define real-

ity has led to domination in various forms; (B) is incorrect. Marxism (C) is hostile toward all forms of domination and seeks to overcome oppression through emancipation of the working class; (C) is inapplicable here. Post-structuralism (D) asserts that analysis—including deconstruction—is difficult because categories are shifting and unstable; (D) does not answer the question.

53. (D)

Miracle plays, morality plays, and interludes typify late medieval drama; drama outside the church was prominent from about 1200 until the end of the medieval period (about 1350). Edwardian drama (A) is so called because it was written during the Edwardian period in the United Kingdom, which spanned from about 1901 to 1910; this was long after the popularity of the morality plays of the late medieval period. The period of romantic drama (B) occurred during the late eighteenth and early nineteenth centuries; again, this was well after the period of medieval drama and the miracle plays. Contemporary drama (C) does not stress morality plays and miracle plays.

54. (B)

George Eliot—the author of *Silas Marner*—was actually Mary Ann Evans. Samuel Langhorne Clemens (A) was the real name of Mark Twain, the author of *The Adventures of Tom Sawyer* and *The Adventures of Huckleberry Finn*. Emily Brontë initially used the pen name of Ellis Bell (C) for her book *Wuthering Heights*. Emily's sister Charlotte Brontë initially used the pen name of Currer Bell (D) for her novel *Jane Eyre*.

55. (A)

The Great Vowel Shift was a feature of the Middle English Period; it occurred about the same time that Chaucer was composing his *Canterbury Tales*. The Great Vowel Shift was a change affecting the vowels of English during the years of 1350 to 1550 especially. Basically, the long vowels shifted to a different place in the mouth. The changes in vowel sounds resulted in implications for orthography, reading, spelling, and understanding English language text. The Old English period (B) was much earlier; usually dated from 600 to 1100, this period was before Chaucer's writing. The Renaissance English period (C) and the Commonwealth period (D) came after the Middle English period: the fifteenth through the seventeenth century for the Renaissance period, and 1649 through 1660 for the Commonwealth period.

56. (D)

The entries on the contents page are generally listed in order of occurrence in the book. The index of a book is arranged in alphabetical order (A) according to topic; the page number is generally given directly after the topic. Content page entries are not arranged according to concrete and abstract arrangements (B) or according to a linear and recursive order (C).

57. (A)

By jokingly suggesting that the two governments contain the positions "lords of the State preserves of loaves and fishes," Dickens mocks their self-assuredness and unflinching certainty that the "preserves" will never be depleted and that "things in general [are] settled for ever." The phrase "clearer than crystal" helps, through its sarcasm, to give this attack more sting. None of the other choices is alluded to or discussed in the passage and are thus incorrect.

58. (A)

The word "drip" is an example of onomatopoeia, that is, a word whose sound suggests its meaning. Other examples of onomatopoeic words are "zip," "whish," and "zoom." The words "waddled" (B), "grub" (C), and "showed" (D) do not suggest sounds and are incorrect.

59. (C)

The sun is, of course, not a person with a face. The statement that "the sun showed its face" is a clear example of personification, or assigning human characteristics to inanimate objects. The predicates in (A), (B), and (D) do not show personification.

60. (D)

While all these poetic forms share characteristics of each other, they can be divided into different categories. An epic is a long narrative poem that deals with heroes in crisis and/or serious subjects. All four of the works listed are examples of epic poetry. Milton's *Paradise Lost* deals with man's fall from God's grace. The anonymously written Beowulf as well as Homer's *The Iliad* and *The Odyssey* chronicle the stories of cultural heroes. Dramatic poetry (A) is when the poet takes on the voice of an invented character. An elegy (C) is a poem for the dead. Lyrical poetry (B) expresses the thoughts and feeling of the poet, and would be much shorter than an epic.

61. (C)

A complex sentence contains an independent clause and a subordinate (or dependent) clause. In the O'Connor sentence, "The grandmother had a peculiar feeling," is the independent clause and "that the bespectled man was someone she knew," is the subordinate clause.

62. (A)

The topic sentence asserts the main point of the paragraphs—it is to the paragraph what the thesis statement is to the entire essay. Often it is the first sentence of the paragraph, but not always. In this paragraph, the first sentence is the topic sentence; the rest of the sentences are details that support the writer's assertion that the bald eagle is being "threatened by a new menace."

63. (B)

The author's use of words such as "mighty bald eagle" and "threatened by a new menace" indicates concern for the topic. For the most part, the author appears concerned; thus, choice (B), concerned interest, is the correct answer. The author does seem to care and is not accepting of the status quo, so (A) and (C) are not appropriate. Suspicion (D) is not part of the writer's attitude.

64. (D)

Persuasive writing attempts to sway the reader to a particular viewpoint; this advertisement does just that. Narrative writing (B) tells a story or recounts an event; it is not appropriate here. Expository writing (A) and explanatory writing (C) may seek to explain; neither of these types of writings seem to apply to this gum advertisement.

65. (C)

Dickinson personifies death as a courtly suitor in this poem.

66. (C)

Dickinson often wrote in ballad meter—iambic tetrameter (four pairs of unstressed, stressed syllables) alternating with iambic trimeter (three pairs of unstressed, stressed syllables). Trochaic tetrameter (A) consists of four pairs of stressed, unstressed syllables. Free verse (B) has no set rhythm or rhyme scheme while blank verse is unrhymed iambic pentameter.

67. (B)

This stanza is a quatrain, consisting of four lines. Two sequential rhyming lines is a couplet (A) while a sonnet (D) is a poem with thirteen or fourteen lines. A refrain (C) is a repeating line or stanza.

68. (C)

The stanza is primarily iambic pentameter (five pairs of unstressed, stressed syllables), though the last lines has eleven syllables rather than ten. Trochaic tetrameter (A) is four pairs of stressed, unstressed syllables while dactylic trimeter (B) is three groups of a stressed syllable followed by two unstressed syllables. Anapestic pentameter (D) is five groups of two unstressed syllables followed by an unstressed syllable.

69. (C)

A caesura is a pause in a line of poetry indicated by a mark of punctuation such as a comma or a dash. An end stopped line (A) is an independent clause, a complete thought expressed in one line. Since this independent clause spans over four lines, it is not end stopped. An enjambed (B) or run-on line (D) runs through to the next line without any pause indicated by punctuation. Finally, (D) is incorrect. As with choice (C), these are all incidental pieces of information or data used to support broader points.

70. (D)

This paragraph is clearly compare/contrast. Jane is weighing the good and bad points of school in order to decide whether she would like to attend. Narration (A) tells a story with a definite plot while description (B) paints a picture with words. Cause and effect (C) analyzes the causes of a particular outcome or the outcome of particular causes.

71. (D)

Jane is conflicted. There are good points and bad points to school, though the positives seem to be outweighing the negatives.

72. (A)

The protagonist is the main character in a work of film, drama, fiction, or narrative poetry. He or she drives the action. The antagonist (B) opposes the protagonist. The antagonist can be another character, or it can be a force such as nature, society, or fate. Foils (C) are pairs of characters who display opposite traits—Jane has a foil in this novel, but that is not the focus of the question. A static character (D) remains the same, does not change and grow, in the course of the novel. Since the question says Jane triumphed over her difficult past, she probably isn't a static character.

73. (C)

First published in Great Britain in 1847, *Jane Eyre* is definitely a Victorian novel. The Elizabethan era would be the 17th century during Shakespeare's time. The British Romantic period directly preceded the Victorian era at the end of the eighteenth and beginning of the nineteenth century. The Modern era would be twentieth century.

74. (A)

The quotation is clearly an example of diction. The quotation exemplifies typical informal speech. The sentence is grammatically incorrect. Because the word "everyone" is singular and the word "their" is plural, the pronouns do not agree in number. Choice (B) is incorrect. The instructor gives directions to the students, but the directions may not be followed. Foreshadowing is not necessarily a result. (C) is also incorrect. One cannot determine from the quotation if the setting is a class for law enforcement officers, an elementary classroom, or a college class. The sentence is not an analogy (D), a comparison of something to something else.

75. (B)

This passage from Herman Melville's *Moby Dick* contains an allusion in the phrase, "like so many Alexanders." Melville is illustrating the strength and power of whalers ("naked Nantucketers") by alluding and comparing them to Alexander the Great, the famous conqueror who died in 323 BCE. Choices (A), (C), and (D) do not use allusions in their illustrations.

76. (A)

This first passage, which opens James Joyce's *A Portrait of the Artist as a Young Man*, illustrates "baby talk" ("moocow," "nicens," "baby tuckoo") to convey to readers the age, speech, and mental state of the narrator. Choices (B), (C), and (D) do not employ distinct voices imitating the speech of the character.

77. (D)

Nineteenth-century novels of manners employed such themes as the importance (or unimportance) of "good breeding," the elation (and suffocation) caused by society, and the interaction of individuals within the confines of a closed country community (to name just a few). This passage, taken from Jane Austen's *Emma*, mentions "opinions" of other characters, the importance of "beauty" and "accomplishment" (which to Emma are saving graces for Mrs. Elton), and the "improvement" of a "country neighborhood." None of the other passages could be categorized as coming from a novel of manners.

78. (B)

In third-person limited point of view, the narrator is in the mind of only one character; in this case the narrator knows what Emma thinks and feels. Third-person pronouns are used by this narrator. First-person narration (A) is from the point of view of a character in the story; the narrator uses the first-person pronoun "I." The third-person omniscient narrator (C) knows what all the characters think and feels, and also knows their pasts and futures. The third-person objective narrator (D), tells the story objectively, without disclosure of the thoughts and feelings of the characters.

79. (C)

An oxymoron is a construction, often but not always adjective noun, that expresses a paradox: "feather of lead," "bright smoke," "cold fire," "sick health," and "still waking sleep." Romeo is expressing through these the paradoxical nature of love that can bring us to complete joy as well as the depths of sorrow.

80. (A)

The first three adverbial phrases are parallel. The sentence is also inverted; that is different from the expected subject verb order. Here the subject "streak" occurs after the verb. A more typical construction of this sentence would be: "The long sparkling streak fled ahead or astern, on one side or the other, at intervals long or short…." In a periodic sentence (B), the essential part of the sentence is saved for the end. The imperative is an command that incorporates the understood "you" as the subject (B). A cumulative sentence (C) is the opposite of the periodic sentence; the most important element is in the beginning followed by clarifying or descriptive elements. This sentence is a compound sentence (C), two joined independent clauses, but since it is not a cumulative sentence, choice (C) is not the best answer. Though it does have parallel elements, the sentence does not ask a question; therefore it is not interrogative (D).

81. (D)

Alliteration is the repetition of sound in words in close proximity, the "s" sound in "sparkling streak." Imagery is language that appeals to the senses and is illustrated by this phrase. The phrase is not a metaphor, an abstract comparison, nor does it sound like what it means, onomatopoeia (A). An allusion (B) is an indirect reference to an earlier work or source. Personification (C) gives human qualities to nonhuman things. Though all words are examples of diction, choice (C) is not the best answer.

82. (A)

Onomatopoeia is when words sound like what they mean, and "whirroo," used as a noun here, is a perfect example of this sound effect. An abstract noun (B) expresses an abstract concept such as love or loyalty, something that cannot be experienced through the senses. Assonance (C) is the repetition of vowel sounds and consonance (D) is the repetition of consonant sounds in words in close proximity. Since "whirroo" is only one word, these sound effects don't apply.

83. (B)

The American writer Stephen Crane (1871–1900) is considered part of the Naturalist movement, an offshoot of the Realistic movement. Naturalists used a technique called impressionism, a psychological approach whereby the writer gives us not an objective reality, but instead creates the reality that the characters perceive. Darwinian theory was another important influence on the Naturalists. American Romanticism (A) preceded Naturalism, and emphasized the individual over society, the emotional over the cerebral, as well as nature over civilization. Transcendentalism (C) was a part of the Romantic movement, with its most famous writers being Ralph Waldo Emerson and Henry David Thoreau. Rationalists (D) are associated with the American Revolution and produced mostly nonfiction prose.

84. (A)

The diction, details, and figurative language (as well as the exclamation points) suggest the speaker is irate. The sarcastic questioning also implies this.

85. (A)

A soliloquy is a poem or speech where the speaker is alone. Since this poem is a soliloquy, we can assume that Brother Lawrence is not present to hear these angry words.

86. (B)

The speaker is angry, and telling Brother Lawrence to literally, "Go to Hell." This figure of speech is an exaggeration, in other words hyperbole. Understatement (A) is the opposite of hyperbole, the language minimizes rather than exaggerates. Inflated language (C) uses overly formal diction and syntax for the situation. Circumlocution (D), often an element of inflated language, is an indirect way of saying something. Certainly the speaker in this poem is not being coy about his feelings.

87. (C)

Answer (C) most clearly denotes the order of collecting data and writing a formal paper; (C) does not, however, form the pattern for all writing. Steps may vary slightly from topic to topic. It is almost impossible to develop a formal thesis statement and outline before one even begins collecting data; (A) is not a good choice. Choice (B) is in error primarily because one does not prepare the outline after writing the paper. Choice (D) is not the best choice primarily because one does not formalize the title as a first step.

88. (D)

The three most frequently used methods of citation are the three listed here: Modern Language Association (MLA) citations (A), American Psychological Association (APA) citations (B), and the *Chicago Manual of Style* (CMS) citations (C). Answer (D) is correct since there is no citation style named AHA.

89. (B)

The sciences most frequently use the American Psychological Association (APA) method of citation. The languages, student research papers, and scholarly research—not of the sciences—most frequently use the Modern Language Association (MLA) method of citation (A). The *Chicago Manual of Style* (CMS), choice (C), is often the method preferred in publishing—particularly social science publications and most historical journals. CMS is not the primary method of the sciences, however. Choice (D), is incorrect because there is no AHA citation style.

90. (C)

A balanced sentence is a parallel construction balancing two usually contrasting ideas. The balanced sentence is divided by a conjunction or punctuation mark that acts as a fulcrum, in the case of the Kennedy quotation, the semicolon.

91. (D)

Because various learning skills are based on environment (e.g., a student can read in some situations but seems unable to read and interpret poetry in class), the teacher should observe the students as they read and study in the classroom. Asking the students to read and reread a text to improve comprehension (A) is not necessarily helpful. Having students write what they read (B) alone does not necessarily help in reading and interpreting texts, and merely watching and documenting students eager to read (C) alone are not sufficient to assist in literary assessment.

92. (A)

Much writing combines methods of exposition, but usually one mode dominates the writer's approach to his or her topic. While this paragraph has elements of choices description (B) and process analysis (C), it is primarily narrative. The paragraph does not explore the causes or the effects of Frankenstein's experiment (D).

93. (A)

The passage is in first-person point of view. Frankenstein narrates the passage, using the first-person pronoun "I." See answer 78 for explanations of the other points of view.

94. (B)

The passage is fearful and ominous. The dreary weather, Frankenstein's "anxiety," and the image of "the yellow eye of the creature" opening combine to create this tone.

95. (C)

Words such as "convulsive" and "infuse" characterize Dr. Frankenstein as an educated man, but the diction straightforward and conversational, not requiring a trip to the dictionary for most educated readers. Choice (A) would entail a much more sophisticated vocabulary, separating the narrator from his audience. Scientific (B) diction would contain jargon. Coarse, colloquial (D) diction would contain slang words and expressions.

96. (C)

This is a complex sentence because it contains both independent and subordinate clauses. Simple sentences (A) only contain one independent clause. Compound sentences (B) contain at least two independent clauses, and compound complex sentences (D) combine two or more complex sentences.

97. (B)

This question is testing your knowledge of the basic types of verbs, of which there are three: action verbs, linking verbs, and auxiliary verbs. In this case, the *main verb* is the action verb "collected," which is the verb that animates the main idea of the sentence, which is the gathering of the "instruments of life." Choices (A), (C) and (D) are action verbs also, but they only support the main idea of the sentence.

98. (C)

An aside is a comment spoken directly to the audience that the other actors on stage are supposedly unable to hear. An aside does not refer to the place an actor takes on the stage (A), to an actor who addresses directly another actor on the stage (B), or to the place another actor on the stage may take (D).

99. (A)

A poem must be written in verse. Rhythm (B) is not a prerequisite to poetry; free verse does not use a set rhythm. A poem does not have to rhyme (C). Onomatopoeia (D)—the use of a word whose sound ("bop," "pow," "bleep") suggests its meaning—is a stylistic device that may appear in a poem, but it is not a requisite.

100. (D)

Sandburg's "Fog" is a free verse poem because it has no formal pattern or structure of rhythm or rhyme. An elegy (A) is a formal poem of mourning. Blank verse (B) is not rhymed, but it is written in iambic pentameter; John Milton's "Paradise Lost" is an example. An ode (C) is a formal poem of praise; although this poem does seem to praise fog, Sand burg is—more accurately—using free verse (D).

101. (D)

This poem comparing the fog to a cat illustrates a metaphor. It is not personification (A) because the cat, though living, is not human. A paradox (B) would marry seemingly contradictory ideas to express a truth. A symbol (C) represents something beyond itself. The fog is being compared to a cat because they share some unlikely characteristics; the cat does not symbolize the fog.

102. (B)

An elegy is a serious poem lamenting the death of an individual or group of individuals. Taken from Robert Herrick's "Upon His Spaniel Tracy," the elegy mourns the death of his favorite dog. An allegory (A) uses figures, characters, or events to represent abstract ideas or principles. A ballad (C) is a narrative folk poem that may have originally been set to verse. A kenning (D) is a poetic phrase, such as "whaleroad" (meaning "ocean") and "ringgiver" (meaning "king"), that consists of figurative language and is used as a descriptive phrase in place of the ordinary name of something.

103. (A)

Enjambment occurs when a line of poetry "runs on" to the next line, causing a slight pause in midsentence or thought. Line 3 reads, "This shall my love do, give thy sad death one." The reader is left wondering, "One what?" It is not until line 4 that the poet explains that he will give one "Tear." Personification (B), or giving human characteristics to an inanimate object, is not appropriate. There is no use of metaphor (C), a figure of speech in which one thing is likened to some wholly different thing. A simile (D) is a comparison using "like" or "as;" there is no simile here.

104. (A)

The speaker of these lines is Berowne, a reluctant student in Shakespeare's *Love's Labour's Lost*. You can discern that the lines are spoken by a student because they are a reaction against study and those who pursue it ("Small have continual plodders won . . ."). It would be highly unusual—incongruous—for a professor (B), a clergyman (C), or a thief (D) to speak these lines.

105. (D)

Restated, the lines mean, "Little (small) have those who constantly (continually) plod through their studies gained (won), except (save) for some common, throwaway knowledge (base authority) from others' books." Choice (D) comes closest to this and is the correct answer.

106. (C)

A supplicant is one who seeks forgiveness in a religious sense. Therefore, by labeling the parishioners as such, the author is implying that they are all guilty of various crimes against their religion and have come to the church seeking forgiveness. The other answers—to celebrate mass (A), devout (B), and hypocrite (D)—do not necessarily follow.

107. (B)

The poem of Byron uses a simple—almost singsong—rhyme scheme. The rhyme scheme is not elaborate (A); in fact it is so simple as to be almost singsong. The writer does not use free verse (C): the pattern is not unrhymed and varying in metrical pattern. The reference to "the glories of Greece and of Rome" is an example of connotation; (D) is incorrect.

108. (A)

The poem is definitely cryptic, sarcastic, or cynical in nature. It is not meant to be humorous (B), and it is not a cliché (C), or an overused expression. Byron (1788–1824) lived and wrote after the medieval period; (D) is incorrect.

109. (A)

The fact that Byron lost his life doing what he warned others against is ironic, not humorous (B), not an exaggeration or a hyperbole (C), and definitely not comedic (D).

110. (A)

Line 2 uses internal rhyme: "combat" and "for that." There is no alliteration (B), metaphor (C), or cliché (D).

111. (D)

All three themes—survival of the unfittest (A), the picaresque, or journey (B), and the reversal of fortune (C)—are frequent in literature; (D) is, therefore, the best answer.

112. (A)

A picaresque novels is comprised of many separate episodes within the overarching story. *The Adventures of Huckleberry Finn* and *Don Quixote* are both examples of this form.

113. (C)

Upon meeting the author at the White House, Lincoln reportedly called Harriet Beecher Stowe, the author of the bestselling abolitionist novel *Uncle Tom's Cabin*, "the little lady who started this big war." All the other works were published after the Civil War, and thus would have to be incorrect.

114. (D)

None of the works was from the 1700s. A review of the works shows that their publication dates were all in the 1800s:

Little Men (1871) by Louisa May Alcott

Little Women (1868) by Louisa May Alcott

The House of the Seven Gables (1851) by Nathaniel Hawthorne

A Wonder-Book (1852) by Nathaniel Hawthorne

The Last of the Mohicans (1826) by James Fenimore Cooper

The Deerslayer (1841) by James Fenimore Cooper

115. (D)

Though Poe, Hawthorne, Irving, and Cooper are considered Romantics, they are not classified as Transcendentalists. Frost and cummings are twentieth century writers, and Transcendentalism is a nineteenth century movement.

116. (A)

Whitman is the first American to establish free verse, poetry not controlled by structured rhyme and meter, as a poetic form. Longfellow, Bryant, and Holmes were popular poets of that time who stayed within the traditional forms of rhythm and rhyme.

117. (C)

Benjamin Franklin is the author of *Poor Richard's Almanack*, a yearly almanac published continuously from 1732 to 1758. Ben Jonson (1572–1637) lived long before the time of Benjamin Franklin and Poor Richard's; (A) is incorrect. William Caxton (B) was the first publisher to publish works especially for children, but he did not publish *Poor Richard's Almanack*. *Poor Richard's Almanack* was published in America; British writers (D) were not a part of the work.

118. (C)

Round characters are those about whom the reader knows the "unique details." Stereotypical characters (A) are without individual characteristics; they are a member of a group and take their characteristics from the group, as the Southern sheriff or the youngest daughter who is the smartest, kindest, and most beautiful. Flat characters (B) may be a part of the author's writing, but the author may not fully describe the figure in the work; the reader may not know about the thoughts or the emotions or even the physical description of the person; (B) is a poor choice. Stock characters (D)—sometimes called stereotyped characters—are immediately recognizable by readers or audiences; most are familiar from their recurrent appearances in literary or folk tradition. (D) is not an acceptable answer.

119. (A)

Two works that the writers meant for adults of the 1700s but that young people promptly adopted were *Robinson Crusoe* by Daniel Defoe (1719) and *Gulliver's Travels* by Jonathan Swift (1726). The works in the other answer choices were all of a later time period: *Little Women* by Louisa May Alcott (1869), *Treasure Island* (1883) by Robert Louis Stevenson, *Rip Van Winkle* (1819) by Washington Irving, *The Pathfinder* (1840) by James Fenimore Cooper, *Kidnapped* (1886) by Robert Louis Stevenson, and *A Christmas Carol* (1843) by Charles Dickens.

120. (B)

Dystopic literature is a genre that amplifies flaws in society or human nature to portray a dark and cautionary view of the future. George Orwell's *1984* and Margaret Atwood's *A Handmaid's Tale* fit this criteria as do *Cooper, Kidnapped* (1886) by Robert Louis Stevenson, and *A Christmas Carol* (1843) by Charles Dickens.

Praxis II English Language, Literature, and Composition: Essays (0042)

The Praxis II English Language, Literature, and Composition: Essays exam (0042) is a two-hour examination for those who plan to teach English in a secondary school. This examination of literature study assesses two main elements:

- The analysis of literature texts/passages

- The ability both to understand and to articulate arguments about key issues in English study

There are four essay questions on the exam. The time limit is two hours, so each of the essays should take about 30 minutes. Each of the answers receives equal weight: 25 percent.

Two of the four questions involve the interpretation of English, American, or world literature of any time period. The first of the two questions focuses on poetry, the second, on prose.

The other two questions are somewhat different. The first of the second pair of questions will ask you to evaluate an argument and the rhetorical features of a passage addressing an issue in English study. Some of the typical topics covered include the value of studying literature, the nature of literary interpretation, the characteristics of the discipline of the study of literature, and what people read and why.

The final question on the Praxis II 0042 requires you to take a position on an issue and defend it; the question will relate to an issue in the study of English. You must use references to literature to support the position you take.

The literary works included in the "Literary Issues and Literary Texts" question will change from test to test. Although Educational Testing Service (ETS) provides a list of sources that might be a part of the literary texts/issues question, the list is changing and nonexhaustive. The list includes these works:

Chinua Achebe, *Things Fall Apart*

Isabel Allende, *The House of the Spirits*

Jane Austen, *Pride and Prejudice*

Pearl S. Buck, *The Good Earth*

Sandra Cisneros, *The House on Mango Street*

Joseph Conrad, *Heart of Darkness*

Charles Dickens, *Great Expectations*

Ralph Ellison, *Invisible Man*

F. Scott Fitzgerald, *The Great Gatsby*

William Golding, *Lord of the Flies*

Lorraine Hansberry, *A Raisin in the Sun*

Ernest Hemingway, *A Farewell to Arms*

Homer, *The Odyssey*

Zora Neale Hurston, *Their Eyes Were Watching God*

Franz Kafka, *The Metamorphosis*

Maxine Hong Kingston, *The Woman Warrior*

Jamaica Kincaid, *Annie John*

Arthur Miller, *Death of a Salesman*

N. Scott Momaday, *House Made of Dawn*

J. D. Salinger, *The Catcher in the Rye*

William Shakespeare, *Romeo and Juliet*

Leslie Marman Silko, *Ceremony*

Mark Twain, *The Adventures of Huckleberry Finn*

Alice Walker, *The Color Purple*

Edith Wharton, *Ethan Frome*

Elie Wiesel, *Night*

Tennessee Williams, *The Glass Menagerie*

(The PRAXIS Series: English Language, Literature, and Composition: Essays (0042), copyright 2008 by the Educational Testing Service)

SCORING GUIDE

To evaluate the response to the first question—which asks you to interpret literature—evaluators use a three-point method of holistic scoring. The scoring method for the other essays also employs this three-point evaluation guide.

Score of 3

To achieve a score of 3, your response must exhibit most or all of the following characteristics:

- The answer indicates that you have a thorough understanding of the selection read.

- The response includes an adequate number of well-chosen examples from the selection and an explanation of how the selected examples support the points that the response makes.

- The answers to all parts of the question are clear and appropriate; the writing is coherent and indicates a control of language, including syntax and diction.

- The analysis of the literary elements is accurate and illustrates some "depth" of knowledge.

- The essay shows that the writer is able to use standard written English correctly.

Score of 2

To achieve a score of 2, your response must exhibit most or all of the following characteristics:

- The answer indicates you have an understanding of the selection read but may have some misreadings.

- The response includes an adequate number of examples from the selection but may fail to explain how the examples support the points.

- The writing is coherent and indicates a control of language, including syntax and diction.

- The analysis of the literary elements is accurate and illustrates some "depth" of knowledge, but the answer may omit or misinterpret some elements.

- The essay shows that you are generally able to use standard written English correctly, but may contain some flaws.

Score of 1

A score of 1 indicates that the response addresses the questions but is illogical or flawed in some ways:

- The answer does not indicate that you have an understanding of the selection read.

- The response fails to include examples to support the points.

- The writing indicates a lack of control of language, a lack of coherence, and difficulty with syntax and diction.

- The analysis of the literary elements is flawed; the analysis may be superficial or it may incorrectly identify literary elements.

- The essay shows repeated and serious writing errors.

Score of 0

A score of 0 indicates that the paper was blank, that the response was inaccurate or incoherent, or even that the response simply repeated the question.

TAKE THE TEST

Now you should take the four essay exams and time yourself. Remember, you should spend approximately 30 minutes on each essay question, and then move on to the next. Each answer is worth 25% of the total score. The answers and analysis begin after the fourth essay exam.

Ruled pages are provided in the back of this book for your essays.

Praxis English Assessment: Essays (0042)

Practice Test 1

Essay Question 1

Read the poem below and then answer the questions that follow.

Ithaca

When you set out on your journey to Ithaca,
pray that the road is long,
full of adventure, full of knowledge.

The Lestrygonians and the Cyclops,
the angry Poseidon—do not fear them:
You will never find such as these on your path,
if your thoughts remain lofty, if a fine
emotion touches your spirit and your body.

The Lestrygonians and the Cyclops,
the fierce Poseidon you will never encounter,
if you do not carry them within your soul,
if your soul does not set them up before you.

Pray that the road is long.
That the summer mornings are many, when,
with such pleasure, with such joy
you will enter ports seen for the first time;
stop at Phoenician markets,
and purchase fine merchandise,
mother-of-pearl and coral, amber and ebony,
and sensual perfumes of all kinds,
as many sensual perfumes as you can;
visit many Egyptian cities,
to learn and learn from scholars.

Always keep Ithaca in your mind.
To arrive there is your ultimate goal.
But do not hurry the voyage at all.
It is better to let it last for many years;
and to anchor at the island when you are old,
rich with all you have gained on the way,
not expecting that Ithaca will offer you riches.

Ithaca has given you the beautiful voyage.
Without her you would have never set out on the road.
She has nothing more to give you.
And if you find her poor, Ithaca has not deceived you.
Wise as you have become, with so much experience,
you must already have understood what Ithacas mean.

—Constantine P. Cavafy (1911)

How does Cavafy use analogy and allusion in the work? Was the use of the devices effective? Explain why or why not.

Essay Question 2

Read the passage below and then answer the essay questions that follow.

From the back-window I can see a narrow brick-yard sloping down to the river-side, strewed with rain-butts and tubs. The river, dull and tawny-colored, *(la belle riviere)* drags itself sluggishly along, tired of the heavy weight of boats and coal-barges. What wonder? When I was a child, I used to fancy a look of weary, dumb appeal upon the face of the negro-like river slavishly bearing its burden day after day. Something of the same idle notion comes to me to-day, when from the street-window I look on the slow stream of human life creeping past, night and morning, to the great mills. Masses of men, with dull, besotted faces bent to the ground, sharpened here and there by pain or cunning; skin and muscle and flesh begrimed with smoke and ashes; stooping all night over boiling caldrons of metal, laired by day in dens of drunkenness and infamy; breathing from infancy to death an air saturated with fog and grease and soot, vileness for soul and body. What do you make of a case like that, amateur psychologist? You call it an altogether serious thing to be alive: to these men it is a drunken jest, a joke,—horrible to angels perhaps, to them commonplace enough. My fancy about the river was an idle one: it is no type of such a life. What if it be stagnant and slimy here? It knows that beyond there waits for it odorous sunlight,—quaint old gardens, dusky with soft, green foliage of apple-trees, and flushing crimson with roses,—air, and fields, and mountains. . . . Stop a moment. I am going to be honest. This is what I want you to do. I want you to hide your disgust, take no heed to your clean clothes, and come right down with me,—here, into the thickest of the fog and mud and foul effluvia. I want you to hear this story. There is a secret down here, in this nightmare fog, that has lain dumb for centuries: I want to make it a real thing to you.

Rebecca Harding Davis, from "Life in the Iron Mills" (Originally appeared anonymously in April 1861 in *The Atlantic Monthly.*)

Cite at least two details/devices that the author uses to help the reader maintain hope for the town near the iron mills. Explain why each is effective.

Essay Question 3

Read carefully the excerpt from the essay "A New Kind of Literacy" by Richard MacManus (July 30, 2004). Then answer the essay questions that follow.

A New Kind of Literacy

The NEA published a report . . . "Reading at Risk," (www.nea.gov/pub/ ReadingAtRisk.pdf) which outlined the findings of a 2002 survey of the reading habits of 17,000 Americans. The survey was also done in 1982 and 1992. The resulting trends? According to the report, literary reading (i.e. novels, short stories, poetry, plays) has declined by 10% since 1982, with 18–24 year olds declining the most—28%! . . .

In this post I want to put the NEA report in a new light. A light that shines from the 21st century. I think the changes in reading habits that were reported are directly related to digital media and the Internet. But, unlike the NEA, I don't think the Internet is a "culprit" or that it "competes" with reading (those are both words used on page 30 of the report). No, what's happening is that reading is changing, metamorphosing. Reading is no longer just a paper-based, solitary activity that people do for leisure. Reading in the 21st century is increasingly digital, social and creative. . . .

To return to the NEA 'Reading at Risk' report. While it is disturbing that reading is apparently declining, there is a new kind of literacy that I believe is rising to take its place. It's like media literacy, but there's more to it as well . . . The new generation of readers aren't content to be passive consumers of books. They want to be able to interact and communicate with words and other media. The NEA report actually has a little clue that helps confirm this trend: it states that creative writing has *increased* over the last 20 years (almost the only thing that did increase!).

I've noted before on this blog that Generation Y is very community-oriented. They use media to form social bonds and reading books doesn't necessarily meet those needs. Maybe that explains the 28% drop in readership among 18–24 year olds.

Two-way media such as blogs and ebooks are the future of reading, because literacy is no longer a one-way consumer culture of 'we write, you read'. Creativity is half the equation now and the new generation want reading books to be a social and productive activity. Digital media and the Internet are the enablers of this new kind of read/write literacy. (*www.readwriteweb.com/archives/a_new_kind_of_l.php*)

In your own words, identify MacManus's central idea in the passage. Show how the method of development and the prose style (sentence structure, word choice, and figurative language) clarify and support his point. Be sure to refer to specific examples from the passage in your discussion.

Essay Question 4

Study the following statement:

> *A book about one character and one country can become a book about other characters and the world.*

Choose TWO works from the list below and then write a well-organized essay in which you SUPPORT the statement above. Develop your thesis using specific references to elements of the works you select (such as characters, plot, and setting).

Literary Works

Maya Angelou, *I Know Why the Caged Bird Sings*

James Baldwin, *Go Tell It on the Mountain*

Charles Dickens, *Great Expectations* **or** *Oliver Twist*

F. Scott Fitzgerald, *The Great Gatsby*

Nathaniel Hawthorne, *The Scarlet Letter*

Isabel Allende, *The House of the Spirits*

Harper Lee, *To Kill a Mockingbird*

Arthur Miller, *The Crucible*

George Orwell, *Animal Farm* **or** *1984*

Answers and Analyses for Essay Question 1

Three-Point Essay

Cavafy uses the analogy of an ordinary person's life to the journey home of the Greek hero Odysseus in Homer's Odyssey *in order to encourage readers to give value to the pursuit, rather than to the end. To assure people that they do not necessarily have to face malice and terror, such as Odysseus did with the monstrous Cyclops, the cannibal Lestrygonians, and vengeful Poseidon, the persona claims that this will not happen if they maintain an elevated spirit. Although he draws the analogy to a journey largely free of amusement and gratification, the persona advocates avoiding strife, and rather focusing on absorbing the sensual pleasures the world has to offer us. He portrays experiences in Mediterranean ports that Odysseus might have had if he had not been embroiled in confrontations with malicious, angry, or jealous monsters, gods, and sorceresses. Contradicting the lesson in Homer's epic, the persona states that Ithaca, the goal of the journey, should be valued only as the cause of the journey in the first place.*

It is at the end of the poem that the most powerful unspoken allusion appears: Penelope. Whereas the persona paints an appealing portrait of a lifestyle in the first five verse paragraphs, in the last one, when he continues to extol the journey over the destination, the reader cannot help but imagine Odysseus's wife, Penelope, who endured many hardships, and was forced to exercise an inhuman amount of faith and patience, as she waited many years for her husband to return. The persona says of Ithaca (implying Penelope): "She has nothing more to give you./And if you find her poor, Ithaca has not deceived you." It is the persona's gently shocking yet powerful way of devaluing intimacy, and praising beauty, experience, and wisdom as more worthy pursuits in life.

Analysis: The test taker's response exhibits the following characteristics:

- The answer indicates the test taker has a thorough understanding of the selection read. The writing indicates that the essayist understands the analogy and the allusions in the poem. The writer explains each device well.

- The response includes an adequate number of well-chosen examples from the selection and an explanation of how the selected examples support the points that the response makes.

- The answers to all parts of the question are clear and appropriate. The question asked the test taker to explain how analogy and allusion are used effectively. The essayist firmly establishes the main analogy (the comparison of ordinary life to the journey of Odysseus), and chooses to focus on the most powerful allusion (Penelope). The essayist explains how the contrast between our sympathetic perception of Penelope and the message in the poem (that intimacy is of less importance than experience) makes the message "shocking yet powerful." The writing is coherent and indicates a control of language. The writing is clearly above average.

- The analysis of the literary elements is accurate and displays notable depth of knowledge. The writer's analysis of the literary elements shows an understanding of stylistic devices and of Greek mythology.

- The essay shows that the writer is able to use standard written English correctly. There are no grammatical, spelling, or punctuation errors. The work is above average: a 3.

One-Point Essay

The analogy is people to creatures. The poem says to watch out for wolfs in sheep clothing. They are out to get you.

Allusions are things that are not as they appear. Like Ithaca is really a woman who will do you wrong. The line "She has nothing left to give you" shows you that Ithaca is an unfaithful woman.

The poem is a depressing tell of bad things to come. The poem did what the poet wanted. Tells us things are bad.

Analysis: To achieve a score of 1, the test taker responded to the questions, but the response is illogical or flawed in some ways.

- The answer does not indicate that the test taker has an understanding of the selection read. The writer gives the analogy as a comparison of people to creatures—a flaw in understanding. The tone is *not* pessimism. The poet does not see Ithaca as an unfaithful woman. The test taker is wrong!

- The response fails to include examples to support the points. The writer does not cite again the creatures in the poem. The examples are flawed.

- The writing indicates a lack of control of language, a lack of coherence, and difficulty with syntax and diction. There is a sentence fragment—"Like Ithaca is really a woman who will do you wrong"—and slang—"out to get you."

- The analysis of the literary elements is flawed; the analysis may be superficial or it may incorrectly identify literary elements. The writer has incorrectly identified the analogy. The writer has confused *allusion* with *illusion*.

- The essay shows repeated and serious writing errors. The sentence fragment, the failure to capitalize *cyclops*, and the misspelled word *wolfs* are serious writing errors for a college student to make.

Answers and Analyses for Essay Question 2

Three-Point Essay

The author of "Life in the Iron Mills" includes messages of hope for the reader. To create this optimistic effect, the writer uses several devices. In my opinion, two are particularly effective in generating an expectation for a better day for the town and the people near the iron mills.

One thing that the writer does is to encourage the reader to look deeper than the physical features of the town. The writer writes that there is promise of "odorous sunlight" for the river—and the town. This is an effective technique because the writer admits having firsthand knowledge of the river from childhood; if the writer is convinced that the future is positive, the reader feels comfortable in feeling that way also.

A second effective device that the writer uses is to tell the reader plainly that she has a great hope. She further emphasizes this hope by noting that there is a secret she must share. This plea is from one who knows the town and is willing to convince the reader that a better life is ahead.

She also tells the reader that the workers have given their best to the iron mills and helps to convince the reader that the price for a better life has been paid. With this expense, the town is due a better life; this is a good way to persuade the reader of the legitimacy of this hope.

Particularly because of the examples of hope, because of the convincing way that the writer uses them, and because of the price that has seemingly already been paid, the reader is left with a feeling of optimism.

Analysis: The test taker's response has fulfilled all or most of the scoring guidelines.

- It is clear that the test taker has an accurate understanding of the passage.

- The response includes three specific examples of literary techniques which the test taker claims support the author's point: a demonstration of how to look beyond the physical qualities of the town, a declaration of the author's own hope and invitation to the mill workers to share it, and the implication that the workers have earned a better life. The third example is inferred by the test taker, who would have benefited from citing specific evidence in the text which supports the idea of entitlement to a reward.

- The essay successfully answers the question, citing at least two literary techniques and explaining how they are used by the author to encourage optimism. The writing is technically accurate, well organized, and coherent, even though the test taker originally intends to discuss two literary devices and ultimately discusses three methods of delivering a powerful message.

- Although there is no particular "depth" of knowledge demonstrated in this essay, the test taker is able to accurately identify and examine three rhetorical techniques.

One-Point Essay

The writer did not convince the reader that better times are a head. The passage was depressing. One feels sad after reading it. I felt almost as sad as I did after I read Charles Dickens's writings about city life.

Speaking of dull water drunkenness grease and soot. These were depressing. There is nothing to convince the reader that it is not a "sentence of death."

The mention of crimsen roses and green apple trees suggests hope somewhere else. Good times not ahead. Because of no examples of hope for the town, the reader is left with a feeling of depression.

Analysis: The test taker's response only marginally addresses the question. The logic of his or her argument is unsupported, and the structure incoherent.

- The essay presents an opinion, not an analysis. The test taker argues that the passage is not promoting optimism; however, the directions ask the test taker to describe the details the author uses to help the reader maintain hope. Although there might be implications of hopelessness in the text, ostensibly this passage delivers a message of hope, which should be the focus of the essay.

- The only literary device addressed in this essay is imagery. It is used as an example to support the test taker's own opinion, but the essay fails to explain how it is used by the author to promote optimism.

- There is no summarization of the passage, one of the requirements of a well-written literary analysis; the passage does not exhibit strong writing skills. The responses to the topic are uncertain; there is as much emphasis on the pessimism as there is on the optimism. Details are random and planning is not evident.

- There are many errors in sentence construction; one might note in particular the incomplete sentences. The first sentence of paragraph 2 is a case in point. This fragment contains other errors as well, notably the omission of the commas in the list (between *water* and *drunkenness* and *drunkenness* and *grease*). The result leaves the reader struggling to comprehend the writer's meaning. There is an unwarranted, confusing shift from present to past tense throughout the essay, along with several misspelled words (e.g., *a head, crimsen*).

This essay demonstrates inadequate command of English grammar, composition mechanics, and literary interpretation; the score would be a 1.

Answers and Analyses for Essay Question 3

Three-Point Essay

Richard MacManus acknowledges the decline in reading since 1982 that the National Education Association noted; he recognizes also the fact that creative writing has increased by 38%. MacManus's central idea, however, is that people write more and that they still read—but in a different way. He calls them "A New Generation of Readers."

Appropriately, MacManus is himself posting his views on the subject on the Internet. He begins his blog by summarizing the NEA article "Literary Reading in Dramatic Decline" of July 8, 2004. He also cites statistics and figures from earlier years. This method development leads the reader from the beginning to believe that the writer is knowledgeable and that he is basing his writing on fact.

MacManus publishes this article informally on his blog and encourages his readers to respond, which is an example of the existing social interchange he recognizes. This prose article is typical of many blogs on the Internet. MacManus's facts clarify and support his points; electronics have indeed brought about a change in the <u>way</u> that people read and the <u>way</u> that people write. "[T]he one-way consumer culture of 'we write, you read'" is changing to a social activity on the Internet and through digital media to a culture of "We write, we read."

The grammar rules that MacManus employs are informal. He places a comma before the word "because"; current punctuation does not separate the dependent clause at the end of a sentence from the independent clause when the "connector" is "because." His use of contractions—"there's" and "aren't"—are another reflection of this casual style. MacManus even uses a sentence fragment: "A light that shines from the 21st century."

MacManus chooses current terms for his writing. He refers to "Generation Y" as being a "community-oriented" group; some decades ago, the term "Generation Y" would have been an unknown quantity. The terms "digital media," "blogs," and "Internet" are other modern words that young people would not freely have used during the Korean War era; the writer reminds us that things have changed.

The writer views the decline in reading, then, as merely a change in what is read and how it is read. He approves the community-oriented writing. His tone, overall, is extremely positive: "A light that shines from the 21st century."

Analysis: The essay above would receive a score of 3. The writing exhibits the following characteristics:

- The answer indicates the test taker has a thorough understanding of the selection read; the writer is able to summarize the central idea of the passage in no uncertain terms.

- The response includes an adequate number of well-chosen examples from the selection and an explanation of how the selected examples support the points that the response makes. The writer indicates the examples through the use of quotation marks; these marks indicate the exact words of MacManus. The writing clearly shows the purpose of the chosen examples.

- The answers to all parts of the question are clear and appropriate. The essayist notes the central idea of the passage, MacManus's method of development, the examples, and the prose style that the question asks the test taker to provide.

- The essayist's writing is coherent and indicates a control of language, including syntax and diction. The writer makes reference to the diction in the NEA article.

- The analysis of the literary elements is accurate and includes some depth. The writer is accurate in the statements made and makes some observations—such as the fact that MacManus's writing appeared on a blog—to reinforce his points.

- The essay shows that the writer is able to use standard written English correctly. The writer makes no errors in grammar or punctuation.

One-Point Essay

Richard MacManus bemones the fact that video games and the Internet have made book reading a thing of the past. He cries for the re-birth of books. No one is going to read the creative writing. Creative writing is on the increase.

MacManus's writing is slow. His writing is for the educated. It is not for the masses. MacManus offers no ansers. Makes the reader sad.

Analysis: To achieve a score of 1, the test taker responded to the questions, but the response is illogical or flawed in some ways.

- The answer does not indicate that the test taker has an understanding of the selection read. Stating that book reading is something of the past and that the author "bemones" this, misses the point entirely. The essayist clearly fails to grasp McManus's thesis: that reading has moved to a different media.

- The response fails to include examples to support the points that the essayist attempts to make.

- The writing indicates a lack of control of language, a lack of coherence, and difficulty with syntax and diction. Misspelled words and a lack of coherence make the essay difficult to read.

- The essayist misunderstands who the audience for the article is. It is an informal blog, not necessarily intended for the educated.

- The tone of MacManus's writing is positive, not negative. The essayist does not identify this literary element correctly.

Answers and Analyses for Essay Question 4

Three-Point Essay

The two books The House of the Spirits *by Isabel Allende and* I Know Why the Caged Bird Sings *by Maya Angelou illustrate very well the statement: "A book about one character and one country can become a book about other characters and the world."*

*Allende's book—*The House of the Spirits*—takes place in an unnamed country in South America about the turn of the twentieth century. The fact that the setting is so unspecific perhaps makes the events in the book even more applicable to the reader in a different country and at another time; this lack of specificity makes the book even more a book for the entire world.*

I Know Why the Caged Bird Sings *is more specific in its setting than is* The House of the Spirits. *The events in Angelou's book occur during the Great Depression; the setting includes events in both the Northern and the Southern regions of the United States. This more specific setting in the United States, however, does not limit the applicability of the book to other parts of the world.*

The main characters in both books are female. The female in The House of the Spirits *lives in an earlier time and in a different country than does Angelou in the autobiographical* I Know Why the Caged Bird Sings. *The interesting feature is that the young females have many things and feelings in common. Again, "A book about one character"—or, in this case, one female—"and one country can become a book about other characters and the world."*

Interestingly, the events of both books include muteness, a coping device that any person could use. In both writings the female protagonist displays the affliction of muteness. The condition in both cases is not one that had been present from birth; instead the condition of noncommunication is brought about by other factors. It is possible for events to change the lives of others in the world—regardless of the time or the place.

The two books I Know Why the Caged Bird Sings *and* The House of the Spirits *both feature females. The stories in the books, the females in the books, the settings in the books are typical of others across the world—regardless of time, place, and gender.*

Analysis: The test taker's response exhibits the following characteristics:

- The response analyzes the literary issue introduced in the statement both systematically and completely.

- The essay develops a thesis and uses appropriate examples from two books to illustrate and support it.

- The writing in the essay is coherent and demonstrates control of the language. The essay employs appropriate diction and syntax. The writing is well-organized.

- The conventions of standard written English are evident in the work.

Zero-Point Essay

To Kill a Mockingbird takes place in Alabama. It is applicable to the whole world. It shows the ugly side of people.

We are all familiar with the ugly side of people. Look at paper. Robbry and murders bound. I know. I had my wallet stolen. Too bad no death penlty for steel.

Analysis: This second essay would receive a score of 0.

- The essay contains off-topic responses. Even though the writer does mention one of the books at the start of the essay, the adherence to the topic does not continue.

- The writing includes many misspellings and sentence fragments.

- The essay contains incoherent statements and is at times disorganized.

Praxis English Assessment:
Essays (0042)

Practice Test 2

Essay Question 1

Read the poem below and then answer the questions that follow.

The Chimney Sweeper

When my mother died I was very young,
And my father sold me while yet my tongue
Could scarcely cry 'weep! 'weep! 'weep! 'weep!'
So your chimneys I sweep, and in soot I sleep.

There's little Tom Dacre, who cried when his head,
That curled like a lamb's back, was shaved: so I said,
"Hush, Tom! never mind it, for when your head's bare,
You know that the soot cannot spoil your white hair."

And so he was quiet; and that very night,
As Tom was a-sleeping, he had such a sight, —
That thousands of sweepers, Dick, Joe, Ned, and Jack,
Were all of them locked up in coffins of black.

And by came an angel who had a bright key,
And he opened the coffins and set them all free;
Then down a green plain leaping, laughing, they run,
And wash in a river, and shine in the sun.

Then naked and white, all their bags left behind,
They rise upon clouds and sport in the wind;
And the angel told Tom, if he'd be a good boy,
He'd have God for his father, and never want joy.

And so Tom awoke; and we rose in the dark,
And got with our bags and our brushes to work.
Though the morning was cold, Tom was happy and warm;
So if all do their duty they need not fear harm.

William Blake, *Songs on Innocence* (1789)

How does Blake use voice, point of view, and symbolism in the work? Was the use of the devices effective? Explain why or why not.

Essay Question 2

Read the passage below by Charles Dickens and cite at least two stylistic devices that the author uses and give an example of each. Explain why each cited device is effective.

> It was the best of times, it was the worst of times, it was the age of wisdom, it was the age of foolishness, it was the epoch of belief, it was the epoch of incredulity, it was the season of Light, it was the season of Darkness, it was the spring of hope, it was the winter of despair, we had everything before us, we had nothing before us, we were all going direct to Heaven, we were all going direct the other way.

> Charles Dickens, *A Tale of Two Cities: A Story of the French Revolution* (1859)

Essay Question 3

Read carefully the excerpt from *Walden* (1854) by Henry David Thoreau and, in your own words, identify Thoreau's central idea in the passage. Indicate two stylistic devices—with examples—that Thoreau uses in his writing.

> I see young men, my townsmen, whose misfortune it is to have inherited farms, houses, barns, cattle, and farming tools; for these are more easily acquired than got rid of. Better if they had been born in the open pasture and suckled by a wolf, that they might have seen with clearer eyes what field they were called to labor in. Who made them serfs of the soil? Why should they eat their sixty acres, when man is condemned to eat only his peck of dirt? Why should they begin digging their graves as soon as they are born? They have got to live a man's life, pushing all these things before them, and get on as well as they can. How many a poor immortal soul have I met well-nigh crushed and smothered under its load, creeping down the road of life, pushing before it a barn seventy-five feet by forty, its Augean stables never cleansed, and one hundred acres of land, tillage, mowing, pasture, and woodlot! The portionless, who struggle with no such unnecessary inherited encumbrances, find it labor enough to subdue and cultivate a few cubic feet of flesh.

> Henry David Thoreau, *Walden* (1854)

Essay Question 4

Study the following statement:

> *Female characters can be assertive protagonists even though the setting of the writing might suggest that a different type of woman would occupy the pages.*

Choose TWO works from the list below and then write a well-organized essay in which you SUPPORT the statement. Develop your thesis using specific references to elements of the works you select; of course, you will need to make reference to the plot, the setting, and the characters.

Literary Works

Maya Angelou, *I Know Why the Caged Bird Sings*

Jane Austen, *Pride and Prejudice*

Pearl S. Buck, *The Good Earth*

Sandra Cisneros, *The House on Mango Street*

Charles Dickens, *Great Expectations*

Ralph Ellison, *Invisible Man*

Lorraine Hansberry, *A Raisin in the Sun*

Ernest Hemingway, *A Farewell to Arms*

Zora Neale Hurston, *Their Eyes Were Watching God*

Maxine Hong Kingston, *The Woman Warrior*

Jamaica Kincaid, *Annie John*

Arthur Miller, *Death of a Salesman*

William Shakespeare, *Romeo and Juliet*

Alice Walker, *The Color Purple*

Tennessee Williams, *The Glass Menagerie*

PRACTICE TEST 2 (0042): ANSWERS AND ANALYSES

Answers and Analyses for Essay Question 1

Three-Point Essay

William Blake uses the voice of a young narrator without parents in the "The Chimney Sweeper." The voice of the child expresses the misery, isolation, and suffering in the common Victorian philosophy: children are merely industrial commodities for exploitation and for disposal when they are of no further use. This first-person point of view makes the suffering real to the reader. The voice of the child pleads for understanding as the child explains that his mother is dead and his father sold him to sweep chimneys. This device of using the words of the child is effective—even more so than having a narrator merely tell what he/she has seen.

The symbolism of death permeates the poem. The child speaks of "coffins of black." The journey to heaven in the poem is to "rise in the cloud." Awaiting his arrival will be an "angel" with a key to open the coffin. A "green plain," a "wash in a river," and the "shine in the sun" symbolize the afterlife. The poem suggests that the relief from toil and want may only come when the coffins open in the end. There is also an admonition to other child laborers: "if all do their duty they need not fear harm."

The symbolism and the point of view of "The Chimney Sweeper" make this poem of the past real to the present-day reader. The effective poem makes one wonder if there are still "Chimney Sweepers" of a different sort in our own society. Certainly Blake attained his purpose in the poem because it is still relevant today.

Overall, the poetic references to an orphaned, weeping child, who was "sold" into a world of perpetual darkness and death pervade "The Chimney Sweeper." Blake's use of narration and his symbolism develop the thematic ideas of a fragile Victorian child's commoditization, his want, his perpetual melancholy, his eventual death, and—hopefully—his life after death.

Analysis: The test taker's response has fulfilled all or most of the scoring guidelines.

- The essay clearly demonstrates that the test taker has a thorough understanding of the poem.

- The essay employs several specific references to the text to support the argument that voice, point-of-view, and symbolism are used effectively by the poet.

- The essay answers all questions posed, demonstrating how the poet uses voice, point-of-view, and symbolism, and clearly explaining how the use of these devices is effective. The test taker interprets the poet's message as one not only of condemnation of the oppression of child laborers in eighteenth-century England, but also of hope for emancipation in the afterlife. Although the test taker might be neglecting the poem's ironic undertones, the thesis presented is thoroughly and coherently supported.

- Although this essay does not demonstrate a particular "depth" of knowledge of poetry, the literary elements have been identified and their employment by the poet has been described accurately.

- The test taker clearly demonstrates aptitude for using the rules of standard written English.

Two-Point Essay

The poem made me really sad. I don't like the idea of little children suffering or dead. Why would Blake write about kids this way? Why are they going to work in the "cold and dark" instead of the daytime?

It says Tom is "a good boy," and yet it seems that he would rather play in the "river" and "in the sun." but instead he has to go to work. Maybe Blake is telling us that work is good for kids. Maybe he wants us to know that without a good day's work the kids won't appreciate their free time as much. They can laugh and play after the work is done. It's really telling us good work values and ethics, since all kids like to play more than they like to work. They are little "angels" who need their moms and dads to support them and give them the love and guidance like all parents give their children. If "Tom" sleeps when the other kids go to work, than maybe he's saying that he's lazy and that lazy is bad while hard work is good. It teaches kids responsibility for when they are adults. I don't think they should be "naked" though when they play. That isn't really teaching them good values like the work ethic part of the poems is.

I think Blake is telling us that hard work is good for kids and that they need to be taught good work ethics and values so they can grow up to be good people like their parents who pray and believe in God. God is in both of these poems because God is a good influence in the life of children and adults. God says that idle hands are the devil's playground, so that the kids won't be just wasting their time playing games all day like they do now, but will be busy working hard and believing in God so they are learning good values for when they grow up and become adults.

Analysis: To achieve a score of 2, the test taker's response is appropriate, but demonstrates some weaknesses.

- The answer indicates the test taker has an understanding of the selection read, but the test taker may have some misreadings. The response does indicate the harsh life of the child laborer, but the writer seems to condone child labor.

- The response includes an adequate number of examples from the selection to support the value of child labor, but the writer fails to acknowledge the cruelty of the system.

- The analysis of the literary elements is misinterpreted in places. The writer does not focus on point of view—one of the requirements of the essay. The life-after-death theme is totally overlooked by the writer; the essayist believes that the reference to a "naked" child is literal.

- There are some flaws in the writing. For instance, the casual use of contractions should not have been a part of the formal essay.

One-Point Essay

This poem is really boring and stupid. If the people don't like their jobs they can just quit and get another one. I had a boss once who was really mean and one day he was mean and rude to me in front of the customers so I told him that it wasn't nice to talk to me like that in front of the customers and he said that I was fired, so I quit and then a week later I got another job making stuffed bears at the mall. It wasn't hard, I just walked in and asked if they needed somebody and they said come back on Thursday and I got the job. So why doesn't Mr. Blake quit his job if isn't happy? He could just not go to work and instead go out and find another job. It's not hard making stuffed toys but sometimes it gets really busy and then we get all rushed but I take my time and do a good job on each one I make.

Sometimes bosses can be mean but some can be nice. I had one boss once who was really nice and he liked the way I put the decorations in the window so he made me in charge of decorating the windows and he said I did a really good job. Once he even said that I made the display look like a Macy's store window and I got embarrassed and laughed because I thought he was making fun of me until he told me that that was a good thing. So I got to do the store windows and one year at Christmas, I brought my friends over to see the windows I decorated and they all really liked it a lot and said it was really cool and I felt really good. So if Mr. Blake didn't like his job or his boss was really mean or rude to him or he just didn't like what he was doing then he could just quit and find a new job instead of complaining like he does in the poems.

Also he could ask his parents for help because parents are supposed to help their kids when they are in trouble or need money and such so why doesn't Mr. Blake just ask his parents for money? If he is a little kid than maybe he could do chores around the house or maybe he could mow lawns for the neighbors of something like that to earn extra money. You could get a paper route or something but then he'd have to get up early every morning and do it everyday even Christmas and New Year's day. But that's ok because my little brother did that until he got enough money for a new bike he wanted and he liked it even more because he got to earn it himself. Maybe Mr. Blake is so sad because he doesn't know how good it'd be for him to earn his own money and get what he wanted by working hard; but if his boss is just too mean or whatever than he should just quit going to his chimney job and find something else that he'd like to do better.

Analysis: To achieve a score of 1, the test taker responded to the questions, but the response is illogical or flawed in some ways.

- The answer does not indicate that the test taker has an understanding of the selection read. The essayist thinks the poem is about a dissatisfied worker.

- The test taker seems to believe the person speaking is "Mr. Blake." This assessment of the point of view is somewhat in error.

- The response fails to include examples of the use and value of symbolism; this was one of the requirements for the essay.

- The writing indicates a lack of control of language, a lack of coherence, and difficulty with syntax and diction.

- The analysis of the literary elements is flawed; the analysis is superficial and there is an omission of some literary elements.

- The essay shows repeated and serious writing errors and misinterpretations.

Answers and Analyses to Essay Question 2

Three-Point Essay

Charles Dickens emphasizes two literary devices in the beginning lines of A Tale of Two Cities. He opens the volume with his depiction of setting and with his use of contrast.

The setting that Dickens uses is a time that is universal: "the best of times . . . the worst of times," "the age of wisdom . . . the age of foolishness." Dickens narrows the time even further when he speaks of "the season of Light . . . the season of Darkness" and "the spring of hope . . . the winter of despair." Dickens's description of time is applicable to almost any era. The often-quoted, haunting, memorable lines have remained for almost two hundred years.

The use of contrasts is an effective literary device in those beginning lines. These descriptive terms help the reader to establish identification with the time in which A Tale of Two Cities occurs; it could be today! Dickens uses the terms "winter" and "spring." He mentions "Darkness" and "Light." These are stark contrasts that still remain today.

Although the writing is prose, it could be poetry with its rhythm, its style, and its purpose. Dickens effectively provided a framework for his novel from the opening lines.

Analysis: The test taker's response exhibits the following characteristics:

- The answer indicates the test taker has a thorough understanding of the selection read. The writing indicates that the essayist understands what a literary device is and how Dickens uses two of them—the setting and contrast—in the passage. The writer explained each well.

- The response includes an adequate number of well-chosen examples from the selection and an explanation of how the selected examples support the points that the response makes. The essayist made reference to examples of the seasons—"the spring of hope" and "the winter of despair"—in the section on the setting. To support his point about contrasts, the writer mentions "Light" and "Darkness," among other examples.

- The answers to all parts of the question are clear and appropriate; the writing is coherent and indicates a control of language. The writing is clearly above average.

- The analysis of the literary elements is accurate and includes some "depth." The writer's analysis of the literary elements shows an understanding of stylistic devices and of the importance of setting to many types of writing.

- The essay shows that the writer is able to use standard written English correctly. There are no grammatical, spelling, or punctuation errors. The work is above average: a 3.

One-Point Essay

The writing by Dickens is poor. The reader has no idea when the book took place. Dickens is vague. The reader begins the book with confusion.

Contrasts are not good. The reader has to think. What the writer is trying to say is like a puzzle. One can remember descriptions and and pictures. Comparisens much better.

I would not recommend these lines by Dickens to any one.

Analysis: To achieve a score of 1, the test taker responds to the questions, but the response is flawed.

- The answer does not indicate that the test taker has an understanding of the selection read. In fact, the writer calls Dickens's writing "poor."

- The response fails to include examples to support the points.

- The writing indicates a lack of control of language, a lack of coherence, and difficulty with syntax and diction. Misspelled words (*comparisen, any one)*, repeated words (*and, and*), and a sentence fragment indicate that the test taker may not have proofread the essay.

- The analysis of the literary elements is flawed. The writer generally denounces the use of contrasts in writing and states that the reader begins the reading with "confusion."

Answers and Analyses for Essay Question 3

Three-Point Essay

In this passage from Walden, *Henry David Thoreau suggests that inheriting material wealth is a "misfortune"—not a fortune. The author compares inheriting land, farms, homes, and buildings to gaining items whose disposal is almost impossible. Through the use of the metaphor and analogy, Thoreau clearly makes his point.*

Important to this passage is the metaphor. Thoreau writes of one's legacy as "burdens" or "loads"; he notes that one must push these burdens all the way to the grave. Thoreau continues this metaphor when he indicates that this "load" has crushed many receivers.

Through analogy Thoreau emphasizes the burden of one's legacy. He says a gift of sixty acres of land is like the chore of having to eat sixty acres of land—not just the "peck of dirt" that legend declares all people eat in a lifetime. He further underscores the tragedy of an inheritance by suggesting that the knowledge of one's inheritance from birth means that one must begin preparing one's grave from birth.

Another literary device that Thoreau employs is alliteration, or the repetition of sounds. An example of alliteration is the phrase "serfs of the soil."

With analogies, with alliteration, and with metaphors, Thoreau makes his point: an inheritance is a burden.

Analysis: The essay above would receive a score of 3. The writing exhibited the following characteristics:

- The answer indicates the test taker has a thorough understanding of the selection read; the writer is able to summarize the central idea of the passage in no uncertain terms.

- The response includes an adequate number of literary devices, well-chosen examples from the selection, and an explanation of how the selected examples support the points that the response makes. The writer uses quotation marks to indicate the examples are the exact words of Thoreau.

- The answers to all parts of the question are clear and appropriate. The essayist notes the central idea of the passage, the devices, and some of the examples.

- The essayist's writing is coherent and indicates a control of language, including syntax and diction.

- The analysis of the literary elements is accurate and includes some "depth."

- The essay shows that the writer is able to use standard written English correctly. The writer makes no errors in grammar or punctuation.

One-Point Essay

The writer is condemning the system that gives the inheritance to the oldest as a birthright. The writer recognizes the hard feelings that can come within a family from this tradition. The oldest whom is to receive the legacy is resented by the other family members. This animousity can lead to anger and murder as in the Bible.

The writer suggests that living with wolves is better than living with those who resent the inheritance that the first-born will recive.

I know about this resentment. I am the oldest of five.

Analysis: To achieve a score of 1, the test taker responded to the questions, but the response is illogical or flawed in some ways:

- The answer does not indicate that the test taker has an understanding of the selection read. The essay by Thoreau is not necessarily indicting the system of giving the holdings to the firstborn. He makes no mention of the resentment of the firstborn by other family members.

- One charge of the essayist is to present the central point; the essayist completely misses Thoreau's point—an inheritance can be a burden and not a blessing.

- The response fails to include examples to support the points that the essayist attempts to make. Of course, finding examples would have been impossible because the test taker has misinterpreted the central point.

- The writing indicates a lack of control of language, a lack of coherence, and difficulty with syntax and diction. Misspelled words—*recive, animousity*—and a lack of coherence makes the essay difficult to read. In addition there is a grammar error because the objective pronoun *whom* replaces the correct pronoun *who*.

Answers and Analyses for Essay Question 4
Three-Point Essay

Even though the setting of both Their Eyes Were Watching God *and* I Know Why the Caged Bird Sings *is mainly in the rural South during the Great Depression, the female characters in both books are assertive females. The characters develop their strength through hardships and trials, but they develop it nevertheless.*

In Their Eyes Were Watching God *the female character copes with the loss of a husband and the problems in managing a store. Her ability to adjust to change and her good business sense earn her the respect of others in the community. Though she has at times been dependent on the men in her life, she is able to endure on her own. Certainly the very fact that a woman operates a business is a credit to her and the community at the time.*

In I Know Why the Caged Bird Sings, *the reader finds Maya Angelou going to live with her aunt in the rural South. This aunt also manages a successful store and cares for her two charges sent South by their caregivers in the North.*

Angelou falls prey to a pedophile in the North, but it is to her credit that she is able to "bounce back" with time. Part of her ability to do so has come as a result of the strong women—her aunt, her teacher, in particular—in her life.

Both books—I Know Why the Caged Bird Sings and Their Eyes Were Watching God—are the works of women writers. Both writers—Maya Angelou and Zora Neale Hurston—recognize the inner strength, the sisterhood, and the value of women and their important place in a society that did not give them their full recognition at the time.

Analysis: The test taker's response exhibited the following characteristics:

- The response analyzes the literary issue introduced in the statement. The essay systematically and completely analyzes the issue.

- The essay uses appropriate examples from two books to illustrate and support the writer's position.

- The writing in the essay is coherent and demonstrates control of the language. The essay employs appropriate diction and syntax. The writing is well organized.

- The conventions of standard written English are evident in the work.

Zero-Point Essay

I Know Why the Cage Bird Sings takes place in the South, primarily. It contains women characters who are beaten down and defeated. Like Their Eyes Were Watching God also contains powerlss women.

Women today are without power. People have asserted power over these women. Little one can say about these Southern women.

Analysis: The second essay received a score of 0.

- The essay contains off-topic responses. Even though the writer does mention the books at the start of the essay, the adherence to the topic does not continue.

- The writing includes misspellings—*powerlss*—and sentence fragments—*Little one can say about these Southern women.*

- The essay is at times disorganized.

Praxis II English Language, Literature, and Composition: Pedagogy (0043)

The Praxis II English Language, Literature, and Composition: Pedagogy exam (0043) is a one-hour examination for those who plan to teach secondary English. This examination of literature study assesses two main elements: the teaching of literature and responses to student writing.

There are two constructed-response questions on the exam. The time limit for the test is one hour, so each of the essays should take about 30 minutes. The two answers receive equal weight: 50 percent each.

TEACHING LITERATURE

The first question on the Praxis II 0043 provides you with a list of literary works that are often a part of the secondary English curriculum and asks you to choose one title from the list and use that work to answer a three-part question.

In response to the three-part question, you should

- indicate two literary devices that are important to the chosen work

- identify two impediments to comprehension that secondary students might encounter when studying the selection

- describe two activities—with specific examples—that might help the students to understand central literary devices, and assist them in overcoming the barriers to comprehension that they might find in the work

For your response to the first question to receive full credit, you must do the following:

- Recognize the use of at least two essential stylistic devices in the chosen literary work and cite examples that are specific to the work. (Discussion that is not specific to the selected work or its literary devices is inappropriate.)

- Demonstrate an understanding of the varying knowledge, abilities, and skills of the secondary students in the English classroom.

- Show that you are aware of obstacles that students might meet in studying the chosen literary work.

- Indicate an ability to plan and explain appropriate activities for a classroom.

SCORING GUIDE

The first question consists of three parts. The score range is 0 to 6. Points are distributed as follows:

Part One: You can receive up to two points—one point for the identification of each appropriate literary feature that is specific to the work selected for review and appropriate for the designated class.

Part Two: You can earn up to two points—one point for the identification of two obstacles to students' understanding a literary work and one point for appropriate, well-chosen obstacles.

Part Three: Part three is worth two points. One point is available for each of the two appropriate activities designed to help students understand the literary feature and/or to help students surmount the obstacle(s) to their understanding. The devised activities must be specific to the selected work and must be appropriate for the grade level.

RESPONDING TO STUDENT WRITING

For your answer to the second question to receive full credit, you must do the following:

- Read a passage of student writing.

- Identify the strengths and weaknesses of the writing.

- Recognize any errors in the student's use of standard written English.

- Develop an assignment that addresses the student's weaknesses and capitalizes on the student's strengths.

These responses must be specific and identify significant problems.

The lesson prepared should include (a) appropriate objectives designed to remedy weaknesses and to capitalize on the strengths of the student; and (b) instructional activities specific to the objectives and commensurate with student abilities; and strategies for teaching composition that recognize the different levels, skills, abilities, rates, interests, cultural differences, and learning modalities of students in an English classroom.

SCORING GUIDE

You may earn a maximum score of 6 on question 2. Identifying a strength in the student's writing is worth one point; likewise, identifying a weakness in the student's writing is worth one point. You may earn two points by specifically noting two errors in standard written English. The last two points are available for preparing objectives specific to the noted weaknesses and/or strengths and providing activities to complement the objectives.

Features of Student Writing

You may wish to note the organization that the student uses and the punctuation choices she makes. The organization is important and can be a strength or a weakness. Two main types of organization may appear in student writing:

1. The **standard American argumentative essay** begins with an introduction that includes the main point of the essay (the thesis). A series of paragraphs give the subpoints. A conclusion sums up the essay.

2. The **inverted pyramid essay** places all the most important details—who, what, when, where, why, and how—in the first paragraph. Supporting—less important—details appear in order of salience in the remainder of the passage. Typical of newspaper reporting, this format enables the reader to stop reading at any point and still have the basic information.

TAKE THE TEST

Now you should take the two essay exams and time yourself. Remember, you should spend approximately 30 minutes on each essay question, and then move on to the next. Each answer is worth 50% of the total score. The answers and analysis begin after the second essay exam.

Ruled pages are provided in the back of this book for your essays.

Praxis English Assessment: Pedagogy (0043)

Practice Test 1

This test is also on CD-ROM in our special interactive TestWare® for the PRAXIS II English Assessment: Pedagogy (0043). It is highly recommended that you first take this exam on computer. You will then have the additional benefit of enforced timed conditions. See page 6 for instructions on how to get the most out of REA's TestWare®.

PRACTICE TEST 1 (0043)
PEDAGOGY

Question 1: Teaching Literature

TIME: 30 minutes

Directions: You are a ninth-grade English teacher. You are preparing a literature unit for a ninth-grade class. A primary goal of the curriculum standards for your district is for you to help the students in your class to identify literary devices in the works that they read.

Your choices of literary works to use as part of this unit are:

William Golding, *Lord of the Flies*

Lorraine Hansberry, *A Raisin in the Sun*

S. E. Hinton, The *Outsiders* **or** *That Was Then, This Is Now*

William Shakespeare, *Romeo and Juliet* **or** *Macbeth*

John Steinbeck, *The Grapes of Wrath* **or** *The Pearl*

Amy Tan, *The Joy Luck Club*

Mildred Taylor, *Roll of Thunder, Hear My Cry*

Mark Twain, *The Adventures of Huckleberry Finn*

From the list, choose ONE work that you know well enough (1) to identify at least two central literary features and (2) to cite specific examples of each literary device. Some examples of literary devices might include—but are not limited to—characterization, narration, genres and subgenres, and poetic techniques. After you select the work of your choice from the list, answer the following three-part question:

Part 1: (a) Identify two literary features in the work of choice and (b) cite two examples of each device from the selected book.

Part 2: Identify two obstacles to the designated students' understanding the literary work. These barriers must be both appropriate and well-chosen.

Part 3: Devise appropriate activities to help the designated students (a) understand the literary features and (b) surmount the obstacles to student understanding.

Question 2: Responses to Student Writing

TIME: 30 minutes

Directions: Below is a sample of a student's writing. After reading the passage, write a response in which you do the following:

1. Identify the strengths and weaknesses of the work.

2. Recognize any errors in standard written English in the passage.

3. Develop an assignment to address the student's weaknesses and to capitalize on the student's strengths.

These responses must be specific and identify significant problems.

Your lesson should include

- appropriate objectives designed to remedy the student's weaknesses and to capitalize on the student's strengths

- activities specific to the objectives and appropriate to the student's level

- strategies for teaching composition that provide for the different levels, skills, abilities, rates, interests, cultural differences, and learning modalities of students in an English classroom

Student Writing Sample

I agree with the many leaders. Who suggest we require young people to serve the public in some way, rather than the military draft.

There are several reasons this could benfit our country. The first is to give the young people, just out of high school and with no job experience, an opportunity to give something to his community and in return for this, the graduate gains self-respect, pride, and some valuable experience.

Whether the service is as simple as taking flowers to shut-ins or stopping for a chat in a rest home, a young person would have gained something and certainly given, perhaps hope, to that elderly person.

I can tell from my own experience how enriched I feel when I visit the elderly. They find joy in the simplest things, which in turn, teaches me I should do the same. This type of universal service would also strengthen the bonds between the younger generation and the older generation.

I am not sure how we would staff the military if people are doing community service instead of enlisting in service. The purpose of this essay is, however, not to answer the question of a lack of military persons. Still it is a question. We will have to depend on those who suggest community service in lew of te military to answer the question.

Praxis English Assessment: Pedagogy (0043)

Answer Explanations
for Practice Test 1

This section presents sample responses along with the standards used in scoring the responses. You should compare your responses to these sample responses to see where you need to improve your answers. When you read these sample responses, keep in mind that they will be less polished than if they had been developed at home, edited, and carefully presented. Examinees do not know what questions will be asked and must decide, on the spot, how to respond. Readers take these circumstances into account when scoring the responses.

Six-Point Response to Question 1: Teaching Literature

Mildred Taylor's Roll of Thunder, Hear My Cry *is a Newbery Award-winning Book and an appropriate selection for a ninth-grade class. The book has two integral literary devices: symbolism and the narration by young Cassie Logan. The students must overcome some obstacles to comprehend the author's intent.*

In Taylor's novel, which is based on fact, symbolism is an important stylistic device and one that may pose an obstacle to the young reader. One of the most important symbols or metaphors in the work is that of the land. To the Logan family, land is symbolic of their freedom. The absence of land ownership, by contrast, is a metaphor of bondage to other families.

A second important symbol in Roll of Thunder, Hear My Cry *is the school bus that the "white" children ride. The bus splatters Cassie and the others with mud. The children aboard the bus yell taunts at the walkers. The bus symbolizes oppression of Cassie and her friends; this symbol may pose an obstacle to modern students. Symbolism is not only significant to Taylor's book set in Mississippi but is also a frequent part of American society at large.*

A second literary device central to Roll of Thunder, Hear My Cry *is the narration by young Cassie Logan. Viewing the events through the eyes of the pre-teen girl makes some events more horrific—like the burning of a neighbor—and other events less terrible—like the loss of the crop.*

Ninth-graders may encounter some obstacles with the literary devices in Roll of Thunder, Hear My Cry*. Inner-city students, in particular, may not understand the symbol of land to represent freedom and the lack of land to represent bondage in the segregated society. These city dwellers may be residents of high-rise apartments and a part of families that do not own land or homes; the importance of land ownership to other families might be difficult for these students to comprehend.*

Likewise, the first-person narration by a young girl may be difficult for students who are accustomed to narration from a third-person point of view to understand. The importance of this device and the use of the word "I" may not be clear to the students. At the end of the unit, the students will be able to identify symbolism and narration from a first-person point of view (objectives).

To help the ninth-graders understand symbolism, the teacher will use several activities. First, the teacher will talk with the students about how an object or picture of an object can represent something else, like American symbols (flag, bald eagles, Statue of Liberty, etc.). Then the teacher will supply each pair of students with a magazine and ask them to cut out in the allotted time at least a) three logos or symbols of products/businesses, and b) the name of the product or business to paste beside it on poster board. If the students encounter American symbols (flag, bald eagles, Statue of Liberty, etc.), these should also be included on the poster board.

To help the student with the first-person narration, the teacher will discuss what the students know about pronouns. They will watch some classmates perform a short skit that may be as simple as three crossing-guards helping a child cross the street before school. The students will then write a sentence about the event from the view of the child (first person), from the standpoint of the guards who are giving directions for crossing the street on a busy morning and using the second-person "you," and from the position of the observers of the scene (third person).

The teacher may read aloud some sections of Roll of Thunder, Hear My Cry which show the reactions of Cassie to events and how her age may affect the telling. For instance, Cassie may not ride a bus to school because of racism; she speaks of the bus passing and the taunts of the children who are riding as they pass.

The location of logos and symbols in the magazines can help students to understand the use of symbolism in Roll of Thunder, Hear My Cry. The use of the scenario can help the students to understand the importance of narration and the use of the word "I" to the book. The scenario may also help students to see the perspective of a pre-teen and how this perspective may affect the way Cassie presents the events— like the passages about the school bus.

Scoring and Analysis

Each of question 1's three parts is worth up to 2 points, for a score range of 0 to 6. The sample response receives the maximum score of 6.

Part One: The test taker received two points—one point for the identification of each appropriate literary feature specific to *Roll of Thunder, Hear My Cry* and appropriate for the designated class of ninth-grade students. Again, the two literary features were symbolism (metaphor) and the point of view (narration).

Part Two: The test taker earned two points—one point for the identification of two obstacles to ninth-graders' understanding the literary work and one point for appropriate, well-chosen obstacles.

Again, the obstacles the test taker noted were the students' lack of understanding of the significance of the symbolism of land and the difficulty that students might have with the first-person narration of Cassie Logan.

Part Three: The test taker earned both of the two possible points for the discussion of the two devised activities to help students (a) understand the literary features and (b) surmount the obstacles to student understanding. The devised activities were specific to *Roll of Thunder, Hear My Cry* and were appropriate to ninth graders.

Six-Point Response to Question 2: Responses to Student Writing

This student essay has major faults. There are misspelled words (lew and benfit) and a lack of organization. In addition, the second paragraph has a long, run-on sentence and the first paragraph has a sentence fragment. The examples of personal observation do strengthen the writing, but the teacher would do well to review for the student—and for others having problems—how to write a good essay.

An appropriate lesson plan will focus on the objective of teaching/reviewing the steps in essay writing. 1) Give the students a work sheet with the essay writing steps (study the task, select the points to be made, organize the information, write it up, give appropriate examples, consult others as needed) listed in scrambled order. 2) Ask the students to number the steps in correct sequence—with consultations with others as needed. 3) Give the students a topic and ask them to use the steps to write an essay in response to the topic. 4) Allow the students to consult with each other at each stage of the essay writing and to use a dictionary to check spelling, as necessary.

Scoring and Analysis

The sample response receives the maximum score of 6. The response of the test taker to the student writing was appropriate. The test taker noted errors in standard written English (two points), both strengths (one point) and weaknesses (one point) in the student writing, and planned the follow-up lesson accordingly (two points). This is in accord with the requirements set in the question itself.

The lesson plan/assignment addressed the student's weaknesses (lack of organization and poor spelling, in particular) and capitalized on the student's strength (noting examples in writing). The examinee developed objectives to address the student's strengths and weaknesses and included activities that address the objectives.

The test taker included strategies to assist the students having problems. The examinee suggested presenting the students with the steps in writing an essay and instructing them to arrange the steps in sequential order. Providing the steps—even in random order—is superior to having to list the steps independently—especially because the student seems to be having some difficulty with organization. In addition, the students may consult with peers and use dictionaries, especially if they are having difficulty. This plan allows for different abilities, learning modalities, and skill levels.

Praxis English Assessment: Pedagogy (0043)

Practice Test 2

Question 1: Teaching Literature

TIME: 30 minutes

Directions: You are a tenth-grade English teacher. You are preparing a literature unit for a tenth-grade class. A primary goal of the curriculum standards for your district is that tenth-grade students should be able to identify literary devices in the works that they read.

Your choices of literary works to use as part of this unit are

Chinua Achebe, *Things Fall Apart*

Anonymous, *Beowulf*

Maya Angelou, *I Know Why the Caged Bird Sings*

James Baldwin, *Go Tell It on the Mountain*

Pearl S. Buck, *The Good Earth*

Sandra Cisneros, *The House on Mango Street*

Stephen Crane, *The Red Badge of Courage*

Charles Dickens, *Great Expectations*

Frederick Douglass, *Narrative of the Life of Frederick Douglass*

F. Scott Fitzgerald, *The Great Gatsby*

Anne Frank, *The Diary of Anne Frank*

William Gibson, *The Miracle Worker*

Lorraine Hansberry, *A Raisin in the Sun*

Nathaniel Hawthorne, *The Scarlet Letter*

Homer, *The Odyssey*

From the list, choose ONE work that you know well enough (1) to identify at least two literary features central to the work and (2) to cite two specific examples of each central literary device in the selected work. Note that literary devices might include—but are not limited to—characterization, narration, genres and subgenres, theme, and poetic techniques. After you select the work of your choice from the list, answer the following three-part question:

Part One: (a) Identify two literary features in the work of choice, and (b) cite two examples of each device from the selected book.

Part Two: Identify two obstacles to the designated students' understanding of the literary work. These barriers must be both appropriate and well-chosen.

Part Three: Devise appropriate activities to help the designated students (a) understand the literary features and (b) surmount the two obstacles to tenth-graders' understanding the literary work.

Question 2: Responses to Student Writing

TIME: 30 minutes

Below is a sample of a student's writing. After reading the passage, write a response in which you do the following:

1. Identify the strengths and weaknesses in the passage.

2. Recognize any errors in standard written English that the student might have used in the passage.

3. Develop an assignment to address the student's weaknesses and to capitalize on the student's strengths. Your lesson should include

   • appropriate objectives designed to remedy the student's weaknesses and to capitalize on the student's strengths

   • activities that are specific to the objectives you devised and are appropriate to the student's level

   • strategies for teaching composition that provide for the different levels, skills, abilities, rates, interests, cultural differences, and learning modalities of students in an English classroom

Your response must be specific and identify significant problems.

Student Writing Sample

When I think of what specific characteristics a person must possess in order to be an effective teacher I think of these: upstanding values, compassion, and a thorough knowledge of their subject matter.

First, a person who becomes a teacher must remember to be a role model to the students in their midst. Both one's private and professional life must be above reproach. A teacher is responsible for setting values as well as for teaching values.

Compassion is a quality that allows the teacher to have a sense of humor and to be supportive of the efforts of the students. Compassion enables the teacher to empathize with the students who are having problems in school or at home; the effective teacher will be supportive and provide positive direction.

Of course, a thorough knowledge of the subject matter is essential to good instruction. This expertise gives the teacher a sense of confidence and allows the teacher to plan effectively. The effective teacher not only knows but also likes teaching. The enthusiasm—or lack of enthusiasm—with which the teacher approaches the subject matter is apparent to the students.

In conclusion, by possessing and demonstrating values, showing compassion, and exhibiting knowledge of the subject matter, the right person can become a good teacher. If students are to learn, a person with all three characteristics can best influence them.

Praxis English Assessment: Pedagogy (0043)

Answer Explanations
for Practice Test 2

Six-Point Response to Question 1: Teaching Literature

The Odyssey is a classic that is appropriate for tenth-graders to read. The genre (traditional vs. modern), the subgenre (epic), the theme (picaresque), and the mythological characters are central to comprehending the epic.

An important literary feature of _The Odyssey_ is its genre. This classic is an example of traditional—as opposed to modern—literature. Tenth-graders should be beginning to recognize genres—especially traditional literature and the epic.

The Odyssey is an epic—a subgenre of traditional literature. An epic is a long, poetic narrative and is another literary feature of the work. An epic usually centers upon a hero—in this case Ulysses; another example of the epic is _Beowulf_. The epic tells of the great achievements of the hero and of the great events in his life. Tenth-graders should be able a) to identify both modern and traditional literature (objectives).

The picaresque theme—an important literary feature of _The Odyssey_—should be readily apparent. Sometimes called the "journey theme," the picaresque theme brings excitement into the lives of the characters—and the readers. In _The Odyssey_, the hero Ulysses does travel—for almost ten years. His travels are a perfect example of the picaresque theme, one of the main themes in traditional literature.

The teacher must help students to recognize main traditional themes (objective): reversal of fortune, survival of the unfittest, picaresque (objective). The teacher will list on the board—as the students name them—some popular fairy tales. The class may review the story line as they talk about each. On the other side of the board in random order the teacher will list the main themes: reversal of fortune, survival of the unfittest, picaresque. In small groups the students will attempt to match the theme with the titles of the fairy tales or other listed literature (activity).

A primary obstacle for many students is their lack of familiarity with the epic and with other types of traditional literature, such as legends, fairy tales, parables, myths, and fables. To help the students recognize genre (traditional) and subgenre (fables, legends, parables, myths, and fairy tales), the teacher will ask the students to work in pairs to define each genre and subgenre appearing on a handout (objective); the students may use a dictionary (activity). The teacher may also give students a paragraph from some traditional and some modern works (activity) and have the students identify the paragraphs as _modern or traditional_ (objective).

A second obstacle in reading this Greek epic is that tenth-graders may feel confusion upon finding that the same mythological character in Greek literature may have a different name in Roman mythology. For instance, the Greek name <u>Ulysses is Odysseus</u> in Roman stories.

To help the students identify the various mythological characters and their descriptions in both Greek and Roman mythology (objective), the teacher will give the students a list of the characters and a dictionary. In pairs, the students will find the characters in the dictionary and write their descriptions on the paper (activity); in doing so, they will note similarities between Greek and Roman literature. Some of the suggested characters to include are Neptune and Poseidon, Odysseus and Ulysses, and Venus and Aphrodite.

Scoring and Analysis

Each of question 1's three parts is worth up to two points, for a score range of 0 to 6. The sample answer receives the maximum score of 6.

Part One: The test taker received two points—one point for the identification of the genre specific to *The Odyssey* and one point for recognizing the themes in traditional literature. Again, identifying (a) the genre and subgenre (traditional literature, epic) and (b) the themes (picaresque, survival of the unfittest, and reversal of fortune) are particularly important.

Part Two: The test taker earned two points—one point for the identification of two obstacles to tenth-graders' understanding the literary work and one point for appropriate, well-chosen obstacles.

Again, the obstacles the test taker noted were (a) the students' lack of familiarity with traditional literature and with the types of traditional literature and (b) the difference between the names of the Greek and Roman mythological characters.

Part Three: The test taker earned both of the two possible points for the discussion of the two devised activities to help students with (a) understanding the literary features and (b) surmounting the obstacles: lack of familiarity with traditional literature and its types and the differences between Greek and Roman mythological characters. The devised activities were specific to the objectives and to *The Odyssey* and were appropriate to tenth graders.

Six-Point Response to Question 2: Responses to Student Writing

This essay has two major faults. The student had a one-sentence paragraph and should have added a comma after the introductory dependent clause in paragraph one. The use of personal observation, however, strengthens the writing.

An appropriate lesson plan will focus on helping the tenth-graders to recognize and punctuate correctly dependent clauses (objective) in order to enhance the understanding of the reader. The teacher will ensure that the students are familiar with a clause and with the difference between independent and dependent clauses. The teacher will want to indicate that a major function of punctuation is to ensure the writing conveys the meaning to the reader. Pausing after the dependent clause at the beginning of the sentence enhances the meaning; a comma is necessary.

To reinforce the use of the punctuation mark, the teacher will give the students a list of six sentences—some with introductory dependent clauses and some without. Working in pairs or alone as their learning style dictates, the students will add commas where needed (activity). Afterwards, the class will discuss the correct punctuation.

The teacher will mention that writers should avoid one-sentence paragraphs (objective). In pairs or individually—to satisfy a learning style—the students will take some examples of short writings with one-sentence paragraphs and expand the one-sentence writings to more than one sentence or combine the one-sentence paragraphs into another paragraph (activity).

Scoring and Analysis

The sample response receives the maximum score of 6. The response of the test-taker to the student writing was appropriate. The test taker noted errors in standard written English (two points), identified both strengths (one point) and weaknesses (one point) in the student writing, and planned the follow-up lesson accordingly (two points). This is in accord with the requirements set in the question itself.

The lesson plan/assignment addressed the student's weaknesses (one-sentence paragraphs and no comma after an introductory dependent clause) and recognized the student's strength (noting examples in writing). The test taker developed objectives to address the student's strengths and weaknesses and included activities that address the objectives.

The test taker included strategies to assist the students having problems. The examinee suggested presenting the students with passages containing one-sentence paragraphs and instructing them either to combine these paragraphs with other paragraphs in the passage or to convert them into two sentences. In addition, the students will have practice in recognizing and punctuating introductory dependent clauses. This plan allows for different abilities, different learning modalities, and varying skill levels.

Praxis II Middle School English Language Arts (0049)

The Praxis II Middle School English Language Arts (0049) is an examination of both the knowledge and competencies necessary for beginning middle school teachers of the English language arts.

This subject examination includes five main content categories:

1. The study of both reading and literature

2. The study of language (the history of and use of the English language)

3. Composition

4. Interpretation of text

5. Teaching reading and/or writing

Each of the main topics includes various subtopics.

The two-hour exam has **90 multiple-choice questions** that constitute 75 percent of your score. These 90 questions cover the first four categories just listed. You should spend about one and a half hours on this first section.

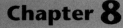

On each Praxis II 0049 exam, there are **two short essay questions** (constructed-response questions) that have equal weight:

1. One question will require the interpretation of a fiction or nonfiction text. The question may ask for interpretation and/or for discussion of an interpretation approach.

2. The other question will ask you to discuss approaches to teaching reading or writing.

You should spend about 30 minutes on the essay section—15 minutes on each question.

THE STUDY OF READING AND LITERATURE

The study of reading and literature, the first topic on the Praxis II 0049 exam, constitutes 45 (50 percent) of the 90 multiple-choice questions and includes several subtopics. These subtopics include the following skills:

- Recognizing/knowing/discussing the major works and authors of adolescent literature

- Paraphrasing, comparing, and interpreting—both inferentially and literally—various types of texts and reading materials: fiction, poetry, drama, graphic representations, and nonfiction

- Identifying and interpreting figurative language and literary elements, which include:

  1. tone: condescension, didacticism, irony, humor, parody, and sentimentality

  2. figurative language: simile, metaphor, analogy, personification, and clichés

  3. allusion

4. diction

5. voice

6. point of view

7. style

8. character

9. setting

10. plot

11. theme

- Identifying characteristics of literary forms and text structures, including prose, poetry, fiction, nonfiction, drama

- Situating and interpreting literature within its cultural contexts and historical periods

- Recognizing various approaches (including shared inquiry and reader-response theory) to critiquing and interpreting text

- Recognizing and applying various instructional approaches to teaching reading; these approaches should include cueing systems, activating prior knowledge, constructing meaning through context, and using metacognitive strategies

Reading Chapter 2 of this volume will give you a quick review of these topics.

LANGUAGE STUDY

Language study, the second topic on the Praxis II 0049 exam, constitutes 16 (18 percent) of the 90 multiple-choice questions and includes several subtopics. These subtopics include the following skills:

- Understanding and applying the conventions of grammar, usage, and mechanics, such as sentence types, sentence structure, parts of speech, modifiers, phrases, clauses, capitalization, and punctuation

- Understanding the development and structure of the English language (e.g., syntax and vocabulary)

- Understanding the principles of first- and second-language acquisition and development, and the nature of dialects

COMPOSITION

This section of the Praxis II 0049 exam accounts for 29 questions (32 percent) of the multiple-choice questions that stresses the importance of strategies for teaching writing in the classroom, with particular emphasis on the following:

- Individual and collaborative approaches to teaching writing (writing processes) and how they work recursively

- Common research and documentation techniques

- Evaluating and assessing student writing

CONSTRUCTED-RESPONSE QUESTIONS

Each Praxis II 0049 examination contains two short-essay questions or constructed-response questions. The constructed-response part of the test comprises 25 percent of your total score. As mentioned earlier, each short-essay question should take about 15 minutes.

Question 1

For question 1, you will read a selection of prose (fiction or nonfiction) or poetry (a complete short poem or an excerpt from a longer work) as a stimulus for the required literary analysis, and then complete two tasks:

1. Describe and give examples of the use of one or two specified literary elements present in the stimulus. These elements might include a metaphor, simile, voice, narrative point of view, tone, style, setting, diction, mood, allusion, irony, cliché, analogy, hyperbole, personification, alliteration, and/or foreshadowing.

2. Discuss the literary elements' role in contributing to the overall meaning and/or the effectiveness of the provided text.

Question 2

For the second essay question, you will be presented with a classroom situation and/or a piece of student work and asked to write a response. For example, the assignment might be to describe an instructional response to the student's work; the response should analyze the work or the situation and reference the strengths and/or the weaknesses of the student or class.

SCORING GUIDE

Score of 3

To achieve a score of 3, your response must:

- Demonstrate an ability to analyze the material thoughtfully and thoroughly.
- Demonstrate a strong knowledge of the subject matter.
- Respond appropriately to all parts of the question.
- Demonstrate use of conventions of standard written English.

Score of 2

To achieve a score of 2, your response must demonstrate some understanding of the topic, but it is limited in one or more of the following ways:

- It indicates a misreading of the material or provides only superficial analysis.
- It demonstrates only superficial knowledge of the subject matter.
- It responds to the question inadequately or not at all.
- It contains significant grammatical errors.

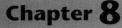

Score of 1

To achieve a score of 1, your response must be seriously flawed in one or more of the following ways:

- It demonstrates poor understanding of the subject matter or of the writing task.
- It fails to respond adequately to the question.
- It is incoherent or severely underdeveloped.
- It contains severe writing errors.

Score of 0

To achieve a score of 0, your response must be blank, irrelevant, totally incorrect, or a mere reiteration of the question.

TAKE THE TEST

Now you should take the two essay exams and time yourself. Remember, you should spend approximately 15 minutes on each essay question, and then move on to the next. Each answer is worth 25% of the total score. The answers and analysis begin after the multiple choice answer explanations.

Ruled pages are provided in the back of this book for your essays.

Praxis English Assessment:
English Language Arts (0049)
Practice Test 1

This test is also on CD-ROM in our special interactive TestWare® for the PRAXIS II English Assessment: English Language Arts (0049). It is highly recommended that you first take this exam on computer. You will then have the additional study features and benefits of enforced timed conditions and instantaneous, accurate scoring. See page 6 for instructions on how to get the most out of REA's TestWare®.

ANSWER SHEET FOR PRACTICE TEST 1 (0049)

1. Ⓐ Ⓑ Ⓒ Ⓓ
2. Ⓐ Ⓑ Ⓒ Ⓓ
3. Ⓐ Ⓑ Ⓒ Ⓓ
4. Ⓐ Ⓑ Ⓒ Ⓓ
5. Ⓐ Ⓑ Ⓒ Ⓓ
6. Ⓐ Ⓑ Ⓒ Ⓓ
7. Ⓐ Ⓑ Ⓒ Ⓓ
8. Ⓐ Ⓑ Ⓒ Ⓓ
9. Ⓐ Ⓑ Ⓒ Ⓓ
10. Ⓐ Ⓑ Ⓒ Ⓓ
11. Ⓐ Ⓑ Ⓒ Ⓓ
12. Ⓐ Ⓑ Ⓒ Ⓓ
13. Ⓐ Ⓑ Ⓒ Ⓓ
14. Ⓐ Ⓑ Ⓒ Ⓓ
15. Ⓐ Ⓑ Ⓒ Ⓓ
16. Ⓐ Ⓑ Ⓒ Ⓓ
17. Ⓐ Ⓑ Ⓒ Ⓓ
18. Ⓐ Ⓑ Ⓒ Ⓓ
19. Ⓐ Ⓑ Ⓒ Ⓓ
20. Ⓐ Ⓑ Ⓒ Ⓓ
21. Ⓐ Ⓑ Ⓒ Ⓓ
22. Ⓐ Ⓑ Ⓒ Ⓓ
23. Ⓐ Ⓑ Ⓒ Ⓓ

24. Ⓐ Ⓑ Ⓒ Ⓓ
25. Ⓐ Ⓑ Ⓒ Ⓓ
26. Ⓐ Ⓑ Ⓒ Ⓓ
27. Ⓐ Ⓑ Ⓒ Ⓓ
28. Ⓐ Ⓑ Ⓒ Ⓓ
29. Ⓐ Ⓑ Ⓒ Ⓓ
30. Ⓐ Ⓑ Ⓒ Ⓓ
31. Ⓐ Ⓑ Ⓒ Ⓓ
32. Ⓐ Ⓑ Ⓒ Ⓓ
33. Ⓐ Ⓑ Ⓒ Ⓓ
34. Ⓐ Ⓑ Ⓒ Ⓓ
35. Ⓐ Ⓑ Ⓒ Ⓓ
36. Ⓐ Ⓑ Ⓒ Ⓓ
37. Ⓐ Ⓑ Ⓒ Ⓓ
38. Ⓐ Ⓑ Ⓒ Ⓓ
39. Ⓐ Ⓑ Ⓒ Ⓓ
40. Ⓐ Ⓑ Ⓒ Ⓓ
41. Ⓐ Ⓑ Ⓒ Ⓓ
42. Ⓐ Ⓑ Ⓒ Ⓓ
43. Ⓐ Ⓑ Ⓒ Ⓓ
44. Ⓐ Ⓑ Ⓒ Ⓓ
45. Ⓐ Ⓑ Ⓒ Ⓓ
46. Ⓐ Ⓑ Ⓒ Ⓓ

47. Ⓐ Ⓑ Ⓒ Ⓓ
48. Ⓐ Ⓑ Ⓒ Ⓓ
49. Ⓐ Ⓑ Ⓒ Ⓓ
50. Ⓐ Ⓑ Ⓒ Ⓓ
51. Ⓐ Ⓑ Ⓒ Ⓓ
52. Ⓐ Ⓑ Ⓒ Ⓓ
53. Ⓐ Ⓑ Ⓒ Ⓓ
54. Ⓐ Ⓑ Ⓒ Ⓓ
55. Ⓐ Ⓑ Ⓒ Ⓓ
56. Ⓐ Ⓑ Ⓒ Ⓓ
57. Ⓐ Ⓑ Ⓒ Ⓓ
58. Ⓐ Ⓑ Ⓒ Ⓓ
59. Ⓐ Ⓑ Ⓒ Ⓓ
60. Ⓐ Ⓑ Ⓒ Ⓓ
61. Ⓐ Ⓑ Ⓒ Ⓓ
62. Ⓐ Ⓑ Ⓒ Ⓓ
63. Ⓐ Ⓑ Ⓒ Ⓓ
64. Ⓐ Ⓑ Ⓒ Ⓓ
65. Ⓐ Ⓑ Ⓒ Ⓓ
66. Ⓐ Ⓑ Ⓒ Ⓓ
67. Ⓐ Ⓑ Ⓒ Ⓓ
68. Ⓐ Ⓑ Ⓒ Ⓓ
69. Ⓐ Ⓑ Ⓒ Ⓓ

70. Ⓐ Ⓑ Ⓒ Ⓓ
71. Ⓐ Ⓑ Ⓒ Ⓓ
72. Ⓐ Ⓑ Ⓒ Ⓓ
73. Ⓐ Ⓑ Ⓒ Ⓓ
74. Ⓐ Ⓑ Ⓒ Ⓓ
75. Ⓐ Ⓑ Ⓒ Ⓓ
76. Ⓐ Ⓑ Ⓒ Ⓓ
77. Ⓐ Ⓑ Ⓒ Ⓓ
78. Ⓐ Ⓑ Ⓒ Ⓓ
79. Ⓐ Ⓑ Ⓒ Ⓓ
80. Ⓐ Ⓑ Ⓒ Ⓓ
81. Ⓐ Ⓑ Ⓒ Ⓓ
82. Ⓐ Ⓑ Ⓒ Ⓓ
83. Ⓐ Ⓑ Ⓒ Ⓓ
84. Ⓐ Ⓑ Ⓒ Ⓓ
85. Ⓐ Ⓑ Ⓒ Ⓓ
86. Ⓐ Ⓑ Ⓒ Ⓓ
87. Ⓐ Ⓑ Ⓒ Ⓓ
88. Ⓐ Ⓑ Ⓒ Ⓓ
89. Ⓐ Ⓑ Ⓒ Ⓓ
90. Ⓐ Ⓑ Ⓒ Ⓓ

PRACTICE TEST 1 (0049)

Middle School English Language Arts

TIME: 2 hours
90 multiple-choice questions and 2 constructed-response questions

In this section, you will find examples of test questions similar to those you are likely to encounter on the Praxis II Middle School English Language Arts exam.

1. Which types of graphs or charts would be appropriate for displaying the following information?

Favorite Books of 45 Surveyed Middle School Students

To Kill a Mockingbird	18
Any of the *Harry Potter* books	12
Call of the Wild	9
Where the Red Fern Grows	4
Forever	2

   I.   Bar graph
   II. Pie (circle) chart
  III. Scatterplot
  IV. Broken-line graph

(A) I and II
(B) III and IV
(C) I and III
(D) II and IV

Consider this excerpt from Louis Sachar's novel *Holes* as you address questions 2 through 6.

> A redheaded woman was there with Trout. Kate could see her rummaging through the cabin, dumping drawers and knocking things from the shelves of cabinets.

2. The antecedent of the possessive pronoun "her" in the second sentence is

(A) woman.
(B) Trout.
(C) Kate.
(D) unknown.

3. The parallel elements in this excerpt are

(A) prepositional phrases.
(B) subordinate clauses.
(C) participial phrases.
(D) relative clauses.

4. The word "redheaded" is an example of a

(A) compound noun.
(B) compound adjective.
(C) compound adverb.
(D) proper adjective.

5. An example of a definite article in this excerpt is

(A) a
(B) with
(C) and
(D) the

6. How many prepositional phrases are in this excerpt?

(A) 1
(B) 2
(C) 3
(D) 4

Consider this excerpt from Mark Twain's *The Adventures of Huckleberry Finn* as you address questions 7 through 19.

It was a monstrous big river down there—sometimes a mile and a half wide; we run nights. . . . Not a sound, anywheres—perfectly still—just like the whole world was asleep, only sometimes the bull-frogs a-cluttering, maybe. The first thing to see, looking away over the water, was a kind of dull line—that was the woods on t'other side—you couldn't make nothing else out; then a pale place in the sky; then more paleness, spreading around; then the river softened up, away off, and warn't black any more, but gray; you could see little dark spots drifting along, ever so far away—trading scows, and such things; and long black streaks—rafts; sometimes you could hear a sweep screaking; or jumbled up voices, it was so still, and sounds come so far; and by-and-by you could see a streak on the water which you know by the look of the streak that there's a snag there in a swift current which breaks on it and makes the streak look that way; and you see the mist curl up off of the water, and the east reddens up, and the river, and you make out a log cabin in the edge of the woods, away on the bank on t'other side of the river, being a wood-yard, likely, and piled by them cheats so you can throw a dog through it anywheres; then the nice breeze springs up, and comes fanning you from over there, so cool and fresh, and sweet to smell, on account of the woods and the flowers; but sometimes not that way, because they've left dead fish laying around, gars, and such, and they do get pretty rank; and next you've got the full day, and everything smiling in the sun, and the song-birds just going it!

7. The dominant method of development of this passage is

   (A) compare/contrast.
   (B) description.
   (C) narration.
   (D) process analysis.

8. The tone of the passage can best be described as

   (A) apathetic and detached.
   (B) disparaging and ominous.
   (C) peaceful and admiring.
   (D) supercilious and didactic.

9. The effect of this passage is achieved predominantly through Twain's use of

   (A) imagery.
   (B) extended metaphor.
   (C) irony.
   (D) abstract diction.

10. The language in the passage is an example of

   (A) abstract diction.
   (B) dialogue.
   (C) dialect.
   (D) hyperbole.

11. Language such as "sweep screaking" and "bull-frogs a-cluttering" are examples of

   (A) onomatopoeia.
   (B) personification.
   (C) inflated language.
   (D) anaphora.

12. "Sweep screaking" is also an example of

   (A) allusion.
   (B) alliteration.
   (C) internal rhyme.
   (D) simile.

13. While the novel as a whole is famously narrated in the first-person from Huck's perspective, this passage incorporates

    (A) third-person limited point of view.
    (B) third-person omniscient point of view.
    (C) third-person objective point of view.
    (D) second-person point of view.

14. This excerpt reveals Huck's thoughts and feelings. Showing a character through his or her thoughts is called

    (A) direct characterization.
    (B) indirect characterization.
    (C) subliminal characterization.
    (D) implied characterization.

15. This novel is associated with which American literary movement?

    (A) Romanticism
    (B) Transcendentalism
    (C) Realism
    (D) Rationalism

16. This novel is considered controversial for use in the classroom because of

    (A) the ungrammatical language.
    (B) Huck's lying and stealing.
    (C) Twain's satiric descriptions of organized religion.
    (D) the use of racial slurs and demeaning images of African Americans.

17. As the main character of the novel, Huck is considered the

    (A) protagonist.
    (B) antagonist.
    (C) foil.
    (D) static character.

18. At the beginning of the novel, Huck introduces himself to the reader, establishes the setting and some of the important characters, and reveals his conflicts with his father as well as with the Widow Douglass's attempt to "sivilize" him. This part of the plot is called the

    (A) exposition.
    (B) point of view.
    (C) rising action.
    (D) resolution.

19. The turning point in the novel is when Huck struggles with his conscience. He must decide once and for all "betwixt two things," whether to help his friend Jim and "go to hell," or to write a letter to Jim's owner Miss Watson, which would send his friend back into slavery. This point in the novel is called the

    (A) climax.
    (B) complications.
    (C) denouement.
    (D) foreshadowing.

20. The scene from the previous question can also be considered an illustration of

    (A) external conflict.
    (B) internal conflict.
    (C) direct characterization.
    (D) stereotyping.

Read the following passage and then answer questions 21 and 22.

> O my luve is like a red, red rose
> That's newly sprung in June;
> O my luve's like the melodie
> That's sweetly played in tune.

21. The passage makes use of

    (A) metaphor.
    (B) simile.
    (C) irony.
    (D) plot.

22. The passage was probably

    (A) a work of the twenty-first century.
    (B) a work of the eighteenth century.
    (C) taken from a work of prose.
    (D) an Anglo-Saxon work.

23. The correct name of a group of lines in a poem is

    (A) a rhyme.
    (B) a verse.
    (C) a stanza.
    (D) a limerick.

24. The name of the literary award given to books for children/young people each year by the American Library Association is

    (A) the Pulitzer Prize.
    (B) the Nobel Prize.
    (C) the Caldecott Award.
    (D) the Newbery Medal.

Consider this excerpt from Truman Capote's *A Christmas Memory* as you answer questions 25 through 28.

> A woman with shorn white hair is standing at the kitchen window. She is wearing tennis shoes and a shapeless gray sweater over a summer calico dress. She is small and sprightly, like a bantam hen; but, due to a long youthful illness, her shoulders are pitifully hunched. Her face is remarkable—not unlike Lincoln's, craggy like that, and tinted by sun and wind; but it is delicate too, finely boned, and her eyes are sherry-colored and timid. "Oh my," she exclaims, her breath smoking the windowpane, "it's fruitcake weather!"

25. What words and phrases directly characterize the woman in the excerpt?

    (A) "white hair," "gray sweater," "hunched"
    (B) "oh my," "fruitcake weather," "standing"

    (C) "sprightly," "remarkable," "timid"
    (D) "finely boned," "not unlike Lincoln's," "tinted"

26. In the clause, "She is small and sprightly, like a bantam hen," "small and sprightly" function as

    (A) predicate adjectives.
    (B) predicate nouns.
    (C) direct objects.
    (D) indirect objects.

27. The clause from the previous question is also an example of

    (A) personification.
    (B) a metaphor.
    (C) a simile.
    (D) an analogy.

28. The diction in this passage is best described as

    (A) academic.
    (B) conversational.
    (C) scientific.
    (D) dialectical.

Read the following pairs of sentences and then answer questions 29 and 30.

I.   Pauline planned to quickly and efficiently finish the cost-analysis report.
     Pauline expected to just barely meet the Friday deadline.

II. The boy took his dog to the vet, crying for fear of what would happen.
     Wiping tears of fear of what might happen, the dog went with the little boy inside the veterinary hospital.

III. She had ten dollars to spend at the fair.
     She had ten dollars to spend on a new purse.

IV. Moviegoers often go to the dollar cinemas wishing to carefully save money.
     Moviegoers wishing to be careful in spending their money often go to the dollar cinema.

29. Which sentences would be useful in discussing split infinitives?

    (A) I and IV
    (B) II and III
    (C) II and IV
    (D) III and IV

30. Which would be useful sentences in a lesson on misplaced modifiers?

    (A) IV, III, and I
    (B) II and III
    (C) II and IV
    (D) I and IV

Read the following lines of poetry and then answer questions 31 through 37.

I.   I celebrate myself, and sing myself.
     And what I assume you shall assume,
     For every atom belonging to me as good belongs to you.

II. Because I could not stop for Death—
     He kindly stopped for me—
     The Carriage held but just Ourselves—
     And Immortality.

III. Two roads diverged in a yellow wood, and I—
     I took the one less traveled by,
     And that has made all the difference.

IV. It was many and many a year ago,
     In a kingdom by the sea,
     That a maiden there lived whom you may know
     By the name of Annabel Lee;

31. Which excerpt begins a poem by Walt Whitman?

    (A) I
    (B) II
    (C) III
    (D) IV

32. What is the tone of the poem that begins "Because I could not stop for Death—"?

    (A) Fear
    (B) Denial
    (C) Acceptance
    (D) Sorrow

33. Which excerpt was written by Edgar Allan Poe?

    (A) I
    (B) II
    (C) III
    (D) IV

34. Which of the following lines includes the best example of personification?

    (A) I celebrate myself, and sing myself.
    (B) Because I could not stop for Death—
        He kindly stopped for me—
    (C) Two roads diverged in a yellow wood,
    (D) For every atom belonging to me as good
        as belongs to you.

35. Which excerpts are examples of free verse?

    (A) I and II
    (B) II and III
    (C) III and IV
    (D) I and III

36. Which excerpt presents an analogy for the difficult choices one makes in life?

    (A) I
    (B) II
    (C) III
    (D) IV

37. Which excerpt is an example of ABAB rhyme?

    (A) I
    (B) II
    (C) III
    (D) IV

Read the following passage and then answer questions 38 and 39.

So Grendel ruled, fought with the righteous,
One against many, and won; so Herot
Stood empty, and stayed deserted for years,
Twelve winters of grief for Hrothgar, king
Of the Danes, sorrow heaped at his door
By hell-forged hands. His misery leaped
The seas, was told and sung in all
Men's ears.

38. The passage is an excerpt from

   (A) *Beowulf.*
   (B) *Everyman.*
   (C) *Le Morte d'Arthur.*
   (D) *The Divine Comedy.*

39. Line 6 from the passage uses which literary device?

   (A) Simile
   (B) Assonance
   (C) Alliteration
   (D) Understatement

40. Though it is essentially a homogenization of many languages, at its roots, English is considered a

   (A) Latinate language.
   (B) Germanic language.
   (C) Romantic language.
   (D) Celtic language.

Read the following lines and then answer questions 41 through 43.

   I.   Call me Ishmael.
   II.   Marley was dead, to begin with.
   III. It was the best of times, it was the worst of times.
   IV.   Whose woods these are I think I know.

41. Which two of the previous quotes are opening lines of novels written by Charles Dickens?

   (A) I and II
   (B) II and III
   (C) IV and I
   (D) II and IV

42. Which line begins Herman Melville's *Moby Dick*?

   (A) I
   (B) II
   (C) III
   (D) IV

43. Which lines use contrasts for effect?

   (A) I and II
   (B) II and III
   (C) IV and I
   (D) II and IV

44. Which of the following is not a traditional folk or literary epic poem?

   (A) "Gilgamesh"
   (B) *The Iliad*
   (C) *Paradise Lost*
   (D) "The Rape of the Lock"

45. Choose the answer that best corrects the following sentence:

   Last night I shot an elephant in my pajamas.

   (A) I shot an elephant last night.
   (B) An elephant was wearing my pajamas when I shot him.
   (C) Last night, while I was wearing my pajamas, I shot an elephant.
   (D) Elephants don't wear pajamas.

46. Choose the answer that best rephrases the following sentence to maintain continuity of thought:

    He noticed a large stain in the rug that was right in the center.

    (A) He noticed a large rug in the center of the room.
    (B) He noticed a large stain right in the center of the rug that was right in the middle of the room.
    (C) He noticed a large stain right in the center of the rug.
    (D) He noticed a rug that had a large stain on it.

47. Which of the following sentences is an example of a present progressive verb form?

    (A) David is writing a novel.
    (B) David wrote a novel last year.
    (C) David will be writing a novel next year.
    (D) David is thinking about writing a novel.

48. Which of the following sentences is NOT written in passive voice?

    (A) The car was parked illegally in the handicapped space near the entrance to the museum.
    (B) Jeannette placed the book back on the shelf before anyone missed it.
    (C) When the votes were finally counted, Adam was named the winner of the election for class president.
    (D) The beaker was placed on the Bunsen burner, and was monitored by the scientist.

49. In the sentence, "We were shocked that Bob hit the home run," the subordinator is

    (A) were.
    (B) that.
    (C) shocked.
    (D) hit.

50. The stages of language acquisition in infancy and young children are

    (A) fluid.
    (B) easily traced.
    (C) set in rigid parameters.
    (D) mirrored in adults.

51. Which of the following statements about grammar is NOT correct?

    (A) Grammar represents a constructed code.
    (B) Grammar rules are at times arbitrary.
    (C) Grammar has a direct relationship to the way people speak.
    (D) Standard English provides a general understanding and competence in the language.

Read the following paragraph and then answer question 52.

[1]Just 12 miles north of San Francisco but with an unmistakably small-town feel, Corte Madera, California, is a kind of metropolitan paradise. [2]Situated near the base of scenic Mt. Tamalpais, the town reflects the mellow, outdoor lifestyle that characterizes the Golden State as a whole, with open space and parks aplenty. [3]Corte Madera is ensconced in the verdant Marin County countryside. [4]Many of its 8,300 residents enjoy running, hiking, and biking, and relish some of the most spectacular vistas in the West.

52. Which of the following is the topic sentence of this paragraph?

    (A) Sentence 1
    (B) Sentence 2
    (C) Sentence 3
    (D) Sentence 4

53. Which of the following sentences is NOT written in active voice?

   (A) Gasping for breath, I ran at full speed down the street, through my yard, and up the back stairs when I heard my mother call me.

   (B) George slammed the money down on the counter and demanded service immediately.

   (C) If I don't slow down, I will spend all my money before the trip is half over.

   (D Though her grades were inconsistent, Kayla was accepted to her first-choice college on the merits of her athletic ability and her record of leadership.

Consider the Prologue from Shakespeare's *Romeo and Juliet* as you answer questions 54 through 59.

Two households, both alike in dignity,
In fair Verona, where we lay our scene,
From ancient grudge break to new mutiny,
Where civil blood makes civil hands unclean.
From forth the fatal loins of these two foes
A pair of star-crossed lovers take their life;
Whose misadventured piteous overthrows
Doth with their death bury their parents' strife.
The fearful passage of their death-marked love,
And the continuance of their parents' rage,
Which, but their children's end, naught could remove,
Is now the two hours' traffic of our stage;
The which if you with patient ears attend,
What here shall miss, our toil shall strive to mend.

54. The Prologue is written in

   (A) blank verse.
   (B) free verse.
   (C) sonnet form.
   (D) ballad form.

55. The line, "A pair of star-crossed lovers take their life," establishes

   (A) a paradox.
   (B) dramatic irony throughout the rest of the play.
   (C) an allusion to an earlier Shakespearian drama.
   (D) a point of conflict between the speaker and the lovers.

56. The poem is written in

   (A) trochaic pentameter.
   (B) dactylic pentameter.
   (C) iambic pentameter.
   (D) anapestic pentameter.

57. One reason Shakespearean language is challenging for students is because of language such as "doth" and "misadventured" that today is considered

   (A) archaic.
   (B) abstract.
   (C) allusive.
   (D) colloquial.

58. This poem is an example of

   (A) internal rhyme.
   (B) external rhyme.
   (C) end rhyme.
   (D) AABB rhyme.

59. The words "love" and "remove" are examples of

   (A) internal rhyme.
   (B) slant rhyme.
   (C) perfect rhyme.
   (D) exact rhyme.

60. Which of the following best describes a language acquisition program that adheres to the basic principles recommended by the Center for Applied Linguistics?

(A) A program of instruction that stresses the commonalities in languages, thereby making the transition from one language to the next phonetically simpler

(B) A program of instruction that tests students' natural language aptitudes and tailors a customized curriculum based on the particular student's abilities and weaknesses

(C) A program of instruction that puts students at ease with the process of language acquisition

(D) A program of instruction that challenges all students academically and linguistically

61. What is a mother tongue?

(A) The language skills acquired from the maternal (mother's) side of the family

(B) The first language a person learns or the native language

(C) The accepted language of the area or region where a person lives

(D) The Latin base from which our modern-day languages developed

62. When two independent clauses are NOT joined correctly, the sentence is known as a

(A) fragmented sentence.

(B) topic sentence.

(C) run-on sentence.

(D) comma-splice sentence.

63. When a student has difficulty with reading retention, the recommended procedure for improving retention skills would include

(A) using classroom materials designated for lower grade levels because these are less intimidating.

(B) increasing the amount of time the student spends on repetition and review.

(C) reading aloud, slowly and clearly, articulating as many words as possible.

(D) designating the child as developmentally disabled and referring him or her to counseling.

64. In Shakespeare's *Romeo and Juliet*, Juliet discovers her new husband, Romeo, has just killed her cousin, Tybalt. In her despair she calls Romeo a "Beautiful tyrant! fiend angelical!" These expressions are examples of

(A) oxymorons.

(B) puns.

(C) mixed metaphors.

(D) anaphora.

65. Which of the following is the best example of onomatopoeia?

(A) Ha-ha, whip, hop, hope

(B) Sneeze, cough, laugh, blink

(C) Buzz, hiss, whoosh, ding-dong

(D) Zip, bump, jump, stump

66. The more common name for a lexicon is

(A) an encyclopedia.

(B) a dictionary.

(C) a catalog.

(D) a textbook.

Read the following passage and then answer questions 67 and 68.

At his birth an oracle prophesied that he would kill his father and marry his mother. His parents abandoned him to die on a mountaintop, but he was saved and adopted by a distant king and queen. As a man, he heard the prophesy and tried to escape his fate by running to another country. He ended up in the land of his birth and unknowingly fulfilled the dire prediction.

67. The passage describes

    (A) Atlas.
    (B) Oedipus.
    (C) Hercules.
    (D) Hydra.

68. Transition in a passage is often brought about by transition words. Which of the following is NOT a transition word?

    (A) When
    (B) While
    (C) Because
    (D) And

Read the following passage and then answer questions 69 through 73.

> One speaks the glory of the British Queen.
> And one describes a charming Indian screen;
> A third interprets motions, looks, and eyes;
> At every word a reputation died.
> Snuff, or the fan, supply each pause of chat.
> While singing, laughing, ogling, and all that.
> Meanwhile, declining from the noon of day,
> The sun obliquely shoots his burning ray;
> The hungry judges soon the sentence sign,
> And wretches hang that jurymen may dine.

69. The last two lines suggest that this society

    (A) takes pride in its justice system.
    (B) speedily administers justice for humanitarian reasons.
    (C) sentences the wrong people to death.
    (D) sentences people for the wrong reasons.

70. Lines 1 though 6 suggest that this society

    I. indulges in gossip that slanders the Queen.
    II. engages in serious discussions about affairs of state.
    III. engages in gossip that ruins reputations.

    (A) I and III
    (B) III only
    (C) II only
    (D) I, II, and III

71. The juxtaposition in lines 1 and 2 suggests that the people

    (A) talk of trivia.
    (B) revere the monarchy and Indian screens equally.
    (C) are Imperialists.
    (D) are Royalists.

72. The word "obliquely" (line 8) in this context could mean or function as all of the following EXCEPT

    (A) "perpendicularly."
    (B) "at a steep angle."
    (C) a pun on hidden meanings.
    (D) a pun on stealth.

73. What is the grammatical function of the word "glory" in the first sentence?

    (A) subject
    (B) direct object
    (C) indirect object
    (D) predicate noun

74. "Like sunshine after storm were the peaceful weeks which followed." This sentence from Louisa May Alcott's *Little Women* is an example of

    (A) a sentence fragment.
    (B) inversion.
    (C) a periodic sentence.
    (D) a balanced sentence.

75. The sentence in the previous question is also an example of

    (A) a simile.
    (B) a metaphor.
    (C) personification.
    (D) an analogy.

Consider the following passage from Harper Lee's *To Kill a Mockingbird* as you answer questions 76 through 83. Here the narrator discusses her mysterious neighbor, Boo Radley.

Inside the house lived a malevolent phantom. People said he existed, but Jem and I had never seen him. People said he went out at night when the moon was down, and peeped in windows. When people's azaleas froze in a cold snap, it was because he had breathed on them. Any stealthy small crimes committed in Maycomb were his work. Once the town was terrorized by a series of morbid nocturnal events: people's chickens and household pets were found mutilated; although the culprit was Crazy Addie, who eventually drowned himself in Barker's Eddy, people still looked at the Radley Place, unwilling to discard their initial suspicions. A Negro would not pass the Radley Place at night, he would cut across to the sidewalk opposite and whistle as he walked. The Maycomb school grounds adjoined the back of the Radley lot; from the Radley chickenyard tall pecan trees shook their fruit into the schoolyard, but the nuts lay untouched by the children: Radley pecans would kill you. A baseball hit into the Radley yard was a lost ball and no questions asked.

76. The dominant method of development of this passage is

(A) narration.
(B) description.
(C) analysis.
(D) cause and effect.

77. The passage is developed through

(A) a series of details that support the main assertion.
(B) a series of incongruous elements that complicate the main assertion.
(C) lush imagery.
(D) citations.

78. The topic sentence of the paragraph is

(A) "Inside the house lived a malevolent phantom."
(B) "People said he existed, but Jem and I had never seen him."
(C) "Any stealthy small crimes committed in Maycomb were his work."
(D) "A baseball hit into the Radley yard was a lost ball and no questions asked."

79. Although acceptable language at the time the novel was written in 1960, the word "negro" in contemporary prose would be considered

(A) a racial slur.
(B) archaic.
(C) unrealistic.
(D) hyperbole.

80. How does the colon function in the underlined portion of the passage?

(A) The colon introduces a list of items.
(B) The colon separates two contrasting ideas.
(C) The colon indicates a cause and effect relationship between the two clauses.
(D) The colon indicates clarification of and expansion upon the first clause.

81. The underlined portion of the passage is an example of

    (A) a cumulative sentence.
    (B) a periodic sentence.
    (C) a balanced sentence.
    (D) a run-on sentence.

82. The word "once" in the underlined portion of the passage is an example of

    (A) a noun.
    (B) an adjective.
    (C) an adverb.
    (D) a preposition.

83. The underlined portion of the passage is an example of

    (A) an interrogative sentence.
    (B) a complex sentence.
    (C) a compound sentence.
    (D) a compound-complex sentence.

84. Which of the following authors are considered primarily fantasy writers?

    (A) William Golding and Robert Cormier
    (B) C.S. Lewis and Roald Dahl
    (C) S. E. Hinton and Carson McCullers
    (D) J.D. Salinger and George Orwell

85. Which of the following is NOT considered a romantic writer?

    (A) Mary Shelley
    (B) Percy Bysshe Shelley
    (C) Edgar Allan Poe
    (D) Stephen Crane

86. Which writers are considered part of the Harlem Renaissance?

    (A) Langston Hughes and Countee Cullen
    (B) Sylvia Plath and Maya Angelou
    (C) T.S. Elliot and Dylan Thomas
    (D) Toni Morrison and Billy Collins

87. Which of the following is NOT an American playwright?

    (A) Tennessee Williams
    (B) Lorraine Hansberry
    (C) Arthur Miller
    (D) Harold Pinter

88. *The Diary of Anne Frank* can best be classified as a

    (A) novel.
    (B) memoir.
    (C) biography.
    (D) drama.

89. Which nineteenth century author wrote novels for children?

    (A) Louisa May Alcott
    (B) E.B. White
    (C) Washington Irving
    (D) Charles Dickens

90. All of the following novels have been controversial in some school settings. Which ones are frequently opposed because of coarse language?

    (A) The *Harry Potter* series and *The Wizard of Oz*
    (B) *Of Mice and Men* and *The Catcher in the Rye*
    (C) *Bridge to Terabithia* and *A Day No Pigs Would Die*
    (D) *The Lord of the Flies* and *Brave New World*

PRACTICE TEST 1 (0049): CONSTRUCTED-RESPONSE QUESTIONS

Question 1: Literary Analysis

Write a critical essay in which you respond to the following poem. The essay must (a) note at least two literary techniques and (b) indicate how the techniques contribute to the text.

The Chimney Sweeper

A little black thing among the snow:
Crying weep, weep, in notes of woe!
Where are thy father & mother? say?
They are both gone up to the church to pray.

Because I was happy upon the heath,
And smil'd among the winters snow:
They clothed me in the clothes of death,
And taught me to sing the notes of woe.

And because I am happy & dance & sing,
They think they have done me no injury:
And are gone to praise God & his Priest & King,
Who make up a heaven of our misery.

William Blake, *Songs of Experience*, 1794

Question 2: Teaching Writing

Read the following classroom situation and then in a well-constructed essay describe the strengths and/or weaknesses of the solution to it.

One of the teachers in the school where you teach has a student who speaks English as a second language. The teacher—Mrs. Jones—has definite ideas about how to deal with that student.

Mrs. Jones tells her entire class that they may not speak any language other than English at any time. She encourages them to eat in the cafeteria where they can eat "American" food. She tells them this is better than bringing ethnic food from home to school. "After all, you are in America," she says.

Mrs. Jones believes that in the United States, English should be the only language.

The purpose of school is to teach that language.

What is your reaction to (a) this teacher and (b) her ideas?

Praxis English Assessment: Middle School English Language Arts (0049)

Answer Explanations for Practice Test 1

ANSWER KEY FOR PRACTICE TEST 1 (0049)

1. (A)	24. (D)	47. (A)	70. (B)
2. (A)	25. (C)	48. (B)	71. (B)
3. (C)	26. (A)	49. (B)	72. (A)
4. (B)	27. (C)	50. (A)	73. (B)
5. (D)	28. (B)	51. (C)	74. (B)
6. (D)	29. (A)	52. (A)	75. (A)
7. (B)	30. (C)	53. (D)	76. (B)
8. (C)	31. (A)	54. (C)	77. (A)
9. (A)	32. (C)	55. (B)	78. (A)
10. (C)	33. (D)	56. (C)	79. (B)
11. (A)	34. (B)	57. (A)	80. (D)
12. (B)	35. (D)	58. (C)	81. (A)
13. (D)	36. (C)	59. (B)	82. (C)
14. (B)	37. (D)	60. (D)	83. (D)
15. (C)	38. (A)	61. (B)	84. (B)
16. (D)	39. (C)	62. (C)	85. (D)
17. (A)	40. (B)	63. (B)	86. (A)
18. (A)	41. (B)	64. (A)	87. (D)
19. (A)	42. (A)	65. (C)	88. (B)
20. (B)	43. (B)	66. (B)	89. (A)
21. (B)	44. (D)	67. (B)	90. (B)
22. (B)	45. (C)	68. (D)	
23. (C)	46. (C)	69. (D)	

PRACTICE TEST 1 (0049): PROGRESS CHART

Reading and the Study of Literature ____/58

1	7	8	9	10	11	12	13	15	16	17	18	19

20	21	22	23	24	25	26	27	31	32	33	34	35

36	37	38	39	40	41	42	43	44	55	56	58	59

63	64	65	67	69	70	71	72	75	76	77	79	84

85	86	87	88	89	90

Language and Linguistics ____/23

2	3	4	5	29	30	45	46	47	48	49	50	51

53	57	60	61	62	63	73	74	80	81

Composition and Rhetoric ____/10

6	14	28	52	54	66	76	78	82	83

1. (A)

A bar graph, choice I, works well here. The height of each of five bars would be determined by the number of votes for each novel. A circle or pie chart, choice II, would also be appropriate. The 18 votes for *To Kill a Mockingbird* give the fraction 18/40, so the book by Harper Lee would have 45 percent of the area of a circle chart. The same approach would tell us the appropriate size for each book on the pie chart and on the bar graph.

A scatter plot (III) illustrates the relationship between sets of data. A broken-line graph (IV) generally illustrates change over time. Neither III nor IV is appropriate for illustrating the given data. Because III or IV or both are a part of (B), (C), and (D), these three answers are not appropriate.

2. (A)

The antecedent of a pronoun is the word that is being replaced. In this sentence, "woman" is the antecedent of the pronoun "her."

3. (C)

Parallelism or parallel construction is the repetition of identical grammatical elements in a sentence. In this sentence, three participial phrases are used in succession: "rummaging . . . dumping . . . knocking . . . ."

4. (B)

In the word "redheaded," two words are combined to form a new one, in this case an adjective, thus we have a compound adjective.

5. (D)

"The" is a type of adjective called a definite article. "A" is an indefinite article (along with "an"), "with" is a preposition, and "and" is a conjunction.

6. (D)

There are four prepositional phrases in this excerpt: "with Trout," "through the cabin," "from the shelves," and "of cabinets."

7. (B)

Though the passage is organized chronologically, Twain's purpose here is descriptive. Writers frequently combine strategies, but in this case, the narration becomes just a way to organize the descriptive details and images that paint a picture of the river.

8. (C)

Nature is celebrated in this passage. The details, images, and diction combine here to create a peaceful and admiring view of the river.

9. (A)

Imagery—language used to appeal to the senses—is the dominant rhetorical strategy of the choices provided. Twain does not use figurative or abstract language in this passage; in fact, his focus on sensory language makes it quite concrete, so choices (B) and (D) are incorrect. Though much of *Huck Finn* is ironic, here Twain and Huck express their true feelings directly and without irony.

10. (C)

The Adventures of Huckleberry Finn is one of the most important examples of dialect used in literature in the English language. Here Twain mimics the diction and syntax of a semi-literate boy from a small town in Missouri. Though nonstandard, the diction is concrete, not abstract (A); neither is it hyperbolic (D) or exaggerated. Also, dialogue (B) is a verbal exchange between two or more characters. In this passage, Huck is only thinking or perhaps speaking directly to the reader, so there is no dialogue here.

11. (A)

This language incorporates onomatopoeia—words that sound like their meaning. Personification (B) is a figure of speech in which nonhuman things are given human characteristics. Inflated language (C) is language too formal and erudite for the occasion; Huck's language here is the opposite of inflated. Nor is anaphora (D), the intentional repetition of words, used here.

12. (B)

The repetition of the "s" sound as well as the long "e" sound make this phrase alliterative. An allusion (A) is an indirect reference to a previous source, and a simile (D) is an abstract comparison using "like" or "as." Internal rhyme are rhyming words within the same line of poetry (C). None of these rhetorical strategies applies to this phrase.

13. (D)

While the novel is famous for its first-person narration, the use of the second-person "you" distinguishes this passage. Huck/Twain uses the second-person here to directly connect to his audience and draw them into the scene.

14. (B)

Direct characterization (A) is the explicit description of a character—words such as "honest," "timid," "strong," and "loving" that *tell* us about the character would be examples of direct characterization. Indirect characterization *shows* rather than *tells*. There are five methods of indirect characterization: the character's thoughts, words, actions, appearance, and the opinion of other characters. In this passage, Huck's character is revealed through his thoughts as well as his language. Choices (C) and (D) are not literary terms.

15. (C)

Though the celebration of nature is generally considered a characteristic of the Romantic movement, *The Adventures of Huckleberry Finn*, published in 1889, is a product of the American Realism. American Romanticism as well as Transcendentalism (about 1830 to 1860) directly precedes this movement, while Rationalism, where the dominant genre was nonfiction prose, is associated with the latter half of the eighteenth century.

16. (D)

Though once condemned for its bad grammar (A), delinquent main character (B), and critical view of organized religion (C), today *Huck Finn* is controversial for its racial slurs and what some consider demeaning images of African Americans.

17. (A)

The main character, the one who drives the action in a work of fiction or drama, is called the protagonist. Though we often use this term interchangeably with the term "hero," many protagonists (Gatsby, Willy Loman, and MacBeth to name a few) are too flawed to really be called heroes. The antagonist (B) is the person or force that opposes the protagonist. Huck is opposed by his alcoholic father, but he is also opposed by a society that does not approve of him and wants to "sivilize" him. Foils (C) are characters who display opposite traits for the purpose of highlighting an important theme in the work. For example, both Jim and Pap are father figures in the novel, but Jim is caring and protective of Huck while Pap, Huck's actual father, abandons Huck and uses him for his money. A static character (D) stays the same throughout the work.

18. (A)

The exposition, sometimes called the basic situation, occurs at the beginning of a story where the characters, settings, and conflicts are introduced. Of course, depending on the work, many people, places, and conflicts may be revealed to us later, but the exposition will set the groundwork for a work of fiction or drama. The point of view (B) is the perspective of the narration. The rising action (C) or complications are the events of the plot, the bulk of the story. The resolution (D) is the end of the plot, where the conflicts will be resolved, or perhaps left unresolved or ambiguous, leaving an opening for a sequel.

19. (A)

The climax is the high point of the work, where the main conflict will be decided one way or another. In *The Adventures of Huckleberry Finn,* Huck's love for his friend Jim is in conflict with the expectations of a racist society where African Americans are considered subhuman. Huck's decision in this scene is the critical point, the climax, of the novel.

20. (B)

This is internal conflict because it occurs within the character. Huck's heart is in conflict with his social conscience. An external conflict (A) is a character's conflict with the outside world. In this novel, Huck's struggle with his father who abuses him and has tried to enslave him is an example of an external conflict.

21. (B)

A simile is a comparison that uses "like" or "as." The poet says his love is like "a red, red rose" and "a melodie." Because these are similes, (B) is the best answer. A metaphor is also a comparative figure of speech, but it does not use "like" or "as;" rather, a metaphor likens one thing, idea, or concept to some other word or phrase whose literal meaning is unrelated to the thing being described; (A) is not the best answer. Irony is the incongruity between what one expects and what actually happens; (C) is not the best answer. A plot—or story line—is not a central element in the poem; (D) is not the best answer.

22. (B)

The passage is a work of the eighteenth century. The passage does not have a current theme or the diction of the present day; it is evidently *not* a work of the twenty-first century (A). By definition, the poem is not a work of prose (C). The Anglo-Saxon period spanned 600 years; it ended with the beginning of the medieval period in 400 CE. This poem is not typical of the Anglo-Saxon period, which has few surviving written remnants, like *Beowulf*. Therefore, (D) is not the best answer.

23. (C)

A stanza is a group of lines in a poem; there is often a metrical order and a repeated rhyme. Students sometimes incorrectly call the grouping a *verse* (B), but the correct term is *stanza*. *Rhyme* (A) can refer to corresponding sounds, to rhyme schemes, and/or to the metrical order; rhyme is not a group of lines, so (A) is incorrect. A limerick (D) is a specific style of poetry; (D) is not the best answer.

24. (D)

The name of the literary award that the American Library Association presents yearly is the Newbery Medal. The ALA also presents the Caldecott Award, but that award goes to a picture book; (C) is not the right answer. The Pulitzer Prize (A) and the Nobel Prize (B) do not have the audience of young people in the requirements for receipt of their awards.

25. (C)

These words directly tell us about the character. The other choices indirectly show us the character.

26. (A)

They are predicate adjectives that modify the subject, "she." Predicate adjectives and nouns (B) follow linking verbs. Direct and indirect objects (C) and (D), follow action verbs. The verb "to be" is the most commonly used linking verb.

27. (C)

A simile is a comparison using the words "like" or "as," while a metaphor (C) makes a more direct comparison without the words "like" or "as." Personification (A) gives human characteristics to nonhuman things, the opposite of what is happening in this example. An analogy is less abstract than the other figures of speech in that it draws a comparison to show how two things are alike, often with the purpose of instruction.

28. (B)

Though the language in this story is beautiful and elegant, it is accessible to the average person; therefore it is not academic (A) nor is it scientific (C). Dialect (D) is the nonstandard language of a particular region or group of people. In addition, journal writing alone is not the same as process writing. (C) is incorrect because the purpose of the journal is much broader, even though the instructor may use some of her journal entries in her formal evaluation. (D) is incorrect because it is too simplistic. If Ms. Axtel were a habitual journal writer, she would be writing about a variety of topics, not just emphasizing those related to teaching.

29. (A)

A split infinitive would have the word *to* separated from a verb form by another word. Examples of the split infinitive would be "to quickly and efficiently finish" in the first sentence in sentence pair I; "to just barely meet" in the second sentence in sentence pair I; and "to carefully save" in the first sentence in sentence pair IV. Answer (A) allows both choices I and IV. The other pairs—listed in (B), (C), and (D)—do not contain split infinitives.

30. (C)

In both sentences in pair II, the modifiers appear near the wrong word. For instance, in the first sentence it is not the vet who is "crying for fear of what would happen." In sentence two of pair II, "wiping tears of fear of what might happen" appears near "the dog"; it is not the dog that is wiping tears, however. In the first sentence of pair IV, "wishing to carefully save money" appears near "cinemas," not near "moviegoers." Choice (C) is the only answer that allows both choices.

31. (A)

These are the opening lines of Walt Whitman's "Song of Myself." (B) begins a poem by Emily Dickinson (1830–86). "Two roads diverged in a yellow wood" is the starting line of "The Road Not Taken" (1916) by Robert Frost.

32. (C)

The poem "Because I Could Not Stop for Death" expresses the acceptance of Emily Dickinson for the visit by Death. There is no evidence of fear (A), denial (B), or sorrow (D).

33. (D)

"Annabel Lee," written in memory of his dead wife Virginia, is one of Edgar Allan Poe's most famous poems. The structured meter and rhyme is also typical of Poe.

34. (B)

In her poem, Emily Dickinson describes Death as a visitor who takes her on a carriage ride; this is an example of personification. None of the other lines quoted include the stylistic device of personification.

35. (D)

Free verse poetry has no structured meter and rhyme scheme; the Whitman poem (I) and the Frost poem (IV) poems are examples of free verse. The Dickinson (II) and Poe poems (IV) both have highly structured meters and rhyme schemes.

36. (C)

Robert Frost uses the choosing of one road over another as a comparison—an analogy—for the choices one makes in life. None of the other examples contains an analogy.

37. (D)

In ABAB is a pattern of end-rhyme where the first and third lines rhyme with each other ("ago" and "know") and the second and fourth line rhyme with each other ("sea" and "Annabel Lee").

38. (A)

These lines depicting Grendel's reign of terror before the coming of the hero Beowulf are from the Old English poem named for the hero. *Everyman* (B) is a sixteenth-century morality play, not a poem. These lines do not come from either Sir Thomas Malory's *Le Morte d'Arthur* (C), which was written in the fifteenth century, or from Dante Alighieri's *The Divine Comedy* (D), written in the early 1300s.

39. (C)

The repetition of the sound of "h" in the phrase "hell-forged hands" illustrates alliteration. A simile (A) is a comparison using "like" or "as;" because neither of those words are present, (A) is not a good choice. Assonance (B) is the repetition of vowel sounds; this repetition is not a characteristic of line 6. (B) is not acceptable. The line certainly does not use understatement (D); if anything, the line uses exaggeration. (D) is not the right answer.

40. (B)

The history of the English language started with the arrival of three invading Germanic tribes during the 5th century CE. These tribes, the Angles, the Saxons and the Jutes, crossed the North Sea from what today is Denmark and northern Germany into England. Although at that time the inhabitants of Britain spoke a Celtic language, English is a member of the Germanic family of languages. Germanic is a branch of the Indo-European language family.

41. (B)

Charles Dickens wrote both II (from *A Christmas Carol*) and III (from *A Tale of Two Cities*). "Call me Ishmael" (III) is the opening line from *Moby Dick* by Herman Melville. "Whose woods these are I think I know" (IV) are the opening words of Robert Frost's "Stopping by Woods on a Snowy Evening." Answer choices (A), (C), and (D) are, therefore, incorrect.

42. (A)

"Call me Ishmael" is the opening line from *Moby Dick* by Herman Melville. "Whose woods these are I think I know" are the opening words of Robert Frost's "Stopping by Woods on a Snowy Evening." Charles Dickens wrote both line II (*A Christmas Carol*) and line III (*A Tale of Two Cities*).

43. (B)

Comparing the best and the worst of times and using the phrase "dead, to begin with"—suggesting that such would not always be the case—are examples of Dickens's uses of contrasts; (B) is the best choice. Neither of the other quoted lines use contrasts, so (A), (C), and (D) are incorrect.

44. (D)

"The Rape of the Lock" was the work of Alexander Pope. The poem is a mock epic; it burlesques the traditional epic. Answers (A), (B), and (C) are examples of traditional and/or literary epics.

45. (C)

In the sentence, "Last night I shot an elephant in my pajamas," the prepositional phrase "in my pajamas" is meant to modify the subject "I," not the object "elephant." Including the information in a new clause—"while I was wearing my pajamas"—and placing it near the word "I" makes the sentence's meaning clear.

46. (C)

In the sentence "He noticed a large stain in the rug that was right in the center," the restrictive clause "that was right in the center" modifies "stain," not "rug." Answer (C) correctly moves the descriptive phrase closer to the word it modifies. The other answers change the meaning of the sentence.

47. (A)

Choice (A) is the best example of present progressive tense; it notes an action in the present that is a continuing action. Choice (B) is in past form, and (C) future tense. While simple and perfect verb tenses have a progressive form, verbs expressing a state of mind or mental activity generally are NOT used in the progressive form; (D), therefore, is incorrect.

48. (B)

Active-voice sentences occur when the subject performs the action—Jeannette "placed." In passive voice sentence, the subject is acted upon—the car "was parked."

49. (B)

Subordinators make a clause or phrase dependent rather than independent. Subordinators introduce embedded clauses in order to reduce ambiguity and increase continuity. In the sentence "We were shocked that Bob hit the home run," the subordinator is "that." The words "were" (A), "shocked" (C), and "hit" (D) are verbs, not subordinators.

50. (A)

Infants and young children move in and out of various stages of language acquisition at different times. There is no strict or inherent logic by which children acquire language. The development is not easily traced (B), set in rigid parameters (C), or mirrored in adults (D).

51. (C)

Grammar often has very little relationship to the way people in the world actually speak; nevertheless, learning Standard English provides a good starting point for students to learn English in all its complexity and nuance. Answers (A), (B), and (D) are all correct.

52. (A)

Sentence 1, in characterizing Corte Madera as a "metropolitan paradise," creates a theme that the subsequent sentences build upon. Sentences 2 (B), 3 (C), and 4 (D) relate to this idea by offering supporting details.

53. (D)

In passive voice sentences, the subject is acted upon—Kayla "was accepted" to her first-choice college. In active voice sentences, the subject performs the action. "Kayla's first-choice college accepted her," would be the active-voice version of this sentence.

54. (C)

The Prologue is an example of a Shakespearean sonnet—fourteen lines of iambic pentameter. The rhyme scheme is ABAB CDCD EFEF GG. Though most of the play is written in blank verse (unrhymed iambic pentameter), this passage has a structured rhyme scheme.

55. (B)

Dramatic irony is when the audience knows something that the characters do not. In this case, we know that the "star-crossed lovers" will commit suicide, but they are unaware of this foreshadowed tragedy until the very end.

56. (C)

The meter of this poem is iambic pentameter, five pairs of unstressed stressed syllables. Trochaic

(A) syllables are stressed unstressed. A dactylic (B) foot is three syllables, stressed followed by two unstressed. An anapest is two unstressed syllables followed by a stressed one.

57. (A)

Archaic words are no longer in common usage today, which makes them difficult for students. Abstract language (B) refers to abstract ideas or concepts such as love, courage, and honesty. Allusions (C) are references to previous sources. Colloquial language (D) is everday speech, the opposite of what is presented here.

58. (C)

End rhyme occurs at the end of lines, which is exactly what we have here. Internal rhyme (A) occurs within a single line of poetry. ABAB (D) would occur in the first four lines of the poem, and we are presented with only two lines here. External rhyme (B) is not a standard literary term.

59. (B)

Slant line is a close but inexact rhyme, descriptive of "love" and "remove." In perfect (C) or exact rhyme (D), the sounds of the words match exactly, as in "scene" and clean." Internal rhymes (A) are words that rhyme within one line of poetry; this poem has end rhyme, words that rhyme at the ends of the lines.

60. (D)

Whether students are learning a single language or multiple languages, the language acquisition program in which they are engaged must challenge them both academically and linguistically. The program need not necessarily stress the commonalities in languages (A), be tailor-made to the individual student (B), or focus on the ease of the student (C).

61. (B)

One's mother tongue is one's indigenous or native language, or the first language one learns to speak. It is not necessarily language acquired from the maternal (mother's) side of the family (A), the accepted language of the area (B), or the Latin base of our modern-day languages.

62. (C)

If two or more independent clauses are run together without a conjunction or proper punctuation, it is a run-on sentence. A fragmented sentence (A) does not have a complete independent clause, so (A) is not a good answer choice. A topic sentence (B) does not necessarily have two or more independent clauses; it may have only one independent clause. (B) is not, therefore, a good answer. Two or more independent clauses may certainly be joined incorrectly by a comma for a comma-splice sentence, but that is not the only way of creating a run-on sentence; (D) is not the best answer choice.

63. (B)

Increasing the amount of time the student spends on repetition and review is the recommended procedure when a student is having difficulty with reading retention. Generally speaking, your lesson plans should include more time for repetition and review than you'd consider necessary. Using materials designed for a lower age group (A) may not be motivating and may insult the students; (A) is inadvisable. Reading aloud, slowly and clearly, articulating as many words as possible (B), would not be advisable if the student were doing the reading; others would be more aware of the affected student's reading skills and that may embarrass the student. Hearing the teacher read aloud slowly (C) would not be a good model for the student. Students who are having difficulty retaining information may not necessarily be developmentally disabled; (D) is incorrect.

64. (A)

Oxymorons are short phrase constructions that present a paradox. A pun (B) is a play on multiple meanings of a word or homonyms cleverly used for an often humorous effect. Romeo says in Act I, "You have dancing shoes/With nimble soles; I have a soul of lead/So stakes me to the ground I cannot move." A mixed metaphor (C) is an inconsistent comparison. For example: She was stretched so far she was almost completely buried. Here we have two separate metaphors, of stretching and burying, competing with each other. An anaphora is an intentional repetition of words. The Bible is filled with this figure of speech, a well-known would be the repetition of "Blessed are the . . . " in Christ's Sermon on the Mount.

65. (C)

Onomatopoeia is evident in nouns that imitate or mimic the sound they represent, as in "buzz, hiss, whoosh," and "ding-dong" (C). Choice (A) includes words that have repetitive consonant sounds; such repetition is known as "alliteration." The words in (B) and (D) are not all examples of onomatopoeia.(C) is the only acceptable answer.

66. (B)

A lexicon is a dictionary. The word's origins stem from Greek, where its original meaning was "vocabulary." The other secondary sources—an encyclopedia (A), a catalog (C), and a textbook (D)—are not correct answers.

67. (B)

The Greek legend of Oedipus is that of a man who kills his father and marries his mother. The other choices are not appropriate. Atlas (A) was a Greek hero punished by having to hold up the weight of the world. Hercules (C) was a Greek hero who performed seven labors; he did not kill his father. The Hydra (D) was the Greek multiheaded sea monster.

68. (D)

The word "and" is not a transition word. Transition words introduce dependent clauses, not complete sentences or independent clauses. Transition words can specify time (e.g., "after, while, before," etc.), place ("where," etc.), cause ("since, because," etc.), condition ("unless, if," etc.), contrast or concession ("despite, although," etc.), and other specifications. All the words listed are transition words except the conjunction "and" (D).

69. (D)

The prisoners are speedily sentenced because the judges and the jurymen are hungry and want to go home for supper as the day ends—the prisoners may be guilty, contrary to what choice (C) suggests, but the wrong reasons determine their sentences (D). No doubt the people do believe in the system (A), but the sarcasm of the piece suggests that this society uses the system for personal selfish benefits—certainly not a humanitarian society (B).

70. (B)

The society depicted is shallow and trivial, engaging in chatty conversations that everyone takes seriously. Serious as the discussions may be, they possibly involve extramarital affairs rather than affairs of state (C, D)—and such gossip ruins reputations (B). The gossiping involves the Queen, but it is not revealed that she is slandered (which would involve maliciousness), which, if you hadn't already done so, eliminates (D) along with (A).

71. (B)

The question wants you to analyze the clash or conflict of two very different concepts in conversation: the glory of the Queen in one breath and a fire screen (or room divider) in another. The juxtaposition is not so much to suggest trivia (A) or seriousness (the Queen's glory is serious but the furniture is not), but that this society holds both in equal reverence (B). The passage offers no real evidence that the people are Imperialists or Royalists (C and D).

72. (A)

There is a clever use of the language in this one adverb. It stands for the angle of the sun as it declines at a steep angle but also for the hidden meanings behind the word as it refers to the society: the deceit, the amorality. It certainly does not mean that the sun is literally at a perpendicular angle (A).

73. (B)

A direct object is a noun or pronoun that follows a transitive verb and answers the question who or what. "One speaks" what? The answer is the noun "glory."

74. (B)

Inverted sentences break from the typical subject verb sentence pattern. In this sentence, "weeks" is the subject of the sentence, "were" is the verb. Though an unusual sentence, it is complete with a subject and verb, and therefore not a

fragment (A). A periodic sentence (C) has the bulk of words at the beginning leading to the most important part of the sentence at the end. A cumulative sentence places the most important element at the beginning, and then develops it with clarifying description and information.

75. (A)

It is a simile, a comparison using "like" or "as."

76. (B)

This is a descriptive paragraph characterizing the narrator's neighbor. Since this is not organized chronologically, it is not narration (A). An analysis (C) breaks a subject into its component parts. Exploring Boo's different character traits would be more characteristic of analysis. A discussion of *why* Boo was perceived as a "phantom" or what caused him to be a "phantom" would be cause and effect (D).

77. (A)

This passage is developed through details, examples that support the assertion. The details are not incongruous or contradictory; in fact, they consistently support the characterization of a "malevolent phantom." Imagery (C), or language that appeals to the senses, is not a rhetorical strategy used in this passage. This is not an academic paper—there are no citations here.

78. (A)

Often, but not always, the first sentence in a paragraph is the topic sentence. In this case, the first sentence asserts the main purpose of the paragraph. The rest of the details are used to support this assertion of Boo as a "malevolent phantom."

79. (B)

Though acceptably polite in Harper Lee's time and not considered a racial slur today, the word "negro" will seem archaic to modern students, and will probably require some context provided by the teacher.

80. (D)

The portion of the sentence after the colon clarifies and expands upon the first clause. Though one function of colons it to introduce lists, this one doesn't (A). The ideas following the colon are not in contrast to the first clause as they might be in a balanced sentence (B), and they do not indicate a cause and effect relationship (C).

81. (A)

A cumulative sentence makes a strong statement at the beginning of the sentence and then further supports, clarifies, expands upon, or describes that statement in the longer rest of the sentence.

82. (C)

"Once" modifies the verb "terrorized" and answers the question "when" in this sentence. When was the town terrorized? "Once." Adverbs modify verbs, adjectives, and other adverbs. They answer the questions "when, where, how," and "to what degree."

83. (D)

There are three independent clauses here making this compound. The last independent clause ("people still looked at the Radley place") also has two subordinate clauses attached to it ("although the culprit was Crazy Addie, who eventually drowned himself in Barker's Eddy"), making the sentence also complex.

84. (B)

Fantasy is a genre where the normal rules of reality are suspended. C.S. Lewis (*The Chronicles of Narnia*) and Roald Dahl (*Willie Wonka and the Chocolate Factory, James and the Giant Peach*) are fantasy writers.

85. (D)

American writer Stephen Crane (*The Red Badge of Courage*) wrote at the end of the nineteenth century. Though his work is considered part of the realistic movement, he is especially associated with a subset of Realism called Naturalism, which emphasized the psychological effects of environment on people as well as Darwinian theory of survival of the fittest. Percy Bysshe and Mary Shelley, husband and wife, were nineteenth-century British Romantics. Poe was an American Romantic writer.

86. (A)

Hughes and Cullen were Harlem Renaissance poets, a period of prolific African American writing in the 1920's and 30's. Harlem Renaissance poets took their cues from other African American forms of expression including jazz and spirituals.

87. (D)

Harold Pinter was a British playwright.

88. (B)

The Diary of Anne Frank is best classified as a memoir: autobiographical writing about a specific event or aspect of a person's life. The story of Anne Frank's life in the annex is nonfiction, so it is not a novel (B). A biography (C) is the true telling of a person's life, but it is written by someone other than the subject. Anne wrote her *Diary*. Drama (D) is a play. While Anne's story has been dramatized in movies and theater, these versions are adapted from her memoir.

89. (A)

Louisa May Alcott's (1832-1888) novels *Little Women, Little Men*, etc., were enjoyed by children and adolescents as well as adults. E.B. White (*Charlotte's Web*) also wrote for children and adults, but he is a twentieth century writer. Though often adapted for children, Washington Irving's complex language in stories such as *Rip Van Winkle* and *The Legend of Sleepy Hollow* make these tales inaccessible to unsophisticated readers. While Dickens often wrote about the difficulties children faced in the nineteenth century (*David Copperfield, Great Expectations*), his novels were aimed at an adult audience.

90. (B)

The subject matter and course language are the most frequent complaints against these two novels. *Harry Potter* and *The Wizard of Oz* have been opposed by religious groups who claim they deal with the occult. Some parents believe the themes in the other four novels (Choices C and D) are too dark and disturbing for students.

Question 1

Three-Point Response

In "The Chimney Sweeper," William Blake presents both the setting on a London street and the image of a lonely child in misery, isolation, and suffering. The child is symbolic of the 18th-century philosophy that children are industrial commodities to be exploited and discarded when they are of no further use.

A prepubescent orphaned narrator voices his misery with sounds of "weeping." The onomatopoeic word "Weep" is reminiscent of the word sweep that the child cries as he advertises his labors on the street and of the word <u>weep</u>, indicating the tears he sheds.

The child's crying is a result of the loss or abandonment of his parents: "father and mother … both gone to the church to pray." The word is also a result of the harsh and hazardous labor he is obligated to perform. The opening lines establish images of an isolated, suffering, exploited child-narrator.

Images of death permeate the poem. The "little black thing" is actually wearing "the clothes of death." These referential images create a dark, "cold," brooding mood reinforcing the fact that the narrator exists in a blackened world fraught with suffering and mortal danger. The poem offers a dim hope of heaven.

Overall, the poetic references to a weeping child "sold" into a world of perpetual darkness and death reinforce the poem's overall thematic ideas of an 18th-century London child's fragile and vulnerable commoditization, resulting in perpetual melancholy and eventually death.

Analysis: This essay would receive a score of 3 because it identifies the literary elements of onomatopoeia and imagery, and describes how one symbol—the weeping child—is developed through these visual and linguistic techniques, to present a powerful indictment of the callous, utilitarian treatment of working-class children in eighteenth-century England. The essay begins by describing the context of the poem and its central symbol. The following paragraphs explicate the poet's use of onomatopoeia and imagery to develop an emotionally moving portrait of the life of an exploited child. The concluding paragraph summarizes the contribution of the literary devices to the poem's theme and effectiveness.

Two-Point Response

A nameless narrator "weep[s] notes of woe!" This image of a child with no name in a snowy setting where the joys of childhood are replaced with the harsh laborious conditions of an industrialized 19th-century England. While England's industrialization produced radical life changes for the better, the history of child labor and child exploitation demonstrates the negative social affects of industrialization.

The proliferation of "chimney's," for example, produces an image of a city abundant with factory "soot" (i.e. pollution) and industrial byproducts. The images of the environment and the "weeping" child suggest that a) the children are a natural resource that industrialization exploits and b), that the city's fragile environment is in jeopardy of destruction and thus, unavailable for future generations.

Overall, the references to "clothes of death" and "notes of woe" apply to both the individual children's suffering as well as the environment's potential to suffer the same "miserable" and deadly fate.

The poem alludes to "churches, God, priests [and] kings." These are the only ones with enough power to change the course of London's environmental future, as shown in the last line where "a heaven," on earth perhaps, can be made "of our misery."

Analysis: This essay would receive a score of 2 because although the essay presents an understanding of the context of the poem, it does not develop an argument as to how effectively the literary elements are used by the poet to enhance his message. The images used as examples are taken for what they denote, rather than for what they imply. The essay fails to treat them as tools of the poet. There is also a sentence fragment in the opening paragraph.

One-Point Response

The poem made me really sad. I don't like the idea of little children "suffering" or dead. Why would Blake write about kids this way? Why are they going to work in the "cold and dark" instead of the daytime?

It says the child likes the heath and yet he has to go to work. Maybe Blake is telling us that work is good for kids. Maybe he wants us to know that without a good day's work the kids won't appreciate their free time as much. They can laugh and play "in the snow" after the work is done. It's really telling us good work values and ethics, since all kids like to play more than they like to work. They all need their moms and dads to support them and give them the love and guidance like all parents give their children. Work teaches kids responsibility for when they are adults.

I think Blake is telling us in these poems that hard work is good for kids and that they need to be taught good work ethics and values so they can grow up to be good people like their parents who pray and believe in God. God, priests, and kings are in this poem because God is a good influence in the life of children and adults and God says that idle hands are the devil's playground, so that the kids won't be just wasting their time playing games all day like they do now, but will be busy working hard and believing in God so they are learning good values for when they grow up and become adults.

Analysis: This essay would receive a score of 1 because the essay fails to follow the directions (to describe the literary elements and discuss their role in contributing to the meaning or effectiveness of the poem). The essay presents a flawed understanding of the poet's message in a poorly crafted presentation ending with a run-on sentence.

Question 2

Three-Point Response

Expecting students and the family to give up their culture and their language entirely is an unreasonable thing to do. Most people are proud of their language, their culture, and their families; rejecting their language and their culture implies rejecting them and the people that they hold most dear.

Rather than asking a student and family to discard beliefs and traditions that are a part of their culture, the teacher might ask the students to share with the class some of the things that are most important to them. The teacher must be prepared to ensure a climate of acceptance and cooperation among those in the classroom; the teacher might even want the student(s) to present their presentations with other classrooms or even with parents on PTA/PTO night. Knowledge may increase acceptance of one another and may encourage the cooperation that will help the school and family and the students within the classroom to work together in harmony.

Analysis: This essay would receive a score of 3 because it very clearly expresses the view that teachers should take in their classrooms. Teachers must accept the students and their families for who they are: unique individuals with worth. Disseminating knowledge can only improve the situation and not worsen it. The suggestion of having a presentation at the parent-teacher association or organization (PTA/PTO) meetings is one that has merit. Hopefully, as the writer stated, the result will be working "together in harmony." The writer makes a statement, supports it in the essay, and presents the ideas clearly in the writing.

Two-Point Response

I would encourage the teacher to work with me on a cooperative project that would result in a compilation of research on various cultures. Each student could take a topic and gather information through interviews, accessing the Internet, and reading. These research projects would focus on ways that people are different and the end result should be the idea that we all have similarities and differences. The United States is like a "salad bowl" and not like the "melting pot" of past generations and this is something that may change but until it does it is something we must deal with in the classroom.

Analysis: This essay approaches the various cultures as having worth. The research is a good idea, but the sentence structure in the last part of the paragraph is not the best.

One-Point Response

I would tell the teacher that speaking only English is important. Like her, I would make the use of any other language unacceptable during class. I would ignore any comments or questions from students who forget to speak English. Only by realizing that they do not fit in will they ever begin to give up their native language and culture. Parents, too, must discard their native language and traditions and if parents come to conferences with me and do not try to communicate clearly with me in English, I will not waste my time trying to decipher their failure to speak in the language of the country in which they reside and will tell them that I do not think speaking a foreign language is good and that they should not receive the benefits of living in the United States.

Analysis: Although the examinee has displayed a well-structured essay with the exception of the last sentences, the content of the essay displays intolerance for the students in the classroom. Such prejudice against certain students and families is totally unacceptable and does not reflect best practices. The elitist view that the writer expresses in the essay is totally unacceptable for a teacher to display toward the students and parents. The essay includes an egocentric view of the language that most U.S. citizens speak. The content of this essay indicates an unaccepting view of the learners in the class. The essay is not adequate.

Praxis English Assessment: Middle School English Language Arts (0049)

Practice Test 2

ANSWER SHEET FOR PRACTICE TEST 2 (0049)

1. Ⓐ Ⓑ Ⓒ Ⓓ
2. Ⓐ Ⓑ Ⓒ Ⓓ
3. Ⓐ Ⓑ Ⓒ Ⓓ
4. Ⓐ Ⓑ Ⓒ Ⓓ
5. Ⓐ Ⓑ Ⓒ Ⓓ
6. Ⓐ Ⓑ Ⓒ Ⓓ
7. Ⓐ Ⓑ Ⓒ Ⓓ
8. Ⓐ Ⓑ Ⓒ Ⓓ
9. Ⓐ Ⓑ Ⓒ Ⓓ
10. Ⓐ Ⓑ Ⓒ Ⓓ
11. Ⓐ Ⓑ Ⓒ Ⓓ
12. Ⓐ Ⓑ Ⓒ Ⓓ
13. Ⓐ Ⓑ Ⓒ Ⓓ
14. Ⓐ Ⓑ Ⓒ Ⓓ
15. Ⓐ Ⓑ Ⓒ Ⓓ
16. Ⓐ Ⓑ Ⓒ Ⓓ
17. Ⓐ Ⓑ Ⓒ Ⓓ
18. Ⓐ Ⓑ Ⓒ Ⓓ
19. Ⓐ Ⓑ Ⓒ Ⓓ
20. Ⓐ Ⓑ Ⓒ Ⓓ
21. Ⓐ Ⓑ Ⓒ Ⓓ
22. Ⓐ Ⓑ Ⓒ Ⓓ
23. Ⓐ Ⓑ Ⓒ Ⓓ

24. Ⓐ Ⓑ Ⓒ Ⓓ
25. Ⓐ Ⓑ Ⓒ Ⓓ
26. Ⓐ Ⓑ Ⓒ Ⓓ
27. Ⓐ Ⓑ Ⓒ Ⓓ
28. Ⓐ Ⓑ Ⓒ Ⓓ
29. Ⓐ Ⓑ Ⓒ Ⓓ
30. Ⓐ Ⓑ Ⓒ Ⓓ
31. Ⓐ Ⓑ Ⓒ Ⓓ
32. Ⓐ Ⓑ Ⓒ Ⓓ
33. Ⓐ Ⓑ Ⓒ Ⓓ
34. Ⓐ Ⓑ Ⓒ Ⓓ
35. Ⓐ Ⓑ Ⓒ Ⓓ
36. Ⓐ Ⓑ Ⓒ Ⓓ
37. Ⓐ Ⓑ Ⓒ Ⓓ
38. Ⓐ Ⓑ Ⓒ Ⓓ
39. Ⓐ Ⓑ Ⓒ Ⓓ
40. Ⓐ Ⓑ Ⓒ Ⓓ
41. Ⓐ Ⓑ Ⓒ Ⓓ
42. Ⓐ Ⓑ Ⓒ Ⓓ
43. Ⓐ Ⓑ Ⓒ Ⓓ
44. Ⓐ Ⓑ Ⓒ Ⓓ
45. Ⓐ Ⓑ Ⓒ Ⓓ
46. Ⓐ Ⓑ Ⓒ Ⓓ

47. Ⓐ Ⓑ Ⓒ Ⓓ
48. Ⓐ Ⓑ Ⓒ Ⓓ
49. Ⓐ Ⓑ Ⓒ Ⓓ
50. Ⓐ Ⓑ Ⓒ Ⓓ
51. Ⓐ Ⓑ Ⓒ Ⓓ
52. Ⓐ Ⓑ Ⓒ Ⓓ
53. Ⓐ Ⓑ Ⓒ Ⓓ
54. Ⓐ Ⓑ Ⓒ Ⓓ
55. Ⓐ Ⓑ Ⓒ Ⓓ
56. Ⓐ Ⓑ Ⓒ Ⓓ
57. Ⓐ Ⓑ Ⓒ Ⓓ
58. Ⓐ Ⓑ Ⓒ Ⓓ
59. Ⓐ Ⓑ Ⓒ Ⓓ
60. Ⓐ Ⓑ Ⓒ Ⓓ
61. Ⓐ Ⓑ Ⓒ Ⓓ
62. Ⓐ Ⓑ Ⓒ Ⓓ
63. Ⓐ Ⓑ Ⓒ Ⓓ
64. Ⓐ Ⓑ Ⓒ Ⓓ
65. Ⓐ Ⓑ Ⓒ Ⓓ
66. Ⓐ Ⓑ Ⓒ Ⓓ
67. Ⓐ Ⓑ Ⓒ Ⓓ
68. Ⓐ Ⓑ Ⓒ Ⓓ
69. Ⓐ Ⓑ Ⓒ Ⓓ

70. Ⓐ Ⓑ Ⓒ Ⓓ
71. Ⓐ Ⓑ Ⓒ Ⓓ
72. Ⓐ Ⓑ Ⓒ Ⓓ
73. Ⓐ Ⓑ Ⓒ Ⓓ
74. Ⓐ Ⓑ Ⓒ Ⓓ
75. Ⓐ Ⓑ Ⓒ Ⓓ
76. Ⓐ Ⓑ Ⓒ Ⓓ
77. Ⓐ Ⓑ Ⓒ Ⓓ
78. Ⓐ Ⓑ Ⓒ Ⓓ
79. Ⓐ Ⓑ Ⓒ Ⓓ
80. Ⓐ Ⓑ Ⓒ Ⓓ
81. Ⓐ Ⓑ Ⓒ Ⓓ
82. Ⓐ Ⓑ Ⓒ Ⓓ
83. Ⓐ Ⓑ Ⓒ Ⓓ
84. Ⓐ Ⓑ Ⓒ Ⓓ
85. Ⓐ Ⓑ Ⓒ Ⓓ
86. Ⓐ Ⓑ Ⓒ Ⓓ
87. Ⓐ Ⓑ Ⓒ Ⓓ
88. Ⓐ Ⓑ Ⓒ Ⓓ
89. Ⓐ Ⓑ Ⓒ Ⓓ
90. Ⓐ Ⓑ Ⓒ Ⓓ

PRACTICE TEST 2 (0049)
Middle School English Language Arts

TIME: 2 hours
90 multiple-choice questions and 2 constructed-response questions

In this section, you will find examples of test questions similar to those you are likely to encounter on the Praxis II Middle School English Language Arts exam.

1. Choose the correctly punctuated sentence below.

   (A) Jodi sells childrens' clothing and lady's shoes at her mothers boutique in the city.
   (B) Jodi sells children's clothing and ladies' shoes at her mother's boutique in the city.
   (C) Jodi sells children's clothing and lady's shoes at her mother's boutique in the city.
   (D) Jodi sells childrens clothing and ladies shoes at her mother's boutique in the city.

2. Which of the following sentences contains a comma-splice error?

   (A) You have missed the bus, so you will need to walk to school.
   (B) I suggest you wake up earlier because you can't afford to be late for school again.
   (C) While I understand you have had a great deal of homework lately, you need to make sure that you get to bed at a reasonable time.
   (D) It is against my better judgment, however, I will drive you to school just this one time.

Read the following passage and then answer questions 3 and 4.

> Hark, hark!
> Bow-wow.

> The watch-dogs bark!
> Bow-wow!
> Hark, hark! I hear
> The strain of strutting chanticleer
> Cry, "Cock-a-doodle-doo!"

3. The passage illustrates the use of

   (A) personification.
   (B) onomatopoeia.
   (C) allusion.
   (D) symbolism.

4. A stylistic device in the passage is

   (A) alliteration.
   (B) foreshadowing.
   (C) simile.
   (D) an argumentative appeal.

Read the following passage and then answer question 5.

> Apparently with no surprise
> To any happy Flower
> The Frost beheads it at its play—
> In accidental power—
> The blonde Assassin passes on—
> The Sun proceeds unmoved
> To measure off another Day
> For an Approving God.

5. "The blonde Assassin" in the passage is the

   (A) Sun.
   (B) Day.
   (C) Frost.
   (D) Flower.

6. Which of the following lines is an example of iambic pentameter?

   (A) The an/gry spot/doth glow/on Cae/sar's brow
   (B) Here goes/the try/I've al/ways known/
   (C) She loves the/way I hold/her hand/
   (D) Although I/knew the road/led home/

Consider the following poem, *Arithmetic*, by Carl Sandburg as you address questions 7 through 12.

   Arithmetic is where numbers fly like pigeons in and out of your head.
   Arithmetic tells you how many you lose or win if you know how many you had before you lost or won.
   Arithmetic is seven eleven all good children go to heaven—or five six bundle of sticks.
   Arithmetic is numbers you squeeze from your head to your hand to your pencil to your paper till you get the answer.

7. The repetition of the word "arithmetic" is called

   (A) allusion.
   (B) alliteration.
   (C) apostrophe.
   (D) anaphora.

8. This form of this poem is

   (A) free verse.
   (B) blank verse.
   (C) ballad meter.
   (D) elegy.

9. The poet says numbers are "like pigeons in and out of your head." This is an example of

   (A) metaphor.
   (B) personification.
   (C) imagery.
   (D) simile.

10. In order to address the audience directly, the poet incorporates

    (A) first-person point of view.
    (B) second-person point of view.
    (C) third-person omniscient point of view.
    (D) third-person limited point of view.

11. The words "seven," "eleven," and "heaven" in the third sentence of the poem form

    (A) end rhyme.
    (B) internal rhyme.
    (C) slant rhyme.
    (D) external rhyme.

12. The expression "squeeze from your head" in the last sentence is meant to be taken

    (A) figuratively.
    (B) literally.
    (C) allusively.
    (D) paradoxically.

13. What is cuneiform script?

    (A) A phonetic form of writing, adaptable to the sounds of any language
    (B) A hybrid script blending hieroglyphs and modern alphanumeric symbols
    (C) The world's earliest known form of written language
    (D) A primitive form of writing developed by Native Americans

14. To help a language-minority student most, research by Elley and Mangubhai suggests that

    (A) listening and speaking proficiency should precede literacy instruction.
    (B) the teacher should help the student develop reading skills coincidentally with speaking skills but independently from writing skills.
    (C) the teacher should help the student develop writing skills before reading skills since motor skills precede reading.

(D) the teacher should seek to help the student to develop reading and writing concomitantly.

15. Teachers who work with language-minority students and wish to help them make the most progress

(A) should consult the research to determine the number of vocabulary words a language-minority student of a given age should have mastered, make sure the student meets that criteria, and then begin reading instruction.

(B) should consult the research to determine the number of vocabulary words a language-minority student of a given age, should recognize orally, make sure the student meets that criteria, and then begin reading instruction.

(C) should ideally conduct separate reading, spelling, speaking, and writing sessions so as not to bombard the child with too much too soon.

(D) should introduce language-minority students to reading and writing experiences as soon as the students enter the classroom.

Consider this line from Martin Luther King's *I Have a Dream* speech as you answer questions 16 and 17.

> I have a dream that one day even the state of Mississippi, a desert state sweltering with the heat of injustice and oppression, will be transformed into an oasis of freedom and justice.

16. In this sentence, the entire phrase "a desert state sweltering with the heat of injustice and oppression" functions as

(A) a subordinate clause.
(B) a participial phrase.
(C) an appositive phrase.
(D) prepositional phrase.

17. The words "injustice," "oppression," "freedom," and "justice" are examples of

(A) abstract nouns.
(B) concrete nouns.
(C) proper adjectives.
(D) proper nouns.

18. What is the definition of "literacy"?

(A) A good thing for children to establish early in life
(B) Essential to functioning well in a wide variety of situations
(C) The ability to write prose and poetry in a manner that listeners and readers find pleasing
(D) The ability to comprehend both reading and writing

19. An important technique for proper literary assessment is to

(A) have students read and reread various texts until they comprehend the symbolic representations.
(B) have students articulate what they have read.
(C) watch and document students, noting the ones who are eager to read.
(D) watch students' performances in authentic learning situations.

20. What is a compound verb?

(A) A compound verb consists of two or more verbs connected by a conjunction such as "and," "but," or "or."
(B) A compound verb is a verb that adds "-ly" to the end, as in "easy" to "easily."
(C) A compound verb is a word that can function as both a noun and a verb: "I was" fishing at the lake; Fishing is my hobby.
(D) A compound verb is a verb supported by adverbs, as in "very upset."

21. In the sentence, "Pull gently on an old rope," the word "gently" is a(n)

    (A) noun.
    (B) verb.
    (C) adjective.
    (D) adverb.

22. What must a sentence contain in order for it to be considered a complete sentence?

    (A) A predicate and a claim
    (B) A noun and a verb
    (C) A verb and an adjective
    (D) A noun and an adjective

23. What is the definition of a "paragraph"?

    (A) A group of sentences that develop the various aspects of certain ideas or claims
    (B) A group of sentences that express the author's emotional response to an issue
    (C) A group of sentences that develop one main (complete) idea
    (D) A group of sentences that express the contemporary views of a society

24. In the phrase "to boldly go where no man has gone before," what is the grammatical term for "to boldly go"?

    (A) Gerund phrase
    (B) Compound verb
    (C) Grammatically correct
    (D) Split infinitive

25. The root of the word *prescription* is

    (A) "pre."
    (B) "script."
    (C) "ion."
    (D) "prescription."

Read the following passage and then answer questions 26 through 31.

Mark Twain has been characterized as "an authentic American author" and as "a representative American author." These descriptions seem to suit the man and his writings. He was born Samuel Clemens in 1835, when Missouri and Louisiana were the only states west of the Mississippi River. His birthplace was less than fifty miles from the river. When Samuel Clemens was four, the family settled in Hannibal, Missouri, and it was there beside the Great River that Samuel lived out the adventurous life he describes in his best-loved novels. In 1853 he set out to see the world as a printer in St. Louis, then in Chicago, Philadelphia, Keokuk, and Cincinnati. In 1857 he impulsively apprenticed himself to Horace Bixby, a riverboat pilot, and traveled all 1,200 miles of the Mississippi River. He said of his years on the river, "I got personally and familiarly acquainted with all the different types of human nature. . . ."

Following a stint in the military, he set out with his brother by stagecoach over the Rockies. He tried prospecting in the West, but found his true calling in journalism. Full public recognition came with the publishing of *Innocents Abroad* (1869), but some of his finest writings were three works based on life on the Mississippi and on his boyhood. In his artfully told stories, Clemens conveyed his powers of observation and perception, his understanding of human nature, and his sense of humor.

26. The purpose of this passage is

    (A) descriptive.
    (B) narrative.
    (C) expository.
    (D) persuasive.

27. The sentence best described as the thesis of the passage is

    (A) Mark Twain has been characterized as "an authentic American author" and as "a representative American author."
    (B) These descriptions seem to suit the man.
    (C) He was born Samuel Clemens in 1835, when Missouri and Louisiana were the only states west of the Mississippi River.
    (D) When Samuel Clemens was four, the family settled in Hannibal, Missouri, and it was there beside the Great river that Samuel lived out the adventurous life he describes in his best-loved novels.

28. The transition between paragraphs two and three is

    (A) the last sentence of paragraph two.
    (B) "Following a stint in the military."
    (C) "he set out with his brother…."
    (D) "He tried prospecting…."

29. The tone of the passage is

    (A) cynical.
    (B) disparaging.
    (C) admiring.
    (D) venerating.

30. The passage alludes to works based on his boyhood. This describes which of these works?

    (A) *The Prince and the Pauper*
    (B) *A Connecticut Yankee in King Arthur's Court*
    (C) *The Celebrated Jumping Frog of Calaveras County*
    (D) *The Adventures of Tom Sawyer*

31. The organization of the article is primarily

    (A) cause and effect.
    (B) comparisons and contrast.
    (C) most important to least important.
    (D) chronological.

Read the following passage and then answer questions 32 through 35.

David would be much better off if he would put aside his fripperies and shoulder his responsibilities. He is the heir to one of the biggest mining concerns in the country, yet he wastes his time and energy on such things as auto racing, support for the arts, and saving whales—saving them for what, I do not know. No one can be a captain of industry unless he pursues his goal with single-minded devotion. If David wants to become a titan, as his father and grandfather were, he must apply his talents and his strength to more important things.

32. The best definition of the word "titan" as the author uses it is a person

    (A) of great power.
    (B) of great physical strength.
    (C) of great intellect.
    (D) considered to be god-like.

33. Which fact would contradict the point of view of the writer?

    (A) Ninety-two percent of all heirs to great fortunes dissipate them.
    (B) A shareholder group is planning to challenge David's control of the large mining company.
    (C) The inflation rate is falling.
    (D) Other captains of industry were people of diverse interests.

34. The type of discourse that the writing represents is

    (A) narrative.
    (B) reflective.
    (C) descriptive.
    (D) persuasive.

35. The passage makes use primarily of

    (A) facts.
    (B) research.
    (C) documentation.
    (D) opinions.

36. The suffix "-ist" as in "realist" or "philanthropist" means

    (A) having the qualities of.
    (B) without.
    (C) one who.
    (D) in the manner or style of.

37. The superlative form of the adjective "happy" is

    (A) happy.
    (B) more happy.
    (C) happier.
    (D) happiest.

38. Which of the following are subordinating conjunctions?

    (A) and, but, or
    (B) although, since, because
    (C) however, therefore, nevertheless
    (D) nor, for, yet

39. Classify the following sentence: "This is the greatest day of my life!"

    (A) declarative sentence
    (B) interrogative sentence
    (C) imperative sentence
    (D) exclamatory sentence

40. An "ad hominem" argument is the technique of attacking the person instead of the issue. Which of the following is an example of an "ad hominem" argument?

    (A) Situations vary, and no prediction of the future is possible.
    (B) One cannot expect a Southerner to present a reasonable opinion.
    (C) The facts prove otherwise.
    (D) There are a number of studies that support this conclusion.

41. Identify the tense of the underlined verb in the following sentence: "By the time we were ready to leave, John *had packed* all of our suitcases into the van."

    (A) present tense
    (B) past tense
    (C) present perfect tense
    (D) past perfect tense

42. Written language has its origin in paintings and drawings. Drawings, diagrams and other records depict facts and events. Abbreviating these visual representations led to letters and alphabets. The philologist studies the relationship between visual forms and the newer forms of expression and communication.

    The passage does NOT support which of the following statements?

    (A) Pictures and drawings preceded written language.
    (B) Letters developed from abbreviations of drawings.
    (C) Language had a civilizing effect on people.
    (D) Philology is the study of the development of visual forms and their relationship to language.

Consider the following passage from *The Lion, the Witch and the Wardrobe* by C.S. Lewis as you answer question 43 and 44.

"This must be a simply enormous wardrobe!" thought Lucy, going still further in and pushing the soft folds of the coats aside to make room for her. Then she noticed that there was something crunching under feet. "I wonder is that more moth-balls?" she thought, stooping down to feel it with her hand. But instead of feeling the hard, smooth wood of the floor of the wardrobe, she felt something soft and powdery and extremely cold.

43. A rhetorical strategy that dominates this passage is

   (A) imagery.
   (B) satire.
   (C) irony.
   (D) anaphora.

44. The point of view of the passage is

   (A) first-person.
   (B) third-person limited.
   (C) third-person omniscient.
   (D) third-person objective.

Consider these opening paragraphs from the short story *The Yellow Wallpaper* by Charlotte Perkins Gilman as you answer questions 45 through 50.

It is very seldom that mere ordinary people like John and myself secure ancestral halls for the summer.

A colonial mansion, a hereditary estate, I would say a haunted house, and reach the height of romantic felicity—but that would be asking too much of fate!

Still I will proudly declare that there is something queer about it.

Else, why should it be let so cheaply? And why have stood so long untenanted?

John laughs at me, of course, but one expects that in marriage.

John is practical in the extreme. He has no patience with faith, an intense horror of superstition, and he scoffs openly at any talk of things not to be felt and seen and put down in figures.

John is a physician, and PERHAPS—(I would not say it to a living soul, of course, but this is dead paper and a great relief to my mind)—PERHAPS that is one reason I do not get well faster.

45. These opening paragraphs of the story are called the

   (A) basic situation or exposition.
   (B) complications or rising action.
   (C) climax.
   (D) denouement.

46. The speaker characterizes John as

   (A) a confidant.
   (B) trustworthy.
   (C) sympathetic.
   (D) realistic.

47. The speaker views writing as

   (A) annoying.
   (B) therapeutic.
   (C) laborious.
   (D) painful.

48. The story, first published in 1892 in the New England Magazine, deals with the psychological breakdown of the narrator as she becomes increasingly oppressed by her environment. These themes are associated with the school of writing called

    (A) Naturalism.
    (B) Transcendentalism.
    (C) Romanticism.
    (D) Rationalism.

49. The passage best illustrates

    (A) the first-person point of view.
    (B) irony.
    (C) an analogy.
    (D) inflated language.

50. The type of writing is

    (A) narrative.
    (B) expressive or poetic.
    (C) informational.
    (D) expository.

Read the following passage and then answer questions 51 through 55.

1   The house of fiction has in short not one window, but a million—a number of possible windows not to be reckoned; rather, every one of which has
5   been pierced, or is still pierceable, in its vast front, by the need and pressure of the individual will. These apertures of dissimilar shape and size, hang so, all together over the human scene
10   that we might have expected of them a greater sameness of report than we find. They are but windows at the best, mere holes in a dead wall, disconnected, perched aloft; they are not hinged
15   doors opening straight upon life. But they have this mark of their own that at each of them stands a figure with a pair of eyes, or at least with a field-glass, which forms, again and again, for

20   observation, a unique instrument, insuring to the person making use of it an impression distinct from every other. He and his neighbors are watching the same show, but one seeing more where the other sees less, one seeing black
25   where the other sees white, and one seeing big where the other sees small, one seeing coarse where the other sees fine. And so on, and so on; there is fortunately no saying on what, for the
30   particular pair of eyes, the window may not open; "fortunately" by season, precisely, of this incalculability of range. The spreading field, the human scene, is the "choice of subject"; the
35   pierced aperture, either broad or balconied or slitlike and low-browed, is the "literary form"; but they are, singly or together, as nothing without the posted presence of the watcher—without, in
40   other words, the consciousness of the artist. Tell me what the artist is, and I will tell you of what he has been conscious. Thereby I shall express to you
45   at once his boundless freedom and his "moral" reference.

51. The author develops the discussion through

    (A) an extended metaphor.
    (B) personal anecdotes.
    (C) syllogistic reasoning.
    (D) stream of consciousness.

52. What is the antecedent of "they" in line 12?

    (A) *Windows* (line 12)
    (B) *Apertures* (line 7)
    (C) *Holes* (line 13)
    (D) *Need* (line 6) and *pressure* (line 6)

53. The phrase "of dissimilar shape and size" is

    (A) a participial phrase modifying "apertures."
    (B) a prepositional phrase modifying "apertures."

(C) a prepositional phrase modifying "hang."

(D) an appositive phrase modifying "apertures."

54. Which of these statements contains an example of antithesis?

(A) "These apertures, of dissimilar shape and size, hang so, all together, over the human scene" (lines 7–9).

(B) "They are but windows at the best, mere holes in a dead wall, disconnected, perched aloft; they are not hinged doors" (lines 12–15).

(C) ". . . at each of them stands a figure with a pair of eyes, or at least with a field-glass" (lines 17–19).

(D) ". . . one seeing more where the other sees less, one seeing black where the other sees white, one seeing big where the other sees small, one seeing coarse where the other sees fine" (lines 24–29).

55. "He and his neighbors are watching the same show, but one seeing more where the other sees less, one seeing black where the other sees white, and one seeing big where the other sees small, one seeing coarse where the other sees fine" (lines 23–29). This sentence is an example of

(A) anaphora.

(B) alliteration.

(C) inversion.

(D) a periodic sentence.

56. Which of the following, according to current linguistic theories, is the best definition of the meaning of a word?

(A) Its general, dictionary definition

(B) Its use in a particular situation

(C) Its referent (the object to which it refers)

(D) Its thought or corresponding idea in the mind

57. Which of the following best describes the acquisition of language by children?

(A) A logical process by which a child learns to express his or her thoughts.

(B) A series of imitative stages occurring in a necessary succession, where each advance is built on the previous one.

(C) A series of imitative stages occurring in a rough, overlapping sequence, including possible regressions.

(D) A random development sequence indivisible into stages.

Consider the following passage from Robert Cormier's *The Chocolate War* as you answer questions 58 through 65.

When he ran, he even loved the pain, the hurt of the running, the burning in his lungs and the spasms that sometimes gripped his calves. He loved it because he knew he could endure the pain, and even go beyond it. He had never pushed himself to the limit but he felt all this reserve strength inside him: more than strength actually—determination. And it sang in him as he ran, his heart pumping blood joyfully through his body.

58. What is the topic sentence of this paragraph?

(A) When he ran, he even loved the pain, the hurt of the running, the burning in his lungs and the spasms that sometimes gripped his calves.

(B) He loved it because he knew he could endure the pain, and even go beyond it.

(C) He had never pushed himself to the limit but he felt all this reserve strength inside him: more than strength actually—determination.

(D) And it sang in him as he ran, his heart pumping blood joyfully through his body.

59. The dominant mode of exposition in this paragraph is

    (A) narration.
    (B) description.
    (C) analysis.
    (D) definition.

60. By showing the joy derived from pain of running, Cormier is creating

    (A) a paradox.
    (B) an extended metaphor.
    (C) an analogy.
    (D) satire.

61. In the first sentence of the passage, the words "pain," "hurt," "burning," and "spasms" function as

    (A) indirect objects.
    (B) direct objects.
    (C) participles.
    (D) objects of prepositions.

62. The first sentence of the passage is an example of a

    (A) compound sentence.
    (B) complex sentence.
    (C) compound sentence.
    (D) compound-complex sentence.

63. The main verb in the first sentence of the passage is in the

    (A) present tense.
    (B) past tense.
    (C) present perfect tense.
    (D) past perfect tense.

64. In the second sentence, the antecedent of the pronoun "it" (both times) is

    (A) running.
    (B) burning.
    (C) pain.
    (D) calves.

65. The antecedent of the pronoun "it" in the last sentence is

    (A) pain.
    (B) strength.
    (C) running.
    (D) determination.

66. In a novel, the epilogue is placed

    (A) after the last chapter.
    (B) before the first chapter.
    (C) between the prologue and the first chapter.
    (D) at any point the author deems appropriate.

For questions 67 through 71, read the paragraph that precedes each question, then choose the type of writing that the student is attempting.

   I like to go to the mall. I enjoy the sights, the sounds and the smells. Sometimes I buy my lunch at the mall before I shop for school supplies and school clothes. Other people may like the city streets. I like the mall.

67. The type of writing in this paragraph is

    (A) persuasive.
    (B) descriptive.
    (C) argumentative.
    (D) comedic.

   Photosynthesis is the way that plants make food. To make foods, plants need chlorophyll and sunshine. After photosynthesis, plants give off carbon dioxide and water.

68. The paragraph is primarily

    (A) informative.
    (B) persuasive.
    (C) entertainment.
    (D) descriptive.

My day started wrong. First I discovered that I had no electricity. This occurred after I washed my hair. I had to dress with a dripping head. The power outage meant that I could not prepare my breakfast. I bought a soft drink and placed it on the trunk of my car while I got my briefcase from the back seat. I realized that I had put the case in the trunk so I pushed the trunk release button inside the dash. I looked over my shoulder just in time to see the trunk "launch" my soft drink.

69. The paragraph is primarily

   (A) an attempt to explain.
   (B) persuasive.
   (C) entertainment.
   (D) informative.

This essay is to give the reasons for my delay in handing in the term paper. I had finished the paper except for typing it. I found that the typewriter I normally use was out of ribbon so I asked my roommate if I could use her word processor. I typed the entire paper. I finished the work at 7:00 a.m.— just in time to print it and get myself dressed for class. I pushed the print button just in time to realize that I had deleted the entire paper. I now have to retype the work. This is why my work is late. It was through no fault of my own and is why I should not receive a penalty.

70. The passage is what type of writing?

   (A) Information
   (B) Description
   (C) Entertainment
   (D) Persuasion

All of us as parents should read aloud to our children. The books should be ones that both parent and child will enjoy. Besides the good feelings that one can derive from reading to a child you love, reading aloud can help the child learn to read and to want to learn to read. Reading aloud is a benefit to all. Read to your child.

71. The primary purpose of the passage is to

   (A) inform.
   (B) describe.
   (C) entertain.
   (D) persuade.

72. The prefix "circum-" as in "circumvent" or "circumlocution" means

   (A) through or across.
   (B) around or about.
   (C) against.
   (D) half.

73. Which of the following authors are known for their science fiction writing?

   (A) Isaac Asimov and Arthur C. Clark
   (B) J.K. Rowling and J.R.R. Tolkien
   (C) Tim O'Brien and Toni Morrison
   (D) Zora Neale Hurston and William Faulkner

74. Which of the following authors received both the Newbery Medal and the Coretta Scott King Award for the same book in the same year?

   (A) Christopher Paul Curtis
   (B) Mildred Taylor
   (C) Virginia Hamilton
   (D) Harper Lee

75. Which of the following authors has never won both the Newbery Medal and the Coretta Scott King Award?

(A) Christopher Paul Curtis
(B) Mildred Taylor
(C) Virginia Hamilton
(D) Cynthia Voigt

76. Which of the following authors has never received the Margaret A. Edwards Award presented by the Young Adult Library Services Association?

(A) Gary Paulsen
(B) S. E. Hinton
(C) Cynthia Voigt
(D) Christopher Paul Curtis

77. Which of the following authors would be appropriate to include in a unit on British writers?

(A) Charles Dickens
(B) Edgar Allan Poe
(C) James Fenimore Cooper
(D) Washington Irving

78. Which of the following authors did not write Gothic literature?

(A) Charlotte Brontë
(B) Emily Brontë
(C) Edgar Allan Poe
(D) Mildred Taylor

79. Which of the following series correctly sequences the steps in process writing?

(A) Drafting, prewriting, revising, editing, publishing, evaluating
(B) Prewriting, revising, drafting, editing, publishing, evaluating
(C) Drafting, revising, prewriting, editing, publishing, evaluating
(D) Prewriting, drafting, revising, editing, publishing, evaluating

80. The approach to understanding literature that focuses on the reader is

(A) IRA.
(B) MLA.
(C) reader-response theory.
(D) arubric.

Read the following passage and then answer questions 81 through 90.

1   Although I am not disposed to maintain that the being born in a workhouse, is in itself the most fortunate and enviable circumstance that can possibly
5 befall a human being, I do mean to say that in this particular instance, it was the best thing for [the child] that could by possibility have occurred.
10 The fact is, that there was considerable difficulty in inducing [the child] to take upon himself the office of respiration, a troublesome practice, but one which custom has rendered necessary to our easy existence; and
15 for some time he lay gasping on a little flock mattress, rather unequally poised between this world and the next: the balance being decidedly in favour of the latter. Now, if, during this brief period, [the child] had been surrounded by careful grandmothers,
20 anxious aunts, experienced nurses, and doctors of profound wisdom, he would most inevitably and indubitably have been killed in no time. There being nobody by, however, but a pauper old woman, who was rendered rather misty by an unwonted allowance
25 of beer; and a parish surgeon who did such matters by contract; [the child] and Nature fought out the point between them.

81. The subject of the main clause of the first sentence is

    (A) "I" in line 1.
    (B) "I" in line 5.
    (C) human being.
    (D) child.

82. When the writer says the child had difficulty taking "taking upon himself the office of respiration" as another way of saying "breathing," he is using

    (A) paradox.
    (B) irony.
    (C) circumlocution.
    (D) incongruity.

83. The words ["the child"] are placed in brackets to indicate

    (A) a parenthetical expression.
    (B) a change in the original text to clarify an ambiguous pronoun reference in the excerpt.
    (C) an allusion to an earlier work.
    (D) a special emphasis placed on the item or idea by the author.

84. The syntax of the passage is characterized by

    (A) lengthy sentences with complex structures.
    (B) a series of balanced sentences.
    (C) the author's strategic use of sentence fragments juxtaposed against run-on sentences.
    (D) parallel construction of relative clauses.

85. These are the opening lines of

    (A) *A Tale of Two Cities.*
    (B) *David Copperfield.*
    (C) *Oliver Twist.*
    (D) *Great Expectations.*

86. The author of these lines is

    (A) Robert Louis Stevenson.
    (B) Charles Dickens.
    (C) Charlotte Brontë.
    (D) Mark Twain.

87. The passage is primarily

    (A) narrative.
    (B) persuasive.
    (C) expository.
    (D) argumentative.

88. The tone of the passage is

    (A) gloomy.
    (B) realistic.
    (C) romantic.
    (D) Gothic.

89. The organization of the passage is

    (A) cause and effect.
    (B) compare and contrast.
    (C) transitional.
    (D) chronological.

90. The thesis statement is

    (A) that being born in a workhouse was good for the child.
    (B) the child had a horrible birth and childhood.
    (C) that the child fought with Nature and Nature won.
    (D) that the child needed an immediate family.

PRACTICE TEST 2 (0049): CONSTRUCTED-RESPONSE QUESTIONS

Question 1

Write a critical essay in which you respond to the following poem. The essay must note at least two literary techniques and indicate how the techniques contribute to the text.

"London"

I wandered through each chartered street,
Near where the chartered Thames does flow,
A mark in every face I meet,
Marks of weakness, marks of woe.

In every cry of every man,
In every infant's cry of fear,
In every voice, in every ban,
The mind-forged manacles I hear:

How the chimney-sweeper's cry
Every blackening church appalls,
And the hapless soldier's sigh
Runs in blood down palace-walls.

But most, through midnight streets I hear
How the youthful harlot's curse
Blasts the new-born infant's tear,
And blights with plagues the marriage-hearse.

William Blake (1757–1827)
Songs of Innocence and Experience

Question 2

After reading the following opening paragraph from a student's preliminary draft of a short story, complete the exercise that follows.

On a warm July evening, Bob and Sally perched themselves on a bluff overlooking the placid little bay. The vista was breathtaking, the sunset sublime. The poor unsuspecting couple had no way of knowing that in less than forty-five minutes, the skies over San Diego, California, would be blackened with over a thousand hostile Taiwanese jet fighters, dropping their destructive cargos on the naval ships sleeping gently in their Pearl Harbor berths below.

Using your knowledge of creative writing, write a response in which you

- describe one type of revision you would make to improve the draft excerpt shown above, and

- explain why this type of revision would enhance the literary quality of the short story.

Praxis English Assessment: Middle School English Language Arts (0049)

Answer Explanations for Practice Test 2

ANSWER KEY FOR PRACTICE TEST 2 (0049)

1. (B)	24. (D)	47. (B)	70. (D)
2. (D)	25. (B)	48. (A)	71. (D)
3. (B)	26. (C)	49. (A)	72. (B)
4. (A)	27. (A)	50. (A)	73. (A)
5. (C)	28. (B)	51. (A)	74. (A)
6. (A)	29. (C)	52. (B)	75. (D)
7. (D)	30. (D)	53. (A)	76. (D)
8. (A)	31. (D)	54. (D)	77. (A)
9. (D)	32. (A)	55. (A)	78. (D)
10. (B)	33. (D)	56. (B)	79. (D)
11. (B)	34. (D)	57. (C)	80. (C)
12. (A)	35. (D)	58. (A)	81. (B)
13. (C)	36. (C)	59. (C)	82. (C)
14. (D)	37. (D)	60. (A)	83. (B)
15. (D)	38. (B)	61. (B)	84. (A)
16. (C)	39. (D)	62. (B)	85. (C)
17. (A)	40. (B)	63. (B)	86. (B)
18. (D)	41. (D)	64. (A)	87. (A)
19. (B)	42. (C)	65. (D)	88. (B)
20. (A)	43. (A)	66. (A)	89. (D)
21. (D)	44. (B)	67. (B)	90. (A)
22. (B)	45. (A)	68. (A)	
23. (C)	46. (D)	69. (C)	

Reading and Understanding ____/38

3	4	5	6	7	8	10	11	12	13	19	30	32

33	45	46	47	48	49	50	51	52	53	54	66	71

72	73	74	75	76	78	80	82	83	85	86	87

Language and Linguistics ____/29

1	2	9	14	10	11	14	15	16	17	18	20	21

22	24	25	36	37	38	56	57	61	62	63	64	65

88	81	84

Composition and Rhetoric ____/23

23	26	27	28	29	31	34	35	40	42	43	44	55

58	59	60	67	68	69	70	79	89	90

1. (B)

The three possessive nouns in Choice (B) are correctly punctuated. "Children" is a plural noun not ending in "s," so an apostrophe "s" is added to form the possessive. The plural "ladies" already ends in "s," so the apostrophe is added to the end of the sentence. "Mother" is singular, so an apostrophe "s" is added to form the possessive.

2. (D)

A comma-splice error is the incorrect joining of two independent clauses with a comma. In Choice (A), the two independent clauses appropriately joined with a comma plus the coordinating conjunction "so." Choice (B) has an independent clause, "I suggest you wake up earlier," followed by a subordinate clause, "because you can't afford to be late for school again," so a comma is not required in this sentence. In Choice (C), the introductory subordinate clause is appropriately followed by a comma and then the independent clause. The comma splice error is in Choice (D) because the conjunctive adverb "however" requires a semicolon to establish the contrast in tone with the prior clause. "It is against my better judgment; however, I will drive you to school just this one time."

3. (B)

Onomatopoeia (B) refers to the formation of words imitating the sound of the animal, the object, or the action; some onomatopoeic words are *buzz*, *clang*, *boom*, and *meow*. The passage contains two examples of onomatopoeia: *bow-wow* to imitate the barking of a dog and *cock-a-doodle-doo* to imitate the sound of the rooster. The animals are not depicted as people, so personification (A) is inappropriate. The passage does not employ allusion (C), or an implied reference to something else. There is a lack of symbolism (D), or an object representing something else, so (D) is not a good choice.

4. (A)

The passage uses repeated sounds, or *alliteration*. Examples of *c* words in the last line include *cry* and *cock*; the writer also uses *d* words: *doodle*, *doo*. There is no foreshadowing (B), or hint of what is to come; or simile (C), comparison using *like* or *as*. There is no argumentative appeal (D), or type of argument, in the passage.

5. (C)

The Frost (C) is the white-haired—or blonde—"Assassin." The personified Frost beheads the unwitting flower and exerts its power in an "accidental" and apparently random manner. There is no reference to the Sun (A), the Day (B), or the Flower (D) as blonde.

6. (A)

Choice (A) is the only correctly scanned line. It contains five iambic feet and is an example of iambic pentameter. The examples in (B), (C), and (D) have incorrectly marked accents and feet.

7. (D)

Anaphora is the purposeful repetition of a word or phrases at the beginning of successive lines, stanzas, sentences, or paragraphs. Allusion (A) is an indirect reference to an earlier source. Alliteration (B) is the repetition of sounds in closely placed words. Apostrophe (C) is an address to an absent person, idea, or inanimate object.

8. (A)

Free verse poetry has no structured rhyme or meter pattern, which describes this poem. Blank verse (B) is unrhymed iambic pentameter, the form of most of the dialogue in Shakespeare's drama. Ballad meter (C) is a highly structured form in which iambic tetrameter alternates with iambic trimeter.

9. (D)

Simile is a figurative comparison using like or as. In contrast, a metaphor (A) makes the comparison directly without the words like or as. Personification (B) gives human characteristics to nonhuman things. Imagery (C) is the use of language that appeals to the senses. Sometimes figurative language incorporates imagery, but not in this case.

10. (B)

The second person directly addresses the audience with the second person pronoun "you." First-person point of view (A) is when the narrator is a character in the text, utilizing the first-person pronoun "I." The third-person objective point of view narrates from outside the story using the third-person pronouns (he, she, it, they), and knows the thoughts and feelings of all the characters as well as the entire past, present, and future of the plot. The third-person limited point of view is similar, but the writer only knows the thoughts and feelings of one character.

11. (B)

These words are examples of internal rhyme, words that rhyme within a single line of poetry. End rhyme (A) is when words rhyme at the ends of lines. Slant rhyme (C) is rhyme that is inexact, such as "remove" and "love"—close but not exact. External rhyme (D) is not a literary term.

12. (A)

The expression is figurative because the numbers cannot literally (B) be "squeezed from your head." The expression is not allusive (C); that is, it does not refer to any other source, and it is not paradoxical (D) because there is no contradiction expressed.

13. (C)

Cuneiform, created by the Sumerians more than 5,000 years ago, is the world's earliest known form of written language. It remained in use up to approximately 75 CE. Choice (A) is incorrect because the language began as pictures (pictoforms), not phonetic forms; the pictorial representations became more abstract with time. Cuneiform form is not alphanumeric and does not include hieroglyphs (B), nor was it developed by Native Americans (D).

14. (D)

Recent research suggests that the concomitant development of the language skills of a language-minority student works best; the development of the skills is not a process that best allows oral language skills to precede written skills—or vice versa. Answers (A), (B), and (C) are, therefore, incorrect.

15. (D)

Research by Elley and Mangubhai suggests that there are no hard-and-fast rules to which a teacher must adhere to help language-minority students. Answers (A), (B), and (C) are not, therefore, the best choices. Choice (D), which suggests introducing students to reading and writing as soon as they enter the classroom, is the best answer.

16. (C)

This is an appositive phrase, a noun or pronoun plus any words that modify them, placed next to another noun or pronoun to identify it or give additional information about it. This phrase modifies "Mississippi." A subordinate clause (A) has a subject and a verb as well as a subordinating conjunction. A participial phrase (B) is a participle, a verb form that functions as an adjective, plus its modifiers. A prepositional phrase (D) is a preposition plus all the words leading to its object.

17. (A)

These words are abstract, dealing with ideas or qualities rather than concrete noun (B) which takes up space or can be recognized by the senses. Proper nouns (D) nouns name a specific person, place, or thing (i.e., Paris), and proper adjectives (C) (i.e., Parisian) are formed from these.

18. (D)

Literacy is the ability to read and write with understanding. Literacy will not be complete for very young children; (A) is not the best answer. One can function adequately in some situations in life without reading and writing skills; (B) is not, therefore, always the case. Answer option (C) is not the best answer because literacy does not necessarily require the ability to write poetry and prose.

19. (B)

To assess students properly, it is necessary to have them articulate what they have read; this way, the teacher can make sure that the reading is not just "word calling." Merely reading and rereading will not ensure comprehension; some diagnosis and reteaching must intervene. (A) is not a good choice. Choice (C) is a very subjective assessment technique; watching and trying to determine which students are eager to read is not objective. Merely "watching" performance is not true assessment; (D) is inadequate.

20. (A)

A compound verb consists of two or more verbs that are connected by a conjunction (*and, but, or*) and that have the same subject, as in *José walked to school and took the big test*. A verb to which *-ly* is added, as in *easy* to *easily* (B), is an adverb, not a compound verb; a word that can function as both noun and verb (C) is a verbal. Any verb, compound or otherwise, can be supported by adverbs (D). Choice (A) is the only correct answer.

21. (D)

An adverb is a word that modifies a verb, an adjective, or another adverb. In the sentence *Pull gently on an old rope*, the adverb *gently* modifies the verb *pull*. *Gently* is not a noun—the name of a person, place, or thing; (A) is incorrect. *Gently* does not show action or a state of being, and is, therefore, not a verb (B). *Gently* does not modify a noun or pronoun, and thus is not an adjective (C).

22. (B)

A complete sentence must have a noun and a verb. A claim ("a red herring," or misleading word) is not necessarily a part of the predicate; (A) is incorrect. Neither a verb and an adjective (C) nor a noun and an adjective (D) alone can make up a complete sentence. Only (B) is a true statement.

23. (C)

A paragraph is a group of sentences that develop one main idea. The other answers—a group of sentences that develop the various aspects of certain ideas or claims (A), a group of sentences that express the author's emotional response to an issue (B), a group of sentences that express the contemporary views of a society (D)—are not correct answers.

24. (D)

To boldly go is a split infinitive because the adverb *boldly* occurs between the *to* and the verb form *go*. A gerund phrase (A) is a phrase that includes a verb form ending in *-ing* and its related words; a gerund phrase acts as a noun in a sentence. A compound verb (B) is made up of two verbs connected by *and*, *but*, or *or*. The phrase is not grammatically correct, so (C) is also incorrect.

25. (B)

The root is the main part of the word, sometimes standing on its own, but often combined with prefixes (added to the beginning of a word) and suffixes (added to the end). In the word "prescrip-tion," "script" is the root, "pre-" (A) is the prefix, and "-ion" (C) is the suffix.

26. (C)

The purpose of expository writing is to explain or inform, exactly the goal of this passage. Though the passage is organized chronologically, it is not narrative (B) because it does not tell a story with a discernible plot. Persuasive (D) writing tries to shape our views and possibly motivate us to act. Though this is a positive portrayal of Twain's, it cannot really be classified as persuasive. Descriptive writing (A) usually appeals to our senses, which is not the case here.

27. (A)

The first sentence of the passage is the thesis statement because it states the main idea. The rest of the passage provides support for the thesis.

28. (B)

In keeping with the chronological order of the passage, the participial phrase, "Following a stint in the military," leads the reader to the next point.

29. (C)

The tone is admiring. Choices (A) and (B) are negative, and this piece is positive. "Venerating" (D) means worshiping, which is too positive for this passage.

30. (D)

The Adventures of Tom Sawyer is based on Twain's boyhood in Hannibal. The others are by Twain, but not specifically autobiographical.

31. (D)

The article is organized chronologically—it largely follows the order in which the events of Clemens's life happened. Cause and effect (A) shows the relationship that occurs when one event influences another. A detailed discussion of the influences on Twain's writing, or the influence of Twain's writing on other writers, would be cause and effect. The passage is not organized as compare and contrast (B), which looks at the similarities and differences between two things, nor is it organized most important to least important points (C).

32. (A)

The author uses the word "titan" to refer to a person of great power. The writer does not encourage David to pursue developing his physical strength (B) or his intellect (C). Choice (D), which encompasses all of the characteristics, is not appropriate.

33. (D)

The author argues that having diverse interests will prevent David from being a captain of industry. Answer (D) directly contradicts that line of reasoning. Choice (A) is incorrect because it strengthens the author's point that it takes exceptional dedication to be a captain of industry. Choice (B) is incorrect because it strengthens the author's claim that David needs to concentrate more on business interests. Choice (C) is incorrect because it is irrelevant to the argument at hand.

34. (D)

The writer is attempting to persuade the reader to a particular point of view toward David; thus, (D), "persuasive," is the best choice. The style is not a story form (narrative), or (A). The writer is not reflecting on past events; (B) is inappropriate.

The writing is not a descriptive passage (C), but is rather one of persuading the reader to adopt a particular point of view.

35. (D)

The writer is asserting an opinion. The author does not rely primarily on facts (A), research (B), or documentation (C) to make his point.

36. (C)

A realist is "one who" sees reality, and a philanthropist is literally "one who" loves mankind or a person who donates large sums to charities. "Having the qualities of" (A) is "-ical" or "-ic"(historical, angelic), and "less" (B) means without (worthless). "In the manner or style of" (D) is "-esque" (e.s., picturesque).

37. (D)

"Happiest" is the superlative form, the most extreme degree, of the adjective "happy" (A), which is the positive form. "Happier" (C) is the comparative form, while "more happy" (B) is not standard English.

38. (B)

Choices (A) and (D) are coordinating conjunctions. "However" and "therefore" (C) are conjunctive adverbs.

39. (D)

An exclamatory sentence expresses a strong emotion and is followed by an exclamation point. A declarative sentence (A) makes a statement, and an interrogative sentence (B) gives a command or makes a request. An interrogative sentence (C) asks a question.

40. (B)

Statement (B) is the only answer option that has "a person"—a Southerner—to attack. All other answers, (A), (C), and (D), address an issue and have no person, place, nor object to attack.

41. (D)

The past perfect tense indicates that one past action began and ended before another past action started. It is formed using the auxiliary verb "had" with the past participle of a verb. The present perfect tense (C) is used to express an action that occurred at some indefinite time in the past. It is formed using the auxiliary verb forms "has" or "have" with the past participle of a verb; thus, "has packed" would be the present participle of the verb to pack.

42. (C)

The conclusion that language had a civilizing effect on people is one historians or philologists might like to draw, but it is not supported in the narrative provided. Statements (A), (B), and (D) find support in the passage.

43. (A)

The passage is dominated by language that appeals to the senses: "soft folds or coats," "something crunching under her feet," "something soft and powdery and extremely cold." Satire (B) is the use of humor to make a persuasive point. The passage is straightforward, neither humorous nor ironic (C). Anaphora (D) is the repetition of initial words and/ or phrases, which also does not apply here.

44. (B)

In each of the third-person points of view, the narrator is not a character in the story, and third-person pronouns are maintained. In the third-person limited point of view, the narrator recounts the thoughts and feelings of only one character, which is the case in this passage. The omniscient (C) narrator knows all the characters' thoughts and feelings. The objective narrator (D) knows only the actions and not the thoughts and feelings of the characters. The first-person narrator (A) is a character in the story.

45. (A)

The basic situation or exposition is at the beginning of a short story where the main characters, conflicts, and settings are introduced. In this passage, we are introduced to the narrator, a woman, and her husband, John. They are staying in a rented home (the setting), which the narrator finds "queer," the first hint at a conflict. The narrator is also ill, and blames her illness to some extent on her husband, another potential conflict. The complications or rising action (B) will be the events that occur after the exposition leading to the climax (C), or the most critical or exciting moment of the story. The denouement (D), or falling action brings us down from the climax to the final resolution of the story. It is usually much briefer than the rising action.

46. (D)

The speaker tells us that her husband laughs at her fears and is very practical; he must be realistic (D). He is not her confidant (A) or a trustworthy sounding board (B). Though he is a doctor, he is not sympathetic (C).

47. (B)

The writer views her writing as a "great relief," in other words, therapeutic (B). Nowhere in the passage does she suggest that writing is annoying (A), laborious (C), or painful (D) to her.

48. (A)

The *Yellow Wallpaper* is a good example of Naturalism, a subset of American Realism that explores psychological themes as well as the effect their environment has on people. Transcendentalists (B) were essentially Romantics (C) who believed in the primacy of the individual and the spirituality of nature. These movements precede Naturalism. Rationalism (D)—a literary and philosophical movement that celebrated logic, human intelligence, and individual rights—produced mostly nonfiction prose, and is associated with the late eighteenth century.

49. (A)

The passage illustrates the first-person point of view. It does not show irony—or the opposite of what one would expect; (B) is incorrect. There are no comparisons or analogies (C) in the writing. Language that incorporates vocabulary and syntax that is overly formal and complex for the occasion is called inflated (D). The language in this passage is direct and conversational—in fact, almost confidential.

50. (A)

The writing is in story form, a narrative. The writing is not expressive/poetic (B), informative (C), or expository (D).

51. (A)

This passage is an excellent example of an extended metaphor, which extends or recurs throughout a work; in this case, fiction is compared to a house through the entire passage. Personal anecdotes (B) are brief, personal narratives used to illustrate a point, not a characteristic of this passage, which is abstract and impersonal. Syllogistic reasoning (C) is a form of deductive reasoning in which a major premise and a minor premise lead to a conclusion (e.g., all three-sided shapes are triangles; this shape has three sides; therefore, this shape is a triangle). Stream of consciousness (D) is a type of first-person narration that flows from the thoughts of the narrator without the feeling of purposeful composition. This piece is highly structured and lacks the emotional affect of stream of consciousness narration.

52. (B)

Apertures (openings) precedes *they* and is synonymous with its predicate, *windows*. Choices (A) and (C) are incorrect because they follow *they* and are its predicates. *Need* and *pressure* (D) describe the formation of the windows, not the windows themselves.

53. (A)

The phrase is prepositional, beginning with the preposition "of" and ending with its object, the noun "shapes." It modifies "apertures," the noun it follows, which is a typical structure for prepositional phrases.

54. (D)

Choice (D), with its parallel pairs of contrasting words, exemplifies antithesis. There are no such contrasts in the other four choices. Shape and size

(A), windows and doors (B), eyes and field-glass (C) are not opposites.

55. (A)

Anaphora is the purposeful repetition of initial words in progressive phrases, clauses, sentences, or paragraphs. The "one sees" pattern is a perfect example of this. Alliteration (B) is the repetition of sounds in closely proximate words, which is not the case here. A periodic sentence (D) places the most important element at the end of the sentence, also not the case here. Inversion (C) is the atypical order of elements in a sentence, i.e., placing the object before the verb: "What light through yonder window breaks?"

56. (B)

Usage is the criterion by which the meaning of a word may be measured. Even if a dictionary offers several possible meanings, it does not provide any method by which to select from the possibilities; choice (A) is incorrect. Words are sometimes used to refer to objects, but this is by no means the only way in which they are used; (C) is not the best answer. Thoughts or ideas "in the mind" are not visible; we can never be sure that what occurs in the speaker's mind when he or she utters a word is the same as what occurs in a listener's mind. Choice (D) is incorrect.

57. (C)

According to most developmental psychologists, there are a number of generally discernible stages in childhood language development. While warning against relying too heavily on artificial divisions, developmental psychologists have identified several particular stages in acquisition of language, although there can be temporary regression in addition to precocious advancement. The conception of the acquisition of language as a child's learning to express his or her thoughts in a coherent notion (A) presupposes a prior language in which the child is having such thoughts; (A) is incorrect. The child's acquisition of language is able to be divided roughly into successive stages, which are not strictly successive (B) but certainly not chaotic and undefinable (D). Both the extreme choices (B) and (D) are incorrect.

58. (A)

This sentence that asserts his love for the pain of running is supported and developed by the rest of the sentences, which show us why he loved the pain of running.

59. (C)

Analysis explains a thing by breaking it down into smaller, separate parts in order to understand it better and draw conclusions from it. The passage is analytical because it breaks down and explains the paradoxical nature of his love for running. The passage has no real plot or chronology, so it is not narrative (A). While it describes the pain of running, this description (B) is used for the purpose of the analysis. Definition (D) seeks to define the essence of something, usually an abstract concept. While pain might be a concept abstract and complex enough to be worthy of this kind of discussion, in this case it's not being defined but rather being used to develop the larger analysis.

60. (A)

Paradoxes are truths revealed through the bringing together of seemingly contradictory things. How can pain bring pleasure? Cormier reveals this truth in the passage. Choices (B) and (C) are not correct because there are no comparisons made in the passage. The passage is not humorous; therefore it is not satiric (D).

61. (B)

These words are all the direct objects of the verb "loved," answering the question what. He loved what? He loved "pain," "hurt," "burning," and "spasms." Direct objects are always nouns or pronouns and follow transitive verbs.

62. (B)

This sentence is complex, the combination of independent and subordinate clause. The introductory subordinate clause in this sentence is "When he ran"; the rest is the independent clause.

63. (B)

It is a simple, past tense verb. Perfect tense verbs are constructed with a form of the auxiliary verb "to have."

64. (A)

The antecedent of a pronoun is the word it is replacing; in this case, "running" is the only choice that makes sense when placed in the sentence. "He loved running because he knew he could endure the pain. . . ."

65. (D)

Replace the pronoun with determination: "And determination sang in him as he ran…."

66. (A)

An epilogue comes at the end of a book, after the last chapter. A prologue comes at the beginning, before the first chapter.

67. (B)

Marvin Klein in his *Development of Writing in Children Pre-K through Grade 8* (Englewood Cliffs, N.J.: Prentice Hall, 1985) gives the types of writing as information, description, explanation, persuasion, and entertainment. The writer is describing the mall and what he or she does there; there is no attempt to persuade (A), to present an argument (C), or to present comedy (D).

68. (A)

The essay is an informative one (A) that might appear in a text. There is no attempt to persuade (B) or entertain (C) the audience. The writing is not descriptive (D).

69. (C)

The paragraph is for entertainment (C). There is no attempt to explain something (A), to persuade the audience (B), or to provide information (D).

70. (D)

The writer intends the paragraph to persuade the teacher not to penalize the late submission. It is not informative (A) in the same manner that a textbook article would be informative. It does provide description (B), but that is not the primary purpose of the work. The writer in no way intends the work to be entertaining (C).

71. (D)

The passage is an attempt to persuade parents to read to their children (D). It is not primarily intended to inform (A), to describe (B), or to entertain (C), although all those characteristics enter into the writing.

72. (B)

Circumlocution is language that is indirect, that speaks around the point. The prefix for "through or across" (A) is "dia-," as in diameter. "Contra-" (C) indicates "against" (contraband), and "hemi-" (D) means "half" (hemisphere).

73. (A)

Asimov and Clark wrote science fiction, while Rowling and Tolkien (B) are fantasy writers. The distinction between the two genres is that science fiction, though sometimes farfetched, tries to work within the realm of accepted scientific laws, or at least tries to offer scientific explanations for the incredible. When we read fantasy, we must completely suspend disbelief and accept a world where magic and the supernatural are the reality. Faulkner's, O'Brien's, and Hurston's stories are realistic in that they do not transcend what we basically understand reality to be. Toni Morrison, as in her masterpiece *Beloved*, sometimes writes in a genre known as magical realism which incorporates elements of realism with touches of fantasy.

74. (A)

Christopher Paul Curtis is the only writer to have won both the Coretta Scott King Award and the Newbery Award in the same year. Both Mildred Taylor (B) and Virginia Hamilton (C) won both awards but not in the same year. Harper Lee (C) was a winner of the Pulitzer Prize but not the Coretta Scott King Award.

75. (D)

Cynthia Voigt (D) has never won the Coretta Scott King Award. Christopher Paul Curtis (A), Mildred Taylor (B), and Virginia Hamilton (C) have won both the Newbery Award and the Coretta Scott King Award.

76. (D)

Christopher Paul Curtis has won both the Newbery Award and the Coretta Scott King Award (in the same year), but he has never won the Margaret A. Edwards Award. Gary Paulsen (A), S. E. Hinton (B), and Cynthia Voigt (C) were all recipients of the Margaret A. Edwards Award.

77. (A)

Charles Dickens would be an appropriate writer to include in a unit on British writers. Edgar Allan Poe (B), James Fenimore Cooper (C), and Washington Irving (D) were all American writers.

78. (D)

Mildred Taylor is a modern writer whose books explore racism through the eyes of her children characters. Charlotte Brontë (A), her sister Emily Brontë (B), and Edgar Allan Poe (C), all authors of the nineteenth century, wrote works that were Gothic in flavor.

79. (D)

The correct order is: prewriting, drafting, revising, editing, publishing, evaluating.

80. (C)

The reader-response theory emphasizes the reader's role in creating the meaning and experience of a literary work. IRA (A) is the abbreviation for the International Reading Association; MLA (B) is the abbreviation for the Modern Lanaguage Association; and a rubric (D) is a scoring "key."

81. (B)

"I" in line 5 is the subject of the main clause, "I do mean to say. . . ." The many phrases and clauses in this complicated sentence makes finding the main clause tricky. Figure that out, and you find the subject.

82. (C)

Circumlocution is literally talking around the point; in other words, using many words to express a simple concept.

83. (B)

Writers and editors use brackets to indicate a change in the original text. In this case, the original text was probably a pronoun, which would be confusing in this excerpted format absent the antecedent.

84. (A)

The lengthy sentences and complex structures are typical of the Victorian time period. None of the other choices applies in this passage.

85. (C)

These beginning lines of *Oliver Twist* are well-known. These lines do not begin *A Tale of Two Cities* (A), *David Copperfield* (B), or *Great Expectations* (D).

86. (B)

Charles Dickens wrote these opening lines of *Oliver Twist*. The lines are not the work of American writer Mark Twain (D). The writer is not Gothic writer Charlotte Brontë (C) or the Scottish writer Robert Louis Stevenson (A).

87. (A)

The passage tells a story, so it is narrative. The passage does not attempt to persuade (B) or to inform as in technical writing (C), nor does it seek to make an argument (D).

88. (B)

The tone of the passage is realistic; it is not excessively gloomy (A) because of the attitude of the narrator. The passage is not better than real life, so romantic (C) is not the tone. The tone is not Gothic (D) because of the absence of haunted houses, castles, and supernatural events.

89. (D)

The passage is in sequential or chronological order. The word "transitional" (C) does not apply to the overall organization. The primary organization is neither cause-and-effect (A) nor compare-and-contrast (B).

90. (A)

The first sentence tells the reader that the rough childhood was the best thing for the child; (A) best summarizes this thesis. The passage does not lament the disadvantaged childhood (B) or bemoan the child's lack of a family (D). The passage in no way suggests that the child lost in the battle with Nature (C).

Question 1

Three-Point Response

> The narrator in William Blake's "London" provides an editorialized commentary of the squalor and abysmal living conditions commonly associated with the late 18th-century Industrial Revolution in Britain. The narrator "wander[s]" the streets of London, which is the setting of the poem. By using the "streets of London" as the setting, the writer implies that anywhere and everywhere he goes, he is met by sad faces "marked" or filled with suffering and "woe." Essentially then, from lowly "harlots" and "chimney sweeps" to "hapless soldiers", no one seems to be safe from London's environmental cruelties and economic miseries. The descriptive adjectives before the nouns—youthful harlots, chimney sweeps, hapless soldiers, blackened church—imply the suffering of all.

> For the narrator, this is not just an opportunity for social exposition, but an opportunity for social commentary on what he sees as the actual cause of the Londoner's suffering: i.e., the self-imposed, "mind-forged manacles."

> The narrator sees the metaphorical manacles to be a result of two things: both ignorance—as in, lack of education and lethargy—and one's own limited or myopic thinking. These shackles are the basis or origin of the people's misery. Their limited thinking prevents them from seeing their own potential for instigating change.

> Without the need or obligation to solve London's social problems, the narrator is free to editorialize or commentate on the current social conditions, while putting the responsibility for solutions squarely on the backs of those who must instigate the change; these catalysts of change must be the Londoners themselves. Yet death's perpetual presence permeates the poem, from birth to the "marriage-hearse." The metaphor suggests a genuine understanding on the narrator's part that social changes are easier spoken about than brought about.

Analysis: This essay would receive a score of 3 because it addresses the use of metaphor as a literary device. The essay elaborates on how the metaphor of the "mind-forged manacles" indicates the narrator's opinion as to the causes of the wretchedness of the life of late-eighteenth century lower-class Londoners.

Two-Point Response

When William Blake speaks of London as a place where he is constantly finding misery and sadness in every face he meets, he is really showing a poetic version of a modern-day Sodom and Gomorrah, complete with all the grief, "misery," suffering, and perversions of its biblical namesake. Infants are crying and harlots are cursed, or perhaps are cursing. The blackened church stands idly by and exploits the people whom it is there to protect. The reader is left to speculate that Blake's London must have been a sad, lonely, corrupt, and dirty place where even the church walls are blackened and stained with unsanctified blood.

Blake seems to be suggesting that the inhabitants of London are manacled or chained to their fears and blights. They are locked to their ultimate consequences and fate. These chains implies that while other, more righteous avenues are available to them, the inhabitants are physically and mentally prevented from following those new avenues of escape.

Blake endlessly wanders about the city, the setting of the poem. The narrator is seemingly like a modern day Lot, looking for one honest "soul" and finding none. London is a contemporary version of Sodom and Gomorrah. Like its biblical namesake, London seems destined for damnation and destruction. The marriage-hearse prepares to depart across the River Jordon, thus reiterating the inevitable fate of those who are cursed to live there.

Analysis: This essay would receive a score of 2 because although it does discuss the metaphor of the "mind-forged manacles," it fails to identify it as a metaphor. Also, the essay is not well written, incorporating its own metaphor—Sodom and Gomorrah—in a far-fetched and unconvincing comparison to 19th-century London. The essay would have benefited from a straightforward treatment of the task at hand.

One-Point Response

I don't get this poem at all. When I went to England with my mom and dad when I was a little kid- it was really fun and nice. The people were pretty friendly but it was kinda hard to understand them sometimes cuz they all have English accents. Duh!!!!! We went to buckinghoard palace and saw the queens knights or something but I wanted to go on the big farist wheel that they have there by the river Times and then my mom tried to get them to laugh, but you cant and they wont laugh no matter what you do, so maybe the poem is about the kings nights who just don't laugh no matter what you do or say and they always look serious and kinda mean.

But 4 me the city of England was kinda funny because - omg - they call soccer football like they do here but its really not like football its like soccer but they call rugby! and money is called pounds like youd weigh something in the local supermarket. Its really hard 2 figure out how much something costs so my dad had a little calculator thing that told him how much itd cost in American money and elevators are called lifts. Do you know what they call a baby stroller? Prams or trams or something stupid like that.... Lol.

I don't think this poem is very good or tells a lot about England like it really is cuz its really pretty fun to go there and if blake really didnt like it very much or isn't happy there he should just move or go somewhere else on his vacation.

Analysis: Even if this essay weren't written in the style of a pre-teen journal entry, it would have received a score of 1 because it fails to answer the question.

Question 2

Three-Point Response

Even though this is supposed to be a fictional account, it's still important that the author gets the facts right. Factual details solidify characters in a believable time and place, giving both the characters and the storyline more credibility. As there is a national holiday commemorating the infamous event, most Americans know that the attack on Pearl Harbor occurred in the Hawaiian Islands (Oahu), on a December morning (7:00 am, December 7, 1941), not in California on a July evening. Additionally, the attack was instigated by the nation of Japan, not Taiwan. So the characters are in no immediate danger, and the storyline feels juvenile, contrived, and completely unrealistic.

This historical inaccuracy will not only corrupt the believability of the characters and storyline, but it will also corrupt the overall tone and timbre of the story. The historical inaccuracies take what could be a suspenseful situation, an unsuspecting couple about to be caught up in a catastrophe, and turn it into a joke that borders more on the edge of parody or satire, rather than on legitimate suspense.

A simple web search or library visit could provide all the fundamental facts and figures necessary to create a believable environment, where the protagonists are in legitimate danger from the impending attack.

Analysis: This essay would receive a score of three because it answers the question with a convincing argument in a well-structured essay. In the first paragraph, the essay identifies a major flaw (historical inaccuracy), citing several elements in the passage to support the argument. The second paragraph explains why this is a serious flaw, and the third paragraph gives advice on how to prevent it.

Two-Point Response

While I'm not exactly sure, I don't think that they had jet fighters in World War II. All the movies I've seen show airplanes with propellers. While this may not seem like a big deal, it is very distracting for me because I don't know where or when the story is supposed to be taking place. Maybe the author is trying to update the story. In that case, he/she could add laser beams, space ships, and other high-tech toys.

Nevertheless, this issue is distracting because I'm not sure if the story is supposed to be taking place in the old days when the war really happened or in a fictional "alternate" time and place. May be the author is using the events of the Second World War as inspiration only. But regardless of the reason he/she chose, the author should make it clear from the onset, where and when this story actually takes place. That way the reader knows from the start, if they are in an imaginary world or in a real world situation. It would make the story more believable and thematically easier for me to understand.

Analysis: This essay would receive a score of 2. Even though the test taker has sensed that there is something wrong with the historical facts in the passage, he or she does not construct as strong an argument and analysis as the test taker who wrote the three-point response above. The test taker describes his or her emotional response to the passage ("it is very distracting to me"), which is not called for in the directions. The test taker speculates instead of analyzes ("Maybe the author is trying to update the story"), and the language employed in the essay is at times colloquial ("big deal").

One-Point Response

Even though I don't know who Bob and Sally are, I think they are going to get married soon. Nothing is more romantic than sitting with your girlfriend by the beach watching the ocean and the sunset. It means he really loves her.

If it were me, I'd bring a blanket and wine and something to eat, and some flowers, and we'd sit on a blanket and watch the boats go by. And we'd watch the sunset, and smell the ocean, and listen to the seagulls and the waves, and it would be really romantic.

The ocean is really romantic. So it'd be a good place for Bob and Sally to get engaged and maybe even have their wedding there. Then they can go back sometimes, and see where they fell in love and got engaged and it'd be even more romantic for many years. I love going to the beach and playing in the sand and the waves or just sitting on the sand and soak up the sun, or watching all the hot girls in their bikinis.

But not if my girlfriend's around. She'd get really jealous. The ocean is a really good spot for a love story.

Analysis: Although the test taker has described a type of revision he or she would make to the courtship of Bob and Sally, he or she has not described what literary revision would benefit the draft. The essay gives an emotional response to the plot, which is a weak form of argument, but above all, it misses the most obvious flaw in the passage: historical inaccuracy. This response would receive a score of 1.

Praxis English Assesment

Index

Index

S

REFERENCES

Answers.com. Symbolism. The New Oxford Companion to Literature in French, Oxford University Press, 1995, 2005. *http://www.answers.com/topic/symbolism.*

Bromley, K. D. 1992. *Language Arts: Exploring Connections*. Upper Saddle River, NJ: Prentice Hall.

Butler, Samuel, trans. 1898 *The Illiad* by Homer. Project Gutenberg. *www.gutenberg.org.*

————. 1900. *The Odyssey* by Homer. Project Gutenberg. *www.gutenberg.org.*

Cook, L., and R. Mayer. 1988. Teaching Readers About the Structure of Scientific Text. *Journal of Educational Psychology*, 80: 448–56.

Cormier, Robert. 1974/1977. *The Chocolate War*. New York: Dell.

Davis, Anita P., and Marla Selvidge. 1995. *Focus on Women*. Westminster, CA: Teacher Created Materials, Inc.

Davis, Anita P., and Thomas R. McMillan. 1999. You've Come a Long Way, Baby—or Have You? *Reading Teacher,* 52: 532–35.

Davis, Anita Price. 1994a. *MAXNotes: I Know Why the Caged Bird Sings*. Piscataway, NJ: Research and Education Association.

————. 1994b. *MAXNotes: To Kill a Mockingbird*. Piscataway, NJ: Research and Education Association.

————. 2005. *Reading Instruction Essentials*. Boston: American Press

Dictionary.com. Drama. *Webster's Revised Unabridged Dictionary*. MICRA, Inc. *http://dictionary.reference.com/browse/drama.*

Goodman, Kenneth 1965. "A Linguistic Study of Cues and Miscues in Reading." Elementary English. 42: 639–43.

Goudvis, Anne, and Stephanie Harvey. 2000. *Strategies that Work*. Portland, ME: Stenhouse.

Great Books Foundation, The. 2008. The shared inquiry method of learning. *www.greatbooks.org/programs-for-all-ages/junior/jgbsharedinquiry/shared-inquiry.html.*

Kinsella, Kim, Kevin Feldman, Colleen Shea, Ph.D., Joyce Armstrong Carroll, and Edward E. Wilson. 2004. *Prentice Hall Literature: The British Tradition*. Upper Saddle River, NJ: Prentice Hall.

Installing REA's TestWare®

SYSTEM REQUIREMENTS

Pentium 75 MHz (300 MHz recommended) or a higher or compatible processor; Microsoft Windows 98 or later; 64 MB available RAM; Internet Explorer 5.5 or higher.

INSTALLATION

1. Insert the PRAXIS English Assessments CD-ROM into the CD-ROM drive.

2. If the installation doesn't begin automatically, from the Start Menu choose the RUN command. When the RUN dialog box appears, type d:\setup (where d is the letter of your CD-ROM drive) at the prompt and click OK.

3. The installation process will begin. A dialog box proposing the directory "C:\Program Files\REA\Praxis_English\" will appear. If the name and location are suitable, click OK. If you wish to specify a different name or location, type it in and click OK.

4. Start the PRAXIS English Assessments TestWare® application by double-clicking on the icon.

REA's PRAXIS English Assessments TestWare® is **EASY** to **LEARN AND USE**. To achieve maximum benefits, we recommend that you take a few minutes to go through the on-screen tutorial on your computer. The "screen buttons" are also explained here to familiarize you with the program.

SSD ACCOMMODATIONS FOR STUDENTS WITH DISABILITIES

Many students qualify for extra time to take the Praxis II English Language Assessments, and our TestWare® can be adapted to accommodate your time extension. This allows you to practice under the same extended-time accommodations that you will receive on the actual test day. To customize your TestWare® to suit the most common extensions, visit our website at www.rea.com/ssd.

TECHNICAL SUPPORT

REA's TestWare® is backed by customer and technical support. For questions about **installation or operation of your software**, contact us at:

> **Research & Education Association**
> **Phone: (732) 819-8880 (9 a.m. to 5 p.m. ET, Monday–Friday)**
> **Fax: (732) 819-8808**
> **Website: www.rea.com**
> **E-mail: info@rea.com**

Note to Windows XP Users: In order for the TestWare® to function properly, please install and run the application under the same computer administrator-level user account. Installing the TestWare® as one user and running it as another could cause file-access path conflicts.